DUMBARTON OAKS
MEDIEVAL LIBRARY

Jan M. Ziolkowski, General Editor

THE VULGATE BIBLE

VOLUME V

DOML 17

The Vulgate Bible

VOLUME V

THE MINOR PROPHETICAL
BOOKS AND MACCABEES

DOUAY-RHEIMS TRANSLATION

Edited by

ANGELA M. KINNEY

Introduction by
SWIFT EDGAR

DUMBARTON OAKS
MEDIEVAL LIBRARY

HARVARD UNIVERSITY PRESS
CAMBRIDGE, MASSACHUSETTS
LONDON, ENGLAND
2012

Library of Congress Cataloging-in-Publication Data
Bible, English. Douai. 2012
  The Vulgate Bible : Douay-Rheims translation / edited by Angela M.
  Kinney.
    v.c. — (Dumbarton Oaks medieval library ; DOML 17)
  English and Latin text on facing pages.
  Includes bibliographical references.
  Contents: v. 1. The Pentateuch. v. 2a. The Historical Books, part a. v. 2b.
  The Historical Books, part b. v. 3. The Poetical Books. v. 4. The Major
  Prophetical Books. v. 5. The Minor Prophetical Books and Maccabees
  ISBN 978-0-674-05534-6 (v. 1: alk. paper)
  ISBN 978-0-674-99667-0 (v. 2a: alk. paper)
  ISBN 978-0-674-06077-7 (v. 2b: alk. paper)
  ISBN 978-0-674-99668-7 (v. 3: alk. paper)
  ISBN 978-0-674-99669-4 (v. 4: alk. paper)
  ISBN 978-0-674-06635-9 (v. 5: alk. paper)
  I. Edgar, Swift, 1985–   II. Dumbarton Oaks.   III. Title.
  BS180 2010
  222′.1047—dc22   2010015238

Contents

CONTENTS

Introduction

The Vulgate Bible is a collection of Latin texts compiled and translated in large part by Saint Jerome (ca. 345–420) in the late fourth and early fifth centuries CE. Roughly speaking, Jerome translated the Old Testament—except for the books of Wisdom, Ecclesiasticus, Baruch and 1 and 2 Maccabees—and he revised existing Latin versions of the Psalms and the Gospels. Jerome's Bible was used widely in the Western European Christian (and later, specifically Catholic) tradition from the early Middle Ages through the twentieth century.

The adjective "Vulgate" (from the Latin verb *vulgare*, meaning "to disseminate") lacks the connotation of coarseness often inherent in its relative "vulgar," but both words imply commonness. Indeed, the Vulgate Bible was so widespread that its significance can hardly be overstated. It made critical contributions to literature, visual art, music and education during the Middle Ages and the Renaissance, and it informed much of the Western theological, intellectual, artistic and even political history of that period. Students of almost any aspect of European civilization from the seventh century (when the Latin Bible existed more or less in the form we know today) through the sixteenth century (when translations of scripture into various European vernaculars

became widely available to the public and acceptable to religious authorities) must refer frequently to the Vulgate Bible and have a thorough knowledge of it.

In this edition, the Latin is presented opposite the first English version of the Bible sanctioned by the Roman Catholic Church. This English Bible is typically referred to as the Douay-Rheims Version, after the present-day names of its places of publication. The New Testament was published in 1582 by the English College at Rheims, and the Old Testament (to call it the Hebrew Bible would be inaccurate, since it includes nine books that have never belonged to the Hebrew canon) was published in 1609 and 1610, in two volumes, by the English College at Douay. The entire Douay-Rheims Bible was revised several times, notably by Bishop Dr. Richard Challoner (1691–1781) in 1749 and 1750.

In this introduction, I use the terms "Catholic" and "Protestant" in their current senses. Adherents to the Church of England in the sixteenth century at times referred to themselves as Catholics and to those who followed the religious authorities in Rome as Popish or Papists. The members of the Roman Church called their Anglican rivals various names, such as heretics, Protestants, Lutherans and Calvinists, but they would not have called them Catholics.

Douay and Rheims were major centers of learning for English-speaking Catholics, who faced hostility in Protestant England. The English College, a prominent Catholic institution, was exiled from Douay to Rheims in 1578, near the beginning of the Eighty Years' War between the Netherlands (to which Douay at the time belonged) and Philip II of Spain, who had founded the college.[1] The exile lasted until 1593. The college undertook these translations of the Bi-

ble primarily in response to the English versions produced under the Church of England that did not treat Jerome's text as the ultimate authority. Protestant English translators did use the Vulgate, but they also consulted the German rendering by Martin Luther (1482–1546), the Greek Septuagint and New Testament, testimonia in Hebrew and other sources. In contrast, the Douay-Rheims Version was directly translated from the Latin Bible as it was known to the professors at the English College in 1582.

While the English College was working on its translations at Douay and Rheims, Pope Sixtus V (r. 1585–1590) called for the preparation of an authoritative Latin text. This Latin Bible was published in 1590, just prior to his death, but it contained errors and was soon suppressed for fear that Protestants would use them to attack the Catholic Church.[2] Three corrected printings followed, in 1592, 1593 and 1598, during the papacy of Clement VIII (r. 1592–1605). These four editions, substantially the same, are referred to collectively as the Sixto-Clementine Version. While it strongly resembles the Latin Bible that evidently served as the basis for the Douay-Rheims translation, the two are not identical. The Dumbarton Oaks Medieval Library (DOML) here presents a reconstructed Latin text of the lost Bible used by the professors at Douay and Rheims, and Challoner's revision of the English translation faces the Latin. Challoner's text, discussed in detail below ("The English Text of This Edition"), sometimes reflects the Sixto-Clementine Bible more closely than did the English College translations of 1582, 1609 and 1610, but many of the revision's features are not at all related to the Sixto-Clementine Bible, and some lead the translation even further from the Latin.

Although the Douay Old Testament was not published until 1609–1610, most of the work on the translation seems to have been completed much earlier, before any Sixto-Clementine edition. Despite its publication date, therefore, this section of the English translation still provides a valuable witness to a Latin text that predated the Sixto-Clementine Version. Most scholars accept the conclusion by Charles Dodd that "the work may be entirely ascribed to Mr. [Gregory] Martin [who died a decade before publication of the Sixto-Clementine edition] . . . He translated the whole Bible; tho' it was not publish'd all at one time."[3] There is good reason to believe that Dodd was right: an entry in the "Douay Diaries,"[4] records of the activities at the young English College, attests that Martin began translating the Bible in October 1578 and that he translated two chapters a day, which were revised by two other professors. Since there are 1,353 chapters in the Bible—including the Books of Tobit, Judith, Wisdom, Ecclesiasticus, Baruch, 1 and 2 Maccabees and 3 and 4 Ezra, and counting the Prayer of Manasseh as one chapter—the task would have taken Martin and his team slightly more than 676 days, far less time than the thirty years that elapsed between the project's commencement and the complete publication of the Bible. Indeed, this calculation is confirmed in the address "To the right vvelbeloved English reader" in the first volume of the Old Testament (1609), which states that the Bible was translated "about thirtie yeares since" (fifth page of the section). The translation thus almost certainly preceded the Sixto-Clementine text, which immediately became the standard edition upon its printing in 1592. The lag between translation and publication is explained on the first page of the

same section: "As for the impediments, which hitherto haue hindered this worke, they al proceded (as manie do know) of one general cause, our poore estate in banishment"—that is, the exile of the English College to Rheims.

The Douay-Rheims translation used here mostly follows the version printed in 1899, a slight revision of Challoner's editions, incorporating elements from the 1749, 1750 and 1752 printings. Challoner's principal contribution was to make the original Douay-Rheims easier to read by updating obscure phraseology and obsolete words. This volume modifies the 1899 version to bring the punctuation and the transliteration of proper nouns and adjectives into line with modern practice (see Alternate Spellings in the endmatter for this edition's policies regarding transliterations) and to restore some readings from Challoner's 1750 and 1752 editions that had been changed (mostly due to printers' errors) in the 1899 version. In addition, the whole text has been prepared according to the guidelines of the fifteenth edition of the *Chicago Manual of Style*. This policy has resulted in significant alterations to Challoner's edition, which superabounds in colons and commas, lacks quotation marks and begins each verse on a new line, sometimes making the text difficult to understand. In contrast to most English Bibles, this volume renders all of the text as prose, even the parts that were originally in verse, since neither the Latin nor the English is poetic. The Latin text has been punctuated according to the English translation to allow easy movement between the two languages. In the rare instances when they diverge, the text in each language has been punctuated according to its most natural meaning (see, for example, Gen 31:1–4).

Readers of the Dumbarton Oaks Medieval Library who wish to compare either the English or the Latin version presented here with another Bible should bear in mind that the versification in the Vulgate and the numbering of psalms differ from those in Bibles translated from languages other than Latin. Furthermore, the books in this volume have been selected and ordered according to Challoner's revisions, which follow the Sixto-Clementine Bible. This policy has resulted in the inclusion of some chapters and books commonly considered "apocryphal" or "deuterocanonical" (Tobit, Judith, Wisdom, Ecclesiasticus, Baruch, 1 and 2 Maccabees, Daniel 3:24–90, Daniel 13 and 14) and the omission of others that were relegated to appendices even in early printed versions of the Bible (3 and 4 Ezra and the Prayer of Mannaseh). The names of some books differ from the ones that may be familiar to many readers: for instance, 1 and 2 Kings in this volume are commonly called 1 and 2 Samuel; 3 and 4 Kings are usually 1 and 2 Kings; 1 and 2 Paralipomenon equate to 1 and 2 Chronicles; 1 Ezra is usually simply Ezra, while 2 Ezra is typically Nehemiah; the Canticle of Canticles is also known as the Song of Songs; Ecclesiasticus is Sirach and in some Latin Bibles is known as Iesu Filii Sirach; and, last, the Apocalypse of St. John the Apostle may be known to most readers as the Book of Revelation.

The Latin Text of This Edition

The Latin in this edition presents as closely as possible the text from which the Douay-Rheims translators worked. It would have been a version of the Bible known to many Europeans from the eighth through the sixteenth century. Be-

fore Jerome, translations of parts of the Bible into Latin existed; we call these disparate texts the Old Latin Bible. After Jerome finished his work, versions of his Vulgate proliferated. According to one count, a third of the biblical manuscripts we have today dating to about one hundred years after Jerome's death are from the Vulgate, and a century later "manuscripts of the Vulgate start to outnumber those of the Old Latin by about two to one. In the seventh century, the ratio has risen to about six to one."[5] The early ninth century brought the stabilization of a recension that was overseen by Alcuin, the schoolmaster from York who played a major role in the cultural revival promoted by Charlemagne. The so-called Alcuin Bibles, of which some thirty survive, became the standard text outside Italy during the Carolingian period. They were the products of monastic copy centers known as scriptoria. In the thirteenth century, the Alcuin Bibles gave way to the so-called Paris Bibles, which were written by professional scribes. The text of the Paris Bibles, a direct descendent of the Alcuin Bibles, was in turn closely related to the Sixto-Clementine Bibles of the late sixteenth century. In large part, the DOML text corresponds to Robert Weber's edition (2007). Most adjustments to bring the Latin closer to the English coincide with an edition of the Sixto-Clementine Bible (1959) that preserves the majority of the readings from the second Clementine edition (1593) and occasionally replaces that text with readings from the other two Clementine editions, which were very similar to each other. For consistency's sake, the spellings and inflections of adjustments based on the Sixto-Clementine Bible have been brought into line with Weber's text.

When neither the Weber nor the Sixto-Clementine text

provides the reading that the Douay-Rheims translators appear to have seen, the critical apparatuses in Weber and in Quentin's edition (1926–[1995]) have been consulted. Often the readings attested in early printed editions of the Bible, such as the famous "42-line Bible" printed by Johannes Gutenberg in 1454, come closest to the translation. In rare instances it has been necessary to print reconstructions of the text theoretically used by the translators, since neither the Sixto-Clementine, Weber and Quentin editions nor the citations in their apparatus provide a suitable reading. These reconstructions, often closer to the Greek Septuagint than to any Vulgate edition, follow the Old Latin Bible.

In trying to identify the Latin source or sources of the Douay-Rheims translation, some scholars have pointed to the Louvain Bible,[6] an early printed edition that strongly resembles the Sixto-Clementine Version. However, the readings in the Douay-Rheims Version do not support the conclusion that Martin based his translation on either the Louvain Bible of 1547 or the correction of that edition published at Rome in 1574. Furthermore, the preface of the Douay-Rheims Version addressed "To the right vvelbeloved English reader" states (and Greenslade accepts) that the editors of the Old Testament "conformed it to the most perfect Latin Edition"—presumably, given the publication date, the Sixto-Clementine Version.[7] To take just one illustration of the danger of assuming that the translators used a single identifiable source, consider Ex 16:29, which in the Douay translation reads in part, "and let none goe forth": of the many sources considered by Quentin (including the Louvain Bible), only two—both early printed editions and neither of them the Sixto-Clementine or the Louvain edition—begin

the relevant Latin clause with a conjunction. Moreover, while the translators claimed their work was "diligently conferred with the Hebrew, Greeke, and other Editions in diuers languages,"[8] the relative paucity of readings different from well-established Latin sources and the inconsistency in the nature of the divergences suggest that they were working with a now lost Latin text of idiosyncratic nature rather than a still extant one that they chose to ignore from time to time. Since several people collaborated on that translation, the translators may also have followed different editions of the Bible and therefore produced a translation for which there is no single surviving Latin source.

Unlike the Latin as edited by Weber, the Sixto-Clementine edition (to whose family the Douay-Rheims translation belongs) often regularizes the language found in earlier manuscripts. In general, the Sixto-Clementine rarely accepts the *lectio difficilior,* while most editors since the eighteenth century, including Weber, tend to choose the "more difficult reading" from among multiple possibilities. For example, at Gen 32:5, the Weber edition reads, "habeo boves et asinos oves et servos atque ancillas," while the Sixto-Clementine editors preferred to avoid the variations of asyndeton after *asinos* and of *atque,* so their text reads, "Habeo boves et asinos et oves et servos et ancillas." In this instance, the Douay-Rheims translators evidently saw a conjunction between *asinos* and *oves* and also between *servos* and *ancillas.* In this edition, an *et* has been inserted in the former case, but the *atque* has remained in the latter, because we cannot know which of the many options for the English "and" the translators encountered in their Latin.

At times, the translation reflects a base text closer to We-

ber's than to the Sixto-Clementine edition. For example, at Gen 1:14, Weber reads "fiant luminaria in firmamento caeli ut dividant diem ac noctem," while for *ut,* the Sixto-Clementine edition reads *et.* However, the Douay-Rheims translation (as revised by Challoner, but here retaining the grammatical construction of the original) reads, "Let there be lights made in the firmament of heaven to divide the day and the night," clearly translating *ut.* The Sixto-Clementine choice was probably made by analogy to verses like Gen 1:6, which reads in both editions "Fiat firmamentum in medio aquarum, et dividat."

The English Text of This Edition

The "Douay-Rheims Version" is an imperfect name for the translation of the Vulgate Bible used in this volume. Indeed, one anonymous scholar in 1836 went so far as to write that calling a translation similar to the one printed here "the Douay or Rhemish version is an abuse of terms."[9] The English here follows a text that was published in 1899. Although this text has been understood routinely as being the Douay-Rheims Version without any qualification, it in fact offers an English translation that derives not directly from the work of the English College of Douay and Rheims, but rather from a nineteenth-century form of a revision by Challoner. Challoner published at least five revisions of the New Testament and two of the Old (the New Testaments appeared in 1749, 1750, 1752, 1764 and 1772, the Old Testaments in 1750 and 1763–1764); after his death, others produced many more. Since the editions of 1582, 1609 and 1610, many subsequent revisions have purported to be simple reprints.

Indeed, the frontispiece to the 1899 edition has a message of approbation by James Cardinal Gibbons, then archbishop of Baltimore, who writes that the text "is an accurate reprint of the Rheims and Douay edition with Dr. Challoner's notes." But if we are to understand the "Rheims and Douay edition" to mean the translations originally printed in those cities in the late sixteenth and early seventeenth centuries, the text we have is by no means an accurate reprint of that.

Because the versions issued between 1610 and 1899 can be difficult to come by, and because the only work approaching a systematic collation of various "Douay-Rheims" Bibles is a bitterly anti-Catholic work from 1855,[10] many scholars regard the Douay-Rheims translation as a text that has barely changed (if at all) since its first printing. Some are aware of Challoner's extensive revisions in the mid-eighteenth century, which updated the language of the Douay-Rheims Version and toned down the polemical annotations, but few know the extent of his alterations, or that they make it more distant from the Latin Vulgate, or that they took place over several editions or that the editions published after his death often contain the work of other scholars.

Many factors complicate analysis of the modifications that the Douay-Rheims Version has undergone over the past four centuries. The most significant is the doctrinal conservatism of the Catholic Church. Owing to both the primacy of Jerome's Vulgate (another inadequate label, since Jerome hardly produced the Latin text by himself), recognized at the Council of Trent (1545–1563), and the desire of the Church to exert some control over access to scripture, the translation of the Bible into vernacular tongues was dis-

couraged. Yet after Protestant churches made the text of the Bible available to speakers of English and German, it became easier for reformist thinkers to disseminate their teachings. Some English-speaking Catholics then sought to produce their own translation, but since the point of this work was to regulate the message read by the flock, the translation required authorization to insure that it was appropriate. A letter of 1580 from William Allen, the president of the English College at Douay, to a colleague, Professor Jean de Vendeville, expresses the need for papal sanctioning of the translation: "We on our part will undertake, if His Holiness shall think proper, to produce a faithful, pure, and genuine version of the Bible in accordance with the version approved by the Church."[11] The printed edition was approved not by the pope but by three professors at Allen's own college (Douay-Rheims 1609, *Approbatio*).

Conservatism demanded the Church's approbation and made revision difficult. How could a reviser supplant something that had already been declared acceptable to the Church? Revisions required approval of their own, yet they could not directly contradict previously approved editions. For this reason, the only reference to a difference between Challoner's 1750 edition and the printings of 1582, 1609 and 1610 comes on the title page, which describes the work as "Newly revised and corrected, according to the Clementine Edition of the Scriptures." As the phrasing shows, Challoner was careful to note that his version derived from the Latin Bible first authorized by Pope Clement VIII in 1592, ten years after the Rheims New Testament, but he obscured the extent of his revisions. Despite the popularity of Challoner's revision and of the Bibles still in print that descend from it,

the English translations and revisions of scripture were not created under a directive from the Vatican. There is no single, indisputably "official" translation of the Latin Bible into English. All the translations lay claim to official status without criticizing other Catholic versions, and none of them has clear primacy.

This confusing (and confused) climate has misled modern readers into believing precisely what the editors and translators of English Catholic Bibles from the sixteenth through the nineteenth century wanted them to think: a single standard English translation of the Bible existed, and the reader in question was holding a copy of it. One well-respected medievalist cautioned against using the King James Version for medieval studies (because it lacks a close relationship to the Vulgate text), implying that the Douay-Rheims Version is preferable. While correct about the King James Version, he shows himself to be unaware of the Douay-Rheims's own modern tradition, writing, "The English translation of [the Vulgate] is the one known as the 'Douai-Rheims' translation . . . also available in many modern editions," and later quoting the translation of Ct 2:4 in the Douay-Rheims as "he set in order charity in me."[12] This quotation comes from Challoner's revision of the translation from 1750; the 1610 translation reads, "he hath ordered in me charitie."

The particular case of Ct 2:4 does not perfectly illustrate the danger of using Challoner's revision of the Douay-Rheims translation, because his rendering still matches the Vulgate text ("ordinavit in me caritatem"). But in many places (italicized in this edition) Challoner strayed from the Latin, usually to revise some particularly awkward phrasing

in the older Douay-Rheims edition. For example, at Gen 6:13, he changed "the earth is replenished with iniquitie from the face of them" to "the earth is filled with iniquity through them." Four points are important about this revision. The first is that Challoner updated the spelling of "iniquitie." Second, here, as elsewhere, he translated very logically an ordinary Latin word *(repleta)* with an equally common English one ("filled"), rather than with a cognate ("replenished"). Thus, he followed a policy that contrasts with the Latinate qualities that pervade the earlier translation. Third, "through" is not found in any Latin edition; while the meaning of "from the face of them" is obscure in English, it is a literal rendition of all the transmitted Vulgate texts of this verse. The fourth point is the trickiest one to address: the preposition "through" instead of "from the face of" is in fact found in the King James Version, which was in Challoner's day the more or less official Anglican (and of course Protestant) Bible.

Gen 6:13 illustrates how Challoner revised the Douay-Rheims Bible on literary grounds. One peculiarity of Bible studies is that many areas of interest are plagued with partisanship, and it can be difficult to make any argument without seeming to side with one religious (or secular) establishment against another. In trying to articulate the relationship between the King James and Douay-Rheims Versions, many otherwise useful sources emphasize the effects of one on the other according to the publisher's disposition: that is to say, Catholic sources underscore the similarities between the 1582 New Testament and the 1611 King James text, while Protestant reference works point to Challoner's alleged in-

debtedness to the King James Version. A notable exception is the anonymous article quoted above, which in its passionate call for a responsible, authorized translation of the Sixto-Clementine Vulgate rightly commented on a difference between the 1582 New Testament and Challoner's revision: "This correction is taken verbatim from the Protestant version."[13] Without delving into the differences in the theological programs of the editors of the Douay-Rheims and King James Versions or calling one preferable to the other, one could argue convincingly (as many have done) that the King James Bible has far greater—or at the very least, more enduring—literary merit than the original Douay-Rheims Version.

To understand the relative qualities of these English Bibles, compare, for example, the translations of Dt 30:19. The Douay-Rheims reads: "I cal for witnesses this day heauen and earth, that I haue proposed to you life and death, blessing and cursing. Choose therefore life, that both thou mayest liue, and thy seede." The King James Version has "I call heauen and earth to record this day against you, that I haue set before you life and death, blessing and cursing: therefore choose life, that both thou and thy seed may liue." Significantly, the King James Version is more natural and memorable; we should also note that the most awkward phrasing in the Douay-Rheims translation ("proposed to") has, in Challoner, been replaced by "set before," the King James reading.

The literary superiority of the King James Version is worth bearing in mind, because Challoner (whose schoolboy nickname, we are told, was Book)[14] revised the Douay-

Rheims text primarily on the basis of literary sensibilities. His version significantly departs from the Douay-Rheims when that text is most stilted, and not infrequently in such instances, Challoner's revision closely matches the sense or wording (or both) of the King James Bible.

A word of caution should be issued to those who would accept the implication of the subtitle of Challoner's Bible: "Newly revised and corrected, according to the Clementine Edition of the Scriptures." This description suggests that Challoner updated the Douay-Rheims translation in light of the standard text of the Bible that had not been available to the translators at the English College. Through oversight, however, his revision skipped a few phrases that the Douay-Rheims translators had missed as well (mostly when similar Latin words appeared on different parts of the page, causing leaps of the eye).[15] These omissions suggest strongly that Challoner's primary task was to make the English of the Douay-Rheims version more readable; it was not a revision on textual grounds. Otherwise, a careful collation of the Douay-Rheims Version with the Sixto-Clementine Bible would have been essential. More often than not, Challoner appears simply to have read the Douay-Rheims and fixed the poor or awkward style, occasionally turning to the King James, Latin, Greek or possibly Hebrew texts for help. He does not seem to have compared the Douay-Rheims systematically with the Latin (or any other version).

If we are not prepared to credit the magnum opus of the Anglican Church as a major source for Challoner, we can say that many of his revisions came from Hebrew and Greek sources (the same texts that the King James editors read,

possibly accounting for the similarities). Why Challoner often turned to sources other than the Latin Vulgate, which had existed in stable and authorized form since 1592, is unclear, especially in view of his title-page statement that he had updated the Douay-Rheims according to the Sixto-Clementine Bible. The period in which Challoner published his first edition of the New Testament (1749) was one of lively productivity for biblical scholars. The monumental edition of the pre-Vulgate Latin Bible credited to Pierre Sabatier, a Benedictine monk, was in production (Rheims 1739, 1749; Paris 1751). This text was meant to reconstruct the Bible as it was known to the Church fathers writing in Latin before the general acceptance of Jerome's text, and it received the approbation of two vicars general and Sabatier's own abbot. It relies frequently on Greek and Hebrew sources, indicating that the study of those texts was not as distasteful to the Church elite in the eighteenth century as it had been in 1609, when the Douay-Rheims translators prefaced their edition with the following words:

> But here an other question may be proposed: VVhy we translate the Latin text, rather than the Hebrew, or Greke, which Protestantes preferre, as the fountaine tongues, wherin holie Scriptures were first written? To this we answer, that if in dede those first pure Editions were now extant, or if such as be extant, were more pure than the Latin, we would also preferre such fountaines before the riuers, in whatsoeuer they should be found to disagree. But the ancient best lerned Fathers, & Doctors of the Church, do much complaine, and

testifie to vs, that both the Hebrew and Greke Editions are fouly corrupted by Iewes, and Heretikes,
since the Latin was truly translated out of them,
whiles they were more pure.[16]

Indeed, by 1750 the Counter-Reformational motives of
the Douay-Rheims Version of 1582, 1609 and 1610 had become largely irrelevant, and the polemical annotations of
the first translation were either omitted or stripped of their
vehemence. Even the notes in the Old Testament of 1609–
1610 contain less vitriol than those in the 1582 New Testament. Strict adherence to the Vulgate Bible mattered less to
Challoner than to the original translators, although he still
evidently favored literalism in his renderings. Consequently,
he may have preferred to replace poorly worded translations
with a new literal translation of a different source, rather
than to print loose constructions of the Latin text. None-
theless, the translation on the whole adheres faithfully to
the Vulgate, the official Bible of the Catholic Church; after
all, Challoner wrote a pamphlet entitled "The Touchstone
of the New Religion: or, Sixty Assertions of Protestants,
try'd by their own Rule of Scripture alone, and condemned
by clear and express Texts of their own Bible" (London 1735).
Interestingly, this tract reveals Challoner's familiarity with,
or at least access to, the King James Version of the Bible. As
one scholar put it, "He sought to establish the Roman
Church's credentials out of the mouths of her enemies."[17]

It may be fitting that the DOML Bible is an artificial one.
After all, in whatever language or languages the texts collectively called the Bible are read, they are heterogeneous, cob-
bled together over centuries, having been composed (or re-

vealed) and varied by oral tradition throughout the preceding millennia. With only minor revisions, we use Challoner's edition of the Douay-Rheims Bible because his text preserves the character of the English translation that brings us closest to the end of the medieval period while still being fairly elegant and readable. This edition differs from the 1899 printing in restoring readings from the 1750 and 1752 editions which had been spuriously altered in the 1899 version and in updating the biblical names and the punctuation of the earlier edition. Challoner's notes have been excised, though his chapter summaries remain.

With its rich and somewhat thorny history, Challoner's English is important to scholars of many disciplines, and its proximity to the literal translation of the most important book of the medieval period—namely, the Latin Bible—makes it invaluable to English-speakers studying the Middle Ages.

A Note on the Translation

Every discussion of the Douay-Rheims translation—whether praising or condemning it, whether acknowledging or ignoring Challoner's contribution to the text—affirms its proximity to the Latin. The translation in this volume has, however, a few characteristics that are either difficult for contemporary English-speakers to understand or that make the English less literal than it could be.

Challoner's word choice may sometimes puzzle readers. In the service of literalism, the Douay-Rheims translators and Challoner usually rendered *postquam* by the now obsolete phrase "after that," regardless of whether the Latin

word was a conjunction or an adverb. For example, at Gen 24:22, the translation reads, "And after that the camels had drunk, the man took out golden earrings weighing two sicles and as many bracelets of ten sicles weight," whereas a natural, more modern rendering would eliminate the word "that." Possibly by analogy to the case of *postquam,* or possibly because in the seventeenth century there was little distinction between the meanings of "after" and "after that," the translators occasionally rendered other words as "after that" where the phrase makes little sense in modern usage; see, for example, the temporal *cum* at Gen 8:6. On the whole, though, Challoner avoided trying to fit the square peg of English translation into the round hole of the Latin text. He shied away from the Douay-Rheims tendency to translate Latin words with awkward cognates, such as "invocate" for forms of *invoco* (for example, Gen 4:26); he frequently rendered relative pronouns with a conjunction followed by a demonstrative (Gen 3:1 and elsewhere); and he and his antecedents were free with temporal constructions, rendering, to take one example, *de nocte* as "very early" at Ex 34:4. Furthermore, Challoner translated many conjunctions as "now" that literally mean "and," "but," "moreover" or "therefore" (for example, Gen 16:1 and 3 Rg 1:1); the King James translators were also liberal in their use of "now."

Challoner's breaches of the rule of strict (some have said excessive) literalism also occur in areas other than word choice. The most frequent deviations appear in the translation of participles, the passive voice and especially passive participles. The translation of Nm 20:6 illustrates this program: the verse in Latin begins, "Ingressusque Moses et Aaron dimissa multitudine Tabernaculum Foederis corruerunt"; the 1609 translation reads, "And Moyses and Aaron,

the multitude being dismissed, entering into the tabernacle of couenant, fel"; whereas Challoner, preferring not to employ the passive voice or more than one construction with a participle, rendered the verse (with my punctuation), "And Moses and Aaron leaving the multitude went into the Tabernacle of the Covenant and fell." The many ablatives absolute and other participial constructions that have been modified by Challoner to fit more neatly into his preferred English style have not been signaled by italics in this volume because they do not illuminate anything about the Latin text and because the renderings are not so loose as to make their relationship to the Latin difficult to perceive.

Another systematic abandonment of literal translations appears in Challoner's rendering of oath formulas and other invocations of God, especially those that begin in Latin *vivo* or *vivit Dominus* or that employ constructions similar to "haec faciat mihi Deus et haec addat." Usually the first two formulas are rendered by adding "as" in English before the subject of the verb, and if the next clause begins with a conjunction, it is excised in translation. See, for example, 1 Rg 14:39, which begins in Latin, "Vivit Dominus, salvator Israhel, quia si" and was translated in the 1609 edition as "Our Lord the sauiour of Israel liueth, that if," which was modified by Challoner to read, "As the Lord liveth who is the saviour of Israel, if." The constructions that substantially resemble "haec faciat mihi Deus et haec addat" as at 1 Rg 14:44 were translated predictably in 1609 as "These thinges doe God to me, and these thinges adde he." Challoner rendered the prayer as "May God do so and so to me and add still more." Both of these divergences from the Latin are anticipated in the English of the King James Version, and because such renderings are pervasive, they have

been noted only here and are not mentioned in the Notes to the Text.

Challoner's antecedents at Douay and Rheims were also at times a bit lax in their translation. The degrees of adjectives and adverbs are not differentiated: *durius* (Gen 31:29) can be rendered as "roughly," *pessima* (Gen 37:20) as "naughtie." *Haec* (Gen 9:8), especially before verbs of saying, is often translated as "thus." Similar lapses in literalism occur with the verbs *volo* and *debeo,* the future tense, the future perfect tense and the subjunctive mood, which are all often rendered as simple futures in English; yet in most cases when the Douay-Rheims translators stuck to a literal translation and Challoner changed it, his variation and its source have been noted. When the Douay-Rheims translators use a turn of phrase that does not square with the Latin, the divergence has been commented upon only if the translation seems to be a useful key to the Latin they worked from; if they seem simply to have rendered the text loosely, no note appears. The most striking translation choices that the professors from Douay and Rheims made were to translate *utinam* (e.g., Ex 16:3) as "would to God," *absit* (e.g., Gen 44:17) as "God forbid," *salve* (e.g., 2 Rg 18:28) as "God save thee" and *vivat Rex* (e.g., 1 Rg 10:24) as "God save the King," even though there is no reference to the Divine. One other consistent policy of the Douay-Rheims translation was to translate *Dominus* as "our Lord." This practice stemmed from theological rather than philological reasons, and Challoner (like the King James translators) rendered this word as "the Lord." In these cases, there can be no other Latin reading, and since the English is not helpful in illuminating a hitherto unknown Latin text, no note has been made.

Last, the translation and Challoner's revision tried to avoid enjambment as much as possible. For example, Nm 7:18–19 reads in Latin, "Secundo die, obtulit Nathanahel, filius Suar, dux de tribu Isachar: / acetabulum argenteum," whereas at verses 24–25 of the same chapter we find "Tertio die, princeps filiorum Zabulon, Heliab, filius Helon, / obtulit acetabulum argenteum." Syntactically, the verses are identical (the colon is placed in the Latin only on the basis of the translation), but because in the first example *obtulit* appears in a separate verse from its direct object, the translation reads, "The second day, Nethanel, the son of Zuar, prince of the tribe of Issachar, made his offering: / a silver dish," while at verses 24–25 we have "The third day, the prince of the sons of Zebulun, Eliab, the son of Helon, / offered a silver dish."

Apart from these few deviations and the occasional italicized words and phrases, the Challoner revision is an exceptionally literal and readable translation of the Vulgate Bible, and it has proved helpful over the past quarter millennium to those who find the meaning of the Latin obscure.

I am grateful to the many people who have helped me with this project, including readers George Carlisle, Bob Edgar, Sally Edgar, Jim Halporn, Scott Johnson and Christopher Osborne; Alexandra Helprin, for her support and encouragement; Terra Dunham, Ian Stevenson and Sharmila Sen at Harvard University Press; Jesse Rainbow, for answering all my questions about Hebrew with clarity, depth, and precision; Christopher Husch, Philip Kim, and Julian Yolles for their excellent proofreading; Maria Ascher, for her thought-

ful editing of the Introduction; Andy Kelly, whose generosity was particularly helpful in the introductory paragraphs on Richard Challoner; Michael Herren and Danuta Shanzer for their careful reading and helpful suggestions; Angela Kinney for her invaluable editorial assistance; and especially Jan Ziolkowski, who conceived of the series, trusted me to see this project through, and supervised my work.

Swift Edgar

I would like to join in thanking those mentioned above and name additional collaborators without whose assistance this project could not have proceeded. Swift Edgar, of course, provided a treasury of advice and guidance. Two outstanding interns became indispensable to me: Christopher Husch helped with sundry scholarly and organizational aspects, including many useful philological remarks; likewise, Anne Marie Creighton added helpful comments while assisting with everything from punctuation to checking variants. Diana Ferrara assisted with formatting the text. Rebecca Frankel's meticulous proofreading was a great help in the final pass. I am grateful to my husband, Robert, for his advice on matters of biblical Greek, his rich library, and his patience. The staff of Dumbarton Oaks and the graduate community and faculty at the University of Illinois continually encouraged me. Special thanks goes to Howard Jacobson for his assistance with Hebrew and to my adviser, Danuta Shanzer, whose brilliance, patience and energy never fail to inspire. Finally, I have the sincerest gratitude for Jan Ziolkowski,

not only for his guidance and consultation on this project, but also for his indefatigable dedication to this series and our field.

Angela M. Kinney

NOTES

1 See Carleton, *The Part of Rheims in the Making of the English Bible,* p. 13.

2 Quentin, *Mémoire sur l'établissement du texte de la Vulgate,* pp. 190–92.

3 Dodd, *The Church History of England,* vol. 2, p. 121, quoted in Pope and Bullough, *English Versions of the Bible,* p. 252.

4 Knox, *The First and Second Diaries of the English College,* p. 145, cited in Carleton, *The Part of Rheims in the Making of the English Bible,* p. 16.

5 de Hamel, *The Book: A History of the Bible,* p. 28.

6 Pope and Bullough, *English Versions of the Bible,* p. 295; Greenslade, *The Cambridge History of the Bible,* p. 163.

7 Greenslade, *The Cambridge History of the Bible,* p. 163.

8 Frontispiece, Douay-Rheims Bible, 1609.

9 A Catholic, "A new Version of the Four Gospels," p. 476, quoted in Cartmell, "English Spiritual Writers," p. 583. Cartmell erroneously cites the passage as appearing on page 276 but attributes it correctly to Nicholas Wiseman, though the review was published anonymously.

10 Cotton, *Rhemes and Doway.*

11 Translated from the Latin by Knox; see Carleton, *The Part of Rheims in the Making of the English Bible,* p. 15.

12 Kaske, *Medieval Christian Literary Imagery,* p. 6.

13 A Catholic, "A new Version of the Four Gospels," p. 476.

14 Duffy, *Challoner and His Church,* p. 6.

15 See Pope and Bullough, *English Versions of the Bible,* pp. 359–71.

16 "To the right vvelbeloved English reader," Douay-Rheims Bible, 1609.

17 Gilley, "Challoner as Controvertionalist," p. 93.

Abbreviations

Gen	Genesis
Ex	Exodus
Lv	Leviticus
Nm	Numbers
Dt	Deuteronomy
Jos	Joshua
Jdg	Judges
Rt	Ruth
1 Kings	1 Kings
2 Kings	2 Kings
3 Kings	3 Kings
4 Kings	4 Kings
1 Par	1 Paralipomenon
2 Par	2 Paralipomenon
1 Ezr	1 Ezra
2 Ezr	2 Ezra
Tb	Tobit
Jdt	Judith
Est	Esther
Job	Job
Ps	Psalms
Prov	Proverbs

Ecl	Ecclesiastes
Ct	Canticle of Canticles
Wis	Wisdom
Sir	Ecclesiasticus
Is	Isaiah
Jer	Jeremiah
Lam	Lamentations
Bar	Baruch
Ez	Ezekiel
Dn	Daniel
Hos	Hosea
Joel	Joel
Am	Amos
Ob	Obadiah
Jon	Jonah
Mi	Micah
Na	Nahum
Hab	Habakkuk
Zeph	Zephaniah
Hag	Haggai
Zech	Zechariah
Mal	Malachi
1 Mcc	1 Maccabees
2 Mcc	2 Maccabees
Mt	Matthew
Mk	Mark
Lk	Luke
John	John
Act	Acts of the Apostles

Rom	Romans
1 Cor	1 Corinthians
2 Cor	2 Corinthians
Gal	Galatians
Eph	Ephesians
Phlp	Philippians
Col	Colossians
1 Th	1 Thessalonians
2 Th	2 Thessalonians
1 Tim	1 Timothy
2 Tim	2 Timothy
Tit	Titus
Phlm	Philemon
Hbr	Hebrews
Ja	James
1 Pt	1 Peter
2 Pt	2 Peter
1 John	1 John
2 John	2 John
3 John	3 John
Jud	Jude
Apc	Apocalypse of St. John the Apostle

LATIN NAMES FOR BOOKS IN THE BIBLE

Gen	Genesis
Ex	Exodi
Lv	Levitici
Nm	Numerorum
Dt	Deuteronomii

Ios	Iosue
Idc	Iudicum
Rt	Ruth
1 Rg	1 Regum
2 Rg	2 Regum
3 Rg	3 Regum
4 Rg	4 Regum
1 Par	1 Paralipomenon
2 Par	2 Paralipomenon
1 Esr	1 Ezrae
2 Esr	2 Ezrae
Tb	Tobiae
Idt	Iudith
Est	Hester
Iob	Iob
Ps	Psalmi
Prv	Proverbiorum
Ecl	Ecclesiastes
Ct	Canticum Canticorum
Sap	Sapientiae
Sir	Sirach (Ecclesiasticus *or* Iesu Filii Sirach)
Is	Isaias
Ier	Hieremias
Lam	Lamentationes
Bar	Baruch
Ez	Hiezechiel
Dn	Danihel
Os	Osee
Ioel	Iohel

Am	Amos
Abd	Abdias
Ion	Iona
Mi	Micha
Na	Naum
Hab	Abacuc
So	Sofonias
Agg	Aggeus
Za	Zaccharias
Mal	Malachi
1 Mcc	1 Macchabeorum
2 Mcc	2 Macchabeorum
Mt	Secundum Mattheum
Mc	Secundum Marcum
Lc	Secundum Lucam
Io	Secundum Iohannem
Act	Actus Apostolorum
Rm	Ad Romanos
1 Cor	Ad Corinthios 1
2 Cor	Ad Corinthios 2
Gal	Ad Galatas
Eph	Ad Ephesios
Phil	Ad Philippenses
Col	Ad Colossenses
1 Th	Ad Thessalonicenses 1
2 Th	Ad Thessalonicenses 2
1 Tim	Ad Timotheum
Tit	Ad Titum
Phlm	Ad Philemonem

Hbr	Ad Hebraeos
Iac	Epistula Iacobi
1 Pt	Epistula Petri 1
2 Pt	Epistula Petri 2
1 Io	Epistula Iohannis 1
2 Io	Epistula Iohannis 2
3 Io	Epistula Iohannis 3
Iud	Epistula Iudae
Apc	Apocalypsis Iohannis

HOSEA

Caput 1

Verbum Domini quod factum est ad Osee, filium Beeri, in diebus Oziae, Ioathan, Ahaz, Ezechiae, regum Iuda, et in diebus Hieroboam, filii Ioas, regis Israhel.

2 Principium loquendi Domino in Osee.

Et dixit Dominus ad Osee, "Vade; sume tibi uxorem fornicationum, et fac filios fornicationum, quia fornicans fornicabitur terra a Domino." 3 Et abiit et accepit Gomer, filiam Debelaim, et concepit et peperit ei filium.

4 Et dixit Dominus ad eum, "Voca nomen eius Hiezrahel, quoniam adhuc modicum et visitabo sanguinem Hiezrahel super domum Hieu, et quiescere faciam regnum domus Israhel. 5 Et in illa die conteram arcum Israhel in valle Hiezrahel."

6 Et concepit adhuc et peperit filiam, et dixit ei, "Voca nomen eius Absque Misericordia, quia non addam ultra misereri domui Israhel, sed oblivione obliviscar eorum.

Chapter 1

By marrying a harlot and by the names of his children, the prophet sets forth the crimes of Israel and their punishment. He foretells their redemption by Christ.

The word of the Lord that came to Hosea, the son of Beeri, in the days of Uzziah, Jotham, Ahaz *and* Hezekiah, kings of Judah, and in the days of Jeroboam, the son of Joash, king of Israel.

2 The beginning of the Lord's speaking by Hosea.

And the Lord said to Hosea, "Go; take thee a wife of fornications, and have *of her* children of fornications, for the land by fornication shall *depart* from the Lord." 3 So he went and took Gomer, the daughter of Diblaim, and she conceived and bore him a son.

4 And the Lord said to him, "Call his name Jezreel, for yet a little while and I will visit the blood of Jezreel upon the house of Jehu, and I will cause to cease the kingdom of the house of Israel. 5 And in that day I will break in pieces the bow of Israel in the valley of Jezreel."

6 And she conceived again and bore a daughter, and he said to him, "Call her name Without Mercy, for I will not add any more to have mercy on the house of Israel, but I will

7 Et domui Iuda miserebor, et salvabo eos in Domino, Deo suo, et non salvabo eos in arcu et gladio et in bello et in equis et in equitibus."

8 Et ablactavit eam quae erat Absque Misericordia, et concepit et peperit filium. 9 Et dixit, "Voca nomen eius Non Populus Meus, quia vos non populus meus et ego non ero vester."

10 Et erit numerus filiorum Israhel quasi harena maris, quae sine mensura est et non numerabitur. Et erit in loco ubi dicetur eis, "Non populus meus vos," dicetur eis, "Filii Dei viventis." 11 Et congregabuntur filii Iuda et filii Israhel pariter, et ponent sibimet caput unum et ascendent de terra, quia magnus dies Hiezrahel.

Caput 2

"Dicite fratribus vestris, 'Populus meus,' et sorori vestrae, 'Misericordiam consecuta.' 2 Iudicate matrem vestram; iudicate, quoniam ipsa non uxor mea et ego non vir eius. Auferat fornicationes suas a facie sua et adulteria sua de medio uberum suorum, 3 ne forte expoliem eam nudam et

utterly forget them. 7 And I will have mercy on the house of Judah, and I will save them by the Lord, their God, and I will not save them by bow nor by sword nor by battle nor by horses nor by horsemen."

8 And she weaned her that was called Without Mercy, and she conceived and bore a son. 9 And he said, "Call his name Not My People, for you are not my people and I will not be yours."

10 And the number of the children of Israel shall be as the sand of the sea, that is without measure and shall not be numbered. And it shall be in the place where it shall be said to them, "You are not my people," it shall be said to them, "Ye are the sons of the living God." 11 And the children of Judah and the children of Israel shall be gathered together, and they shall appoint themselves one head and shall come up out of the land, for great is the day of Jezreel.

Chapter 2

Israel is justly punished for leaving God. The abundance of grace in the church of Christ.

"Say ye to your brethren, 'You are my people,' and to your sister, 'Thou hast obtained mercy.' 2 Judge your mother; judge her, because she is not my wife and I am not her husband. Let her put away her fornications from her face and her adulteries from between her breasts, 3 *lest* I strip her

statuam eam secundum diem nativitatis suae. Et ponam eam quasi solitudinem et statuam eam velut terram inviam et interficiam eam siti. 4 Et filiorum illius non miserebor, quoniam filii fornicationum sunt. 5 Quia fornicata est mater eorum; confusa est quae concepit eos, quia dixit, 'Vadam post amatores meos qui dant panes mihi et aquas meas, lanam meam et linum meum, oleum meum et potum meum.' 6 Propter hoc ecce: ego sepiam viam tuam spinis, et sepiam eam maceria, et semitas suas non inveniet. 7 Et sequetur amatores suos et non adprehendet eos, et quaeret eos et non inveniet, et dicet, 'Vadam et revertar ad virum meum priorem, quia bene mihi erat tunc magis quam nunc.' 8 Et haec nescivit quia ego dedi ei frumentum et vinum et oleum et argentum multiplicavi ei et aurum, quae fecerunt Baal. 9 Idcirco convertar et sumam frumentum meum in tempore suo et vinum meum in tempore suo, et liberabo lanam meam et linum meum, quae operiebant ignominiam eius. 10 Et nunc revelabo stultitiam eius in oculis amatorum eius, et vir non eruet eam de manu mea. 11 Et cessare faciam omne gaudium eius, sollemnitatem eius, neomeniam eius, sabbatum eius et omnia festa tempora eius. 12 Et corrumpam vineam eius et ficum eius, de quibus dixit, 'Mercedes hae meae sunt quas dederunt mihi amatores mei.' Et ponam eam in saltum, et comedet illam bestia agri. 13 Et visitabo super eam dies Baalim, quibus accendebat incensum et ornabatur inaure sua et monili suo et ibat post amatores suos et mei obliviscebatur," dicit Dominus.

naked and set her as in the day that she was born. And I will make her as a wilderness and will set her as a land that none can pass through and will kill her with drought. 4 And I will not have mercy on her children, for they are the children of fornications. 5 For their mother hath committed fornication; she that conceived them is covered with shame, for she said, 'I will go after my lovers that give me my bread and my water, my wool and my flax, my oil and my drink.' 6 Wherefore behold: I will hedge up thy way with thorns, and I will stop it up with a wall, and she shall not find her paths. 7 And she shall follow after her lovers and shall not overtake them, and she shall seek them and shall not find, and she shall say, 'I will go and return to my first husband, because it was better with me then than now.' 8 And she did not know that I gave her corn and wine and oil and multiplied her silver and gold, which they have used in the service of Baal. 9 Therefore will I return and take away my corn in its season and my wine in its season, and I will set at liberty my wool and my flax, which covered her disgrace. 10 And now I will lay open her folly in the eyes of her lovers, and no man shall deliver her out of my hand. 11 And I will cause all her mirth to cease, her solemnities, her new moons, her sabbaths and all her festival times. 12 And I will destroy her vines and her fig trees, of which she said, 'These are my rewards which my lovers have given me.' And I will make her as a forest, and the beasts of the field shall devour her. 13 And I will visit upon her the days of Baalim, to whom she burnt incense and decked herself out with her earrings and with her jewels and went after her lovers and forgot me," saith the Lord.

14 "Propter hoc ecce: ego lactabo eam et ducam eam in solitudinem, et loquar ad cor eius. 15 Et dabo ei vinitores eius ex eodem loco et Vallem Achor ad aperiendam spem, et canet ibi iuxta dies iuventutis suae et iuxta dies ascensionis suae de terra Aegypti.

16 "Et erit in die illa," ait Dominus, "vocabit me 'vir meus,' et non vocabit me ultra 'Baali.' 17 Et auferam nomina Baalim de ore eius, et non recordabitur ultra nominis eorum. 18 Et percutiam cum eis foedus in die illa, cum bestia agri et cum volucre caeli et cum reptili terrae. Et arcum et gladium et bellum conteram de terra, et dormire eos faciam fiducialiter. 19 Et sponsabo te mihi in sempiternum, et sponsabo te mihi in iustitia et iudicio et in misericordia et in miserationibus, 20 et sponsabo te mihi in fide, et scies quia ego Dominus.

21 "Et erit in illa die: exaudiam," dicit Dominus. "Exaudiam caelos, et illi exaudient terram, 22 et terra exaudiet triticum et vinum et oleum, et haec exaudient Hiezrahel. 23 Et seminabo eam mihi in terram, et miserebor eius quae fuit Absque Misericordia. 24 Et dicam Non Populo Meo, 'Populus meus es tu,' et ipse dicet, 'Deus meus es tu.'"

14 "Therefore behold: I will allure her and will lead her into the wilderness, and I will speak to her heart. 15 And I will give her vinedressers out of the same place and the Valley of Achor for an opening of hope, and she shall sing there according to the days of her youth and according to the days of her coming up out of the land of Egypt.

16 "And it shall be in that day," saith the Lord, "that she shall call me 'my husband,' and she shall call me no more 'Baali.' 17 And I will take away the names of Baalim out of her mouth, and she shall no more remember their name. 18 And in that day I will make a covenant with them, with the beasts of the field and with the fowls of the air and with the creeping things of the earth. And I will destroy the bow and the sword and war out of the land, and I will make them sleep secure. 19 And I will espouse thee to me for ever, and I will espouse thee to me in justice and judgment and in mercy and in commiserations, 20 and I will espouse thee to me in faith, and thou shalt know that I am the Lord.

21 "And it shall come to pass in that day: I will hear," saith the Lord. "I will hear the heavens, and they shall hear the earth, 22 and the earth shall hear the corn and the wine and the oil, and these shall hear Jezreel. 23 And I will sow her unto me *in* the earth, and I will have mercy on her that was Without Mercy. 24 And I will say to *that which was* Not My People, 'Thou art my people,' and they shall say, 'Thou art my God.'"

Caput 3

Et dixit Dominus ad me, "Adhuc vade; dilige mulierem dilectam amico et adulteram sicut diligit Dominus filios Israhel, et ipsi respiciunt ad deos alienos et diligunt vinacea uvarum."

2 Et fodi eam mihi quindecim argenteis et choro hordei et dimidio choro hordei. 3 Et dixi ad eam, "Dies multos expectabis me; non fornicaberis, et non eris viro, sed et ego expectabo te."

4 Quia dies multos sedebunt filii Israhel sine rege et sine principe et sine sacrificio et sine altari et sine ephod et sine therafin. 5 Et post haec revertentur filii Israhel et quaerent Dominum, Deum suum, et David, regem suum. Et pavebunt ad Dominum et ad bonum eius in novissimo dierum.

Chapter 3

The prophet is commanded again to love an adulteress to signify God's love to the synagogue. The wretched state of the Jews for a long time till at last they shall be converted.

And the Lord said to me, "Go yet again, *and* love a woman beloved of her friend and an adulteress as the Lord loveth the children of Israel, and they look to strange gods and love the husks of the grapes."

2 And I *bought* her to me for fifteen pieces of silver and for a core of barley and for half a core of barley. 3 And I said to her, "Thou shalt wait for me many days; thou shalt not play the harlot, and thou shalt be no man's, and I also will wait for thee."

4 For the children of Israel shall sit many days without king and without prince and without sacrifice and without altar and without ephod and without theraphim. 5 And after this the children of Israel shall return and shall seek the Lord, their God, and David, their king. And they shall fear the Lord and his goodness in the last days.

Caput 4

Audite verbum Domini, filii Israhel, quia iudicium Domino cum habitatoribus terrae, non est enim veritas, et non est misericordia, et non est scientia Dei in terra.

2 "Maledictum et mendacium et homicidium et furtum et adulterium inundaverunt, et sanguis sanguinem tetigit. 3 Propter hoc lugebit terra, et infirmabitur omnis qui habitat in ea in bestia agri et in volucre caeli, sed et pisces maris congregabuntur. 4 Verumtamen unusquisque non iudicet, et non arguatur vir, populus enim tuus sicut hii qui contradicunt sacerdoti. 5 Et corrues hodie, et corruet etiam propheta tecum. Nocte tacere feci matrem tuam. 6 Conticuit populus meus eo quod non habuerit scientiam; quia tu scientiam reppulisti repellam te, ne sacerdotio fungaris mihi. Et oblita es legis Dei tui; obliviscar filiorum tuorum et ego. 7 Secundum multitudinem eorum, sic peccaverunt mihi. Gloriam eorum in ignominiam commutabo. 8 Peccata populi mei comedent et ad iniquitatem eorum sublevabunt animas

Chapter 4

God's judgment against the sins of Israel. Judah is warned not to follow their example.

Hear the word of the Lord, ye children of Israel, for the Lord *shall enter into* judgment with the inhabitants of the land, for there is no truth, and there is no mercy, and there is no knowledge of God in the land.

2 "Cursing and lying and killing and theft and adultery have overflowed, and blood hath touched blood. 3 Therefore shall the land mourn, and every one that dwelleth in it shall languish with the beasts of the field and with the fowls of the air, yea, the fishes of the sea also shall be gathered together. 4 But yet let not any man judge, and let not a man be rebuked, for thy people are as they that contradict the priest. 5 And thou shalt fall today, and the prophet also shall fall with thee. In the night I have made thy mother to be silent. 6 My people have been silent because they had no knowledge; because thou hast rejected knowledge I will reject thee, that thou shalt not do the office of priesthood to me. And thou hast forgotten the law of thy God; I also will forget thy children. 7 According to the multitude of them, so have they sinned against me. I will change their glory into shame. 8 They shall eat the sins of my people and shall lift up

eorum. 9 Et erit sicut populus, sic sacerdos. Et visitabo super eum vias eius, et cogitationes eius reddam ei, 10 et comedent et non saturabuntur. Fornicati sunt et non cessaverunt quoniam Dominum reliquerunt in non custodiendo.

11 "Fornicatio et vinum et ebrietas auferunt cor. 12 Populus meus in ligno suo interrogavit, et baculus eius adnuntiavit ei, spiritus enim fornicationum decepit eos et fornicati sunt a Deo suo. 13 Super capita montium sacrificabant et super colles accendebant thymiama subtus quercum et populum et terebinthum, quia bona erat umbra eius. Ideo fornicabuntur filiae vestrae, et sponsae vestrae adulterae erunt. 14 Non visitabo super filias vestras cum fuerint fornicatae et super sponsas vestras cum adulteraverint, quoniam ipsi cum meretricibus conversabantur et cum effeminatis sacrificabant, et populus non intellegens vapulabit.

15 "Si fornicaris tu, Israhel, non delinquat saltim Iuda. Et nolite ingredi in Galgala, et ne ascenderitis in Bethaven, neque iuraveritis, 'Vivit Dominus.' 16 Quoniam sicut vacca lasciviens declinavit Israhel. Nunc pascet eos Dominus quasi agnum in latitudine. 17 Particeps idolorum Ephraim; dimitte eum. 18 Separatum est convivium eorum; fornicatione fornicati sunt; dilexerunt adferre ignominiam protectores eius. 19 Ligavit spiritus eum in alis suis, et confundentur a sacrificiis suis."

their souls to their iniquity. 9 And there shall be like people, like priest. And I will visit their ways upon them, and I will repay them their devices, 10 and they shall eat and shall not be filled. They have committed fornication and have not ceased because they have forsaken the Lord in not observing *his law.*

11 "Fornication and wine and drunkenness take away the understanding. 12 My people have consulted *their stocks,* and their staff hath declared unto them, for the spirit of fornication hath deceived them and they have committed fornication against their God. 13 They offered sacrifice upon the tops of the mountains and burnt incense upon the hills under the oak and the poplar and the turpentine tree, because the shadow thereof was good. Therefore shall your daughters commit fornication, and your spouses shall be adulteresses. 14 I will not visit upon your daughters when they shall commit fornication and upon your spouses when they shall commit adultery, because themselves conversed with harlots and offered sacrifice with the effeminate, and the people that doth not understand shall be beaten.

15 "If thou play the harlot, O Israel, at least let not Judah offend. And go ye not into Gilgal, and come not up into Beth-aven, and do not swear, 'The Lord liveth.' 16 For Israel hath gone astray like a wanton heifer. Now will the Lord feed them as a lamb in a spacious place. 17 Ephraim is a partaker with idols; let him alone. 18 Their banquet is separated; they have gone astray by fornication; they that *should* have protected them have loved to bring shame upon them. 19 The wind hath bound them up in its wings, and they shall be confounded because of their sacrifices."

Caput 5

"Audite hoc, sacerdotes, et adtendite, domus Israhel, et domus regis, auscultate, quia vobis iudicium est quoniam laqueus facti estis speculationi et rete expansum super Thabor, 2 et victimas declinastis in profundum, et ego eruditor omnium eorum. 3 Ego scio Ephraim, et Israhel non est absconditus a me, quia nunc fornicatus est Ephraim; contaminatus est Israhel.

4 "Non dabunt cogitationes suas ut revertantur ad Deum suum, quia spiritus fornicationum in medio eorum et Dominum non cognoverunt. 5 Et respondebit arrogantia Israhel in facie eius, et Israhel et Ephraim ruent in iniquitate sua; ruet etiam Iudas cum eis. 6 In gregibus suis et in armentis suis vadent ad quaerendum Dominum et non invenient; ablatus est ab eis. 7 In Dominum praevaricati sunt, quia filios alienos genuerunt. Nunc devorabit eos mensis cum partibus suis.

8 "Clangite bucina in Gabaa, tuba in Rama; ululate in Bethaven, post tergum tuum, Beniamin. 9 Ephraim in desolatione erit in die correptionis; in tribubus Israhel ostendi fidem. 10 Facti sunt principes Iuda quasi adsumentes

Chapter 5

God's threats against the priests, the people and princes of Israel for their idolatry.

"Hear ye this, O priests, and hearken, O ye house of Israel, and give ear, O house of the king, for there is a judgment against you because you have been a snare to *them whom you should have watched over* and a net spread upon Tabor, 2 and you have turned aside victims into the depth, and I am the teacher of them all. 3 I know Ephraim, and Israel is not hid from me, for now Ephraim hath committed fornication; Israel is defiled.

4 "They will not set their thoughts to return to their God, for the spirit of fornication is in the midst of them and they have not known the Lord. 5 And the pride of Israel shall answer in his face, and Israel and Ephraim shall fall in their iniquity; Judah also shall fall with them. 6 With their flocks and with their herds they shall go to seek the Lord and shall not find him; he is withdrawn from them. 7 They have transgressed against the Lord, for they have begotten children that are strangers. Now shall a month devour them with their portions.

8 "Blow ye the cornet in Gibeah, the trumpet in Ramah; howl ye in Beth-aven, behind thy back, O Benjamin. 9 Ephraim shall be in desolation in the day of rebuke; among the tribes of Israel I have shewn *that which shall surely be.* 10 The princes of Judah are become as they that take up the

terminum. Super eos effundam quasi aquam iram meam.
11 Calumniam patiens est Ephraim fractus iudicio quoniam
coepit abire post sordem. 12 Et ego quasi tinea Ephraim et
quasi putredo domui Iuda. 13 Et vidit Ephraim languorem
suum, et Iuda vinculum suum. Et abiit Ephraim ad Assur et
misit ad regem ultorem. Et ipse non poterit sanare vos, nec
solvere poterit a vobis vinculum, 14 quoniam ego quasi leaena
Ephraim et quasi catulus leonis domui Iuda. Ego, ego capiam et vadam. Tollam, et non est qui eruat. 15 Vadens revertar ad locum meum donec deficiatis et quaeratis faciem
meam."

Caput 6

"In tribulatione sua mane consurgent ad me: 'Venite, et
revertamur ad Dominum, 2 quia ipse cepit et sanabit nos.
Percutiet, et curabit nos. 3 Vivificabit nos post duos dies; in
die tertia suscitabit nos, et vivemus in conspectu eius. Scie-
mus, sequemurque ut cognoscamus Dominum. Quasi dilu-
culum praeparatus est egressus eius, et veniet quasi imber
nobis temporaneus et serotinus terrae.'

bound. I will pour out my wrath upon them like water. 11 Ephraim is under oppression and broken in judgment because he began to go after filthiness. 12 And I will be like a moth to Ephraim and like rottenness to the house of Judah. 13 And Ephraim saw his sickness, and Judah his band. And Ephraim went to the Assyrian and sent to the avenging king. And he shall not be able to heal you, neither shall he be able to take off the band from you, 14 for I will be like a lioness to Ephraim and like a lion's whelp to the house of Judah. I, I will catch and go. I will take away, and there is none that can rescue. 15 I will go and return to my place until you are consumed and seek my face."

Chapter 6

Affliction shall be a means to bring many to Christ. A complaint of the untowardness of the Jews. God loves mercy more than sacrifice.

"In their affliction they will rise early to me: 'Come, and let us return to the Lord, 2 for he hath taken us and he will heal us. He will strike, and he will cure us. 3 He will revive us after two days; on the third day he will raise us up, and we shall live in his sight. We shall know, and we shall follow on that we may know the Lord. His going forth is prepared as the morning light, and he will come to us as the early and the latter rain to the earth.'

4 "Quid faciam tibi, Ephraim? Quid faciam tibi, Iuda? Misericordia vestra quasi nubes matutina et quasi ros mane pertransiens. 5 Propter hoc dolavi in prophetis; occidi eos in verbis oris mei, et iudicia tua quasi lux egredientur. 6 Quia misericordiam volui et non sacrificium, et scientiam Dei plus quam holocausta. 7 Ipsi autem sicut Adam transgressi sunt pactum; ibi praevaricati sunt in me. 8 Galaad civitas operantium idolum, subplantata sanguine. 9 Et quasi fauces virorum latronum particeps sacerdotum in via interficientium pergentes de Sychem, quia scelus operati sunt. 10 In domo Israhel vidi horrendum: ibi fornicationes Ephraim. Contaminatus est Israhel. 11 Sed et, Iuda, pone messem tibi, cum convertero captivitatem populi mei."

Caput 7

"Cum sanare vellem Israhel, revelata est iniquitas Ephraim et malitia Samariae, quia operati sunt mendacium et fur ingressus est spolians, latrunculus foris. 2 Et ne forte

4 "What shall I do to thee, O Ephraim? What shall I do to thee, O Judah? Your mercy is as a morning cloud and as the dew that goeth away in the morning. 5 For this reason have I hewed them by the prophets; I have slain them by the words of my mouth, and thy judgments shall go forth as the light. 6 For I desired mercy and not sacrifice, and the knowledge of God more than holocausts. 7 But they like Adam have transgressed the covenant; there have they dealt treacherously against me. 8 Gilead is a city of workers of idols, supplanted with blood. 9 And like the jaws of highway robbers they conspire with the priests who murder in the way those that pass out of Shechem, for they have wrought wickedness. 10 I have seen a horrible thing in the house of Israel: the fornications of Ephraim there. Israel is defiled. 11 And thou also, O Judah, set thee a harvest, when I shall bring back the captivity of my people."

Chapter 7

The manifold sins of Israel and of their kings hinder the Lord from healing them.

"When I would have healed Israel, the iniquity of Ephraim was discovered and the wickedness of Samaria, for they have committed falsehood and the thief is come in *to* steal; the robber is without. 2 And *lest* they may say in their

dicant in cordibus suis omnem malitiam eorum me recorda-
tum, nunc circumdederunt eos adinventiones suae; coram
facie mea factae sunt. 3 In malitia sua laetificaverunt regem
et in mendaciis suis principes. 4 Omnes adulterantes, quasi
clibanus succensus a coquente. Quievit paululum civitas a
commixtione fermenti donec fermentaretur totum. 5 Dies
regis nostri: coeperunt principes furere a vino; extendit manum suam cum inlusoribus. 6 Quia adplicuerunt quasi cliba-
num cor suum cum insidiaretur eis, tota nocte dormivit
coquens eos; mane ipse succensus quasi ignis flammae.
7 Omnes calefacti sunt quasi clibanus et devoraverunt iudices suos; omnes reges eorum ceciderunt. Non est qui clamet
in eis ad me. 8 Ephraim in populis ipse commiscebatur;
Ephraim factus est subcinericius panis qui non reversatur.
9 Comederunt alieni robur eius, et ipse nescivit. Sed et cani
effusi sunt in eo, et ipse ignoravit. 10 Et humiliabitur superbia Israhel in facie eius, nec reversi sunt ad Dominum, Deum
suum, et non quaesierunt eum in omnibus his.

11 "Et factus est Ephraim quasi columba seducta, non habens cor. Aegyptum invocabant; ad Assyrios abierunt. 12 Et
cum profecti fuerint, expandam super eos rete meum; quasi
volucrem caeli detraham eos; caedam eos secundum auditionem coetus eorum. 13 Vae eis, quoniam recesserunt a me.
Vastabuntur quia praevaricati sunt in me, et ego redemi eos,
et ipsi locuti sunt contra me mendacia. 14 Et non clamaverunt ad me in corde suo, sed ululabant in cubilibus suis.

hearts that I *remember* all their wickedness, their own devices now have beset them about; they have been done before my face. 3 They have made the king glad with their wickedness and the princes with their lies. 4 They are all adulterers, like an oven heated by the baker. The city rested a little from the mingling of the leaven till the whole was leavened. 5 The day of our king: the princes began to be mad with wine; he stretched out his hand with scorners. 6 Because they have applied their heart like an oven when he laid snares for them, he slept all the night baking them; in the morning he himself was heated as a flaming fire. 7 They were all heated like an oven and have devoured their judges; all their kings have fallen. There is none amongst them that calleth unto me. 8 Ephraim himself is mixed among the nations; Ephraim is become as bread baked under the ashes that is not turned. 9 Strangers have devoured his strength, and he knew it not. Yea, grey hairs also are spread about upon him, and he is ignorant of it. 10 And the pride of Israel shall be humbled before his face, and they have not returned to the Lord, their God, nor have they sought him in all these.

11 "And Ephraim is become as a dove that is decoyed, not having a heart. They called upon Egypt; they went to the Assyrians. 12 And when they shall go, I will spread my net upon them; I will bring them down as the fowl of the air; I will strike them as their congregation hath heard. 13 Woe to them, for they have departed from me. They shall be wasted because they have transgressed against me, and I redeemed them, and they have spoken lies against me. 14 And they have not cried to me with their heart, but they howled in their

Super triticum et vinum ruminabant; recesserunt a me. 15 Et ego erudivi eos et confortavi brachia eorum, et in me cogitaverunt malitiam. 16 Reversi sunt ut essent absque iugo; facti sunt quasi arcus dolosus. Cadent in gladio principes eorum a furore linguae suae. Ista subsannatio eorum in terra Aegypti."

Caput 8

"In gutture tuo sit tuba quasi aquila super domum Domini pro eo quod transgressi sunt foedus meum et legem meam praevaricati sunt. 2 Me invocabunt: 'Deus meus, cognovimus te Israhel.' 3 Proiecit Israhel bonum; inimicus persequetur eum. 4 Ipsi regnaverunt et non ex me; principes extiterunt, et non cognovi. Argentum suum et aurum suum fecerunt sibi idola ut interirent. 5 Proiectus est vitulus tuus, Samaria; iratus est furor meus in eos. Usquequo non poterunt emundari? 6 Quia ex Israhel et ipse est; artifex fecit illum, et non est deus, quoniam in aranearum telas erit vitulus Samariae. 7 Quia ventum seminabunt et turbinem metent. Culmus stans non est in eo; germen non faciet farinam, quod

beds. They have thought upon wheat and wine; they are departed from me. 15 And I have chastised them and strengthened their arms, and they have imagined evil against me. 16 They returned that they might be without yoke; they became like a deceitful bow. Their princes shall fall by the sword for the rage of their tongue. This is their derision in the land of Egypt."

Chapter 8

The Israelites are threatened with destruction for their impiety and idolatry.

"Let there be a trumpet in thy throat like an eagle upon the house of the Lord because they have transgressed my covenant and have violated my law. 2 They shall call upon me: 'O my God, we, Israel, know thee.' 3 Israel hath cast off the thing that is good; the enemy shall pursue him. 4 They have reigned *but* not by me; they have been princes, and I knew not. Of their silver and their gold they have made idols to themselves that they might perish. 5 Thy calf, O Samaria, is cast off; my wrath is kindled against them. How long will they be incapable of being cleansed? 6 For itself also is *the invention* of Israel; a workman made it, and it is no god, for the calf of Samaria shall be turned to spiders' webs. 7 For they shall sow wind and reap a whirlwind. There is no standing stalk in it; the bud shall yield no meal, and if it should yield

et si fecerit alieni comedent eam. 8 Devoratus est Israhel; nunc factus est in nationibus quasi vas inmundum. 9 Quia ipsi ascenderunt ad Assur, onager solitarius sibi; Ephraim munera dederunt amatoribus. 10 Sed et cum mercede conduxerint nationes, nunc congregabo eos, et quiescent paulisper ab onere regis et principum.

11 "Quia multiplicavit Ephraim altaria ad peccandum, factae sunt ei arae in delictum. 12 Scribam ei multiplices leges meas, quae velut alienae conputatae sunt. 13 Hostias offerent; immolabunt carnes et comedent, et Dominus non suscipiet eas. Nunc recordabitur iniquitatis eorum et visitabit peccata eorum; ipsi in Aegyptum convertentur. 14 Et oblitus est Israhel factoris sui et aedificavit delubra, et Iudas multiplicavit urbes munitas. Et mittam ignem in civitates eius, et devorabit aedes illius."

Caput 9

Noli laetari, Israhel; noli exultare sicut populi, quia fornicatus es a Deo tuo; dilexisti mercedem super omnes areas tritici. 2 Area et torcular non pascet eos, et vinum mentietur

strangers shall eat it. 8 Israel is swallowed up; now is he become among the nations like an unclean vessel. 9 For they are gone up to Assyria, a wild ass alone by himself; Ephraim hath given gifts to his lovers. 10 But even though they shall have hired the nations, now will I gather them together, and they shall rest a while from the burden of the king and the princes.

11 "Because Ephraim hath made many altars to sin, altars are become to him unto sin. 12 I shall write to him my manifold laws, which have been accounted as foreign. 13 They shall offer victims; they shall sacrifice flesh and shall eat it, and the Lord will not receive them. Now will he remember their iniquity and will visit their sins; they shall return to Egypt. 14 And Israel hath forgotten his maker and hath built temples, and Judah hath built many fenced cities. And I will send a fire upon his cities, and it shall devour the houses thereof."

Chapter 9

The distress and captivity of Israel for their sins and idolatry.

Rejoice not, O Israel; rejoice not as the nations do, for thou hast committed fornication against thy God; thou hast loved a reward upon every corn-floor. 2 The floor and the winepress shall not feed them, and the wine shall deceive

eis. 3 Non habitabunt in terra Domini. Reversus est Ephraim in Aegyptum et in Assyriis pollutum comedit. 4 Non libabunt Domino vinum, et non placebunt ei. Sacrificia eorum quasi panis lugentium; omnes qui comedent eum contaminabuntur, quia panis eorum animae ipsorum: non intrabit in domum Domini.

5 Quid facietis in die sollemni, in die festivitatis Domini? 6 Ecce enim: profecti sunt a vastitate. Aegyptus congregabit eos; Memphis sepeliet eos. Desiderabile argentum eorum urtica hereditabit; lappa in tabernaculis eorum. 7 Venerunt dies visitationis; venerunt dies retributionis. Scitote, Israhel, stultum prophetam, insanum virum spiritalem propter multitudinem iniquitatis tuae et multitudinem amentiae. 8 Speculator Ephraim cum Deo meo. Propheta laqueus ruinae factus est super omnes vias eius; insania in domo Dei eius. 9 Profunde peccaverunt sicut in diebus Gabaa. Recordabitur iniquitatis eorum et visitabit peccata eorum.

10 "Quasi uvas in deserto inveni Israhel; quasi prima poma ficulneae in cacumine eius vidi patres eorum. Ipsi autem intraverunt ad Beelphegor et abalienati sunt in confusionem et facti sunt abominabiles sicut ea quae dilexerunt. 11 Ephraim, quasi avis avolavit gloria eorum a partu et ab utero et a conceptu. 12 Quod et si enutrierint filios suos, absque liberis eos faciam in hominibus, sed et vae eis cum recessero ab eis. 13 Ephraim, ut vidi, Tyrus erat fundata in pulchritudine, et Ephraim educet ad interfectorem filios suos."

them. 3 They shall not dwell in the Lord's land. Ephraim is returned to Egypt and hath eaten unclean things among the Assyrians. 4 They shall not offer wine to the Lord, neither shall they please him. Their sacrifices shall be like the bread of mourners; all that shall eat it shall be defiled, for their bread is *life* for their soul: it shall not enter into the house of the Lord.

5 What will you do in the solemn day, in the day of the feast of the Lord? 6 For behold: they are gone because of destruction. Egypt shall gather them together; Memphis shall bury them. Nettles shall inherit their beloved silver; the bur shall be in their tabernacles. 7 The days of visitation are come; the days of repaying are come. Know ye, O Israel, that the prophet was foolish, the spiritual man was mad for the multitude of thy iniquity and the multitude of thy madness. 8 The watchman of Ephraim was with my God. The prophet is become a snare of ruin upon all his ways; madness is in the house of his God. 9 They have sinned deeply as in the days of Gibeah. He will remember their iniquity and will visit their sin.

10 "I found Israel like grapes in the desert; I saw their fathers like the firstfruits of the fig tree in the top thereof. But they went in to Baal-peor and alienated themselves to *that* confusion and became abominable as those things were which they loved. 11 As for Ephraim, their glory hath flown away like a bird from the birth and from the womb and from the conception. 12 And though they should bring up their children, I will make them without children among men, yea, and woe to them when I shall depart from them. 13 Ephraim, as I saw, was a Tyre founded in beauty, and Ephraim shall bring out his children to the murderer."

14 Da eis, Domine. Quid dabis eis? Da eis vulvam sine liberis et ubera arentia.

15 "Omnes nequitiae eorum in Galgal, quia ibi exosos habui eos. Propter malitiam adinventionum eorum de domo mea eiciam eos. Non addam ut diligam eos; omnes principes eorum recedentes. 16 Percussus est Ephraim; radix eorum exsiccata est; fructum nequaquam facient. Quod et si genuerint, interficiam amantissima uteri eorum."

17 Abiciet eos Deus meus quia non audierunt eum, et erunt vagi in nationibus.

Caput 10

Vitis frondosa: Israhel; fructus adaequatus est ei. Secundum multitudinem fructus sui multiplicavit altaria; iuxta ubertatem terrae suae exuberavit simulacris. 2 Divisum est cor eorum; nunc interibunt. Ipse confringet simulacra eorum; depopulabitur aras eorum.

3 Quia nunc dicent, "Non est rex nobis, non enim timemus Dominum. Et rex quid faciet nobis?" 4 Loquimini verba visionis inutilis, et ferietis foedus, et germinabit quasi

14 Give them, O Lord. What wilt thou give them? Give them a womb without children and dry breasts.

15 "All their wickedness is in Gilgal, for there I hated them. For the wickedness of their devices I will cast them forth out of my house. I will love them no more; all their princes are revolters. 16 Ephraim is struck; their root is dried up; they shall yield no fruit. *And* if they should have issue, I will slay the best beloved *fruit* of their womb."

17 My God will cast them away because they hearkened not to him, and they shall be wanderers among the nations.

Chapter 10

After many benefits great affliction shall fall upon the ten tribes for their ingratitude to God.

Israel: a vine full of branches; the fruit is agreeable to it. According to the multitude of his fruit he hath multiplied altars; according to the plenty of his land he hath abounded with idols. 2 Their heart is divided; now they shall perish. He shall break down their idols; he shall destroy their altars.

3 For now they shall say, "We have no king, because we fear not the Lord. And what shall a king do to us?" 4 You speak words of an unprofitable vision, and you shall make a covenant, and judgment shall spring up as bitterness in the

amaritudo iudicium super sulcos agri. 5 Vaccas Bethaven coluerunt habitatores Samariae, quia luxit super eum populus eius et aeditui eius super eum exultaverunt in gloria eius, quia migravit ab eo. 6 Siquidem et ipse in Assur delatus est, munus regi ultori. Confusio Ephraim capiet, et confundetur Israhel in voluntate sua. 7 Transire fecit Samaria regem suum quasi spumam super faciem aquae. 8 Et disperdentur excelsa idoli, peccatum Israhel. Lappa et tribulus ascendet super aras eorum, et dicent montibus, "Operite nos," et collibus, "Cadite super nos."

9 "Ex diebus Gabaa peccavit Israhel; ibi steterunt. Non conprehendet eos in Gabaa proelium super filios iniquitatis. 10 Iuxta desiderium meum corripiam eos, et congregabuntur super eos populi cum corripientur propter duas iniquitates suas. 11 Ephraim vitula docta diligere trituram, et ego transivi super pulchritudinem colli eius. Ascendam super Ephraim; arabit Iudas; confringet sibi sulcos Iacob. 12 Seminate vobis in iustitia, et metite in ore misericordiae; innovate vobis novale, tempus autem requirendi Dominum cum venerit qui docebit vos iustitiam. 13 Arastis impietatem; iniquitatem messuistis; comedistis frugem mendacii quia confisus es in viis tuis, in multitudine fortium tuorum. 14 Consurget tumultus in populo tuo, et omnes munitiones tuae vastabuntur sicut vastatus est Salmana a domo eius qui iudicavit Baal in die proelii, matre super filios adlisa. 15 Sic fecit vobis Bethel a facie malitiae nequitiarum vestrarum."

furrows of the field. 5 The inhabitants of Samaria have worshipped the kine of Beth-aven, for the people thereof have mourned over it and the wardens of its temple *that* rejoiced over it in its glory, because it is departed from it. 6 For itself also is carried into Assyria, a present to the avenging king. Shame shall fall upon Ephraim, and Israel shall be confounded in his own will. 7 Samaria hath made her king to pass as froth upon the face of the water. 8 And the high places of the idol, the sin of Israel, shall be destroyed. The bur and the thistle shall grow up over their altars, and they shall say to the mountains, "Cover us," and to the hills, "Fall upon us."

9 "From the days of Gibeah Israel hath sinned; there they stood. The battle in Gibeah against the children of iniquity shall not overtake them. 10 According to my desire I will chastise them, and the nations shall be gathered together against them when they shall be chastised for their two iniquities. 11 Ephraim is a heifer taught to love to tread out *corn, but* I passed over upon the beauty of her neck. I will ride upon Ephraim; Judah shall plough; Jacob shall break the furrows for himself. 12 Sow for yourselves in justice, and reap in the mouth of mercy; break up your fallow ground, but the time to seek the Lord is when he shall come that shall teach you justice. 13 You have ploughed wickedness; you have reaped iniquity; you have eaten the fruit of lying because thou hast trusted in thy ways, in the multitude of thy strong ones. 14 A tumult shall arise among thy people, and all thy fortresses shall be destroyed as Shalman was destroyed by the house of him that judged Baal in the day of battle, the mother being dashed in pieces upon her children. 15 So hath Bethel done to you *because* of the evil of your iniquities."

Caput 11

"Sicuti mane transiit pertransiit rex Israhel. Quia puer Israhel, et dilexi eum, et ex Aegypto vocavi filium meum. 2 Vocaverunt eos, sic abierunt a facie eorum; Baalim immolabant et simulacris sacrificabant. 3 Et ego quasi nutricius Ephraim; portabam eos in brachiis meis, et nescierunt quod curarem eos. 4 In funiculis Adam traham eos, in vinculis caritatis, et ero eis quasi exaltans iugum super maxillas eorum, et declinavi ad eum ut vesceretur. 5 Non revertetur in terram Aegypti, et Assur ipse rex eius, quoniam noluerunt converti. 6 Coepit gladius in civitatibus eius, et consumet electos eius et comedet capita eorum. 7 Et populus meus pendebit ad reditum meum, iugum autem inponetur eis simul quod non auferetur.

8 "Quomodo dabo te, Ephraim? Protegam te, Israhel? Quomodo dabo te sicut Adama? Ponam te ut Seboim? Conversum est in me cor meum; pariter conturbata est paenitudo mea. 9 Non faciam furorem irae meae; non convertar ut disperdam Ephraim, quoniam Deus ego et non homo, in medio tui Sanctus, et non ingrediar civitatem.

10 "Post Dominum ambulabunt; quasi leo rugiet, quia ipse

Chapter 11

God proceeds in threatening Israel for their ingratitude, yet he will not utterly destroy them.

"As the morning passeth, *so* hath the king of Israel passed away. Because Israel was a child, and I loved him, and I called my son out of Egypt. 2 *As* they called them, *they* went away from before their face; they offered victims to Baalim and sacrificed to idols. 3 And I was like a foster father to Ephraim; I carried them in my arms, and they knew not that I healed them. 4 I will draw them with the cords of Adam, with the bands of love, and I will be to them as one that *taketh off* the yoke on their jaws, and I *put his meat* to him that he might eat. 5 He shall not return into the land of Egypt, *but* the Assyrian shall be his king, because they would not be converted. 6 The sword hath begun in his cities, and it shall consume his chosen men and shall devour their heads. 7 And my people shall long for my return, but a yoke shall be put upon them together which shall not be taken off.

8 "How shall I *deal with* thee, O Ephraim? Shall I protect thee, O Israel? How shall I make thee as Admah? Shall I set thee as Zeboiim? My heart is turned within me; my repentance is stirred *up*. 9 I will not execute the fierceness of my wrath; I will not return to destroy Ephraim, because I am God and not man, the Holy One in the midst of thee, and I will not enter into the city.

10 "They shall walk after the Lord; he shall roar as a lion,

rugiet et formidabunt filii maris. 11 Et avolabunt quasi avis ex Aegypto et quasi columba de terra Assyriorum, et conlocabo eos in domibus suis," dicit Dominus.

12 "Circumdedit me in negatione Ephraim, et in dolo domus Israhel, Iudas autem testis descendit cum Deo et cum sanctis fidelis."

Caput 12

Ephraim pascit ventum et sequitur aestum; tota die mendacium et vastitatem multiplicat, et foedus cum Assyriis iniit et oleum in Aegyptum ferebat. 2 Iudicium ergo Domini cum Iuda et visitatio super Iacob; iuxta vias eius et iuxta adinventiones eius reddet ei. 3 In utero subplantavit fratrem suum, et in fortitudine sua directus est cum angelo. 4 Et invaluit ad angelum et confortatus est; flevit et rogavit eum; in Bethel invenit eum, et ibi locutus est nobiscum. 5 Et Dominus, Deus exercituum, Dominus, memoriale eius. 6 Et tu ad Deum tuum converteris; misericordiam et iudicium custodi, et spera in Deo tuo semper.

7 Chanaan: in manu eius statera dolosa; calumniam dilexit. 8 Et dixit Ephraim, "Verumtamen dives effectus sum; inveni

because he shall roar and the children of the sea shall fear. 11 And they shall fly away like a bird out of Egypt and like a dove out of the land of the Assyrians, and I will place them in their own houses," saith the Lord.

12 "Ephraim hath compassed me about with denials, and the house of Israel with deceit, but Judah went down as a witness with God and is faithful with the saints."

Chapter 12

Israel is reproved for sin. God's favours to them.

Ephraim feedeth on the wind and followeth the burning heat; all the day long he multiplieth lies and desolation, and he hath made a covenant with the Assyrians and carried oil into Egypt. 2 Therefore there is a judgment of the Lord with Judah and a visitation for Jacob; he will render to him according to his ways and according to his devices. 3 In the womb he supplanted his brother, and by his strength he had success with an angel. 4 And he prevailed over the angel and was strengthened; he wept and made supplication to him; he found him in Bethel, and there he spoke with us. 5 Even the Lord, the God of hosts, the Lord, is his memorial. 6 *Therefore* turn thou to thy God; keep mercy and judgment, and hope in thy God always.

7 *He is like* Canaan: there is a deceitful balance in his hand; he hath loved oppression. 8 And Ephraim said, "But yet I am

idolum mihi. Omnes labores mei non invenient mihi iniquitatem quam peccavi."

9 "Et ego Dominus, Deus tuus ex terra Aegypti, adhuc
sedere te faciam in tabernaculis sicut in diebus festivitatis.
10 Et locutus sum super prophetas, et ego visionem multiplicavi, et in manu prophetarum adsimilatus sum. 11 Si Galaad
idolum, ergo frustra erant in Galgal bubus immolantes, nam
et altaria eorum quasi acervi super sulcos agri. 12 Fugit Iacob
in regionem Syriae, et servivit Israhel in uxorem et in uxorem servavit. 13 In propheta autem eduxit Dominus Israhel
de Aegypto, et in propheta servatus est. 14 Ad iracundiam
me provocavit Ephraim in amaritudinibus suis, et sanguis
eius super eum veniet, et obprobrium eius restituet ei Dominus suus."

Caput 13

Loquente Ephraim, horror invasit Israhel, et deliquit in
Baal et mortuus est. 2 Et nunc addiderunt ad peccandum, fe-
ceruntque sibi conflatile de argento suo quasi similitudinem idolorum; factura artificum totum est. His ipsi dicunt,
"Immolate, homines, vitulos adorantes." 3 Idcirco erunt
quasi nubes matutina et sicut ros matutinus praeteriens,

become rich; I have found me an idol. All my labours shall not find me the iniquity that I have committed."

9 "And I that am the Lord, thy God from the land of Egypt, will yet cause thee to dwell in tabernacles as in the days of the feast. 10 And I have spoken by the prophets, and I have multiplied visions, and I have used similitudes by the ministry of the prophets. 11 If Gilead be an idol, then in vain were they in Gilgal offering sacrifices with bullocks, for their altars also are as heaps in the furrows of the field. 12 Jacob fled into the country of Syria, and Israel served for a wife and was a keeper for a wife. 13 But the Lord by a prophet brought Israel out of Egypt, and he was preserved by a prophet. 14 Ephraim hath provoked me to wrath with his bitterness, and his blood shall come upon him, and his Lord will render his reproach unto him."

Chapter 13

The judgments of God upon Israel for their sins. Christ shall one day redeem them.

When Ephraim spoke, a horror seized Israel, and he sinned in Baal and died. 2 And now they have sinned more and more, and they have made to themselves a molten thing of their silver as the likeness of idols; the whole is the work of craftsmen. To these they say, "Sacrifice, men, ye that adore calves." 3 Therefore they shall be as a morning cloud and as

sicut pulvis turbine raptus ex area et sicut fumus de fumario.

4 "Ego autem Dominus, Deus tuus ex terra Aegypti, et Deum absque me nescies, et salvator non est praeter me. 5 Ego cognovi te in deserto, in terra solitudinis.

6 "Iuxta pascua sua adimpleti sunt et saturati sunt; elevaverunt cor suum et obliti sunt mei. 7 Et ero eis quasi leaena, sicut pardus in via Assyriorum. 8 Occurram eis quasi ursa raptis catulis, et disrumpam interiora iecoris eorum, et consumam eos ibi quasi leo, bestia agri, scindet eos.

9 "Perditio tua, Israhel; tantummodo in me auxilium tuum. 10 Ubi est rex tuus? Maxime nunc salvet te in omnibus urbibus tuis et iudices tui, de quibus dixisti, 'Da mihi reges et principes.' 11 Dabo tibi regem in furore meo et auferam in indignatione mea.

12 "Conligata est iniquitas Ephraim; absconditum peccatum eius. 13 Dolores parturientis venient ei; ipse filius non sapiens, nunc enim non stabit in contritione filiorum. 14 De manu mortis liberabo eos; de morte redimam eos. Ero mors tua, O mors; ero morsus tuus, inferne. Consolatio abscondita est ab oculis meis."

15 Quia ipse inter fratres dividet, adducet urentem ventum Dominus de deserto ascendentem, et siccabit venas eius et desolabit fontem eius. Et ipse diripiet thesaurum omnis vasis desiderabilis.

the early dew that passeth away, as the dust that is driven with a whirlwind out of the floor and as the smoke out of the chimney.

4 "But I am the Lord, thy God from the land of Egypt, and thou shalt know no God but me, and there is no saviour beside me. 5 I knew thee in the desert, in the land of the wilderness.

6 "According to their pastures they were filled and were made full, *and* they lifted up their heart and have forgotten me. 7 And I will be to them as a lioness, as a leopard in the way of the Assyrians. 8 I will meet them as a bear that is robbed of her whelps, and I will rend the inner parts of their liver, and I will devour them there as a lion, the beast of the field, shall tear them.

9 "Destruction is thy own, O Israel; thy help is only in me. 10 Where is thy king? Now especially let him save thee in all thy cities and thy judges, of whom thou saidst, 'Give me kings and princes.' 11 I will give thee a king in my wrath and will take him away in my indignation.

12 "The iniquity of Ephraim is bound up; his sin is hidden. 13 The sorrows of a woman in labour shall come upon him; he is an unwise son, for now he shall not stand in the breach of the children. 14 I will deliver them out of the hand of death; I will redeem them from death. O death, I will be thy death; O hell, I will be thy bite. Comfort is hidden from my eyes."

15 Because he shall make a separation between brothers, the Lord will bring a burning wind that shall rise from the desert, and it shall dry up his springs and shall make his fountain desolate. And he shall carry off the treasure of every desirable vessel.

Caput 14

Pereat Samaria, quoniam ad amaritudinem concitavit Deum suum. In gladio pereant; parvuli eorum elidantur, et fetae eius discindantur.

2 Convertere, Israhel, ad Dominum, Deum tuum, quoniam corruisti in iniquitate tua. 3 Tollite vobiscum verba, et convertimini ad Dominum, et dicite ei, "Omnem aufer iniquitatem, et accipe bonum, et reddemus vitulos labiorum nostrorum. 4 Assur non salvabit nos; super equum non ascendemus, nec dicemus ultra, 'Dii nostri opera manuum nostrarum,' quia eius qui in te est misereberis pupilli."

5 "Sanabo contritiones eorum; diligam eos spontanee, quia aversus est furor meus ab eis. 6 Ero quasi ros; Israhel germinabit quasi lilium, et erumpet radix eius ut Libani. 7 Ibunt rami eius, et erit quasi oliva gloria eius, et odor eius ut Libani. 8 Convertentur sedentes in umbra eius; vivent tritico, et germinabunt quasi vinea. Memoriale eius sicut vinum Libani. 9 Ephraim, 'Quid mihi ultra idola?' Ego exau-

Chapter 14

Samaria shall be destroyed. An exhortation to repentance.
God's favour through Christ to the penitent.

Let Samaria perish, because she hath stirred up her God to bitterness. Let them perish by the sword; let their little ones be dashed, and let the women with child be ripped up.

2 Return, O Israel, to the Lord, thy God, for thou hast fallen down by thy iniquity. 3 Take with you words, and return to the Lord, and say to him, "Take away all iniquity, and receive the good, and we will render the calves of our lips. 4 Assyria shall not save us; we will not ride upon horses, neither will we say any more, 'The works of our hands are our gods,' for thou wilt have mercy on the fatherless that is in thee."

5 "I will heal their breaches; I will love them freely, for my wrath is turned away from them. 6 I will be as the dew; Israel shall spring as the lily, and his root shall shoot forth as that of Lebanon. 7 His branches shall *spread,* and his glory shall be as the olive tree, and his smell as that of Lebanon. 8 They shall be converted that sit under his shadow; they shall live upon wheat, and they shall blossom as a vine. His memorial shall be as the wine of Lebanon. 9 Ephraim *shall say,* 'What have I to do any more with idols?' I will hear him, and I will

diam, et dirigam eum ego ut abietem virentem; ex me fructus tuus inventus est."

10 Quis sapiens, et intelleget ista? Intellegens, et sciet haec? Quia rectae viae Domini, et iusti ambulabunt in eis, praevaricatores vero corruent in eis.

make him flourish like a green fir tree; from me is thy fruit found."

10 Who is wise, and he shall understand these things? Prudent, and he shall know these things? For the ways of the Lord are right, and the just shall walk in them, but the transgressors shall fall in them.

JOEL

Caput 1

Verbum Domini quod factum est ad Iohel, filium Fatuhel.

2 Audite hoc, senes, et auribus percipite, omnes habitatores terrae. Si factum est istud in diebus vestris aut in diebus patrum vestrorum? 3 Super hoc filiis vestris narrate, et filii vestri filiis suis, et filii eorum generationi alterae.

4 Residuum erucae comedit lucusta, et residuum lucustae comedit bruchus, et residuum bruchi comedit rubigo.

5 Expergescimini, ebrii, et flete, et ululate, omnes qui bibitis vinum in dulcedine, quoniam periit ab ore vestro. 6 Gens enim ascendit super terram meam fortis et innumerabilis; dentes eius ut dentes leonis, et molares eius ut catuli leonis. 7 Posuit vineam meam in desertum et ficum meam decorticavit; nudans spoliavit eam et proiecit; albi facti sunt rami eius.

Chapter 1

The prophet describes the judgments that shall fall upon the people and invites them to fasting and prayer.

The word of the Lord that came to Joel, the son of Pethuel.

2 Hear this, ye old men, and give ear, all ye inhabitants of the land. Did this ever happen in your days or in the days of your fathers? 3 Tell ye of this to your children, and *let* your children *tell* their children, and their children to another generation.

4 That which the palmer-worm hath left the locust hath eaten, and that which the locust hath left the bruchus hath eaten, and that which the bruchus hath left the mildew hath destroyed.

5 Awake, ye that are drunk, and weep, and mourn, all ye that *take delight in drinking sweet* wine, for it is cut off from your mouth. 6 For a nation is come up upon my land strong and without number; his teeth are like the teeth of a lion, and his cheek teeth as of a lion's whelp. 7 He hath laid my vineyard waste and hath pilled off the bark of my fig tree; he hath stripped it bare and cast it away; the branches thereof are made white.

8 Plange quasi virgo accincta sacco super virum pubertatis suae. 9 Periit sacrificium et libatio de domo Domini; luxerunt sacerdotes, ministri Domini. 10 Depopulata est regio;
luxit humus, quoniam devastatum est triticum, confusum
est vinum, elanguit oleum. 11 Confusi sunt agricolae; ulula-
verunt vinitores super frumento et hordeo quia periit messis
agri. 12 Vinea confusa est, et ficus elanguit; malogranatum et
palma et malum et omnia ligna agri aruerunt quia confusum
est gaudium a filiis hominum.

13 Accingite vos, et plangite, sacerdotes; ululate, ministri
altaris. Ingredimini; cubate in sacco, ministri Dei mei, quoniam interiit de domo Dei vestri sacrificium et libatio.
14 Sanctificate ieiunium; vocate coetum; congregate senes,
omnes habitatores terrae in domum Dei vestri, et clamate
ad Dominum.

15 A, a, a diei! Quia prope est dies Domini, et quasi vastitas a potente veniet. 16 Numquid non coram oculis vestris
alimenta perierunt, de domo Dei nostri laetitia et exultatio?
17 Conputruerunt iumenta in stercore suo; demolita sunt
horrea; dissipatae sunt apothecae quoniam confusum est
triticum. 18 Quid ingemuit animal, mugierunt greges armenti? Quia non est pascua eis, sed et greges pecorum disperierunt.

19 Ad te, Domine, clamabo, quia ignis comedit speciosa
deserti et flamma succendit omnia ligna regionis. 20 Sed et

8 Lament like a virgin girded with sackcloth for the husband of her youth. 9 Sacrifice and libation is cut off from the house of the Lord; the priests, the Lord's ministers, have mourned. 10 The country is destroyed; the ground hath mourned, for the corn is wasted, the wine is confounded, the oil hath languished. 11 The husbandmen are ashamed; the vinedressers have howled for the wheat and for the barley because the harvest of the field is perished. 12 The vineyard is confounded, and the fig tree hath languished; the pomegranate tree and the palm tree and the apple tree and all the trees of the field are withered because joy is *withdrawn* from the children of men.

13 Gird yourselves, and lament, O ye priests; howl, ye ministers of the altars. Go in; lie in sackcloth, ye ministers of my God, because sacrifice and libation is cut off from the house of your God. 14 Sanctify ye a fast; call an assembly; gather together the ancients, all the inhabitants of the land into the house of your God, and cry ye to the Lord.

15 Ah, ah, ah for the day! Because the day of the Lord is at hand, and it shall come like destruction from the mighty. 16 Is not your food cut off before your eyes, joy and gladness from the house of our God? 17 The beasts have rotted in their dung; the barns are destroyed; the storehouses are broken down because the corn is confounded. 18 Why did the beast groan; why did the herds of cattle low? Because there is no pasture for them, yea and the flocks of sheep are perished.

19 To thee, O Lord, will I cry, because fire hath devoured the beautiful places of the wilderness and the flame hath burnt all the trees of the country. 20 Yea and the beasts of the

bestiae agri quasi area sitiens imbrem suspexerunt ad te, quoniam exsiccati sunt fontes aquarum et ignis devoravit speciosa deserti.

Caput 2

Canite tuba in Sion; ululate in monte sancto meo. Conturbentur omnes habitatores terrae quia venit dies Domini, quia prope est: 2 dies tenebrarum et caliginis, dies nubis et turbinis. Quasi mane expansum super montes populus multus et fortis: similis ei non fuit a principio et post eum non erit usque in annos generationis et generationis. 3 Ante faciem eius ignis vorans, et post eum exurens flamma. Quasi hortus voluptatis terra coram eo, et post eum solitudo deserti, neque est qui effugiat eum. 4 Quasi aspectus equorum aspectus eorum, et quasi equites sic current. 5 Sicut sonitus quadrigarum super capita montium exilient, sicut sonitus flammae ignis devorantis stipulam, velut populus fortis praeparatus ad proelium. 6 A facie eius cruciabuntur populi;

field have looked up to thee as a garden bed that thirsteth after rain, for the springs of waters are dried up and fire hath devoured the beautiful places of the wilderness.

Chapter 2

The prophet foretells the terrible day of the Lord, exhorts sinners to a sincere conversion and comforts God's people with promises of future blessings under Christ.

Blow ye the trumpet in Zion; sound *an alarm* in my holy mountain. Let all the inhabitants of the land tremble because the day of the Lord cometh, because it is nigh at hand: 2 a day of darkness and of gloominess, a day of clouds and whirlwinds. A numerous and strong people as the morning spread upon the mountains: the like to it hath not been from the beginning nor shall be after it even to the years of generation and generation. 3 Before the face thereof a devouring fire, and behind it a burning flame. The land is like a garden of pleasure before it, and behind it a desolate wilderness, neither is there any one that can escape it. 4 The appearance of them is as the appearance of horses, and they shall run like horsemen. 5 They shall leap like the noise of chariots upon the tops of mountains, like the noise of a flame of fire devouring the stubble, as a strong people prepared to battle. 6 At their presence the people shall be in grievous pains;

omnes vultus redigentur in ollam. 7 Sicut fortes current; quasi viri bellatores ascendent murum. Viri in viis suis gradientur, et non declinabunt a semitis suis. 8 Unusquisque fratrem suum non coartabit; singuli in calle suo ambulabunt, sed et per fenestras cadent et non demolientur. 9 Urbem ingredientur; in muro current; domos conscendent; per fenestras intrabunt quasi fur. 10 A facie eius contremuit terra, moti sunt caeli, sol et luna obtenebrati sunt, et stellae retraxerunt splendorem suum. 11 Et Dominus dedit vocem suam ante faciem exercitus sui, quia multa sunt nimis castra eius, quia fortia et facientia verbum eius. Magnus enim dies Domini et terribilis valde. Et quis sustinebit eum?

12 "Nunc ergo," dicit Dominus, "convertimini ad me in toto corde vestro in ieiunio et in fletu et in planctu."

13 Et scindite corda vestra et non vestimenta vestra, et convertimini ad Dominum, Deum vestrum, quia benignus et misericors est, patiens et multae misericordiae et deprecabilis super malitia. 14 Quis scit si convertatur et ignoscat et relinquat post se benedictionem, sacrificium et libamen Domino, Deo vestro? 15 Canite tuba in Sion; sanctificate ieiunium; vocate coetum. 16 Congregate populum; sanctificate ecclesiam; coadunate senes; congregate parvulos et sugentes ubera. Egrediatur sponsus de cubili suo, et sponsa de thalamo suo.

17 Inter vestibulum et altare plorabunt sacerdotes, ministri Domini, et dicent, "Parce, Domine; parce populo tuo, et

all faces shall be made like a kettle. 7 They shall run like valiant men; like men of war they shall scale the wall. The men shall march every one on his way, and they shall not turn aside from their ranks. 8 No one shall press upon his brother; they shall walk every one in his path, yea and they shall fall through the windows and shall take no harm. 9 They shall enter into the city; they shall run upon the wall; they shall climb up the houses; they shall come in at the windows as a thief. 10 At their presence the earth hath trembled, the heavens are moved, the sun and moon are darkened, and the stars have withdrawn their shining. 11 And the Lord hath uttered his voice before the face of his army, for his armies are exceeding great, for they are strong and execute his word. For the day of the Lord is great and very terrible. And who *can* stand it?

12 "Now therefore," saith the Lord, "be converted to me with all your heart in fasting and in weeping and in mourning."

13 And rend your hearts and not your garments, and turn to the Lord, your God, for he is gracious and merciful, patient and rich in mercy and *ready to repent of the evil.* 14 Who knoweth but he will return and forgive and leave a blessing behind him, sacrifice and libation to the Lord, your God? 15 Blow the trumpet in Zion; sanctify a fast; call a *solemn* assembly. 16 Gather together the people; sanctify the church; assemble the ancients; gather together the little ones and them that suck at the breasts. Let the bridegroom go forth from his bed, and the bride out of her bride chamber.

17 Between the porch and the altar the priests, the Lord's ministers, shall weep and shall say, "Spare, O Lord; spare thy

ne des hereditatem tuam in obprobrium, ut dominentur eis nationes. Quare dicunt in populis, 'Ubi est Deus eorum?'"

18 Zelatus est Dominus terram suam et pepercit populo suo. 19 Et respondit Dominus et dixit populo suo, "Ecce: ego mittam vobis frumentum et vinum et oleum, et replebimini eis, et non dabo vos ultra obprobrium in gentibus. 20 Et eum qui ab aquilone est procul faciam a vobis, et expellam eum in terram inviam et desertam, faciem eius contra mare orientale et extremum eius ad mare novissimum, et ascendet fetor eius, et ascendet putredo eius, quia superbe egit.

21 "Noli timere, terra; exulta, et laetare, quoniam magnificavit Dominus ut faceret. 22 Nolite timere, animalia regionis, quia germinaverunt speciosa deserti, quia lignum adtulit fructum suum; ficus et vinea dederunt virtutem suam. 23 Et filii Sion, exultate, et laetamini in Domino, Deo vestro, quia dedit vobis doctorem iustitiae et descendere faciet ad vos imbrem matutinum et serotinum sicut in principio, 24 et implebuntur areae frumento, et redundabunt torcularia vino et oleo. 25 Et reddam vobis annos quos comedit lucusta, bruchus et rubigo et eruca, fortitudo mea magna quam misi in vos. 26 Et comedetis vescentes et saturabimini, et laudabitis nomen Domini, Dei vestri, qui fecit vobiscum mirabilia. Et non confundetur populus meus in sempiternum. 27 Et scietis quia in medio Israhel ego sum et ego Dominus, Deus

people, and give not thy inheritance to reproach, that the heathen should rule over them. Why *should* they say among the nations, 'Where is their God?'"

18 The Lord hath been zealous for his land and hath spared his people. 19 And the Lord answered and said to his people, "Behold: I will send you corn and wine and oil, and you shall be filled with them, and I will no more make you a reproach among the nations. 20 And I will remove far off from you the northern *enemy,* and I will drive him into a land unpassable and desert, with his face towards the east sea and his hinder part towards the utmost sea, and his stench shall ascend, and his rottenness shall go up, because he hath done proudly.

21 "Fear not, O land; be glad, and rejoice, for the Lord hath *done great things.* 22 Fear not, ye beasts of the fields, for the beautiful places of the wilderness are sprung, for the tree hath brought forth its fruit; the fig tree and the vine have yielded their strength. 23 And you, O children of Zion, rejoice, and be joyful in the Lord, your God, because he hath given you a teacher of justice and he will make the early and the latter rain to come down to you as in the beginning, 24 and the floors shall be filled with wheat, and the presses shall overflow with wine and oil. 25 And I will restore to you the years which the locust *and* the bruchus and the mildew and the palmer-worm have eaten, my great *host* which I sent upon you. 26 And you shall eat in plenty and shall be filled, and you shall praise the name of the Lord, your God, who hath done wonders with you. And my people shall not be confounded for ever. 27 And you shall know that I am in the midst of Israel and I am the Lord, your God, and there is

vester, et non est amplius, et non confundetur populus meus in aeternum.

28 "Et erit post haec effundam spiritum meum super omnem carnem, et prophetabunt filii vestri et filiae vestrae; senes vestri somnia somniabunt, et iuvenes vestri visiones videbunt. 29 Sed et super servos meos et ancillas in diebus illis effundam spiritum meum. 30 Et dabo prodigia in caelo et in terra: sanguinem et ignem et vaporem fumi. 31 Sol vertetur in tenebras, et luna in sanguinem, antequam veniat dies Domini magnus et horribilis. 32 Et erit omnis qui invocaverit nomen Domini salvus erit, quia in Monte Sion et in Hierusalem erit salvatio, sicut dixit Dominus, et in residuis quos Dominus vocaverit."

Caput 3

"Quia ecce: in diebus illis et in tempore illo cum convertero captivitatem Iuda et Hierusalem, 2 congregabo omnes gentes et deducam eas in vallem Iosaphat, et disceptabo

none besides, and my people shall not be confounded for ever.

28 "And it shall come to pass after this that I will pour out my spirit upon all flesh, and your sons and your daughters shall prophesy; your old men shall dream dreams, and your young men shall see visions. 29 Moreover upon my servants and handmaids in those days I will pour forth my spirit. 30 And I will shew wonders in heaven and in earth: blood and fire and vapour of smoke. 31 The sun shall be turned into darkness, and the moon into blood, before the great and dreadful day of the Lord doth come. 32 And it shall come to pass that every one that shall call upon the name of the Lord shall be saved, for in Mount Zion and in Jerusalem shall be salvation, as the Lord hath said, and in the residue whom the Lord shall call."

Chapter 3

The Lord shall judge all nations in the valley of Jehoshaphat.
The evils that shall fall upon the enemies of God's people.
His blessing upon the church of the saints.

"For behold: in those days and in that time when I shall bring back the captivity of Judah and Jerusalem, 2 I will gather together all nations and will bring them down into the valley of Jehoshaphat, and I will plead with them there

cum eis ibi super populo meo et hereditate mea, Israhel, quos disperserunt in nationibus et terram meam diviserunt. 3 Et super populum meum miserunt sortem, et posuerunt puerum in prostibulum, et puellam vendiderunt pro vino ut biberent.

4 "Verum quid vobis et mihi, Tyrus et Sidon et omnis terminus Palestinorum? Numquid ultionem vos reddetis mihi? Et si ulciscimini vos contra me, cito velociter reddam vicissitudinem vobis super caput vestrum. 5 Argentum enim meum et aurum meum tulistis, et desiderabilia mea et pulcherrima intulistis in delubra vestra. 6 Et filios Iuda et filios Hierusalem vendidistis filiis Graecorum ut longe faceretis eos de finibus suis. 7 Ecce: ego suscitabo eos de loco in quo vendidistis eos, et convertam retributionem vestram in caput vestrum. 8 Et vendam filios vestros et filias vestras in manibus filiorum Iuda, et venundabunt eos Sabeis, genti longinquae, quia Dominus locutus est.

9 "Clamate hoc in gentibus: 'Sanctificate bellum; suscitate robustos; accedant; ascendant omnes viri bellatores. 10 Concidite aratra vestra in gladios et ligones vestros in lanceas. Infirmus dicat quia "fortis ego sum."'

11 "Erumpite, et venite, omnes gentes de circuitu, et congregamini; ibi occumbere faciet Dominus robustos tuos. 12 Consurgant, et ascendant gentes in vallem Iosaphat, quia ibi sedebo ut iudicem omnes gentes in circuitu. 13 Mittite falces, quoniam maturavit messis. Venite, et descendite, quia plenum est torcular; exuberant torcularia, quia multiplicata est malitia eorum. 14 Populi, populi in valle concisionis,

for my people and for my inheritance, Israel, whom they have scattered among the nations and have parted my land. 3 And they have cast lots upon my people, and the boy they have put in the stews, and the girl they have sold for wine that they might drink.

4 "But what have you to do with me, O Tyre and Sidon and all the coast of the Philistines? Will you revenge yourselves on me? And if you revenge yourselves on me, I will very soon return you a recompense upon your own head. 5 For you have taken away my silver and my gold, and my desirable and most beautiful things you have carried into your temples. 6 And the children of Judah and the children of Jerusalem you have sold to the children of the Greeks that you might remove them far off from their own country. 7 Behold: I will raise them up out of the place wherein you have sold them, and I will return your recompense upon your own heads. 8 And I will sell your sons and your daughters by the hands of the children of Judah, and they shall sell them to the Sabeans, a nation far off, for the Lord hath spoken it.

9 "Proclaim ye this among the nations: *'Prepare* war; rouse up the strong; let them come; let all the men of war come up. 10 Cut your ploughshares into swords and your spades into spears. Let the weak say *"I* am strong."'

11 "Break forth, and come, all ye nations from round about, and gather yourselves together; there will the Lord cause all thy strong ones to fall down. 12 Let them arise, and let the nations come up into the valley of Jehoshaphat, for there I will sit to judge all nations round about. 13 Put ye in the sickles, for the harvest is ripe. Come, and go down, for the press is full; the fats run over, for their wickedness is multiplied. 14 Nations, nations in the valley of destruction,

quia iuxta est dies Domini in valle concisionis. 15 Sol et luna obtenebrati sunt, et stellae retraxerunt splendorem suum. 16 Et Dominus de Sion rugiet et de Hierusalem dabit vocem suam, et movebuntur caeli et terra, et Dominus spes populi sui et fortitudo filiorum Israhel.

17 "Et scietis quia ego Dominus, Deus vester, habitans in Sion, monte sancto meo, et erit Hierusalem sancta, et alieni non transibunt per eam amplius. 18 Et erit in die illa stillabunt montes dulcedinem, et colles fluent lacte, et per omnes rivos Iuda ibunt aquae, et fons de domo Domini egredietur et inrigabit torrentem spinarum. 19 Aegyptus in desolationem erit, et Idumea in desertum perditionis, pro eo quod inique egerint in filios Iuda et effuderint sanguinem innocentem in terra sua. 20 Et Iudaea in aeternum habitabitur, et Hierusalem in generationem et generationem. 21 Et mundabo sanguinem eorum, quem non mundaveram, et Dominus commorabitur in Sion."

for the day of the Lord is near in the valley of destruction. 15 The sun and the moon are darkened, and the stars have withdrawn their shining. 16 And the Lord shall roar out of Zion and utter his voice from Jerusalem, and the heavens and the earth shall be moved, and the Lord shall be the hope of his people and the strength of the children of Israel.

17 "And you shall know that I am the Lord, your God, dwelling in Zion, my holy mountain, and Jerusalem shall be holy, and strangers shall pass through it no more. 18 And it shall come to pass in that day that the mountains shall drop down sweetness, and the hills shall flow with milk, and waters shall flow through all the rivers of Judah, and a fountain shall come forth of the house of the Lord and shall water the torrent of thorns. 19 Egypt shall be a desolation, and Edom a wilderness destroyed, because they have done unjustly against the children of Judah and have shed innocent blood in their land. 20 And Judea shall be inhabited for ever, and Jerusalem to generation and generation. 21 And I will cleanse their blood, which I had not cleansed, and the Lord will dwell in Zion."

AMOS

Caput 1

V erba Amos, qui fuit in pastoribus de Thecuae, quae vidit super Israhel in diebus Oziae, regis Iuda, et in diebus Hieroboam, filii Ioas, regis Israhel, ante duos annos terraemotus.

2 Et dixit, "Dominus de Sion rugiet et de Hierusalem dabit vocem suam, et luxerunt speciosa pastorum, et exsiccatus est vertex Carmeli."

3 Haec dicit Dominus: "Super tribus sceleribus Damasci et super quattuor non convertam eum, eo quod trituraverint in plaustris ferreis Galaad. 4 Et mittam ignem in domum Azahel, et devorabit domos Benadad. 5 Et conteram vectem Damasci, et disperdam habitatorem de campo idoli et tenentem sceptrum de domo voluptati, et transferetur populus Syriae Cyrenen," dicit Dominus.

6 Haec dicit Dominus: "Super tribus sceleribus Gazae et super quattuor non convertam eum, eo quod transtulerint

Chapter 1

The prophet threatens Damascus, Gaza, Tyre, Edom and
Ammon with the judgments of God for their obstinacy
in sin.

The words of Amos, who was among herdsmen of Tekoa,
which he saw concerning Israel in the days of Uzziah, king
of Judah, and in the days of Jeroboam, the son of Joash, king
of Israel, two years before the earthquake.

2 And he said, "The Lord will roar from Zion and utter his
voice from Jerusalem, and the beautiful places of the shepherds have mourned, and the top of Carmel is withered."

3 Thus saith the Lord: "For three crimes of Damascus and
for four I will not convert it, because they have threshed
Gilead with iron wains. 4 And I will send a fire into the house
of Hazael, and it shall devour the houses of Ben-hadad.
5 And I will break the bar of Damascus, and I will cut off the
inhabitants from the plain of the idol and him that holdeth
the sceptre from the house of pleasure, and the people of
Syria shall be carried away to Cyrene," saith the Lord.

6 Thus saith the Lord: "For three crimes of Gaza and for
four I will not convert it, because they have carried away a

captivitatem perfectam ut concluderent eam in Idumea. 7 Et mittam ignem in murum Gazae, et devorabit aedes eius. 8 Et disperdam habitatorem de Azoto et tenentem sceptrum de Ascalone, et convertam manum meam super Accaron, et peribunt reliqui Philisthinorum," dicit Dominus Deus.

9 Haec dicit Dominus: "Super tribus sceleribus Tyri et super quattuor non convertam eum, eo quod concluserint captivitatem perfectam in Idumea et non sint recordati foederis fratrum. 10 Et mittam ignem in murum Tyri, et devorabit aedes eius."

11 Haec dicit Dominus: "Super tribus sceleribus Edom et super quattuor non convertam eum, eo quod persecutus sit in gladio fratrem suum et violaverit misericordiam eius et tenuerit ultra furorem suum et indignationem suam servaverit usque in finem. 12 Mittam ignem in Theman, et devorabit aedes Bosrae."

13 Haec dicit Dominus: "Super tribus sceleribus filiorum Ammon et super quattuor non convertam eum, eo quod dissecuerit praegnantes Galaad ad dilatandum terminum suum. 14 Et succendam ignem in muro Rabbae, et devorabit aedes eius in ululatu in die belli et in turbine in die commotionis. 15 Et ibit Melchom in captivitatem, ipse et principes eius simul," dicit Dominus.

perfect captivity to shut them up in Edom. 7 And I will send a fire on the wall of Gaza, and it shall devour the houses thereof. 8 And I will cut off the inhabitant from Ashdod and him that holdeth the sceptre from Ashkelon, and I will turn my hand against Ekron, and the rest of the Philistines shall perish," saith the Lord God.

9 Thus saith the Lord: "For three crimes of Tyre and for four I will not convert it, because they have shut up an entire captivity in Edom and have not remembered the covenant of brethren. 10 And I will send a fire upon the wall of Tyre, and it shall devour the houses thereof."

11 Thus saith the Lord: "For three crimes of Edom and for four I will not convert him, because he hath pursued his brother with the sword and hath *cast off all* pity and hath carried on his fury and hath kept his wrath to the end. 12 I will send a fire into Teman, and it shall devour the houses of Bozrah."

13 Thus saith the Lord: "For three crimes of the children of Ammon and for four I will not convert him, because he hath ripped up the women with child of Gilead to enlarge his border. 14 And I will kindle a fire in the wall of Rabbah, and it shall devour the houses thereof with shouting in the day of battle and with a whirlwind in the day of trouble. 15 And Milcom shall go into captivity, both he and his princes together," saith the Lord.

Caput 2

Haec dicit Dominus: "Super tribus sceleribus Moab et super quattuor non convertam eum, eo quod incenderit ossa regis Idumeae usque ad cinerem. 2 Et mittam ignem in Moab, et devorabit aedes Carioth, et morietur in sonitu Moab, in clangore tubae. 3 Et disperdam iudicem de medio eius et omnes principes eius interficiam cum eo," dicit Dominus.

4 Haec dicit Dominus: "Super tribus sceleribus Iuda et super quattuor non convertam eum, eo quod abiecerit legem Domini et mandata eius non custodierit, deceperunt enim eos idola sua, post quae abierunt patres eorum. 5 Et mittam ignem in Iuda, et devorabit aedes Hierusalem."

6 Haec dicit Dominus: "Super tribus sceleribus Israhel et super quattuor non convertam eum, pro eo quod vendiderit pro argento iustum et pauperem pro calciamentis. 7 Qui conterunt super pulverem terrae capita pauperum et viam humilium declinant, et filius ac pater eius ierunt ad puellam ut violarent nomen sanctum meum. 8 Et super vestimentis pigneratis accubuerunt iuxta omne altare et vinum damnatorum bibebant in domo Dei sui.

Chapter 2

The judgments with which God threatens Moab, Judah and Israel for their sins and their ingratitude.

Thus saith the Lord: "For three crimes of Moab and for four I will not convert him, because he hath burnt the bones of the king of Edom even to ashes. 2 And I will send a fire into Moab, and it shall devour the houses of Kerioth, and Moab shall die with a noise, with the sound of the trumpet. 3 And I will cut off the judge from the midst thereof and will slay all his princes with him," saith the Lord.

4 Thus saith the Lord: "For three crimes of Judah and for four I will not convert him, because he hath cast away the law of the Lord and hath not kept his commandments, for their idols have caused them to err, after which their fathers have walked. 5 And I will send a fire into Judah, and it shall devour the houses of Jerusalem."

6 Thus saith the Lord: "For three crimes of Israel and for four I will not convert him, because he hath sold the just man for silver and the poor man for *a pair of* shoes. 7 They bruise the heads of the poor upon the dust of the earth and turn aside the way of the humble, and the son and his father have gone to the *same* young woman to profane my holy name. 8 And they sat down upon garments laid to pledge by every altar and drank the wine of the condemned in the house of their God.

9 "Ego autem exterminavi Amorreum a facie eorum, cuius altitudo cedrorum altitudo eius et fortis ipse quasi quercus, et contrivi fructum eius desuper et radices eius subter. 10 Ego sum qui ascendere vos feci de terra Aegypti, et duxi vos in deserto quadraginta annis ut possideretis terram Amorrei. 11 Et suscitavi de filiis vestris in prophetas et de iuvenibus vestris Nazareos. Numquid non ita est, filii Israhel?" dicit Dominus.

12 "Et propinabatis Nazareis vinum et prophetis mandabatis, dicentes, 'Ne prophetetis.' 13 Ecce: ego stridebo subter vos sicut stridet plaustrum onustum faeno. 14 Et peribit fuga a veloce, et fortis non obtinebit virtutem suam, et robustus non salvabit animam suam. 15 Et tenens arcum non stabit, et velox pedibus suis non salvabitur, et ascensor equi non salvabit animam suam. 16 Et robustus corde inter fortes nudus fugiet in die illa," dicit Dominus.

Caput 3

"Audite verbum quod locutus est Dominus super vos, filii Israhel, super omni cognatione quam eduxi de terra Aegypti, dicens, 2 'Tantummodo vos cognovi ex omnibus cognationibus terrae; idcirco visitabo super vos omnes iniquitates vestras.'"

9 "Yet I cast out the Amorite before their face, whose height was *like* the height of cedars and who was strong as an oak, and I destroyed his fruit from above and his roots beneath. 10 It is I that brought you up out of the land of Egypt, and I led you forty years through the wilderness that you might possess the land of the Amorite. 11 And I raised up of your sons for prophets and of your young men *for* Nazirites. Is it not so, O ye children of Israel?" saith the Lord.

12 "And you *will present* wine to the Nazirites and *command* the prophets, saying, 'Prophesy not.' 13 Behold: I will screak under you as a wain screaketh that is laden with hay. 14 And flight shall perish from the swift, and the valiant shall not possess his strength, neither shall the strong save his life. 15 And he that holdeth the bow shall not stand, and the swift of foot shall not escape, neither shall the rider of the horse save his life. 16 And the stout of heart among the valiant shall flee away naked in that day," saith the Lord.

Chapter 3

The evils that shall fall upon Israel for their sins.

"Hear the word that the Lord hath spoken concerning you, O ye children of Israel, concerning the whole family that I brought up out of the land of Egypt, saying: 2 'You only have I known of all the families of the earth; therefore will I visit upon you all your iniquities.'"

3 Numquid ambulabunt duo pariter nisi convenerit eis? 4 Numquid rugiet leo in saltu nisi habuerit praedam? Numquid dabit catulus leonis vocem de cubili suo nisi aliquid adprehenderit? 5 Numquid cadet avis in laqueum terrae absque aucupe? Numquid auferetur laqueus de terra antequam quid ceperit? 6 Si clanget tuba in civitate, et populus non expavescet? Si erit malum in civitate quod Dominus non fecerit? 7 Quia non faciet Dominus Deus verbum nisi revelaverit secretum suum ad servos suos, prophetas. 8 Leo rugiet; quis non timebit? Dominus Deus locutus est; quis non prophetabit?

9 Auditum facite in aedibus Azoti et in aedibus terrae Aegypti, et dicite: "Congregamini super montes Samariae, et videte insanias multas in medio eius et calumniam patientes in penetralibus eius."

10 "Et nescierunt facere rectum," dicit Dominus, "thesaurizantes iniquitatem et rapinas in aedibus suis." 11 Propterea haec dicit Dominus Deus: "Tribulabitur et circumietur terra, et detrahetur ex te fortitudo tua, et diripientur aedes tuae."

12 Haec dicit Dominus: "Quomodo si eruat pastor de ore leonis duo crura aut extremum auriculae, sic eruentur filii Israhel qui habitant in Samaria in plaga lectuli et in Damasci grabato."

13 "Audite, et contestamini in domo Iacob," dicit Dominus, Deus exercituum, 14 "quia in die cum visitare coepero praevaricationes Israhel, super eum visitabo et super altaria Bethel, et amputabuntur cornua altaris et cadent in terram.

3 Shall two walk together except they be agreed? 4 Will a lion roar in the forest if he have no prey? Will the lion's whelp cry out of his den if he have taken nothing? 5 Will the bird fall into the snare upon the earth if there be no fowler? Shall the snare be taken up from the earth before it hath taken somewhat? 6 Shall the trumpet sound in a city, and the people not be afraid? Shall there be evil in a city which the Lord hath not done? 7 For the Lord God *doth* nothing without *revealing* his secret to his servants, the prophets. 8 The lion shall roar; who will not fear? The Lord God hath spoken; who shall not prophesy?

9 Publish it in the houses of Ashdod and in the houses of the land of Egypt, and say: "Assemble yourselves upon the mountains of Samaria, and behold the many follies in the midst thereof and them that suffer oppression in the inner rooms thereof."

10 "And they have not known to do the right thing," saith the Lord, "storing up iniquity and robberies in their houses." 11 Therefore thus saith the Lord God: "The land shall be in tribulation and shall be compassed about, and thy strength shall be taken away from thee, and thy houses shall be spoiled."

12 Thus saith the Lord: "As if a shepherd should get out of the lion's mouth two legs or the tip of the ear, so shall the children of Israel be taken out that dwell in Samaria in a piece of a bed and in the couch of Damascus."

13 "Hear ye, and testify in the house of Jacob," saith the Lord, the God of hosts, 14 "that in the day when I shall begin to visit the transgressions of Israel, I will visit upon him and upon the altars of Bethel, and the horns of the altars shall be

15 Et percutiam domum hiemalem cum domo aestiva, et peribunt domus eburneae, et dissipabuntur aedes multae," dicit Dominus.

Caput 4

Audite verbum hoc, vaccae pingues quae estis in monte Samariae, quae calumniam facitis egenis et confringitis pauperes, quae dicitis dominis vestris, "Adferte, et bibemus."

2 "Iuravit Dominus Deus in sancto suo quia ecce: dies venient super vos, et levabunt vos in contis et reliquias vestras in ollis ferventibus. 3 Et per aperturas exibitis altera contra alteram, et proiciemini in Armon," dicit Dominus.

4 "Venite ad Bethel, et impie agite, ad Galgalam, et multiplicate praevaricationem. Et offerte mane victimas vestras, tribus diebus decimas vestras. 5 Et sacrificate de fermentato laudem, et vocate voluntarias oblationes, et adnuntiate, sic enim voluistis, filii Israhel," dicit Dominus Deus.

cut off and shall fall to the ground. 15 And I will strike the winter house with the summer house, and the houses of ivory shall perish, and many houses shall be destroyed," saith the Lord.

Chapter 4

The Israelites are reproved for their oppressing the poor,
for their idolatry and their incorrigibleness.

Hear this word; ye fat kine that are in the *mountains* of Samaria, you that oppress the needy and crush the poor, that say to your masters, "Bring, and we will drink."

2 "The Lord God hath sworn by his holiness that lo: the days shall come upon you *when* they shall lift you up on pikes and what shall remain of you in boiling pots. 3 And you shall go out at the breaches one over against the other, and you shall be cast forth into Harmon," saith the Lord.

4 "Come ye to Bethel, and do wickedly, to Gilgal, and multiply transgressions. And bring in the morning your victims, your tithes in three days. 5 And offer a sacrifice of praise *with leaven,* and call free offerings, and proclaim it, for so you would do, O children of Israel," saith the Lord God.

6 "Unde et ego dedi vobis stuporem dentium in cunctis urbibus vestris et indigentiam panum in omnibus locis vestris, et non estis reversi ad me," dicit Dominus. 7 "Ego quoque prohibui a vobis imbrem cum adhuc tres menses superessent usque ad messem, et plui super civitatem unam et super civitatem alteram non plui; pars una conpluta est, et pars super quam non plui aruit. 8 Et venerunt duae et tres civitates ad civitatem unam ut biberent aquam et non sunt satiatae, et non redistis ad me," dicit Dominus. 9 "Percussi vos in vento urente et in aurugine; multitudinem hortorum vestrorum et vinearum vestrarum, oliveta vestra et ficeta vestra comedit eruca, et non redistis ad me," dicit Dominus. 10 "Misi in vos mortem in via Aegypti. Percussi in gladio iuvenes vestros usque ad captivitatem equorum vestrorum, et ascendere feci putredinem castrorum vestrorum in nares vestras, et non redistis ad me," dicit Dominus. 11 "Subverti vos sicut subvertit Deus Sodomam et Gomorram, et facti estis quasi torris raptus de incendio, et non redistis ad me," dicit Dominus.

12 "Quapropter haec faciam tibi, Israhel, postquam autem haec fecero tibi, praeparare in occursum Dei tui, Israhel."

13 Quia ecce: formans montes et creans ventum et adnuntians homini eloquium suum, faciens matutinam nebulam et gradiens super excelsa terrae, Dominus, Deus exercituum, nomen eius.

6 "Whereupon I also have given you dullness of teeth in all your cities and want of bread in all your places, *yet* you have not returned to me," saith the Lord. 7 "I also have withholden the rain from you when there were yet three months to the harvest, and I caused it to rain upon one city and caused it not to rain upon another city; one piece was rained upon, and the piece whereupon I rained not withered. 8 And two and three cities went to one city to drink water and were not filled, *yet* you returned not to me," saith the Lord. 9 "I struck you with a burning wind and with mildew; the palmerworm hath eaten up your many gardens and your vineyards, your olive groves and fig groves, *yet* you returned not to me," saith the Lord. 10 "I sent death upon you in the way of Egypt. I slew your young men with the sword even to the captivity of your horses, and I made the *stink* of your camp to come up into your nostrils, *yet* you returned not to me," saith the Lord. 11 "I destroyed *some of* you as God destroyed Sodom and Gomorrah, and you were as a firebrand plucked out of the burning, *yet* you returned not to me," saith the Lord.

12 *"Therefore* I will do these things to thee, O Israel, and after I shall have done these things to thee, be prepared to meet thy God, O Israel."

13 For behold: he that formeth the mountains and createth the wind and declareth his word to man, he that maketh the morning mist and walketh upon the high places of the earth, the Lord, the God of hosts, is his name.

Caput 5

Audite verbum istud quod ego levo super vos planctum.

Domus Israhel cecidit, et non adiciet ut resurgat. 2 Virgo Israhel proiecta est in terram suam; non est qui suscitet eam.

3 Quia haec dicit Dominus Deus: "Urbs de qua egrediebantur mille, relinquentur in ea centum, et de qua egrediebantur centum, relinquentur in ea decem in domo Israhel."

4 Quia haec dicit Dominus domui Israhel: "Quaerite me, et vivetis. 5 Et nolite quaerere Bethel, et in Galgalam nolite intrare, et in Bersabee non transibitis, quia Galgala captiva ducetur et Bethel erit inutilis."

6 Quaerite Dominum, et vivite, ne forte conburatur ut ignis domus Ioseph, et devorabit, et non erit qui extinguat Bethel. 7 Qui convertitis in absinthium iudicium et iustitiam in terra relinquitis, 8 facientem Arcturum et Orionem et convertentem in mane tenebras et diem in noctem mutantem, qui vocat aquas maris et effundit eas super faciem terrae: Dominus nomen est eius, 9 qui subridet vastitatem super robustum et depopulationem super potentem adfert.

10 Odio habuerunt in porta corripientem, et loquentem perfecte abominati sunt. 11 Idcirco pro eo quod diripiebatis

Chapter 5

A lamentation for Israel. An exhortation to return to God.

Hear ye this word which I take up concerning you for a lamentation.

The house of Israel is fallen, and it shall rise no more. 2 The virgin of Israel is cast down upon her land; there is none to raise her up.

3 For thus saith the Lord God: 'The city out of which came forth a thousand, there shall be left in it a hundred, and out of which there came a hundred, there shall be left in it ten in the house of Israel.'

4 For thus saith the Lord to the house of Israel: "Seek ye me, and you shall live. 5 *But* seek not Bethel, and go not into Gilgal, neither shall you pass over to Beer-sheba, for Gilgal shall go into captivity and Bethel shall be unprofitable."

6 Seek ye the Lord, and live, *lest* the house of Joseph be burnt *with* fire, and it shall devour, and there shall be none to quench Bethel. 7 You that turn judgment into wormwood and forsake justice in the land, 8 *seek* him that maketh Arcturus and Orion and that turneth darkness into morning and that changeth day into night, that calleth the waters of the sea and poureth them out upon the face of the earth: the Lord is his name, 9 he that with a smile bringeth destruction upon the strong and waste upon the mighty.

10 They have hated him that rebuketh in the gate, and have abhorred him that speaketh perfectly. 11 Therefore

pauperem et praedam electam tollebatis ab eo, domos quadro lapide aedificabitis et non habitabitis in eis; vineas amantissimas plantabitis et non bibetis vinum earum. 12 Quia cognovi multa scelera vestra et fortia peccata vestra, hostes iusti, accipientes munus et pauperes in porta deprimentes. 13 Ideo prudens in tempore illo tacebit, quia tempus malum est.

14 Quaerite bonum et non malum, ut vivatis, et erit Dominus, Deus exercituum, vobiscum, sicut dixistis. 15 Odite malum, et diligite bonum, et constituite in porta iudicium; si forte misereatur Dominus, Deus exercituum, reliquiis Ioseph.

16 Propterea haec dicit Dominus, Deus exercituum, Dominator: "In omnibus plateis planctus, et in cunctis quae foris sunt, dicetur, 'Vae, vae!' Et vocabunt agricolam ad luctum et ad planctum eos qui sciunt plangere. 17 Et in omnibus vineis erit planctus, quia pertransibo in medio tui," dicit Dominus.

18 Vae desiderantibus diem Domini! Ad quid eam vobis? Dies Domini ista tenebrae et non lux. 19 Quomodo si fugiat vir a facie leonis et occurrat ei ursus, et ingrediatur domum et innitatur manu sua super parietem et mordeat eum coluber. 20 Numquid non tenebrae dies Domini et non lux et caligo et non splendor in ea?

21 "Odi et proieci festivitates vestras, et non capiam odorem coetuum vestrorum. 22 Quod si obtuleritis mihi holocaustomata et munera vestra, non suscipiam, et vota pinguium vestrorum non respiciam. 23 Aufer a me tumultum

because you robbed the poor and took the choice prey from him, you shall build houses with square stone and shall not dwell in them; you shall plant most delightful vineyards and shall not drink the wine of them. 12 Because I know your manifold crimes and your grievous sins, enemies of the just, taking bribes and oppressing the poor in the gate. 13 Therefore the prudent shall keep silence at that time, for it is an evil time.

14 Seek ye good and not evil, that you may live, and the Lord, the God of hosts, will be with you, as you have said. 15 Hate evil, and love good, and establish judgment in the gate; it may be the Lord, the God of hosts, may have mercy on the remnant of Joseph.

16 Therefore thus saith the Lord, the God of hosts, the sovereign Lord: "In every street there shall be wailing, and in all places that are without, they shall say, 'Alas, alas!' And they shall call the husbandman to mourning and such as are skillful in lamentation to lament. 17 And in all vineyards there shall be wailing, because I will pass through in the midst of thee," saith the Lord.

18 Woe to them that desire the day of the Lord! To what end is it for you? The day of the Lord is darkness and not light. 19 As if a man should flee from the face of a lion and a bear should meet him, *or* enter into the house and lean with his hand upon the wall and a serpent should bite him. 20 Shall not the day of the Lord be darkness and not light and obscurity and no brightness in it?

21 "I hate and have rejected your festivities, and I will not receive the odour of your assemblies. 22 And if you offer me holocausts and your gifts, I will not receive them, neither will I regard the vows of your fat beasts. 23 Take away from

carminum tuorum, et cantica lyrae tuae non audiam. 24 Et revelabitur quasi aqua iudicium, et iustitia quasi torrens fortis. 25 Numquid hostias et sacrificium obtulistis mihi in deserto quadraginta annis, domus Israhel? 26 Et portastis tabernaculum Moloch vestro et imaginem idolorum vestrorum, sidus dei vestri, quae fecistis vobis. 27 Et migrare vos faciam trans Damascum," dicit Dominus; Deus exercituum nomen eius.

Caput 6

Vae qui opulenti estis in Sion et confiditis in monte Samariae, optimates, capita populorum, ingredientes pompatice domum Israhel. 2 Transite in Chalanne, et videte, et ite inde in Emath magnam, et descendite in Geth Palestinorum et ad optima quaeque regna horum, si latior terminus eorum termino vestro est, 3 qui separati estis in diem malum et adpropinquatis solio iniquitatis, 4 qui dormitis in lectis eburneis et lascivitis in stratis vestris, qui comeditis agnum de grege et vitulos de medio armenti, 5 qui canitis ad vocem

me the tumult of thy songs, and I will not hear the canticles of thy harp. 24 *But* judgment shall be revealed as water, and justice as a mighty torrent. 25 Did you offer victims and sacrifices to me in the desert for forty years, O house of Israel? 26 *But* you carried a tabernacle for your Molech and the image of your idols, the star of your god, which you made to yourselves. 27 And I will cause you to go *into captivity* beyond Damascus," saith the Lord; the God of hosts is his name.

Chapter 6

The desolation of Israel for their pride and luxury.

Woe to you that are wealthy in Zion and to you that have confidence in the mountain of Samaria, ye great men, heads of the people, that go in with state into the house of Israel. 2 Pass ye over to Calneh, and see, and go from thence into Hamath the great, and go down into Gath of the Philistines and to all the best kingdoms of these, if their border be larger than your border, 3 you that are separated unto the evil day and that approach to the throne of iniquity, 4 you that sleep upon beds of ivory and are wanton on your couches, that eat the lambs out of the flock and the calves out of the midst of the herd, 5 you that sing to the sound of

psalterii (sicut David putaverunt se habere vasa cantici), 6 bibentes in fialis vinum et optimo unguento delibuti, et nihil patiebantur super contritione Ioseph. 7 Quapropter nunc migrabunt in capite transmigrantium, et auferetur factio lascivientium.

8 "Iuravit Dominus Deus in anima sua," dicit Dominus, Deus exercituum. "Detestor ego superbiam Iacob, et domos eius odi, et tradam civitatem cum habitatoribus suis."

9 Quod si reliqui fuerint decem viri in domo una, et ipsi morientur. 10 Et tollet eum propinquus suus et conburet eum, ut efferat ossa de domo, et dicet ei qui in penetralibus domus est, "Numquid adhuc est apud te?"

11 Et respondebit, "Finis est."

Et dicet ei, "Tace, et non recorderis nominis Domini."

12 Quia ecce: Dominus mandavit, et percutiet domum maiorem ruinis et domum minorem scissionibus. 13 Numquid currere queunt in petris equi? Aut arari potest in bubalis? Quoniam convertistis in amaritudinem iudicium et fructum iustitiae in absinthium, 14 qui laetamini in nihilo, qui dicitis, "Numquid non in fortitudine nostra adsumpsimus nobis cornua?"

15 "Ecce enim: suscitabo super vos, domus Israhel," dicit Dominus, Deus exercituum, "gentem, et conterent vos ab introitu Emath usque ad torrentem deserti."

the psaltery (they have thought themselves to have instruments of music like David), 6 that drink wine in bowls and anoint themselves with the best ointments, and they *are not concerned* for the affliction of Joseph. 7 Wherefore now they shall go captive at the head of them that go into captivity, and the faction of the luxurious ones shall be taken away.

8 "The Lord God hath sworn by his own soul," saith the Lord, the God of hosts. "I detest the pride of Jacob, and I hate his houses, and I will deliver up the city with the inhabitants thereof."

9 And if there remain ten men in one house, they also shall die. 10 And a man's kinsman shall take him up and shall burn him, that he may carry the bones out of the house, and he shall say to him that is in the inner rooms of the house, "Is there yet any with thee?"

11 And he shall answer, "There is an end."

And he shall say to him, "Hold thy peace, and mention not the name of the Lord."

12 For behold: the Lord hath commanded, and he will strike the greater house with breaches and the lesser house with clefts. 13 Can horses run upon the rocks? Or can any one plough with buffles? For you have turned judgment into bitterness and the fruit of justice into wormwood, 14 you that rejoice in a thing of nought, you that say, "Have we not taken unto us horns by our own strength?"

15 "But behold: I will raise up a nation against you, O house of Israel," saith the Lord, the God of hosts, "and they shall destroy you from the entrance of Hamath even to the torrent of the desert."

Caput 7

Haec ostendit mihi Dominus Deus, et ecce: fictor lucustae in principio germinantium serotini imbris, et ecce: serotinus post tonsionem regis. 2 Et factum est cum consummasset comedere herbam terrae dixi, "Domine Deus, propitius esto, obsecro. Quis suscitabit Iacob, quia parvulus est?"

3 Misertus est Dominus super hoc. "Non erit," dixit Dominus.

4 Haec ostendit mihi Dominus Deus, et ecce: vocabat iudicium ad ignem Dominus Deus, et devoravit abyssum multam et comedit simul partem. 5 Et dixi, "Domine Deus, quiesce, obsecro. Quis suscitabit Iacob, quia parvulus est?"

6 Misertus est Dominus super hoc. "Sed et istud non erit," dixit Dominus Deus.

7 Haec ostendit mihi Dominus, et ecce: Dominus stans super murum litum, et in manu eius trulla cementarii.

8 Et dixit Dominus ad me, "Quid tu vides, Amos?"

Et dixi, "Trullam cementarii."

Chapter 7

The prophet sees in three visions evils coming upon Israel.
He is accused of treason by the false priest of Bethel.

These things the Lord God shewed to me, and behold: the locust *was formed* in the beginning of the shooting up of the latter rain, and lo: it was the latter rain after the king's mowing. 2 And it came to pass that when they had made an end of eating the grass of the land I said, "O Lord God, be merciful, I beseech thee. Who shall raise up Jacob, for he is very little?"

3 The Lord had pity upon this. "It shall not be," said the Lord.

4 These things the Lord God shewed to me, and behold: the *Lord* called for judgment unto fire, and it devoured the great deep and ate up a part at the same time. 5 And I said, "O Lord God, cease, I beseech thee. Who shall raise up Jacob, for he is a little one?"

6 The Lord had pity upon this. "Yea this also shall not be," said the Lord God.

7 These things the Lord shewed to me, and behold: the Lord was standing upon a plastered wall, and in his hand a mason's trowel.

8 And the Lord said to me, "What seest thou, Amos?"

And I said, "A mason's trowel."

Et dixit Dominus, "Ecce: ego ponam trullam in medio populi mei Israhel; non adiciam ultra superinducere eum. 9 Et demolientur excelsa idoli, et sanctificationes Israhel desolabuntur, et consurgam super domum Hieroboam in gladio."

10 Et misit Amasias, sacerdos Bethel, ad Hieroboam, regem Israhel, dicens, "Rebellavit contra te Amos in medio domus Israhel; non poterit terra sustinere universos sermones eius. 11 Haec enim dicit Amos: 'In gladio morietur Hieroboam, et Israhel captivus migrabit de terra sua.'"

12 Et dixit Amasias ad Amos, "Qui vides, gradere; fuge in terram Iuda, et comede ibi panem, et ibi prophetabis. 13 Et in Bethel non adicies ultra ut prophetes, quia sanctificatio regis est et domus regni est."

14 Et respondit Amos et dixit ad Amasiam, "Non sum propheta, et non sum filius prophetae, sed armentarius ego sum vellicans sycomoros. 15 Et tulit me Dominus cum sequerer gregem, et dixit ad me Dominus, 'Vade; propheta ad populum meum Israhel.'

16 "Et nunc audi verbum Domini. Tu dicis, 'Non prophetabis super Israhel, et non stillabis super domum idoli.' 17 Propter hoc haec dicit Dominus: 'Uxor tua in civitate fornicabitur, et filii tui et filiae tuae in gladio cadent, et humus tua funiculo metietur, et tu in terra polluta morieris, et Israhel captivus migrabit de terra sua.'"

And the Lord said, "Behold: I will lay down the trowel in the midst of my people Israel; I will plaster them over no more. 9 And the high places of the idol shall be thrown down, and the sanctuaries of Israel shall be laid waste, and I will rise up against the house of Jeroboam with the sword."

10 And Amaziah, the priest of Bethel, sent to Jeroboam, king of Israel, saying, "Amos hath rebelled against thee in the midst of the house of Israel; the land is not able to bear all his words. 11 For thus saith Amos: 'Jeroboam shall die by the sword, and Israel shall be carried away captive out of their own land.'"

12 And Amaziah said to Amos, "Thou seer, go; flee away into the land of Judah, and eat bread there, and *prophesy* there. 13 *But* prophesy not again any more in Bethel, because it is the king's sanctuary and it is the house of the kingdom."

14 And Amos answered and said to Amaziah, "I am not a prophet, nor am I the son of a prophet, but I am a herdsman plucking wild figs. 15 And the Lord took me when I followed the flock, and the Lord said to me, 'Go; prophesy to my people Israel.'

16 "And now hear thou the word of the Lord. Thou sayest, 'Thou shalt not prophesy against Israel, and thou shalt not drop thy word upon the house of the idol.' 17 Therefore thus saith the Lord: 'Thy wife shall play the harlot in the city, and thy sons and thy daughters shall fall by the sword, and thy land shall be measured by a line, and thou shalt die in a polluted land, and Israel shall go into captivity out of their land.'"

Caput 8

Haec ostendit mihi Dominus Deus, et ecce: uncinus pomorum.

2 Et dixit, "Quid tu vides, Amos?"

Et dixi, "Uncinum pomorum."

Et dixit Dominus ad me, "Venit finis super populum meum Israhel; non adiciam ultra ut pertranseam eum. 3 Et stridebunt cardines templi in die illa," dicit Dominus Deus. "Multi morientur; in omni loco proicietur silentium."

4 Audite hoc, qui conteritis pauperem et deficere facitis egenos terrae, 5 dicentes, "Quando transibit mensis, et venundabimus merces, et sabbatum, et aperiemus frumentum, ut inminuamus mensuram et augeamus siclum et subponamus stateras dolosas, 6 ut possideamus in argento egenos et pauperes pro calciamentis et quisquilias frumenti vendamus?"

7 Iuravit Dominus in superbiam Iacob: "Si oblitus fuero usque ad finem omnia opera eorum. 8 Numquid super isto non commovebitur terra, et lugebit omnis habitator eius et ascendet quasi fluvius universus et eicietur et defluet quasi rivus Aegypti?"

9 "Et erit in die illa," dicit Dominus Deus, "occidet sol meridie, et tenebrescere faciam terram in die luminis.

Chapter 8

Under the figure of a hook which bringeth down the fruit,
the approaching desolation of Israel is foreshewed for their
avarice and injustices.

These things the *Lord* shewed to me, and behold: a hook
to draw down the fruit.

2 And he said, "What seest thou, Amos?"

And I said, "A hook *to draw down* fruit."

And the Lord said to me, "The end is come upon my people Israel; I will not again pass by them any more. 3 And the
hinges of the temple shall screak in that day," saith the Lord
God. "Many shall die; silence shall be cast in every place."

4 Hear this, you that crush the poor and make the needy
of the land to fail, 5 saying, "When will the month be over,
and we shall sell our wares, and the sabbath, and we shall
open the corn, that we may lessen the measure and increase
the sicle and may convey in deceitful balances, 6 that we may
possess the needy for money and the poor for *a pair of* shoes
and may sell the refuse of the corn?"

7 The Lord hath sworn against the pride of Jacob: "Surely
I will never forget all their works. 8 Shall not the land tremble for this, and every one mourn that dwelleth therein and
rise up altogether as a river and be cast out and run down as
the river of Egypt?"

9 "And it shall come to pass in that day," saith the Lord
God, "that the sun shall go down at midday, and I will make

10 Et convertam festivitates vestras in luctum et omnia cantica vestra in planctum, et inducam super omne dorsum vestrum saccum et super omne caput calvitium, et ponam eam quasi luctum unigeniti et novissima eius quasi diem amarum."

11 "Ecce: dies veniunt," dicit Dominus, "et mittam famem in terram, non famem panis neque sitim aquae sed audiendi verbum Domini. 12 Et commovebuntur a mari usque ad mare et ab aquilone usque ad orientem; circumibunt quaerentes verbum Domini et non invenient. 13 In die illa deficient virgines pulchrae et adulescentes in siti. 14 Qui iurant in delicto Samariae et dicunt, 'Vivit Deus tuus, Dan, et vivit via Bersabee,' et cadent et non resurgent ultra."

Caput 9

Vidi Dominum stantem super altare, et dixit, "Percute cardines, et commoveantur superliminaria, avaritia enim in capite omnium, et novissimum eorum in gladio interficiam. Non erit fuga eis; fugient, et non salvabitur ex eis qui

the earth dark in the day of light. 10 And I will turn your feasts into mourning and all your songs into lamentation, and I will bring up sackcloth upon every back of yours and baldness upon every head, and I will make it as the mourning of an only son and the latter end thereof as a bitter day."

11 "Behold: the days come," saith the Lord, "and I will send forth a famine into the land, not a famine of bread nor a thirst of water but of hearing the word of the Lord. 12 And they shall move from sea to sea and from the north to the east; they shall go about seeking the word of the Lord and shall not find it. 13 In that day the fair virgins and the young men shall faint for thirst. 14 They that swear by the sin of Samaria and say, 'Thy God, O Dan, liveth, and the way of Beersheba liveth,' and they shall fall and shall rise no more."

Chapter 9

The certainty of the desolation of Israel. The restoring of
the tabernacle of David and the conversion of the Gentiles
to the church, which shall flourish for ever.

I saw the Lord standing upon the altar, and he said, "Strike the hinges, and let the lintels be shook, for there is covetousness in the head of them all, and I will slay the last of them with the sword. There shall be no flight for them; they shall flee, and he that shall flee of them shall not be

fugerit. 2 Si descenderint usque ad infernum, inde manus mea educet eos, et si ascenderint usque ad caelum, inde detraham eos. 3 Et si absconditi fuerint in vertice Carmeli, inde scrutans auferam eos, et si celaverint se ab oculis meis in profundo maris, ibi mandabo serpenti, et mordebit eos. 4 Et si abierint in captivitatem coram inimicis suis, ibi mandabo gladio, et occidet eos. Et ponam oculos meos super eos in malum et non in bonum."

5 Et Dominus, Deus exercituum, qui tangit terram, et tabescet, et lugebunt omnes habitantes in ea, et ascendet sicut rivus omnis et defluet sicut fluvius Aegypti. 6 Qui aedificat in caelo ascensionem suam et fasciculum suum super terram fundavit, qui vocat aquas maris et effundit eas super faciem terrae, Dominus nomen eius.

7 "Numquid non ut filii Aethiopum vos estis mihi, filii Israhel?" ait Dominus. "Numquid non Israhel ascendere feci de terra Aegypti et Palestinos de Cappadocia et Syros de Cyrene? 8 Ecce: oculi Domini Dei super regnum peccans, et conteram illud a facie terrae, verumtamen conterens non conteram domum Iacob," dicit Dominus.

9 "Ecce enim: ego mandabo, et concutiam in omnibus gentibus domum Israhel sicut concutitur triticum in cribro, et non cadet lapillus super terram. 10 In gladio morientur omnes peccatores populi mei, qui dicunt, 'Non adpropinquabit et non veniet super nos malum.' 11 In die illa suscitabo tabernaculum David quod cecidit, et reaedificabo aperturas murorum eius et ea quae corruerant instaurabo, et

delivered. 2 Though they go down even to hell, thence shall my hand bring them out, and though they climb up to heaven, thence will I bring them down. 3 And though they be hid in the top of Carmel, I will search and take them away from thence, and though they hide themselves from my eyes in the depth of the sea, there will I command the serpent, and he shall bite them. 4 And if they go into captivity before their enemies, there will I command the sword, and it shall kill them. And I will set my eyes upon them for evil and not for good."

5 And the Lord, the God of hosts, is he who toucheth the earth, and it shall melt, and all that dwell therein shall mourn, and it *shall* rise up as a river and shall run down as the river of Egypt. 6 He that buildeth his ascension in heaven and hath founded his bundle upon the earth, who calleth the waters of the sea and poureth them out upon the face of the earth, the Lord is his name.

7 "Are not you as the children of the Ethiopians unto me, O children of Israel?" saith the Lord. "Did not I bring up Israel out of the land of Egypt and the Philistines out of Cappadocia and the Syrians out of Cyrene? 8 Behold: the eyes of the Lord God are upon the sinful kingdom, and I will destroy it from the face of the earth, but yet I will not utterly destroy the house of Jacob," saith the Lord.

9 "For behold: I will command, and I will sift the house of Israel among all nations as corn is sifted in a sieve, and there shall not a little stone fall to the ground. 10 All the sinners of my people shall fall by the sword, who say, 'The evils shall not approach and shall not come upon us.' 11 In that day I will raise up the tabernacle of David that is fallen, and I will *close up* the breaches of the walls thereof and repair what was

reaedificabo eum sicut in diebus antiquis, 12 ut possideant reliquias Idumeae et omnes nationes, eo quod invocatum sit nomen meum super eos," dicit Dominus faciens haec.

13 "Ecce: dies veniunt," dicit Dominus, "et conprehendet arator messorem, et calcator uvae mittentem semen, et stillabunt montes dulcedinem, et omnes colles culti erunt. 14 Et convertam captivitatem populi mei Israhel, et aedificabunt civitates desertas et habitabunt, et plantabunt vineas et bibent vinum earum et facient hortos et comedent fructus eorum. 15 Et plantabo eos super humum suam, et non evellam eos ultra de terra sua quam dedi eis," dicit Dominus, Deus tuus.

fallen, and I will rebuild it as in the days of old, 12 that they may possess the remnant of Edom and all nations, because my name is invoked upon them," saith the Lord that doth these things.

13 "Behold: the days come," saith the Lord, *"when* the ploughman shall overtake the reaper, and the treader of grapes him that soweth seed, and the mountains shall drop sweetness, and every hill shall be tilled. 14 And I will bring back the captivity of my people Israel, and they shall build the abandoned cities and inhabit them, and they shall plant vineyards and drink the wine of them and shall make gardens and eat the fruits of them. 15 And I will plant them upon their own land, and I will no more pluck them out of their land which I have given them," saith the Lord, thy God.

OBADIAH

Caput 1

Visio Abdiae.

Haec dicit Dominus Deus ad Edom. Auditum audivimus a Domino, et legatum ad gentes misit: "Surgite, et consurgamus adversum eum in proelium."

2 "Ecce: parvulum te dedi in gentibus; contemptibilis tu es valde. 3 Superbia cordis tui extulit te habitantem in scissuris petrarum, exaltantem solium tuum, qui dicis in corde tuo, 'Quis detrahet me in terram?' 4 Si exaltatus fueris ut aquila et si inter sidera posueris nidum tuum, inde detraham te," dicit Dominus.

5 "Si fures introissent ad te, si latrones per noctem, quomodo conticuisses? Nonne furati essent sufficientia sibi? Si vindemiatores introissent ad te, numquid saltim racemum reliquissent tibi? 6 Quomodo scrutati sunt Esau, investigaverunt abscondita eius? 7 Usque ad terminum emiserunt te. Omnes viri foederis tui inluserunt tibi; invaluerunt adversum te viri pacis tuae; qui comedunt tecum ponent insidias subter te. Non est prudentia in eo.

Chapter 1

The destruction of Edom for their pride and the wrongs
they did to Jacob. The salvation and victory of Israel.

The vision of Obadiah.

Thus saith the Lord God to Edom. We have heard a rumour from the Lord, and he hath sent an ambassador to the nations: "Arise, and let us rise up to battle against him."

2 "Behold: I have made thee small among the nations; thou art exceeding contemptible. 3 The pride of thy heart hath lifted thee up who dwellest in the clefts of the rocks and settest up thy throne on high, who sayest in thy heart, 'Who shall bring me down to the ground?' 4 *Though* thou *be* exalted as an eagle and *though* thou *set* thy nest among the stars, thence will I bring thee down," saith the Lord.

5 "If thieves had gone in to thee, if robbers by night, how wouldst thou have held thy peace? Would they not have stolen *till they had* enough? If the grape-gatherers had come in to thee, would they not have left thee at the least a cluster? 6 How have they searched Esau? How have they sought out his hidden things? 7 They have sent thee out even to the border. All the men of thy confederacy have deceived thee; the men of thy peace have prevailed against thee; they that eat with thee shall lay snares under thee. There is no wisdom in him.

8 "Numquid non in die illa," dicit Dominus, "perdam sapientes de Idumea et prudentiam de Monte Esau? 9 Et timebunt fortes tui a meridie ut intereat vir de Monte Esau. 10 Propter interfectionem et propter iniquitatem in fratrem tuum Iacob operiet te confusio, et peribis in aeternum. 11 In die cum stares adversus eum, quando capiebant alieni exercitum eius et extranei ingrediebantur portas eius et super Hierusalem mittebant sortem, tu quoque eras quasi unus ex eis. 12 Et non despicies in die fratris tui, in die peregrinationis eius, et non laetaberis super filios Iuda in die perditionis eorum, et non magnificabis os tuum in die angustiae. 13 Neque ingredieris portam populi mei in die ruinae eorum, neque despicies et tu in malis eius in die vastitatis illius, et non emitteris adversum exercitum eius in die vastitatis illius. 14 Neque stabis in exitibus ut interficias eos qui fugerint, et non concludes reliquos eius in die tribulationis.

15 "Quoniam iuxta est dies Domini super omnes gentes. Sicut fecisti, fiet tibi. Retributionem tuam convertet in caput tuum. 16 Quomodo enim bibisti super montem sanctum meum, bibent omnes gentes iugiter, et bibent et absorbebunt, et erunt quasi non sint. 17 Et in Monte Sion erit salvatio, et erit sanctus, et possidebit domus Iacob eos qui se possederant. 18 Et erit domus Iacob ignis, et domus Ioseph flamma, et domus Esau stipula, et succendentur in eis et

8 "Shall not I in that day," saith the Lord, "destroy the wise out of Edom and understanding out of the Mount of Esau? 9 And thy valiant men of the south shall be afraid that man may be cut off from the Mount of Esau. 10 For the slaughter and for the iniquity against thy brother Jacob confusion shall cover thee, and thou shalt perish for ever. 11 In the day when thou stoodest against him, when strangers carried away his army captive and foreigners entered into his gates and cast lots upon Jerusalem, thou also wast as one of them. 12 *But* thou shalt not look on in the day of thy brother, in the day of his leaving his country, and thou shalt not rejoice over the children of Judah in the day of their destruction, and thou shalt not magnify thy mouth in the day of distress. 13 Neither shalt thou enter into the gate of my people in the day of their ruin, neither shalt thou also look on in his evils in the day of his calamity, and thou shalt not be sent out against his army in the day of his desolation. 14 Neither shalt thou stand in the *crossways* to kill them that flee, and thou shalt not shut up them that remain of him in the day of tribulation.

15 "For the day of the Lord is at hand upon all nations. As thou hast done, so shall it be done to thee. He will turn thy reward upon thy own head. 16 For as you have drunk upon my holy mountain, so all nations shall drink continually, and they shall drink and sup up, and they shall be as though they were not. 17 And in Mount Zion shall be salvation, and it shall be holy, and the house of Jacob shall possess those that *possessed* them. 18 And the house of Jacob shall be a fire, and the house of Joseph a flame, and the house of Esau stubble, and they shall be kindled in them and shall devour them.

devorabunt eos. Et non erunt reliquiae domus Esau, quia Dominus locutus est."

19 Et hereditabunt hii qui ad austrum sunt Montem Esau, et qui in campestribus Philisthim. Et possidebunt regionem Ephraim et regionem Samariae, et Beniamin possidebit Galaad. 20 Et transmigratio exercitus huius filiorum Israhel omnia loca Chananeorum usque ad Saraptham, et transmigratio Hierusalem quae in Bosforo est possidebit civitates austri. 21 Et ascendent salvatores in Montem Sion iudicare Montem Esau, et erit Domino regnum.

And there shall be no remains of the house of Esau, for the Lord hath spoken it."

19 And they that are toward the south shall inherit the Mount of Esau, and they that are in the plains the Philistines. And they shall possess the country of Ephraim and the country of Samaria, and Benjamin shall possess Gilead. 20 And the captivity of this host of the children of Israel all the places of the Canaanites even to Zarephath, and the captivity of Jerusalem that is in Bosphorus shall possess the cities of the south. 21 And saviours shall come up into Mount Zion to judge the Mount of Esau, and the kingdom shall be for the Lord.

JONAH

Caput 1

Et factum est verbum Domini ad Ionam, filium Amathi, dicens, 2 "Surge, et vade in Nineven, civitatem grandem, et praedica in ea, quia ascendit malitia eius coram me." 3 Et surrexit Ionas ut fugeret in Tharsis a facie Domini. Et descendit in Ioppen et invenit navem euntem in Tharsis, et dedit naulum eius et descendit in eam ut iret cum eis in Tharsis a facie Domini. 4 Dominus autem misit ventum magnum in mare, et facta est tempestas magna in mari, et navis periclitabatur conteri. 5 Et timuerunt nautae, et clamaverunt viri ad deum suum, et miserunt vasa quae erant in navi in mare ut adleviaretur ab eis. Et Ionas descendit ad interiora navis et dormiebat sopore gravi.

6 Et accessit ad eum gubernator et dixit ei, "Quid tu sopore deprimeris? Surge; invoca Deum tuum, si forte recogitet Deus de nobis et non pereamus."

Chapter 1

Jonah, being sent to preach in Nineveh, fleeth away by sea.
A tempest riseth, of which he, being found by lot to be the
cause, is cast into the sea, which thereupon is calmed.

Now the word of the Lord came to Jonah, the son of Amittai, saying, 2 "Arise, and go to Nineveh, the great city, and preach in it, for the wickedness thereof is come up before me." 3 And Jonah rose up to flee into Tarshish from the face of the Lord. And he went down to Joppa and found a ship going to Tarshish, and he paid the fare thereof and went down into it to go with them to Tarshish from the face of the Lord. 4 But the Lord sent a great wind into the sea, and a great tempest was *raised* in the sea, and the ship was in danger to be broken. 5 And the mariners were afraid, and the men cried to their god, and they cast forth the *wares* that were in the ship into the sea to lighten it of them. And Jonah went down into the inner part of the ship and fell into a deep sleep.

6 And the shipmaster came to him and said to him, "Why art thou fast asleep? Rise up; call upon thy God, if so be that God will think of us *that* we may not perish."

7 Et dixit vir ad collegam suum, "Venite, et mittamus sortes, et sciamus quare hoc malum sit nobis." Et miserunt sortes, et cecidit sors super Ionam. 8 Et dixerunt ad eum, "Indica nobis cuius causa malum istud sit nobis. Quod est opus tuum? Quae terra tua? Et quo vadis? Vel ex quo populo es tu?"

9 Et dixit ad eos, "Hebraeus ego sum, et Dominum, Deum caeli, ego timeo, qui fecit mare et aridam."

10 Et timuerunt viri timore magno, et dixerunt ad eum, "Quid hoc fecisti?" Cognoverunt enim viri quod a facie Domini fugeret quia indicaverat eis. 11 Et dixerunt ad eum, "Quid faciemus tibi, et cessabit mare a nobis?" Quia mare ibat et intumescebat.

12 Et dixit ad eos, "Tollite me, et mittite in mare, et cessabit mare a vobis, scio enim ego quoniam propter me tempestas grandis est haec super vos."

13 Et remigabant viri ut reverterentur ad aridam, et non valebant quia mare ibat et intumescebat super eos. 14 Et clamaverunt ad Dominum et dixerunt, "Quaesumus, Domine, ne pereamus in anima viri istius, et ne des super nos sanguinem innocentem, quia tu, Domine, sicut voluisti fecisti." 15 Et tulerunt Ionam et miserunt in mare, et quievit mare a fervore suo. 16 Et timuerunt viri timore magno Dominum et immolaverunt hostias Domino et voverunt vota.

7 And they said every one to his fellow, "Come, and let us cast lots, *that* we may know why this evil is upon us." And they cast lots, and the lot fell upon Jonah. 8 And they said to him, "Tell us for what cause this evil is upon us. What is thy business? *Of* what country *art thou?* And whither goest thou? Or of what people art thou?"

9 And he said to them, "I am a Hebrew, and I fear the Lord, the God of heaven, who made both the sea and the dry land."

10 And the men were greatly afraid, and they said to him, "Why hast thou done this?" For the men knew that he fled from the face of the Lord because he had told them. 11 And they said to him, "What shall we do to thee, *that* the sea *may be* calm to us?" For the sea flowed and swelled.

12 And he said to them, "Take me up, and cast me into the sea, and the sea shall be calm to you, for I know that for my sake this great tempest is upon you."

13 And the men rowed *hard* to return to land, *but* they were not able because the sea *tossed* and swelled upon them. 14 And they cried to the Lord and said, "We beseech thee, O Lord, let us not perish for this man's life, and lay not upon us innocent blood, for thou, O Lord, hast done as it pleased thee." 15 And they took Jonah and cast him into the sea, and the sea ceased from raging. 16 And the men feared the Lord exceedingly and sacrificed victims to the Lord and made vows.

Caput 2

Et praeparavit Dominus piscem grandem ut degluttiret Ionam, et erat Ionas in ventre piscis tribus diebus et tribus noctibus. 2 Et oravit Ionas ad Dominum, Deum suum, de ventre piscis.

3 Et dixit, "Clamavi de tribulatione mea ad Dominum, et exaudivit me. De ventre inferni clamavi, et exaudisti vocem meam. 4 Et proiecisti me in profundum in corde maris, et flumen circumdedit me; omnes gurgites tui et fluctus tui super me transierunt. 5 Et ego dixi, 'Abiectus sum a conspectu oculorum tuorum, verumtamen rursus videbo templum sanctum tuum.' 6 Circumdederunt me aquae usque ad animam; abyssus vallavit me; pelagus operuit caput meum. 7 Ad extrema montium descendi; terrae vectes concluserunt me in aeternum. Et sublevabis de corruptione vitam meam, Domine, Deus meus. 8 Cum angustiaretur in me anima mea, Domini recordatus sum, ut veniat ad te oratio mea, ad templum sanctum tuum. 9 Qui custodiunt vanitates frustra misericordiam suam derelinquunt. 10 Ego autem in voce laudis immolabo tibi; quaecumque vovi reddam pro salute Domino."

11 Et dixit Dominus pisci, et evomuit Ionam in aridam.

Chapter 2

Jonah is swallowed up by a great fish. He prayeth with confidence in God, and the fish casteth him out on the dry land.

Now the Lord prepared a great fish to swallow up Jonah, and Jonah was in the belly of the fish three days and three nights. 2 And Jonah prayed to the Lord, his God, out of the belly of the fish.

3 And he said, "I cried out of my affliction to the Lord, and he heard me. I cried out of the belly of hell, and thou hast heard my voice. 4 And thou hast cast me forth into the deep in the heart of the sea, and a flood hath compassed me; all thy billows and thy waves have passed over me. 5 And I said, 'I am cast away out of the sight of thy eyes, but yet I shall see thy holy temple again.' 6 The waters compassed me about even to the soul; the deep hath closed me round about; the sea hath covered my head. 7 I went down to the lowest parts of the mountains; the bars of the earth have shut me up for ever. And thou wilt bring up my life from corruption, O Lord, my God. 8 When my soul was in distress within me, I remembered the Lord, that my prayer may come to thee, unto thy holy temple. 9 They that in vain observe vanities forsake their own mercy. 10 But I with the voice of praise will sacrifice to thee; I will pay whatsoever I have vowed for my salvation to the Lord."

11 And the Lord spoke to the fish, and it vomited out Jonah upon the dry land.

Caput 3

Et factum est verbum Domini ad Ionam secundo, dicens, 2 "Surge, et vade in Nineven, civitatem magnam, et praedica in ea praedicationem quam ego loquor ad te." 3 Et surrexit Ionas et abiit in Nineven iuxta verbum Domini. Et Nineve erat civitas magna itinere dierum trium.

4 Et coepit Ionas introire in civitatem itinere diei unius, et clamavit et dixit, "Adhuc quadraginta dies et Nineve subvertetur." 5 Et crediderunt viri Ninevitae in Deum, et praedicaverunt ieiunium et vestiti sunt saccis, a maiore usque ad minorem. 6 Et pervenit verbum ad regem Nineve. Et surrexit de solio suo et abiecit vestimentum suum a se et indutus est sacco et sedit in cinere.

7 Et clamavit et dixit in Nineve ex ore regis et principum eius, dicens, "Homines et iumenta et boves et pecora non gustent quicquam. Nec pascantur, et aquam non bibant. 8 Et operiantur saccis homines et iumenta et clament ad Dominum in fortitudine, et convertatur vir a via sua mala et ab iniquitate quae est in manibus eorum. 9 Quis scit si convertatur et ignoscat Deus et revertatur a furore irae suae, et non

Chapter 3

Jonah is sent again to preach in Nineveh. Upon their fasting and repentance, God recalleth the sentence by which they were to be destroyed.

And the word of the Lord came to Jonah the second time, saying, 2 "Arise, and go to Nineveh, the great city, and preach in it the preaching that I *bid* thee." 3 And Jonah arose and went to Nineveh according to the word of the Lord. Now Nineveh was a great city of three days' journey.

4 And Jonah began to enter into the city one day's journey, and he cried and said, "Yet forty days and Nineveh shall be destroyed." 5 And the men of Nineveh believed in God, and they proclaimed a fast and put on sackcloth, from the greatest to the least. 6 And the word came to the king of Nineveh. And he rose up out of his throne and cast away his robe from him and was clothed with sackcloth and sat in ashes.

7 And he *caused it to be proclaimed* and *published* in Nineveh from the mouth of the king and of his princes, saying, "Let neither men nor *beasts,* oxen nor sheep taste any thing. Let them not feed, nor drink water. 8 And let men and beasts be covered with sackcloth and cry to the Lord with *all their* strength, and let them turn every one from his evil way and from the iniquity that is in their hands. 9 Who *can tell* if God will turn and forgive and will turn away from his *fierce* anger,

peribimus?" 10 Et vidit Deus opera eorum, quia conversi sunt a via sua mala. Et misertus est Deus super malitiam quam locutus fuerat ut faceret eis, et non fecit.

Caput 4

Et adflictus est Ionas adflictione magna et iratus est. 2 Et oravit ad Dominum et dixit, "Obsecro, Domine, numquid non hoc est verbum meum cum adhuc essem in terra mea? Propter hoc praeoccupavi ut fugerem in Tharsis, scio enim quia tu Deus clemens et misericors es, patiens et multae miserationis et ignoscens super malitia. 3 Et nunc, Domine, tolle, quaeso, animam meam a me, quia melior est mihi mors quam vita."

4 Et dixit Dominus, "Putasne bene irasceris tu?"

5 Et egressus est Ionas de civitate et sedit contra orientem civitatis, et fecit sibimet ibi umbraculum. Et sedebat subter illud in umbra donec videret quid accideret civitati. 6 Et praeparavit Dominus Deus hederam, et ascendit super caput Ionae ut esset umbra super caput eius et protegeret eum, laboraverat enim, et laetatus est Ionas super hedera laetitia

and we shall not perish?" 10 And God saw their works, that they were turned from their evil way. And God had mercy with regard to the evil which he had said that he would do to them, and he did it not.

Chapter 4

Jonah, repining to see that his prophecy is not fulfilled, is reproved by the type of the ivy.

And Jonah was exceedingly troubled and was angry. 2 And he prayed to the Lord and said, "I beseech thee, O Lord, is not this *what I said* when I was yet in my own country? Therefore I went before to flee into Tarshish, for I know that thou art a gracious and merciful God, patient and of much compassion and easy to forgive evil. 3 And now, O Lord, I beseech thee, take my life from me, for it is better for me *to die* than *to live.*"

4 And the Lord said, "Dost thou think thou *hast reason to be* angry?"

5 Then Jonah went out of the city and sat toward the east side of the city, and he made himself a booth there. And he sat under it in the shadow till he might see what would befall the city. 6 And the Lord God prepared an ivy, and it came up over the head of Jonah to be a shadow over his head and to cover him, for he was fatigued, and Jonah was exceeding glad

magna. 7 Et paravit Deus vermem ascensu diluculi in crastinum, et percussit hederam, et exaruit. 8 Et cum ortus fuisset sol, praecepit Dominus vento calido et urenti, et percussit sol super caput Ionae, et ab ardore aestuabat. Et petivit animae suae ut moreretur et dixit, "Melius est mihi mori quam vivere."

9 Et dixit Dominus ad Ionam, "Putasne bene irasceris tu super hedera?"

Et dixit, "Bene irascor ego usque ad mortem."

10 Et dixit Dominus, "Tu doles super hederam, in qua non laborasti neque fecisti ut cresceret, quae sub una nocte nata est et sub una nocte periit. 11 Et ego non parcam Nineve, civitati magnae, in qua sunt plus quam centum viginti milia hominum qui nesciunt quid sit inter dexteram et sinistram suam, et iumenta multa?"

of the ivy. 7 *But* God prepared a worm when the morning arose on the following day, and it struck the ivy, and it withered. 8 And when the sun was risen, the Lord commanded a hot and burning wind, and the sun beat upon the head of Jonah, and he broiled with the heat. And he desired for his soul that he might die and said, "It is better for me to die than to live."

9 And the Lord said to Jonah, "Dost thou think thou *hast reason to be* angry for the ivy?"

And he said, "I am angry *with reason* even unto death."

10 And the Lord said, "Thou art grieved for the ivy, for which thou hast not laboured nor made it to grow, which in one night came up and in one night perished. 11 And shall not I spare Nineveh, that great city, in which there are more than a hundred and twenty thousand persons that know not *how to distinguish* between their right hand and their left, and many beasts?"

MICAH

Caput 1

Verbum Domini quod factum est ad Micham, Morasthiten, in diebus Ioatham, Ahaz et Ezechiae, regum Iuda, quod vidit super Samariam et Hierusalem.

2 "Audite, populi omnes, et adtendat terra et plenitudo eius, et sit Dominus Deus vobis in testem, Dominus de templo sancto suo. 3 Quia ecce: Dominus egredietur de loco suo, et descendet et calcabit super excelsa terrae, 4 et consumentur montes subtus eum, et valles scindentur sicut cera a facie ignis et sicut aquae quae decurrunt in praeceps. 5 In scelere Iacob omne istud et in peccatis domus Israhel. Quod scelus Iacob? Nonne Samaria? Et quae excelsa Iudae? Nonne Hierusalem? 6 Et ponam Samariam quasi acervum lapidum in agro cum plantatur vinea, et detraham in vallem lapides eius

Chapter 1

Samaria for her sins shall be destroyed by the Assyrians.
They shall also invade Judah and Jerusalem.

The word of the Lord that came to Micah, the Moreshethite, in the days of Jotham, Ahaz and Hezekiah, kings of Judah, which he saw concerning Samaria and Jerusalem. 2 "Hear, all ye people, and let the earth give ear and all that is therein, and let the Lord God be a witness to you, the Lord from his holy temple. 3 For behold: the Lord will come forth out of his place, and he will come down and will tread upon the high places of the earth, 4 and the mountains shall be *melted* under him, and the valleys shall be cleft as wax before the fire and as waters that run down a steep place. 5 For the wickedness of Jacob is all this and for the sins of the house of Israel. What is the wickedness of Jacob? Is it not Samaria? And what are the high places of Judah? Are they not Jerusalem? 6 And I will make Samaria as a heap of stones in the field when a vineyard is planted, and I will bring down the stones thereof into the valley and will lay her

et fundamenta eius revelabo. 7 Et omnia sculptilia eius concidentur, et omnes mercedes eius conburentur igni, et omnia idola eius ponam in perditionem, quia de mercedibus meretricis congregata sunt et usque ad mercedem meretricis revertentur."

8 Super hoc plangam et ululabo; vadam spoliatus et nudus; faciam planctum velut draconum et luctum quasi strutionum. 9 Quia desperata est plaga eius, quia venit usque ad Iudam; tetigit portam populi mei usque ad Hierusalem. 10 In Geth nolite adnuntiare; lacrimis ne ploretis; in Domo Pulveris pulvere vos conspergite. 11 Et transite vobis, Habitatio Pulchra, confusa ignominia. Non est egressa quae habitat in exitu. Planctum Domus Vicina accipiet ex vobis, quae stetit sibimet, 12 quia infirmata est in bonum quae habitat in amaritudinibus, quia descendit malum a Domino in portam Hierusalem. 13 Tumultus quadrigae stuporis habitanti Lachis; principium peccati est filiae Sion, quia in te inventa sunt scelera Israhel. 14 Propterea dabit emissarios super hereditatem Geth, domus mendacii in deceptionem regibus Israhel. 15 Adhuc heredem adducam tibi quae habitas in Maresa; usque ad Odollam veniet gloria Israhel. 16 Decalvare, et tondere super filios deliciarum tuarum; dilata calvitium tuum sicut aquila, quoniam captivi ducti sunt ex te.

foundations bare. 7 And all her graven things shall be cut in pieces, and all her wages shall be burnt with fire, and I will bring to destruction all her idols, for they were gathered together of the hire of a harlot and unto the hire of a harlot they shall return."

8 Therefore will I lament and howl; I will go stripped and naked; I will make a wailing like the dragons and a mourning like the ostriches. 9 Because her wound is desperate, because it is come even to Judah; it hath touched the gate of my people even to Jerusalem. 10 Declare ye it not in Gath; weep ye not with tears; in the House of Dust sprinkle yourselves with dust. 11 And pass *away, O thou that dwellest in the* Beautiful Place, covered with thy shame. She went not forth that dwelleth in the confines. The House Adjoining shall receive mourning from you, which stood by herself, 12 for she is become weak unto good that dwelleth in bitterness, for evil is come down from the Lord into the gate of Jerusalem. 13 A tumult of chariots *hath astonished* the inhabitants of Lachish; it is the beginning of sin to the daughter of Zion, for in thee were found the crimes of Israel. 14 Therefore shall she send messengers to the inheritance of Gath, the houses of lying to deceive the kings of Israel. 15 Yet will I bring an heir to thee that dwellest in Mareshah; even to Adullam shall the glory of Israel come. 16 Make thee bald, and be polled for *thy delicate* children; enlarge thy baldness as the eagle, for they are carried into captivity from thee.

Caput 2

Vae qui cogitatis inutile et operamini malum in cubilibus vestris; in luce matutina faciunt illud quoniam contra Deum est manus eorum. 2 Et concupierunt agros et violenter tulerunt, et domos rapuerunt et calumniabantur virum et domum eius, virum et hereditatem eius.

3 Idcirco haec dicit Dominus: "Ecce: ego cogito super familiam istam malum unde non auferetis colla vestra, et non ambulabitis superbi, quoniam tempus pessimum est. 4 In die illa sumetur super vos parabola, et cantabitur canticum cum suavitate dicentium, 'Depopulatione vastati sumus; pars populi mei commutata est. Quomodo recedet a me, cum revertatur qui regiones nostras dividat?' 5 Propter hoc non erit tibi mittens funiculum sortis in coetu Domini.

6 Ne loquamini, loquentes, "Non stillabit super istos; non conprehendet confusio."

7 Dicit domus Iacob, "Numquid adbreviatus est spiritus Domini, aut tales sunt cogitationes eius?"

Nonne verba mea bona sunt cum eo qui recte graditur? 8 Et e contrario populus meus in adversarium consurrexit. Desuper tunica pallium sustulistis, et eos qui transiebant simpliciter convertistis in bellum. 9 Mulieres populi mei

Chapter 2

The Israelites by their crying injustices provoke God to punish them. He shall at last restore Jacob.

Woe to you that devise that which is unprofitable and work evil in your beds; in the morning light they execute it because their hand is against God. 2 And they have coveted fields and taken them by violence, and houses they have forcibly taken away and oppressed a man and his house, a man and his inheritance.

3 Therefore thus saith the Lord: "Behold: I devise an evil against this family from which you shall not withdraw your necks, and you shall not walk haughtily, for this is a very evil time. 4 In that day a parable shall be taken up upon you, and a song shall be sung with *melody* by them that say, 'We are laid waste and spoiled; the portion of my people is changed. How shall he depart from me, whereas he is returning that will divide our land?' 5 Therefore thou shalt have none that shall cast the cord of a lot in the assembly of the Lord.

6 Speak ye not, saying, *"The prophecy* shall not drop upon these; confusion shall not take them."

7 The house of Jacob saith, "Is the spirit of the Lord *straitened,* or are *these* his thoughts?"

Are not my words good to him that walketh uprightly? 8 *But* my people on the contrary are risen up as an enemy. You have taken away the cloak off from the coat, and them that passed harmless you have turned to war. 9 You have cast

eiecistis de domo deliciarum suarum; a parvulis earum tulistis laudem meam in perpetuum. 10 Surgite, et ite, quia non habetis hic requiem. Propter inmunditiam eius corrumpetur putredine pessima. 11 Utinam non essem vir habens spiritum et mendacium potius loquerer; stillabo tibi in vinum et in ebrietatem, et erit super quem stillatur populus iste.

12 "Congregatione congregabo, Iacob, totum te in unum; conducam reliquias Israhel. Pariter ponam illum quasi gregem in ovili, quasi pecus in medio caularum. Tumultuabuntur a multitudine hominum, 13 ascendet enim pandens iter ante eos. Divident et transibunt portam et ingredientur per eam, et transibit rex eorum coram eis et Dominus in capite eorum."

Caput 3

Et dixi, "Audite, principes Iacob et duces domus Israhel. Numquid non vestrum est scire iudicium, 2 qui odio habetis bonum et diligitis malum, qui violenter tollitis pelles eorum

out the women of my people from *their houses, in which they took delight*; you have taken my praise for ever from their children. 10 Arise ye, and depart, for there is no rest here for you. For *that* uncleanness of *the land* it shall be corrupted with a grievous corruption. 11 Would God I were not a man that hath the spirit and that I rather spoke a lie; I will let drop to thee *of* wine and *of* drunkenness, and it shall be this people upon whom it shall drop.

12 "I will assemble and gather together all of thee, O Jacob; I will bring together the remnant of Israel. I will put them together as a flock in the fold, as the sheep in the midst of the sheepcotes. They shall make a tumult by reason of the multitude of men, 13 for he shall go up that shall open the way before them. They shall divide and pass through the gate and shall come in by it, and their king shall pass before them and the Lord at the head of them."

Chapter 3

For the sins of the rich oppressing the poor, of false prophets flattering for lucre and of judges perverting justice, Jerusalem and the temple shall be destroyed.

And I said, "Hear, O ye princes of Jacob and ye chiefs of the house of Israel. Is it not your part to know judgment, 2 you that hate good and love evil, that violently pluck off

desuper eis et carnem eorum desuper ossibus eorum, 3 qui comederunt carnem populi mei et pellem eorum desuper excoriaverunt et ossa eorum confregerunt et conciderunt sicut in lebete et quasi carnem in medio ollae? 4 Tunc clamabunt ad Dominum, et non exaudiet eos, et abscondet faciem suam ab eis in tempore illo, sicut nequiter egerunt in adinventionibus suis.

5 "Haec dicit Dominus super prophetas qui seducunt populum meum, qui mordent dentibus suis et praedicant pacem, et si quis non dederit in ore eorum quippiam, sanctificant super eum proelium: 6 'Propterea nox vobis pro visione erit, et tenebrae vobis pro divinatione, et occumbet sol super prophetas, et obtenebrabitur super eos dies. 7 Et confundentur qui vident visiones, et confundentur divini, et operient vultus suos omnes quia non est responsum Dei.'

8 "Verumtamen ego repletus sum fortitudine spiritus Domini, iudicio et virtute ut adnuntiem Iacob scelus suum et Israhel peccatum suum. 9 Audite hoc, principes domus Iacob et iudices domus Israhel, qui abominamini iudicium et omnia recta pervertitis, 10 qui aedificatis Sion in sanguinibus, et Hierusalem in iniquitate. 11 Principes eius in muneribus iudicabant, et sacerdotes eius in mercede docebant, et prophetae eius in pecunia divinabant, et super Dominum requiescebant, dicentes, 'Numquid non Dominus in medio nostrum? Non venient super nos mala.' 12 Propter hoc causa vestri Sion quasi ager arabitur, et Hierusalem quasi acervus lapidum erit, et mons templi in excelsa silvarum."

their skins from them and their flesh from their bones, 3 who have eaten the flesh of my people and have flayed their skin from off them and have broken and chopped their bones as for the kettle and as flesh in the midst of the pot? 4 Then shall they cry to the Lord, and he will not hear them, and he will hide his face from them at that time, as they have behaved wickedly in their devices.

5 "Thus saith the Lord concerning the prophets that make my people err, that bite with their teeth and preach peace, and if a man give not something into their mouth, they *prepare* war against him: 6 'Therefore night shall be to you instead of vision, and darkness to you instead of divination, and the sun shall go down upon the prophets, and the day shall be darkened over them. 7 And they shall be confounded that see visions, and the diviners shall be confounded, and they shall all cover their faces because there is no answer of God.'

8 "But yet I am filled with the strength of the spirit of the Lord, with judgment and power to declare unto Jacob his wickedness and to Israel his sin. 9 Hear this, ye princes of the house of Jacob and ye judges of the house of Israel, you that abhor judgment and pervert all that is right, 10 you that build up Zion with blood, and Jerusalem with iniquity. 11 Her princes have judged for bribes, and her priests have taught for hire, and her prophets divined for money, and they leaned upon the Lord, saying, 'Is not the Lord in the midst of us? No evil shall come upon us.' 12 Therefore because of you Zion shall be ploughed as a field, and Jerusalem shall be as a heap of stones, and the mountain of the temple as the high places of the forests."

Caput 4

Et erit in novissimo dierum erit mons domus Domini praeparatus in vertice montium et sublimis super colles, et fluent ad eum populi.

2 Et properabunt gentes multae et dicent, "Venite; ascendamus ad montem Domini et ad domum Dei Iacob, et docebit nos de viis suis, et ibimus in semitis eius, quia de Sion egredietur lex, et verbum Domini de Hierusalem."

3 Et iudicabit inter populos multos et corripiet gentes fortes usque in longinquum, et concident gladios suos in vomeres, et hastas suas in ligones; non sumet gens adversus gentem gladium, et non discent ultra belligerare. 4 Et sedebit vir subtus vineam suam et subtus ficum suam, et non erit qui deterreat, quia os Domini exercituum locutum est. 5 Quia omnes populi ambulabunt unusquisque in nomine dei sui, nos autem ambulabimus in nomine Domini, Dei nostri, in aeternum et ultra.

Chapter 4

The glory of the church of Christ by the conversion of the Gentiles. The Jews shall be carried captives to Babylon and be delivered again.

And it shall come to pass in the last days that the mountain of the house of the Lord shall be prepared in the top of mountains and high above the hills, and people shall flow to it.

2 And many nations shall come in haste and say, "Come; let us go up to the mountain of the Lord and to the house of the God of Jacob, and he will teach us of his ways, and we will walk in his paths, for the law shall go forth out of Zion, and the word of the Lord out of Jerusalem."

3 And he shall judge among many people and rebuke strong nations afar off, and they shall beat their swords into ploughshares, and their spears into spades; nation shall not take sword against nation, neither shall they learn war any more. 4 And every man shall sit under his vine and under his fig tree, and there shall be none to make them afraid, for the mouth of the Lord of hosts hath spoken. 5 For all people will walk every one in the name of his god, but we will walk in the name of the Lord, our God, for ever and ever.

6 "In die illa," dicit Dominus, "congregabo claudicantem, et eam quam eieceram colligam, et quam adflixeram. 7 Et ponam claudicantem in reliquias et eam quae laboraverat in gentem robustam, et regnabit Dominus super eos in Monte Sion ex hoc nunc et usque in aeternum.

8 "Et tu, turris gregis nebulosa filiae Sion, usque ad te veniet; et veniet potestas prima, regnum filiae Hierusalem. 9 Nunc quare maerore contraheris? Numquid rex non est tibi, aut consiliarius tuus periit quia conprehendit te dolor sicut parturientem? 10 Dole, et satage, filia Sion, quasi parturiens, quia nunc egredieris de civitate et habitabis in regione et venies usque ad Babylonem. Ibi liberaberis; ibi redimet te Dominus de manu inimicorum tuorum.

11 "Et nunc congregatae sunt super te gentes multae, quae dicunt, 'Lapidetur, et aspiciat in Sion oculus noster.' 12 Ipsi autem non cognoverunt cogitationes Domini et non intellexerunt consilium eius, quia congregavit eos quasi faenum areae.

13 "Surge, et tritura, filia Sion, quia cornu tuum ponam ferreum, et ungulas tuas ponam aereas, et comminues populos multos et interficies Domino rapinas eorum et fortitudinem eorum Domino universae terrae."

6 "In that day," saith the Lord, "I will gather up her that halteth, and her that I had cast out I will gather up, and her whom I had afflicted. 7 And I will make her that halted a remnant and her that hath been afflicted a mighty nation, and the Lord will reign over them in Mount Zion from this time now and for ever.

8 "And thou, O cloudy tower of the flock of the daughter of Zion, unto thee shall it come; yea the first power shall come, the kingdom to the daughter of Jerusalem. 9 Now why art thou drawn together with grief? Hast thou no king in thee, or is thy counsellor perished because sorrow hath taken thee as a woman in labour? 10 Be in pain, and labour, O daughter of Zion, as a woman that bringeth forth, for now shalt thou go out of the city and shalt dwell in the country and shalt come even to Babylon. There thou shalt be delivered; there the Lord will redeem thee out of the hand of thy enemies.

11 "And now many nations are gathered together against thee, and they say, 'Let her be stoned, and let our eye look upon Zion.' 12 But they have not known the thoughts of the Lord and have not understood his counsel, because he hath gathered them together as the hay of the floor.

13 "Arise, and tread, O daughter of Zion, for I will make thy horn iron, and thy hoofs I will make brass, and thou shalt beat in pieces many peoples and shalt *immolate* the spoils of them to the Lord and their strength to the Lord of the whole earth."

Caput 5

Nunc vastaberis, filia latronis; obsidionem posuerunt super nos. In virga percutient maxillam iudicis Israhel.

2 Et tu, Bethleem Ephrata, parvulus es in milibus Iuda; ex te mihi egredietur qui sit dominator in Israhel, et egressus eius ab initio, a diebus aeternitatis. 3 Propter hoc dabit eos usque ad tempus in quo parturiens pariet, et reliquiae fratrum eius convertentur ad filios Israhel. 4 Et stabit et pascet in fortitudine Domini, in sublimitate nominis Domini, Dei sui, et convertentur, quia nunc magnificabitur usque ad terminos terrae. 5 Et erit iste pax Assyrius cum venerit in terram nostram et quando calcaverit in domibus nostris, et suscitabimus super eum septem pastores et octo primates homines.

6 Et pascent terram Assur in gladio et terram Nemrod in lanceis eius, et liberabit ab Assur cum venerit in terram nostram et cum calcaverit in finibus nostris. 7 Et erunt reliquiae Iacob in medio populorum multorum quasi ros a Domino et quasi stillae super herbam, quae non expectat virum et non praestolatur filios hominum. 8 Et erunt reliquiae

Chapter 5

The birth of Christ in Bethlehem. His reign and spiritual conquests.

Now shalt thou be laid waste, O daughter of the robber; they have laid siege against us. With a rod shall they strike the cheek of the judge of Israel.

2 And thou, Bethlehem Ephrathah, art a little one among the thousands of Judah; out of thee shall he come forth unto me that is to be the ruler in Israel, and his going forth is from the beginning, from the days of eternity. 3 Therefore will he give them up even till the time wherein she that travaileth shall bring forth, and the remnant of his brethren shall be converted to the children of Israel. 4 And he shall stand and feed in the strength of the Lord, in the height of the name of the Lord, his God, and they shall be converted, for now shall he be magnified even to the ends of the earth. 5 And this man shall be our peace when the Assyrian shall come into our land and when he shall set his foot in our houses, and we shall raise against him seven shepherds and eight principal men.

6 And they shall feed the land of Assyria with the sword and the land of Nimrod with the spears thereof, and he shall deliver us from the Assyrian when he shall come into our land and when he shall tread in our borders. 7 And the remnant of Jacob shall be in the midst of many peoples as a dew from the Lord and as drops upon the grass, which waiteth not for man nor tarrieth for the children of men. 8 And the

Iacob in Gentibus in medio populorum multorum quasi leo in iumentis silvarum et quasi catulus leonis in gregibus pecorum, qui, cum transierit et conculcaverit et ceperit, non est qui eruat. 9 Exaltabitur manus tua super hostes tuos, et omnes inimici tui interibunt.

10 "Et erit in die illa," dicit Dominus, "auferam equos tuos de medio tui et disperdam quadrigas tuas. 11 Et perdam civitates terrae tuae et destruam omnes munitiones tuas, et auferam maleficia de manu tua, et divinationes non erunt in te. 12 Et perire faciam sculptilia tua et statuas tuas de medio tui, et non adorabis ultra opera manuum tuarum. 13 Et evellam lucos tuos de medio tui et conteram civitates tuas. 14 Et faciam in furore et in indignatione ultionem in omnibus gentibus quae non audierunt."

Caput 6

Audite quae Dominus loquitur: "Surge; contende iudicio adversum montes, et audiant colles vocem tuam. 2 Audiant montes iudicium Domini, et fortia fundamenta terrae, quia

remnant of Jacob shall be among the Gentiles in the midst of many peoples as a lion among the beasts of the forests and as a young lion among the flocks of sheep, who, when he shall go through and tread down and take, there is none to deliver. 9 Thy hand shall be lifted up over thy enemies, and all thy enemies shall be cut off.

10 "And it shall come to pass in that day," saith the Lord, "that I will take away thy horses out of the midst of thee and will destroy thy chariots. 11 And I will destroy the cities of thy land and will throw down all thy strongholds, and I will take away sorceries out of thy hand, and there shall be no divinations in thee. 12 And I will destroy thy graven things and thy statues out of the midst of thee, and thou shalt no more adore the works of thy hands. 13 And I will pluck up thy groves out of the midst of thee and will crush thy cities. 14 And I will execute vengeance in wrath and in indignation among all the nations that have not given ear."

Chapter 6

God expostulates with the Jews for their ingratitude and sins, for which they shall be punished.

Hear ye what the Lord saith: "Arise; contend thou in judgment against the mountains, and let the hills hear thy voice. 2 Let the mountains hear the judgment of the Lord, and the strong foundations of the earth, for the

iudicium Domini cum populo suo, et cum Israhel diiudica-
bitur.

3 "Popule meus, quid feci tibi, aut quid molestus fui tibi?
Responde mihi, 4 quia eduxi te de terra Aegypti et de domo
servientium liberavi te, et misi ante faciem tuam Mosen et
Aaron et Mariam. 5 Popule meus, memento, quaeso, quid
cogitaverit Balac, rex Moab, et quid responderit ei Balaam,
filius Beor, de Setthim usque ad Galgalam, ut cognosceres
iustitias Domini."

6 Quid dignum offeram Domino? Curvabo genu Deo excelso? Numquid offeram ei holocaustomata et vitulos anni-
culos? 7 Numquid placari potest Dominus in milibus arie-
tum aut in multis milibus hircorum pinguium? Numquid
dabo primogenitum meum pro scelere meo, fructum ventris
mei pro peccato animae meae? 8 Indicabo tibi, O homo,
quid sit bonum et quid Dominus requirat a te: utique facere
iudicium et diligere misericordiam et sollicitum ambulare
cum Deo tuo.

9 Vox Domini ad civitatem clamat (et salus erit timentibus nomen tuum): "Audite, tribus, et quis adprobabit illud?
10 Adhuc ignis in domo impii, thesauri iniquitatis et mensura
minor irae plena. 11 Numquid iustificabo stateram impiam
et saccelli pondera dolosa? 12 In quibus divites eius repleti
sunt iniquitate, et habitantes in ea loquebantur mendacium,
et lingua eorum fraudulenta in ore eorum.

13 "Et ego ergo coepi percutere te perditione super peccatis tuis. 14 Tu comedes et non saturaberis, et humiliatio
tua in medio tui. Et adprehendes et non salvabis, et quos

Lord will enter into judgment with his people, and he will plead against Israel.

3 "O my people, what have I done to thee, or in what have I molested thee? Answer thou me, 4 for I brought thee up out of the land of Egypt and delivered thee out of the house of slaves, and I sent before thy face Moses and Aaron and Miriam. 5 O my people, remember, I pray thee, what Balak, the king of Moab, purposed and what Balaam, the son of Beor, answered him, from Shittim to Gilgal, that thou mightest know the justices of the Lord."

6 What shall I offer to the Lord that is worthy? *Wherewith* shall I kneel before the high God? Shall I offer holocausts unto him and calves of a year old? 7 May the Lord be appeased with thousands of rams or with many thousands of fat he-goats? Shall I give my firstborn for my wickedness, the fruit of my *body* for the sin of my soul? 8 I will shew thee, O man, what is good and what the Lord requireth of thee: verily to do judgment and to love mercy and to walk solicitous with thy God.

9 The voice of the Lord crieth to the city (and salvation shall be to them that fear thy name): "Hear, O ye tribes, and who shall approve it? 10 As yet there is a fire in the house of the wicked, the treasures of iniquity and a scant measure full of wrath. 11 Shall I justify wicked balances and the deceitful weights of the bag? 12 By which her rich men were filled with iniquity, and the inhabitants thereof have spoken lies, and their tongue was deceitful in their mouth.

13 "And I therefore began to strike thee with desolation for thy sins. 14 Thou shalt eat *but* shalt not be filled, and thy humiliation shall be in the midst of thee. And thou shalt take hold *but* shalt not save, and those whom thou shalt save

salvaveris in gladium dabo. 15 Tu seminabis et non metes. Tu calcabis olivam et non ungueris oleo, et mustum et non bibes vinum. 16 Et custodisti praecepta Amri et omne opus domus Achab, et ambulasti in voluntatibus eorum ut darem te in perditionem et habitantes in ea in sibilum, et obprobrium populi mei portabitis."

Caput 7

Vae mihi, quia factus sum sicut qui colligit in autumno racemos vindemiae. Non est botrus ad comedendum; praecoquas ficus desideravit anima mea.

2 Periit sanctus de terra, et rectus in hominibus non est. Omnes in sanguine insidiantur; vir fratrem suum venatur ad mortem. 3 Malum manuum suarum dicunt bonum. Princeps postulat, et iudex in reddendo est, et magnus locutus est desiderium animae suae, et conturbaverunt eam. 4 Qui optimus in eis est quasi paliurus, et qui rectus quasi spina de

I will give up to the sword. 15 Thou shalt sow *but* shalt not reap. Thou shalt tread the olives *but* shalt not be anointed with the oil, and the new wine *but* shalt not drink the wine. 16 *For* thou hast kept the statutes of Omri and all the works of the house of Ahab, and thou hast walked according to their wills that I should make thee a desolation and the inhabitants thereof a hissing, and you shall bear the reproach of my people."

Chapter 7

The prophet laments that notwithstanding all his preaching the generality are still corrupt in their manners. Therefore their desolation is at hand, but they shall be restored again and prosper, and all mankind shall be redeemed by Christ.

Woe is me, for I am become as one that gleaneth in autumn the grapes of the vintage. There is no cluster to eat; my soul desired the first ripe figs.

2 The holy man is perished out of the earth, and there is none upright among men. They all lie in wait for blood; every one hunteth his brother to death. 3 The evil of their hands they call good. The prince requireth, and the judge is for giving, and the great man hath uttered the desire of his soul, and they have troubled it. 4 He that is best among them is as a brier, and he that is righteous as the thorn of the

sepe. Dies speculationis tuae, visitatio tua venit; nunc erit vastitas eorum.

5 Nolite credere amico, et nolite confidere in duce. Ab ea quae dormit in sinu tuo custodi claustra oris tui, 6 quia filius contumeliam facit patri et filia consurgit adversus matrem suam, nurus contra socrum suam, et inimici hominis domestici eius.

7 Ego autem ad Dominum aspiciam; expectabo Deum, salvatorem meum; audiet me Deus meus.

8 Ne laeteris, inimica mea, super me quia cecidi. Consurgam cum sedero in tenebris; Dominus lux mea est. 9 Iram Domini portabo quoniam peccavi ei, donec iudicet causam meam et faciat iudicium meum. Educet me in lucem; videbo iustitiam eius.

10 Et aspiciet inimica mea, et operietur confusione quae dicit ad me, "Ubi est Dominus, Deus tuus?" Oculi mei videbunt in eam; nunc erit in conculcationem ut lutum platearum. 11 Dies ut aedificentur maceriae tuae, in die illa longe fiet lex. 12 In die illa et usque ad te veniet Assur et usque ad civitates munitas et a civitatibus munitis usque ad flumen et ad mare de mari et ad montem de monte. 13 Et erit terra in desolationem propter habitatores suos et propter fructum cogitationum eorum.

14 Pasce populum tuum in virga tua, gregem hereditatis tuae, habitantes solos in saltu in medio Carmeli. Pascentur Basan et Galaad iuxta dies antiquos.

hedge. The day of thy inspection, thy visitation cometh; now shall be their destruction.

5 Believe not a friend, and trust not in a prince. Keep the doors of thy mouth from her that sleepeth in thy bosom, 6 for the son dishonoureth the father and the daughter riseth up against her mother, the daughter-in-law against her mother-in-law, and a man's enemies are they of his own household.

7 But I will look towards the Lord; I will wait for God, my saviour; my God will hear me.

8 Rejoice not thou, my enemy, over me because I am fallen. I shall arise when I sit in darkness; the Lord is my light. 9 I will bear the wrath of the Lord because I have sinned against him, until he judge my cause and execute judgment for me. He will bring me forth into the light; I shall behold his justice.

10 And my enemy shall behold, and she shall be covered with shame who saith to me, "Where is the Lord, thy God?" My eyes shall look down upon her; now shall she be trodden under foot as the mire of the streets. 11 The day *shall come* that thy walls may be built up; in that day shall the law be far removed. 12 In that day *they* shall come even *from* Assyria to thee and to the fortified cities and from the fortified cities even to the river and from sea to sea and from mountain to mountain. 13 And the land shall be made desolate because of the inhabitants thereof and for the fruit of their devices.

14 Feed thy people with thy rod, the flock of thy inheritance, them that dwell alone in the forest in the midst of Carmel. They shall feed in Bashan and Gilead according to the days of old.

15 "Secundum dies egressionis tuae de terra Aegypti ostendam ei mirabilia."

16 Videbunt gentes et confundentur super omni fortitudine sua. Ponent manum super os; aures eorum surdae erunt. 17 Lingent pulverem sicut serpentes, velut reptilia terrae; perturbabuntur in aedibus suis; Dominum, Deum nostrum, formidabunt et timebunt te.

18 Quis Deus similis tui, qui aufers iniquitatem et transis peccatum reliquiarum hereditatis tuae? Non inmittet ultra furorem suum quoniam volens misericordiam est. 19 Revertetur et miserebitur nostri. Deponet iniquitates nostras, et proiciet in profundum maris omnia peccata nostra. 20 Dabis veritatem Iacob, misericordiam Abraham, quae iurasti patribus nostris a diebus antiquis.

15 "According to the days of thy coming out of the land of Egypt I will shew him wonders."

16 The nations shall see and shall be confounded at all their strength. They shall put the hand upon the mouth; their ears shall be deaf. 17 They shall lick the dust like serpents, as the creeping things of the earth; they shall be disturbed in their houses; they shall dread the Lord, our God, and shall fear thee.

18 Who is a God like to thee, who takest away iniquity and passest by the sin of the remnant of thy inheritance? He will send his fury in no more because he delighteth in mercy. 19 He will turn again and have mercy on us. He will put away our iniquities, and he will cast all our sins into the bottom of the sea. 20 Thou wilt perform the truth of Jacob, the mercy to Abraham, which thou hast sworn to our fathers from the days of old.

NAHUM

Caput 1

Onus Nineve. Liber visionis Naum, Helcesei.

2 Deus aemulator et ulciscens Dominus; ulciscens Dominus et habens furorem; ulciscens Dominus in hostes suos, et irascens ipse inimicis suis. 3 Dominus patiens et magnus fortitudine et mundans non faciet innocentem. Dominus: in tempestate et turbine viae eius, et nebulae pulvis pedum eius. 4 Increpans mare et exsiccans illud et omnia flumina ad desertum deducens. Infirmatus est Basan et Carmelus, et flos Libani elanguit.

5 Montes commoti sunt ab eo, et colles desolati sunt, et contremuit terra a facie eius, et orbis et omnes habitantes in eo. 6 Ante faciem indignationis eius quis stabit? Et quis resistet in ira furoris eius? Indignatio eius effusa est ut ignis, et petrae dissolutae sunt ab eo.

Chapter 1

The majesty of God. His goodness to his people and severity to his enemies.

The burden of Nineveh. The book of the vision of Nahum, the Elkoshite.

2 The Lord is a jealous God and a revenger; the Lord is a revenger and hath wrath; the Lord taketh vengeance on his adversaries, and he is angry with his enemies. 3 The Lord is patient and great in power and *will not cleanse* and *acquit the guilty.* The Lord's ways are in a tempest and a whirlwind, and clouds are the dust of his feet. 4 He rebuketh the sea and drieth it up and bringeth all the rivers to *be* a desert. Bashan languisheth and Carmel, and the flower of Lebanon fadeth away.

5 The mountains tremble at him, and the hills are made desolate, and the earth hath quaked at his presence, and the world and all that dwell therein. 6 Who *can* stand before the face of his indignation? And who shall resist in the fierceness of his anger? His indignation is poured out like fire, and the rocks are melted by him.

7 Bonus Dominus et confortans in die tribulationis et sciens sperantes in se. 8 Et in diluvio praetereunte consummationem faciet loci eius, et inimicos eius persequentur tenebrae.

9 Quid cogitatis contra Dominum? Consummationem ipse faciet; non consurget duplex tribulatio. 10 Quia sicut spinae se invicem conplectuntur, sic convivium eorum pariter potantium consumentur quasi stipula ariditate plena. 11 Ex te exibit cogitans contra Dominum malitiam, mente pertractans praevaricationem.

12 Haec dicit Dominus: "Si perfecti fuerint, et ita plures, sic quoque adtondebuntur, et pertransibit; adflixi te, et non adfligam te ultra. 13 Et nunc conteram virgam eius de dorso tuo, et vincula tua disrumpam."

14 Et praecipiet super te Dominus; non seminabitur ex nomine tuo amplius: "De domo Dei tui interficiam sculptile et conflatile; ponam sepulchrum tuum, quia inhonoratus es."

15 Ecce: super montes pedes evangelizantis et adnuntiantis pacem. Celebra, Iuda, festivitates tuas, et redde vota tua, quia non adiciet ultra ut pertranseat in te Belial; universus interiit.

7 The Lord is good and giveth strength in the day of trouble and knoweth them that hope in him. 8 *But* with a flood that passeth by he will make an utter end of the place thereof, and darkness shall pursue his enemies.

9 What do ye devise against the Lord? He will make an utter end; there shall not rise a double affliction. 10 For as thorns embrace one another, so *while they are feasting and drinking* together they shall be consumed as stubble that is fully dry. 11 Out of thee shall come forth one that imagineth evil against the Lord, contriving treachery in his mind.

12 Thus saith the Lord: *"Though* they *were* perfect, and many of them so, *yet* thus shall they be cut off, and he shall pass; I have afflicted thee, and I will afflict thee no more. 13 And now I will break in pieces his rod *with which he struck* thy back, and I will burst thy bonds asunder."

14 And the Lord will give a commandment concerning thee *that* no more of thy name shall be sown: "I will destroy the graven and molten thing out of the house of thy God; I will make *it* thy grave, for thou art disgraced."

15 Behold: upon the mountains the feet of him that bringeth good tidings and that preacheth peace. O Judah, keep thy festivals, and pay thy vows, for Belial shall no more pass through thee again; he is utterly cut off.

Caput 2

Ascendit qui dispergat coram te, qui custodiat obsidionem. Contemplare viam; conforta lumbos; robora virtutem valde.

2 Quia reddidit Dominus superbiam Iacob sicut superbiam Israhel, quia vastatores dissipaverunt eos et propagines eorum corruperunt.

3 Clypeus fortium eius ignitus, viri exercitus in coccineis. Igneae habenae currus in die praeparationis eius, et agitatores consopiti sunt. 4 In itineribus conturbati sunt; quadrigae conlisae sunt in plateis. Aspectus eorum quasi lampades, quasi fulgura discurrentia. 5 Recordabitur fortium suorum; ruent in itineribus suis. Velociter ascendent muros eius, et praeparabitur umbraculum. 6 Portae fluviorum apertae sunt, et templum ad solum dirutum. 7 Et miles captivus abductus est, et ancillae eius minabantur gementes ut columbae, murmurantes in cordibus suis.

8 Et Nineve, quasi piscina aquarum aquae eius, ipsi vero fugerunt. "State, state," et non est qui revertatur. 9 Diripite argentum, diripite aurum, et non est finis divitiarum ex omnibus vasis desiderabilibus. 10 Dissipata est et scissa et dilacerata, et cor tabescens, et dissolutio geniculorum, et

Chapter 2

God sends his armies against Nineveh to destroy it.

He is come up that shall destroy before thy face, that shall keep the siege. Watch the way; fortify thy loins; strengthen thy power exceedingly.

2 For the Lord hath rendered the pride of Jacob as the pride of Israel, because the spoilers have laid them waste and have marred their vine branches.

3 The shield of his mighty men is *like* fire; the men of the army are clad in scarlet. The reins of the chariot are flaming in the day of his preparation, and the drivers are stupefied. 4 They are in csonfusion in the ways; the chariots jostle one against another in the streets. Their looks are like torches, like lightning running to and fro. 5 He will *muster up* his valiant men; they shall *stumble* in their march. They shall quickly get upon the walls thereof, and a covering shall be prepared. 6 The gates of the rivers are opened, and the temple is thrown down to the ground. 7 And the soldier is led away captive, and her bondwomen were led away mourning as doves, murmuring in their hearts.

8 And as for Nineveh, her waters are like a *great pool,* but the men flee away. *They cry,* "Stand, stand," *but* there is none that will return back. 9 Take ye the spoil of the silver, take the spoil of the gold, *for* there is no end of the riches of all the precious *furniture.* 10 She is destroyed and rent and torn; *the* heart melteth, and the knees fail, and all the loins lose

defectio in cunctis renibus, et facies omnium eorum sicut nigredo ollae.

11 Ubi est habitaculum leonum et pascua catulorum leonum, ad quam ivit leo ut ingrederetur illuc, catulus leonis, et non est qui exterreat? 12 Leo cepit sufficienter catulis suis et necavit leaenis suis, et implevit praeda speluncas suas et cubile suum rapina.

13 "Ecce: ego ad te," dicit Dominus exercituum, "et succendam usque ad fumum quadrigas tuas, et leunculos tuos comedet gladius, et exterminabo de terra praedam tuam, et non audietur ultra vox nuntiorum tuorum."

Caput 3

Vae, civitas sanguinum, universa mendacii dilaceratione plena; non recedet a te rapina. 2 Vox flagelli et vox impetus rotae et equi frementis et quadrigae ferventis et equitis ascendentis 3 et micantis gladii et fulgurantis hastae et multitudinis interfectae et gravis ruinae, nec est finis cadaverum, et corruent in corporibus suis.

their strength, and the faces of them all are as the blackness of a kettle.

11 Where is *now* the dwelling of the lions and the feeding place of the young lions, to which the lion went to enter in thither, the young lion, and there was none to make them afraid? 12 The lion caught enough for his whelps and killed for his lionesses, and he filled his holes with prey and his den with rapine.

13 "Behold: I come against thee," saith the Lord of hosts, "and I will burn thy chariots even to smoke, and the sword shall devour thy young lions, and I will cut off thy prey out of the land, and the voice of thy messengers shall be heard no more."

Chapter 3

The miserable destruction of Nineveh.

Woe to thee, O city of blood, all full of lies and violence; rapine shall not depart from thee. 2 The noise of the whip and the noise of the *rattling* of the wheels and of the *neighing* horse and of the running chariot and of the horsemen coming up 3 and of the shining sword and of the glittering spear and of a multitude slain and of a grievous destruction, and there is no end of carcasses, and they shall fall down on their *dead* bodies.

4 "Propter multitudinem fornicationum meretricis speciosae et gratae et habentis maleficia, quae vendidit gentes in fornicationibus suis et familias in maleficiis suis, 5 ecce: ego ad te," dicit Dominus exercituum. "Et revelabo pudenda tua in facie tua et ostendam gentibus nuditatem tuam, et regnis ignominiam tuam, 6 et proiciam super te abominationes et contumeliis te adficiam et ponam te in exemplum. 7 Et erit omnis qui viderit te resiliet a te et dicet, 'Vastata est Nineve; quis commovebit super te caput? Unde quaeram consolatorem tibi?'"

8 Numquid melior es Alexandria populorum quae habitat in fluminibus? Aquae in circuitu eius, cuius divitiae mare; aquae muri eius. 9 Aethiopia fortitudo eius et Aegyptus, et non est finis; Africa et Lybies fuerunt in auxilio tuo. 10 Sed et ipsa in transmigrationem ducta est in captivitatem; parvuli eius elisi sunt in capite omnium viarum, et super inclitos eius miserunt sortem, et omnes optimates eius confixi sunt in conpedibus.

11 Et tu ergo inebriaberis et eris despecta, et tu quaeres auxilium ab inimico. 12 Omnes munitiones tuae sicuti ficus cum grossis suis: si concussae fuerint, cadent in os comedentis. 13 Ecce: populus tuus mulieres in medio tui; inimicis tuis adapertione pandentur portae terrae tuae; devorabit ignis vectes tuos.

14 Aquam propter obsidionem hauri tibi; extrue munitiones tuas. Intra in lutum, et calca; subigens, tene laterem. 15 Ibi comedet te ignis; peribis gladio: devorabit te ut bruchus. Congregare ut bruchus; multiplicare ut lucusta.

4 "Because of the multitude of the fornications of the harlot that was beautiful and agreeable and that made use of witchcraft, that sold nations through her fornications and families through her witchcrafts, 5 behold: I come against thee," saith the Lord of hosts. "And I will discover thy shame to thy face and will shew thy nakedness to the nations, and thy shame to kingdoms, 6 and I will cast abominations upon thee and will disgrace thee and will make an example of thee. 7 And it shall come to pass that every one that shall see thee shall flee from thee and shall say, 'Nineveh is laid waste; who shall *bemoan* thee? Whence shall I seek a comforter for thee?'"

8 Art thou better than the populous Alexandria that dwelleth among the rivers? Waters are round about it; the sea is its riches; the waters are its walls. 9 Ethiopia and Egypt were the strength thereof, and there is no end; Africa and the Libyans were thy helpers. 10 Yet she also was removed and carried into captivity; her young children were dashed in pieces at the top of every street, and they cast lots upon her nobles, and all her great men were bound in fetters.

11 Therefore thou also shalt be made drunk and shalt be despised, and thou shalt seek help from the enemy. 12 All thy strongholds shall be like fig trees with their green figs: if they be shaken, they shall fall into the mouth of the eater. 13 Behold: thy people in the midst of thee are women; the gates of thy land shall be set wide open to thy enemies; the fire shall devour thy bars.

14 Draw thee water for the siege; build up thy bulwarks. Go into the clay, and tread; work it, and *make* brick. 15 There shall the fire devour thee; thou shalt perish by the sword: it shall devour thee like the bruchus. Assemble together like the bruchus; make thyself many like the locust.

16 Plures fecisti negotiationes tuas quam stellae sint caeli; bruchus expansus est et avolavit. 17 Custodes tui quasi lucustae, et parvuli tui quasi lucustae lucustarum quae considunt in sepibus in die frigoris; sol ortus est, et avolaverunt, et non est cognitus locus earum ubi fuerint.

18 Dormitaverunt pastores tui, rex Assur; sepelientur principes tui; latitavit populus tuus in montibus, et non est qui congreget. 19 Non est obscura contritio tua; pessima est plaga tua. Omnes qui audierunt auditionem tuam conpresserunt manum super te, quia super quem non transiit malitia tua semper?

16 Thou hast multiplied thy merchandises above the stars of heaven; the bruchus hath spread himself and flown away. 17 Thy guards are like the locusts, and thy little ones like the locusts of locusts which swarm on the hedges in the day of cold; the sun arose, and they flew away, and their place was not known where they were.

18 Thy shepherds have slumbered, O king of Assyria; thy princes shall be buried; thy people are hid in the mountains, and there is none to gather them together. 19 Thy destruction is not hidden; thy wound is grievous. All that have heard the fame of thee have clapped their hands over thee, for upon whom hath not thy wickedness passed continually?

HABAKKUK

Caput 1

Onus quod vidit Abacuc, propheta.

2 Usquequo, Domine, clamabo, et non exaudies? Vociferabor ad te vim patiens, et non salvabis? 3 Quare ostendisti mihi iniquitatem et laborem, videre praedam et iniustitiam contra me? Et factum est iudicium, et contradictio potentior. 4 Propter hoc lacerata est lex, et non pervenit usque ad finem iudicium, quia impius praevalet adversus iustum; propterea egreditur iudicium perversum.

5 "Aspicite in gentibus, et videte; admiramini, et obstupescite, quia opus factum est in diebus vestris quod nemo credet cum narrabitur. 6 Quia ecce: ego suscitabo Chaldeos, gentem amaram et velocem ambulantem super latitudinem terrae, ut possideat tabernacula non sua. 7 Horribilis et terribilis est; ex semet ipsa iudicium et onus eius egredietur. 8 Leviores pardis equi eius et velociores lupis vespertinis, et

Chapter 1

The prophet complains of the wickedness of the people.
God reveals to him the vengeance he is going to take of
them by the Chaldeans.

The burden that Habakkuk, the prophet, saw.

2 How long, O Lord, shall I cry, and thou wilt not hear?
Shall I cry out to thee suffering violence, and thou wilt not
save? 3 Why hast thou shewn me iniquity and grievance, to
see rapine and injustice before me? And there is a judgment,
but opposition is more powerful. 4 Therefore the law is torn
in pieces, and judgment cometh not to the end, because the
wicked prevaileth against the just; therefore wrong judgment goeth forth.

5 "Behold ye among the nations, and see; wonder, and be
astonished, for a work is done in your days which no man
will believe when it shall be told. 6 For behold: I will raise up
the Chaldeans, a bitter and swift nation marching upon the
breadth of the earth, to possess the dwelling places that are
not their own. 7 They are dreadful and terrible; from themselves shall their judgment and their burden proceed. 8 Their
horses are lighter than leopards and swifter than evening

diffundentur equites eius, equites namque eius de longe venient; volabunt quasi aquila festinans ad comedendum. 9 Omnes ad praedam venient; facies eorum ventus urens, et congregabit quasi harenam captivitatem. 10 Et ipse de regibus triumphabit, et tyranni ridiculi eius erunt, et ipse super omnem munitionem ridebit et conportabit aggerem et capiet eam. 11 Tunc mutabitur spiritus, et pertransibit et corruet; haec est fortitudo eius dei sui."

12 Numquid non tu a principio, Domine, Deus meus, Sancte meus, et non moriemur? Domine, in iudicium posuisti eum et fortem ut corriperes fundasti eum. 13 Mundi sunt oculi tui ne videas malum, et respicere ad iniquitatem non poteris. Quare non respicis super iniqua agentes et taces devorante impio iustiorem se? 14 Et facies homines quasi pisces maris et quasi reptile non habens principem.

15 Totum in hamo sublevavit; traxit illud in sagena sua et congregavit in rete suum; super hoc laetabitur et exultabit. 16 Propterea immolabit sagenae suae, et sacrificabit reti suo, quia in ipsis incrassata est pars eius et cibus eius electus. 17 Propter hoc ergo expandit sagenam suam et semper interficere gentes non parcet.

wolves, and their horsemen shall be spread abroad, for their horsemen shall come from afar; they shall fly as an eagle that maketh haste to eat. 9 They shall all come to the prey; their face is like a burning wind, and they shall gather together captives as the sand. 10 And *their prince* shall triumph over kings, and princes shall be his laughingstock, and he shall laugh at every stronghold and shall cast up a mount and shall take it. 11 Then shall his spirit be changed, and he shall pass and fall; this is his strength of his god."

12 Wast thou not from the beginning, O Lord, my God, my Holy One, and we shall not die? Lord, thou hast appointed him for judgment and made him strong for correction. 13 Thy eyes are *too* pure *to* behold evil, and thou canst not look on iniquity. Why lookest *thou* upon them that do unjust things and holdest thy peace when the wicked devoureth the man that is more just than himself? 14 And thou wilt make men as the fishes of the sea and as the creeping things that have no ruler.

15 He lifted up all them with his hook; he drew them in his drag and gathered them into his net; for this he will be glad and rejoice. 16 Therefore will he offer victims to his drag, and he will sacrifice to his net, because through them his portion is made fat and his meat dainty. 17 For this cause therefore he spreadeth his net and will not spare continually to slay the nations.

Caput 2

Super custodiam meam stabo et figam gradum meum super munitionem, et contemplabor ut videam quid dicatur mihi et quid respondeam ad arguentem me.

2 Et respondit mihi Dominus et dixit, "Scribe visum, et explana eum super tabulas, ut percurrat qui legerit eum. 3 Quia adhuc visus procul, et apparebit in finem et non mentietur; si moram fecerit, expecta illum, quia veniens veniet, et non tardabit. 4 Ecce: qui incredulus est, non erit recta anima eius in semet ipso, iustus autem in fide sua vivet. 5 Et quomodo vinum potantem decipit, sic erit vir superbus. Et non decorabitur qui dilatavit quasi infernus animam suam et ipse quasi mors, et non adimpletur et congregabit ad se omnes gentes et coacervabit ad se omnes populos."

6 Numquid non omnes isti super eum parabolam sument et loquellam enigmatum eius, et dicetur, "Vae ei qui multiplicat non sua"? Usquequo et adgravat contra se densum lutum? 7 Numquid non repente consurgent qui mordeant te, et suscitabuntur lacerantes te, et eris in rapinam eis? 8 Quia tu spoliasti gentes multas, spoliabunt te omnes qui reliqui

Chapter 2

The prophet is admonished to wait with faith. The enemies
of God's people shall assuredly be punished.

I will stand upon my watch and fix my foot upon the tower,
and I will watch to see what will be said to me and what I
may answer to him that reproveth me.

2 And the Lord answered me and said, "Write the vision,
and make it plain upon tables, that he that readeth it may
run over it. 3 For as yet the vision is far off, and it shall appear at the end and shall not lie; if it make any delay, wait for
it, for it shall surely come, and it shall not be slack. 4 Behold:
he that is unbelieving, his soul shall not be right in himself,
but the just shall live in his faith. 5 And as wine deceiveth
him that drinketh it, so shall the proud man be. And he shall
not be honoured who hath enlarged his *desire* like hell and is
himself like death, and he is *never* satisfied *but* will gather together unto him all nations and heap together unto him all
people."

6 Shall not all these take up a parable against him and a
dark speech concerning him, and it shall be said, "Woe to
him that *heapeth together* that which is not his own"? How
long also doth he load *himself* with thick clay? 7 Shall they
not rise up suddenly that shall bite thee, and they be stirred
up that shall tear thee, and thou shalt be a spoil to them?
8 Because thou hast spoiled many nations, all that shall be

fuerint de populis propter sanguinem hominis et iniquitatem terrae, civitatis et omnium habitantium in ea.

9 Vae qui congregat avaritiam malam domui suae, ut sit in
excelso nidus eius, et liberari se putat de manu mali. 10 Cogi-
tasti confusionem domui tuae; concidisti populos multos, et
peccavit anima tua. 11 Quia lapis de pariete clamabit, et lignum quod inter iuncturas aedificiorum est respondebit.

12 Vae qui aedificat civitatem in sanguinibus et praeparat
urbem in iniquitate. 13 Numquid non haec a Domino sunt
exercituum? Laborabunt enim populi in multo igni et gentes
in vacuum, et deficient. 14 Quia replebitur terra ut cognoscant gloriam Domini quasi aquae operientes mare.

15 Vae qui potum dat amico suo, mittens fel suum et ine-
brians ut aspiciat nuditatem eius. 16 Repletus es ignominia
pro gloria; bibe tu quoque, et consopire; circumdabit te ca-
lix dexterae Domini, et vomitus ignominiae super gloriam
tuam. 17 Quia iniquitas Libani operiet te, et vastitas anima-
lium deterrebit eos de sanguinibus hominum et iniquitate
terrae et civitatis et omnium habitantium in ea.

18 Quid prodest sculptile, quia sculpsit illud fictor suus,
conflatile et imaginem falsam? Quia speravit in figmento
fictor eius ut faceret simulacra muta. 19 Vae qui dicit ligno
"Expergiscere," "Surge" lapidi tacenti. Numquid ipse docere

left of the people shall spoil thee because of men's blood and for the iniquity of the land, of the city and of all that dwell therein.

9 Woe to him that gathereth together an evil covetousness to his house, that his nest may be on high, and thinketh he may be delivered out of the hand of evil. 10 Thou hast devised confusion to thy house; thou hast cut off many people, and thy soul hath sinned. 11 For the stone shall cry out of the wall, and the timber that is between the joints of the building shall answer.

12 Woe to him that buildeth a town with blood and prepareth a city by iniquity. 13 Are not these things from the Lord of hosts? For the people shall labour in a great fire and the nations in vain, and they shall faint. 14 For the earth shall be filled that men may know the glory of the Lord as waters covering the sea.

15 Woe to him that giveth drink to his friend and presenteth his gall and maketh him drunk that he may behold his nakedness. 16 Thou art filled with shame instead of glory; drink thou also, and fall fast asleep; the cup of the right hand of the Lord shall compass thee, and shameful vomiting shall be on thy glory. 17 For the iniquity of Lebanon shall cover thee, and the ravaging of beasts shall terrify them because of the blood of men and the iniquity of the land and of the city and of all that dwell therein.

18 What doth the graven thing avail, because the maker thereof hath graven it, a molten and a false image? Because the forger thereof hath trusted in a thing of his own forging to make dumb idols. 19 Woe to him that saith to wood, "Awake," to the dumb stone, "Arise." Can it teach? Behold: it

poterit? Ecce: iste coopertus est auro et argento, et omnis spiritus non est in visceribus eius.

20 Dominus autem in templo sancto suo; sileat a facie eius omnis terra.

Caput 3

Oratio Abacuc, prophetae, pro ignorationibus.

2 Domine, audivi auditionem tuam et timui. Domine, opus tuum in medio annorum, vivifica illud. In medio annorum notum facies; cum iratus fueris, misericordiae recordaberis. 3 Deus ab austro veniet, et Sanctus de Monte Pharan; operuit caelos gloria eius, et laudis eius plena est terra. 4 Splendor eius ut lux erit; cornua in manibus eius: ibi abscondita est fortitudo eius. 5 Ante faciem eius ibit mors, et egredietur diabolus ante pedes eius. 6 Stetit et mensus est terram. Aspexit et dissolvit gentes, et contriti sunt montes saeculi. Incurvati sunt colles mundi ab itineribus aeternitatis eius. 7 Pro iniquitate vidi tentoria Aethiopiae; turbabuntur pelles terrae Madian.

8 Numquid in fluminibus iratus es, Domine? Aut in fluminibus furor tuus, vel in mari indignatio tua? Qui ascendes super equos tuos, et quadrigae tuae salvatio. 9 Suscitans suscitabis arcum tuum, iuramenta tribubus quae locutus es. Fluvios scindes terrae. 10 Viderunt te et doluerunt montes;

is laid over with gold and silver, and there is no spirit in the bowels thereof.

20 But the Lord is in his holy temple; let all the earth keep silence before him.

Chapter 3

A prayer of Habakkuk, the prophet, for ignorances.

2 O Lord, I have heard thy hearing and was afraid. O Lord, thy work in the midst of the years, bring it to life. In the midst of the years thou shalt make it known; when thou art angry, thou wilt remember mercy. 3 God will come from the south, and the Holy One from Mount Paran; his glory covered the heavens, and the earth is full of his praise. 4 His brightness shall be as the light; horns are in his hands: there is his strength hid. 5 Death shall go before his face, and the devil shall go forth before his feet. 6 He stood and measured the earth. He beheld and melted the nations, and the ancient mountains were crushed to pieces. The hills of the world were bowed down by the journeys of his eternity. 7 I saw the tents of Ethiopia for their iniquity; the curtains of the land of Midian shall be troubled.

8 Wast thou angry, O Lord, with the rivers? Or was thy wrath upon the rivers, or thy indignation in the sea? Who will ride upon thy horses, and thy chariots are salvation. 9 Thou wilt surely take up thy bow *according to* the oaths which thou hast spoken to the tribes. Thou wilt divide the rivers of the earth. 10 The mountains saw thee and were

gurges aquarum transiit. Dedit abyssus vocem suam; altitudo manus suas levavit. 11 Sol et luna steterunt in habitaculo suo; in luce sagittarum tuarum ibunt, in splendore fulgurantis hastae tuae.

12 In fremitu conculcabis terram; in furore obstupefacies gentes. 13 Egressus es in salutem populi tui, in salutem cum Christo tuo. Percussisti caput de domo impii; denudasti fundamentum usque ad collum. 14 Maledixisti sceptris eius, capiti bellatorum eius, venientibus ut turbo ad dispergendum me. Exultatio eorum sicut eius qui devorat pauperem in abscondito. 15 Viam fecisti in mari equis tuis in luto aquarum multarum.

16 Audivi, et conturbatus est venter meus; a voce contremuerunt labia mea. Ingrediatur putredo in ossibus meis et subter me scateat ut requiescam in die tribulationis, ut ascendam ad populum accinctum nostrum.

17 Ficus enim non florebit, et non erit germen in vineis. Mentietur opus olivae, et arva non adferent cibum; abscidetur de ovili pecus, et non erit armentum in praesepibus. 18 Ego autem in Domino gaudebo, et exultabo in Deo, Iesu meo. 19 Dominus Deus fortitudo mea, et ponet pedes meos quasi cervorum, et super excelsa mea deducet me, victor, in psalmis canentem.

grieved; the great body of waters passed away. The deep put forth its voice; the deep lifted up its hands. 11 The sun and the moon stood still in their habitation; in the light of thy arrows they shall go, in the brightness of thy glittering spear.

12 In thy *anger* thou wilt tread the earth under foot; in thy wrath thou wilt astonish the nations. 13 Thou wentest forth for the salvation of thy people, for salvation with thy Christ. Thou struckest the head of the house of the wicked; thou hast laid bare *his* foundation even to the neck. 14 Thou hast cursed his sceptres, the head of his warriors, them that came out as a whirlwind to scatter me. Their joy was like that of him that devoureth the poor man in secret. 15 Thou madest a way in the sea for thy horses in the mud of many waters.

16 I have heard, and my bowels were troubled; my lips trembled at the voice. Let rottenness enter into my bones and swarm under me that I may rest in the day of tribulation, that I may go up to our people that are girded.

17 For the fig tree shall not blossom, and there shall be no spring in the vines. The labour of the olive tree shall *fail,* and the fields shall yield no food; the flock shall be cut off from the fold, and there shall be no herd in the stalls. 18 But I will rejoice in the Lord, and I will joy in God, my Jesus. 19 The Lord God is my strength, and he will make my feet like the feet of harts, and he, the conqueror, will lead me upon my high places singing psalms.

ZEPHANIAH

Caput I

Verbum Domini quod factum est ad Sofoniam, filium Chusi, filii Godoliae, filii Amariae, filii Ezechiae, in diebus Iosiae, filii Amon, regis Iudae.

2 "Congregans congregabo omnia a facie terrae," dicit Dominus, 3 "congregans hominem et pecus, congregans volatilia caeli et pisces maris, et ruinae impiorum erunt, et disperdam homines a facie terrae," dicit Dominus. 4 "Et extendam manum meam super Iudam et super omnes habitantes Hierusalem, et disperdam de loco hoc reliquias Baal et nomina aedituorum cum sacerdotibus 5 et eos qui adorant super tecta militiam caeli et adorant et iurant in Domino et iurant in Melchom 6 et qui avertuntur de post tergum Domini et qui non quaesierunt Dominum nec investigaverunt eum.

7 "Silete a facie Domini Dei, quia iuxta est dies Domini, quia praeparavit Dominus hostiam; sanctificavit vocatos

Chapter 1

For divers enormous sins the kingdom of Judah is threatened with severe judgment.

The word of the Lord that came to Zephaniah, the son of Cushi, the son of Gedaliah, the son of Amariah, the son of Hezekiah, in the days of Josiah, the son of Amon, king of Judah.

2 "Gathering I will gather together all things from off the face of the land," saith the Lord. 3 "I will gather man and beast; I will gather the birds of the air and the fishes of the sea, and the ungodly shall meet with ruin, and I will destroy men from off the face of the land," saith the Lord. 4 "And I will stretch out my hand upon Judah and upon all the inhabitants of Jerusalem, and I will destroy out of this place the remnant of Baal and the names of the wardens of the temples with the priests 5 and them that worship the host of heaven upon the tops of houses and them that adore and swear by the Lord and swear by Milcom 6 and them that turn away from following after the Lord and that have not sought the Lord nor searched after him.

7 "Be silent before the face of the Lord God, for the day of the Lord is near, for the Lord hath prepared a victim; he

suos. 8 Et erit in die hostiae Domini visitabo super principes et super filios regis et super omnes qui induti sunt veste peregrina. 9 Et visitabo super omnem qui arroganter ingreditur super limen in die illa, qui conplent domum Domini, Dei sui, iniquitate et dolo.

10 "Et erit in die illa," dicit Dominus "vox clamoris a porta piscium et ululatus a Secunda et contritio magna a collibus. 11 Ululate, habitatores Pilae. Conticuit omnis populus Chanaan; disperierunt omnes involuti argento. 12 Et erit in tempore illo scrutabor Hierusalem in lucernis et visitabo super viros defixos in fecibus suis, qui dicunt in cordibus suis, 'Non faciet bene Dominus, et non faciet male.' 13 Et erit fortitudo eorum in direptionem, et domus eorum in desertum, et aedificabunt domos et non habitabunt, et plantabunt vineas et non bibent vinum earum.

14 "Iuxta est dies Domini magnus; iuxta est et velox nimis. Vox diei Domini amara; tribulabitur ibi fortis. 15 Dies irae dies illa, dies tribulationis et angustiae, dies calamitatis et miseriae, dies tenebrarum et caliginis, dies nebulae et turbinis, 16 dies tubae et clangoris super civitates munitas et super angulos excelsos.

17 "Et tribulabo homines, et ambulabunt ut caeci quia Domino peccaverunt, et effundetur sanguis eorum sicut humus et corpora eorum sicut stercora. 18 Sed et argentum eorum et aurum eorum non poterit liberare eos in die irae

hath sanctified his *guests*. 8 And it shall come to pass in the day of the victim of the Lord that I will visit upon the princes and upon the king's sons and upon all such as are clothed with strange apparel. 9 And I will visit in that day upon every one that entereth arrogantly over the threshold, them that fill the house of the Lord, their God, with iniquity and deceit.

10 "And there shall be in that day," saith the Lord, "the noise of a cry from the fish gate and a howling from the Second and a great destruction from the hills. 11 Howl, ye inhabitants of the Morter. All the people of Canaan is hush; all are cut off that were wrapped up in silver. 12 And it shall come to pass at that time that I will search Jerusalem with lamps and will visit upon the men that are settled on their lees, that say in their hearts, 'The Lord will not do good, nor will he do evil.' 13 And their strength shall become a booty, and their houses as a desert, and they shall build houses and shall not dwell in them, and they shall plant vineyards and shall not drink the wine of them.

14 "The great day of the Lord is near; it is near and exceeding swift. The voice of the day of the Lord is bitter; the mighty man shall there meet with tribulation. 15 That day is a day of wrath, a day of tribulation and distress, a day of calamity and misery, a day of darkness and obscurity, a day of clouds and whirlwinds, 16 a day of the trumpet and alarm against the fenced cities and against the high *bulwarks*.

17 "And I will distress men, and they shall walk like blind men because they have sinned against the Lord, and their blood shall be poured out as earth and their bodies as dung. 18 *Neither* shall their silver and their gold be able to deliver

Domini; in igne zeli eius devorabitur omnis terra, quia consummationem cum festinatione faciet cunctis habitantibus
terram."

Caput 2

Convenite; congregamini, gens non amabilis, 2 priusquam
pariat iussio quasi pulverem transeuntem diem, antequam
veniat super vos ira furoris Domini, antequam veniat super
vos dies indignationis Domini. 3 Quaerite Dominum, omnes
mansueti terrae, qui iudicium eius estis operati. Quaerite iustum; quaerite mansuetum, si quo modo abscondamini in die
furoris Domini. 4 Quia Gaza destructa erit, et Ascalon in desertum; Azotum in meridie eicient, et Accaron eradicabitur.

5 Vae qui habitatis funiculum maris, gens perditorum; verbum Domini super vos, Chanaan, terra Philisthinorum, et
disperdam te ita ut non sit inhabitator. 6 Et erit funiculus
maris requies pastorum et caulae pecorum, 7 et erit funiculus eius qui remanserit de domo Iuda. Ibi pascentur; in

them in the day of the wrath of the Lord; all the land shall be devoured by the fire of his jealousy, for he shall make *even* a speedy *riddance of* all them that dwell in the land."

Chapter 2

An exhortation to repentance. The judgment of the Philistines, of the Moabites and the Ammonites, of the Ethiopians and the Assyrians.

Assemble yourselves together; be gathered together, O nation not worthy to be loved, 2 before the decree bring forth the day as dust passing away, before the *fierce* anger of the Lord come upon you, before the day of the Lord's indignation come upon you. 3 Seek the Lord, all ye meek of the earth, you that have wrought his judgment. Seek the just; seek the meek, if by any means you may be hid in the day of the Lord's indignation. 4 For Gaza shall be destroyed, and Ashkelon shall be a desert; they shall cast out Ashdod at noonday, and Ekron shall be rooted up.

5 Woe to you that inhabit the sea coast, O nation of reprobates; the word of the Lord upon you, O Canaan, the land of the Philistines, and I will destroy thee so that there shall not be an inhabitant. 6 And the sea coast shall be the resting place of shepherds and folds for cattle, 7 and it shall be the portion of him that shall remain of the house of Judah.

domibus Ascalonis ad vesperam requiescent, quia visitabit eos Dominus, Deus eorum, et avertet captivitatem eorum.

8 "Audivi obprobrium Moab et blasphemias filiorum Ammon quae exprobraverunt populo meo et magnificati sunt super terminos eorum. 9 Propterea vivo ego," dicit Dominus exercituum, Deus Israhel, "quia Moab ut Sodoma erit, et filii Ammon quasi Gomorra: siccitas spinarum et acervi salis et desertum usque in aeternum. Reliquiae populi mei diripient eos, et residui gentis meae possidebunt eos. 10 Hoc eis eveniet pro superbia sua, quia blasphemaverunt et magnificati sunt super populum Domini exercituum. 11 Horribilis Dominus super eos et adtenuabit omnes deos terrae, et adorabunt eum, vir de loco suo, omnes insulae Gentium. 12 Sed et vos Aethiopes interfecti gladio meo eritis."

13 Et extendet manum suam super aquilonem et perdet Assur, et ponet speciosam in solitudinem et in invium et quasi desertum. 14 Et accubabunt in medio eius greges, omnes bestiae gentium, et onocrotalus et ericius in liminibus eius morabuntur, vox cantantis in fenestra, corvus in superliminari, quoniam adtenuabo robur eius. 15 Haec est civitas gloriosa habitans in confidentia, quae dicebat in corde suo, "Ego sum, et extra me non est alia amplius." Quomodo facta est in desertum, cubile bestiae? Omnis qui transit per eam sibilabit et movebit manum suam.

There they shall feed; in the houses of Ashkelon they shall rest in the evening, because the Lord, their God, will visit them and *bring back* their captivity.

8 "I have heard the reproach of Moab and the blasphemies of the children of Ammon with which they reproached my people and have magnified themselves upon their borders. 9 Therefore as I live," saith the Lord of hosts, the God of Israel, "Moab shall be as Sodom, and the children of Ammon as Gomorrah: the dryness of thorns and heaps of salt and a desert even for ever. The remnant of my people shall make a spoil of them, and the residue of my nation shall possess them. 10 This shall befall them for their pride, because they have blasphemed and have been magnified against the people of the Lord of hosts. 11 The Lord shall be terrible upon them and shall consume all the gods of the earth, and they shall adore him, every man from his own place, all the islands of the Gentiles. 12 *You* Ethiopians also shall be slain with my sword."

13 And he will stretch out his hand upon the north and will destroy Assyria, and he will make the beautiful *city* a wilderness and as a place not passable and as a desert. 14 And flocks shall lie down in the midst thereof, all the beasts of the nations, and the bittern and the urchin shall lodge in the threshold thereof, the voice of the singing *bird* in the window, the raven on the upper post, for I will consume her strength. 15 This is the glorious city that *dwelt* in security, that said in her heart, "I am, and there is *none* beside me." How is she become a desert, a place for beasts to lie down in? Every one that passeth by her shall hiss and wag his hand.

Caput 3

Vae provocatrix et redempta civitas, columba. 2 Non audivit vocem, et non suscepit disciplinam. In Domino non est confisa; ad Deum suum non adpropiavit. 3 Principes eius in medio eius quasi leones rugientes; iudices eius lupi vespere; non relinquebant in mane. 4 Prophetae eius vesani viri infideles; sacerdotes eius polluerunt sanctum; iniuste egerunt contra legem. 5 Dominus iustus in medio eius; non faciet iniquitatem. Mane, mane iudicium suum dabit in lucem, et non abscondetur, nescivit autem iniquus confusionem.

6 "Disperdidi gentes, et dissipati sunt anguli earum; desertas feci vias eorum dum non est qui transeat. Desolatae sunt civitates eorum, non remanente viro nec ullo habitatore. 7 Dixi, 'Attamen timebis me; suscipies disciplinam, et non peribit habitaculum eius propter omnia in quibus visitavi eam.' Verumtamen diluculo surgentes corruperunt omnes cogitationes suas.

8 "Quapropter expecta me," dicit Dominus, "in die resurrectionis meae in futurum, quia iudicium meum ut congregem Gentes et colligam regna et effundam super eas indignationem meam, omnem iram furoris mei, in igne enim zeli

Chapter 3

A woe to Jerusalem for her sins. A prophecy of the conversion of the Gentiles and of the poor of Israel; God shall be with them. The Jews shall be converted at last.

Woe to the provoking and redeemed city, the dove. 2 She hath not hearkened to the voice, neither hath she received discipline. She hath not trusted in the Lord; she drew not near to her God. 3 Her princes are in the midst of her as roaring lions; her judges are evening wolves; they left nothing for the morning. 4 Her prophets are senseless men without faith; her priests have polluted the sanctuary; they have acted unjustly against the law. 5 The just Lord is in the midst thereof; he will not do iniquity. In the morning, in the morning he will bring his judgment to light, and it shall not be hid, but the wicked man hath not known shame.

6 "I have destroyed the nations, and their *towers* are beaten down; I have made their ways desert so that there is none that passeth by. Their cities are desolate; there is not a man remaining nor any inhabitant. 7 I said, 'Surely thou wilt fear me; thou wilt receive correction, and her dwelling shall not perish for all things wherein I have visited her.' But they rose early and corrupted all their thoughts.

8 "Wherefore expect me," saith the Lord, "in the day of my resurrection that is to come, for my judgment is to assemble the Gentiles and to gather the kingdoms and to pour upon them my indignation, all *my fierce* anger, for with the

mei devorabitur omnis terra. 9 Quia tunc reddam populis labium electum, ut invocent omnes in nomine Domini et serviant ei umero uno. 10 Ultra flumina Aethiopiae, inde supplices mei, filii dispersorum meorum, deferent munus mihi.

11 "In die illa non confunderis super cunctis adinventionibus tuis quibus praevaricata es in me, quia tunc auferam de medio tui magniloquos superbiae tuae, et non adicies exaltari amplius in monte sancto meo. 12 Et derelinquam in medio tui populum pauperem et egenum, et sperabunt in nomine Domini. 13 Reliquiae Israhel non facient iniquitatem nec loquentur mendacium, et non invenietur in ore eorum lingua dolosa, quoniam ipsi pascentur et accubabunt, et non erit qui exterreat."

14 Lauda, filia Sion; iubila, Israhel; laetare, et exulta in omni corde, filia Hierusalem. 15 Abstulit Dominus iudicium tuum; avertit inimicos tuos. Rex Israhel, Dominus, in medio tui; non timebis malum ultra.

16 In die illa dicetur Hierusalem, "Noli timere." Sion: "Non dissolvantur manus tuae. 17 Dominus, Deus tuus in medio tui, fortis. Ipse salvabit; gaudebit super te in laetitia; silebit in dilectione sua; exultabit super te in laude."

18 "Nugas qui a lege recesserant congregabo quia ex te erant, ut non ultra habeas super eis obprobrium. 19 Ecce: ego interficiam omnes qui adflixerunt te in tempore illo, et salvabo claudicantem et eam quae eiecta fuerat congregabo, et

fire of my jealousy shall all the earth be devoured. 9 Because then I will restore to the people a chosen lip, that all may call upon the name of the Lord and may serve him with one shoulder. 10 From beyond the rivers of Ethiopia shall my suppliants, the children of my dispersed people, bring me an offering.

11 "In that day thou shalt not be ashamed for all thy doings wherein thou hast transgressed against me, for then I will take away out of the midst of thee *thy proud* boasters, and thou shalt no more be lifted up because of my holy mountain. 12 And I will leave in the midst of thee a poor and needy people, and they shall hope in the name of the Lord. 13 The remnant of Israel shall not do iniquity nor speak lies, nor shall a deceitful tongue be found in their mouth, for they shall feed and shall lie down, and there shall be none to make them afraid."

14 Give praise, O daughter of Zion; shout, O Israel; be glad, and rejoice with all thy heart, O daughter of Jerusalem. 15 The Lord hath taken away thy judgment; he hath turned away thy enemies. The King of Israel, the Lord, is in the midst of thee; thou shalt fear evil no more.

16 In that day it shall be said to Jerusalem, "Fear not." To Zion: "Let not thy hands be weakened. 17 The Lord, thy God in the midst of thee, is mighty. He will save; he will rejoice over thee with gladness; he will be silent in his love; he will be joyful over thee in praise."

18 "The triflers that were departed from the law I will gather together because they were of thee, that thou mayest no more suffer reproach for them. 19 Behold: I will cut off all that have afflicted thee at that time, and I will save her that halteth and will gather her that was cast out, and I

ponam eos in laudem et in nomen in omni terra confusionis eorum [20] in tempore illo quo adducam vos et in tempore quo congregabo vos, dabo enim vos in nomen et in laudem omnibus populis terrae cum convertero captivitatem vestram coram oculis vestris," dicit Dominus.

will *get* them *praise* and a name in all the land *where they had been put to* confusion 20 at that time when I will bring you and at the time that I will gather you, for I will give you a name and praise among all the people of the earth when I shall have brought back your captivity before your eyes," saith the Lord.

HAGGAI

Caput 1

In anno secundo Darii, regis, in mense sexto, in die una mensis, factum est verbum Domini in manu Aggei, prophetae, ad Zorobabel, filium Salathihel, ducem Iuda, et ad Iesum, filium Iosedech, sacerdotem magnum, dicens, 2 "Haec ait Dominus exercituum, dicens, 'Populus iste dicit, "Nondum venit tempus domus Domini aedificandae."'"

3 Et factum est verbum Domini in manu Aggei, prophetae, dicens, 4 "Numquid tempus vobis est ut habitetis in domibus laqueatis, et domus ista deserta?"

5 Et nunc haec dicit Dominus exercituum: "Ponite corda vestra super vias vestras. 6 Seminastis multum et intulistis parum; comedistis et non estis satiati; bibistis et non estis inebriati; operuistis vos et non estis calefacti, et qui mercedes congregavit misit eas in sacculum pertusum."

Chapter 1

The people are reproved for neglecting to build the temple.
They are encouraged to set about the work.

In the second year of Darius, the king, in the sixth month, in the first day of the month, the word of the Lord came by the hand of Haggai, the prophet, to Zerubbabel, the son of Shealtiel, governor of Judah, and to Joshua, the son of Jehozadak, the high priest, saying, 2 "Thus saith the Lord of hosts, saying, 'This people saith, "The time is not yet come for building the house of the Lord."'"

3 And the word of the Lord came by the hand of Haggai, the prophet, saying, 4 "Is it time for you to dwell in ceiled houses, and this house lie desolate?"

5 And now thus saith the Lord of hosts: "Set your hearts *to consider* your ways. 6 You have sowed much and brought in little; you have eaten *but* have not had enough; you have drunk *but* have not been filled with drink; you have clothed yourselves *but* have not been warmed, and he that hath *earned* wages put them into a bag with holes."

7 Haec dicit Dominus exercituum: "Ponite corda vestra super vias vestras. 8 Ascendite in montem; portate ligna, et aedificate domum, et acceptabilis mihi erit, et glorificabor," dicit Dominus. 9 "Respexistis ad amplius, et ecce: factum est minus, et intulistis in domum, et exsuflavi illud. Quam ob causam?" dicit Dominus exercituum. "Quia domus mea deserta est, et vos festinatis, unusquisque in domum suam. 10 Propter hoc super vos prohibiti sunt caeli ne darent rorem, et terra prohibita est ne daret germen suum, 11 et vocavi siccitatem super terram et super montes et super triticum et super vinum et super oleum et quaecumque profert humus et super homines et super iumenta et super omnem laborem manuum."

12 Et audivit Zorobabel, filius Salathihel, et Iesus, filius Iosedech, sacerdos magnus, et omnes reliquiae populi vocem Dei sui et verba Aggei, prophetae, sicut misit eum Dominus, Deus eorum, ad ipsos. Et timuit populus a facie Domini.

13 Et dixit Aggeus, nuntius Domini, de nuntiis Domini, populo dicens, "'Ego vobiscum sum,' dicit Dominus." 14 Et suscitavit Dominus spiritum Zorobabel, filii Salathihel, ducis Iuda, et spiritum Iesu, filii Iosedech, sacerdotis magni, et spiritum reliquorum de omni populo, et ingressi sunt et faciebant opus in domo Domini exercituum, Dei sui.

7 Thus saith the Lord of hosts: "Set your hearts upon your ways. 8 Go up to the mountain; bring timber, and build the house, and it shall be acceptable to me, and I shall be glorified," saith the Lord. 9 "You have looked for more, and behold: it became less, and you brought it home, and I blowed it away. Why?" saith the Lord of hosts. "Because my house is desolate, and you make haste, every man to his own house. 10 Therefore the heavens over you were stayed from giving dew, and the earth was hindered from yielding her *fruits,* 11 and I called for a drought upon the land and upon the mountains and upon the corn and upon the wine and upon the oil and upon all that the ground bringeth forth and upon men and upon beasts and upon all the labour of the hands."

12 Then Zerubbabel, the son of Shealtiel, and Joshua, the son of Jehozadak, the high priest, and all the remnant of the people hearkened to the voice of *the Lord,* their God, and to the words of Haggai, the prophet, as the Lord, their God, sent him to them. And the people feared before the Lord.

13 And Haggai, the messenger of the Lord, as one of the messengers of the Lord, spoke, saying to the people, "'I am with you,' saith the Lord." 14 And the Lord stirred up the spirit of Zerubbabel, the son of Shealtiel, governor of Judah, and the spirit of Joshua, the son of Jehozadak, the high priest, and the spirit of all the rest of the people, and they went in and did the work in the house of the Lord of hosts, their God.

Caput 2

In die vicesima et quarta mensis, in sexto mense, in anno secundo Darii, regis. 2 In septimo mense, vicesima et prima mensis, factum est verbum Domini in manu Aggei, prophetae, dicens, 3 "Loquere ad Zorobabel, filium Salathihel, ducem Iuda, et ad Iesum, filium Iosedech, sacerdotem magnum, et ad reliquos populi, dicens, 4 'Quis in vobis est derelictus qui vidit domum istam in gloria sua prima, et quid vos videtis hanc nunc? Numquid non ita est quasi non sit in oculis vestris? 5 "Et nunc confortare, Zorobabel," dicit Dominus, "et confortare, Iesu, fili Iosedech, sacerdos magne, et confortare, omnis popule terrae," dicit Dominus exercituum, "et facite, quoniam ego vobiscum sum," dicit Dominus exercituum, 6 "verbum quod pepigi vobiscum cum egrederemini de terra Aegypti, et spiritus meus erit in medio vestrum; nolite timere." 7 Quia haec dicit Dominus exercituum: "Adhuc unum modicum est, et ego commovebo caelum et terram et mare et aridam, 8 et movebo omnes gentes, et veniet desideratus cunctis gentibus, et implebo domum istam gloria," dicit Dominus exercituum. 9 "Meum est argentum, et meum est aurum," dicit Dominus exercituum. 10 "Magna erit gloria domus istius novissimae plus quam

Chapter 2

Christ by his coming shall make the latter temple more glorious than the former. The blessing of God shall reward their labour in building. God's promise to Zerubbabel.

In the four and twentieth day of the month, in the sixth month, in the second year of Darius, the king, *they began.* 2 *And* in the seventh *month,* the word of the Lord came by the hand of Haggai, the prophet, saying, 3 "Speak to Zerubbabel, the son of Shealtiel, the governor of Judah, and to Joshua, the son of Jehozadak, the high priest, and to the rest of the people, saying, 4 'Who is left among you that saw this house in its first glory, and how do you see it now? Is it not *in comparison to that* as nothing in your eyes? 5 "*Yet* now take courage, O Zerubbabel," saith the Lord, "and take courage, O Joshua, the son of Jehozadak, the high priest, and take courage, all ye people of the land," saith the Lord of hosts, "and perform, for I am with you," saith the Lord of hosts, 6 "the word that I covenanted with you when you came out of the land of Egypt, and my spirit shall be in the midst of you; fear not." 7 For thus saith the Lord of hosts: "Yet one little while, and I will move the heaven and the earth and the sea and the dry land, 8 and I will move all nations, and the desired of all nations shall come, and I will fill this house with glory," saith the Lord of hosts. 9 "The silver is mine, and the gold is mine," saith the Lord of hosts. 10 "Great shall be the glory of this last house more than of the first," saith

primae," dicit Dominus exercituum, "et in loco isto dabo pacem," dicit Dominus exercituum.'"

11 In vicesima et quarta noni mensis, in anno secundo Darii, regis, factum est verbum Domini ad Aggeum, prophetam, dicens, 12 "Haec dicit Dominus exercituum: 'Interroga sacerdotes legem, dicens, 13 "Si tulerit homo carnem sanctificatam in ora vestimenti sui et tetigerit de summitate eius panem aut pulmentum aut vinum aut oleum aut omnem cibum, numquid sanctificabitur?"'"

Respondentes autem sacerdotes dixerunt, "Non."

14 Et dixit Aggeus, "Si tetigerit pollutus in anima ex omnibus his, numquid contaminabitur?"

Et responderunt sacerdotes et dixerunt, "Contaminabitur."

15 Et respondit Aggeus et dixit, "'Sic populus iste, et sic gens ista ante faciem meam,' dicit Dominus, 'et sic omne opus manuum eorum, et omnia quae obtulerunt ibi contaminata erunt.

16 "'Et nunc ponite corda vestra a die hac et supra, antequam poneretur lapis super lapidem in templo Domini, 17 cum accederetis ad acervum viginti modiorum, et fierent decem, et intraretis ad torcular ut exprimeretis quinquaginta lagoenas, et fiebant viginti. 18 Percussi vos vento urente, et aurugine et grandine omnia opera manuum vestrarum, et non fuit in vobis qui reverteretur ad me,' dicit Dominus. 19 'Ponite corda vestra ex die ista et in futurum, a die vicesima et quarta noni mensis, a die qua fundamenta iacta sunt templi Domini; ponite in cordibus vestris. 20 Numquid iam semen in germine est? Et adhuc vinea et ficus et malogranatum et lignum olivae non floruit? Ex die ista benedicam.'"

the Lord of hosts, "and in this place I will give peace," saith the Lord of hosts.'"

11 In the four and twentieth day of the ninth month, in the second year of Darius, the king, the word of the Lord came to Haggai, the prophet, saying, 12 "Thus saith the Lord of hosts: 'Ask the priests the law, saying, 13 "If a man carry sanctified flesh in the skirt of his garment and touch with his skirt bread or pottage or wine or oil or any meat, shall it be sanctified?"'"

And the priests answered and said, "No."

14 And Haggai said, "If one that is unclean by occasion of a soul touch any of all these things, shall it be defiled?"

And the priests answered and said, "It shall be defiled."

15 And Haggai answered and said, "'So is this people, and so is this nation before my face,' saith the Lord, 'and so is all the work of their hands, and all that they have offered there shall be defiled.

16 "And now consider in your hearts from this day and upward, before there was a stone laid upon a stone in the temple of the Lord, 17 when you went to a heap of twenty bushels, and they became ten, and you went into the press to press out fifty vessels, and they became twenty. 18 I struck you with a blasting wind, and all the works of your hand with the mildew and with hail, *yet* there was none among you that returned to me,' saith the Lord. 19 'Set your hearts from this day and henceforward, from the four and twentieth day of the ninth month, from the day that the foundations of the temple of the Lord were laid, *and* lay it up in your hearts. 20 Is the seed as yet sprung up? *Or hath* the vine and the fig tree and the pomegranate and the olive tree as yet flourished? From this day I will bless *you*.'"

21 Et factum est verbum Domini secundo ad Aggeum in vicesima et quarta mensis, dicens, 22 "Loquere ad Zorobabel, ducem Iuda, dicens, '"Ego movebo caelum pariter et terram. 23 Et subvertam solium regnorum et conteram fortitudinem regni Gentium, et subvertam quadrigam et ascensorem eius, et descendent equi et ascensores eorum vir in gladio fratris sui. 24 In die illa," dicit Dominus exercituum, "adsumam te, Zorobabel, fili Salathihel, serve meus," dicit Dominus, "et ponam te quasi signaculum, quia te elegi," dicit Dominus exercituum.'"

21 And the word of the Lord came a second time to Haggai in the four and twentieth day of the month, saying, 22 "Speak to Zerubbabel, the governor of Judah, saying, '"I will move both heaven and earth. 23 And I will overthrow the throne of kingdoms and will destroy the strength of the kingdom of the Gentiles, and I will overthrow the chariot and him that rideth therein, and the horses and their riders shall come down every one by the sword of his brother. 24 In that day," saith the Lord of hosts, "I will take thee, O Zerubbabel, the son of Shealtiel, my servant," saith the Lord, "and will make thee as a signet, for I have chosen thee," saith the Lord of hosts.'"

ZECHARIAH

Caput 1

In mense octavo, in anno secundo Darii Regis, factum est verbum Domini ad Zacchariam, filium Barachiae, filii Addo, prophetam, dicens, 2 "Iratus est Dominus super patres vestros iracundia. 3 Et dices ad eos, 'Haec dicit Dominus exercituum: "Convertimini ad me," ait Dominus exercituum, "et convertar ad vos," dicit Dominus exercituum. 4 "Ne sitis sicut patres vestri, ad quos clamabant prophetae priores, dicentes, 'Haec dicit Dominus exercituum: "Convertimini de viis vestris malis et de cogitationibus vestris pessimis."'

""Et non audierunt, neque adtenderunt ad me," dicit Dominus. 5 "Patres vestri, ubi sunt? Et prophetae, numquid in sempiternum vivent? 6 Verumtamen verba mea et legitima mea quae mandavi servis meis, prophetis, numquid non conprehenderunt patres vestros? Et conversi sunt et dixerunt, 'Sicut cogitavit Dominus exercituum facere nobis secundum vias nostras et secundum adinventiones nostras, fecit nobis.'"'"

7 In die vicesima et quarta undecimi mensis, Sabath, in

Chapter 1

The prophet exhorts the people to return to God and declares his visions, by which he puts them in hopes of better times.

In the eighth month, in the second year of King Darius, the word of the Lord came to Zechariah, the son of Berechiah, the son of Iddo, the prophet, saying, 2 "The Lord hath been exceeding angry with your fathers. 3 And thou shalt say to them, 'Thus saith the Lord of hosts: "Turn ye to me," saith the Lord of hosts, "and I will turn to you," saith the Lord of hosts. 4 "Be not as your fathers, to whom the former prophets have cried, saying, 'Thus saith the Lord of hosts: "Turn ye from your evil ways and from your wicked thoughts."'

"'"*But* they did not give ear, neither did they hearken to me," saith the Lord. 5 "Your fathers, where are they? And the prophets, shall they live always? 6 But yet my words and my ordinances which I gave in charge to my servants, the prophets, did they not take hold of your fathers? And they returned and said, 'As the Lord of hosts thought to do to us according to our ways and according to our devices, so he hath done to us.'"'"

7 In the four and twentieth day of the eleventh month,

anno secundo Darii, factum est verbum Domini ad Zacchariam, filium Barachiae, filii Addo, prophetam, dicens, 8 "Vidi per noctem, et ecce: vir ascendens super equum rufum, et ipse stabat inter myrteta quae erant in profundo, et post eum equi rufi, varii et albi."

9 Et dixi, "Quid sunt isti, Domine mi?"

Et dixit ad me angelus qui loquebatur in me, "Ego ostendam tibi quid sint haec."

10 Et respondit vir qui stabat inter myrteta et dixit, "Isti sunt quos misit Dominus ut perambularent terram."

11 Et responderunt angelo Domini qui stabat inter myrteta et dixerunt, "Perambulavimus terram, et ecce: omnis terra habitatur et quiescit."

12 Et respondit angelus Domini et dixit, "Domine exercituum, usquequo tu non misereberis Hierusalem et urbium Iuda quibus iratus es? Iste iam septuagesimus annus est."

13 Et respondit Dominus angelo qui loquebatur in me verba bona, verba consolatoria.

14 Et dixit ad me angelus qui loquebatur in me, "Clama, dicens, 'Haec dicit Dominus exercituum: "Zelatus sum Hierusalem et Sion zelo magno. 15 Et ira magna ego irascor super gentes opulentas, quia ego iratus sum parum, ipsi vero adiuverunt in malum." 16 Propterea haec dicit Dominus: "Revertar ad Hierusalem in misericordiis; domus mea aedificabitur in ea," ait Dominus exercituum, "et perpendiculum extendetur super Hierusalem."'

17 "Adhuc clama, dicens, 'Haec dicit Dominus exerci-

which is called Shebat, in the second year of Darius, the word of the Lord came to Zechariah, the son of Berechiah, the son of Iddo, the prophet, saying, 8 "I saw by night, and behold: a man riding upon a red horse, and he stood among the myrtle trees that were in the bottom, and behind him were horses red, speckled and white."

9 And I said, "What are these, my Lord?"

And the angel that spoke in me said to me, "I will shew thee what these are."

10 And the man that stood among the myrtle trees answered and said, "These are they whom the Lord hath sent to walk through the earth."

11 And they answered the angel of the Lord that stood among the myrtle trees and said, "We have walked through the earth, and behold: all the earth is inhabited and is at rest."

12 And the angel of the Lord answered and said, "O Lord of hosts, how long wilt thou not have mercy on Jerusalem and on the cities of Judah with which thou hast been angry? This is now the seventieth year."

13 And the Lord answered the angel that spoke in me good words, comfortable words.

14 And the angel that spoke in me said to me, "Cry thou, saying, 'Thus saith the Lord of hosts: "I am zealous for Jerusalem and Zion with a great zeal. 15 And I am angry with a great anger with the wealthy nations, for I was angry a little, but they helped *forward* the evil." 16 Therefore thus saith the Lord: "I will return to Jerusalem in mercies; my house shall be built in it," saith the Lord of hosts, "and the building line shall be stretched forth upon Jerusalem.""

17 "Cry yet, saying, 'Thus saith the Lord of hosts: "My cit-

tuum: 'Adhuc affluent civitates meae bonis, et consolabitur Dominus adhuc Sion, et eliget adhuc Hierusalem.'"'"

18 Et levavi oculos meos et vidi, et ecce: quattuor cornua. 19 Et dixi ad angelum qui loquebatur in me, "Quid sunt haec?"

Et dixit ad me, "Haec sunt cornua quae ventilaverunt Iudam et Israhel et Hierusalem."

20 Et ostendit mihi Dominus quattuor fabros. 21 Et dixi, "Quid isti veniunt facere?"

Qui ait, dicens, "Haec sunt cornua quae ventilaverunt Iudam per singulos viros, et nemo eorum levavit caput suum. Et venerunt isti deterrere ea, ut deiciant cornua gentium quae levaverunt cornu super terram Iuda ut dispergerent eam."

Caput 2

Et levavi oculos meos et vidi, et ecce: vir et in manu eius funiculus mensorum. 2 Et dixi, "Quo tu vadis?"

Et dixit ad me, "Ut metiar Hierusalem et videam quanta sit latitudo eius et quanta longitudo eius."

ies shall yet flow with good things, and the Lord will yet comfort Zion, and he will yet choose Jerusalem.'"'"

18 And I lifted up my eyes and saw, and behold: four horns. 19 And I said to the angel that spoke in me, "What are these?"

And he said to me, "These are the horns that have scattered Judah and Israel and Jerusalem."

20 And the Lord shewed me four smiths. 21 And I said, "What come these to do?"

And he spoke, saying, "These are the horns which have scattered Judah every man apart, and none of them lifted up his head. And these are come to fray them, to cast down the horns of the nations that have lifted up the horn upon the land of Judah to scatter it."

Chapter 2

Under the name of Jerusalem he prophesieth the progress of the church of Christ by the conversion of some Jews and many Gentiles.

And I lifted up my eyes and saw, and behold: a man with a measuring line in his hand. 2 And I said, "Whither goest thou?"

And he said to me, "To measure Jerusalem and to see how great is the breadth thereof and how great the length thereof."

3 Et ecce: angelus qui loquebatur in me egrediebatur, et angelus alius egrediebatur in occursum eius. 4 Et dixit ad eum, "Curre; loquere ad puerum istum, dicens, "Absque muro habitabitur Hierusalem prae multitudine hominum et iumentorum in medio eius. 5 Et ego ero ei," ait Dominus, "murus ignis in circuitu, et in gloria ero in medio eius.

6 ""O, O fugite de terra aquilonis," dicit Dominus, "quoniam in quattuor ventos caeli dispersi vos," dicit Dominus. 7 "O Sion, fuge, quae habitas apud filiam Babylonis," 8 quia haec dicit Dominus exercituum: "Post gloriam misit me ad gentes quae spoliaverunt vos, qui enim tetigerit vos tangit pupillam oculi mei. 9 Quia ecce: ego levo manum meam super eos, et erunt praedae his qui serviebant sibi, et cognoscetis quia Dominus exercituum misit me.

10 ""Lauda, et laetare, filia Sion, quia ecce: ego venio, et habitabo in medio tui," ait Dominus. 11 "Et adplicabuntur gentes multae ad Dominum in die illa, et erunt mihi in populum, et habitabo in medio tui, et scies quia Dominus exercituum misit me ad te. 12 Et possidebit Dominus Iudam, partem suam in terra sanctificata, et eliget adhuc Hierusalem. 13 Sileat omnis caro a facie Domini, quia consurrexit de habitaculo sancto suo.""

3 And behold: the angel that spoke in me went forth, and another angel went out to meet him. 4 And he said to him, "Run; speak to this young man, saying, 'Jerusalem shall be inhabited without walls by reason of the multitude of men and of the beasts in the midst thereof. 5 And I will be to it," saith the Lord, "a wall of fire round about, and I will be in glory in the midst thereof.

6 ""O, O flee ye out of the land of the north," saith the Lord, "for I have scattered you into the four winds of heaven," saith the Lord. 7 "O Zion, flee, thou that dwellest with the daughter of Babylon," 8 for thus saith the Lord of hosts: "After the glory he hath sent me to the nations that have robbed you, for he that toucheth you toucheth the apple of my eye. 9 For behold: I lift up my hand upon them, and they shall be a prey to those that served them, and you shall know that the Lord of hosts sent me.

10 ""Sing praise, and rejoice, O daughter of Zion, for behold: I come, and I will dwell in the midst of thee," saith the Lord. 11 "And many nations shall be joined to the Lord in that day, and they shall be my people, and I will dwell in the midst of thee, and thou shalt know that the Lord of hosts hath sent me to thee. 12 And the Lord shall possess Judah, his portion in the sanctified land, and he shall yet choose Jerusalem. 13 Let all flesh be silent at the presence of the Lord, for he is risen up out of his holy habitation."""

Caput 3

Et ostendit mihi Dominus Iesum, sacerdotem magnum, stantem coram angelo Domini, et Satan stabat a dextris eius ut adversaretur ei. 2 Et dixit Dominus ad Satan, "Increpet Dominus in te, Satan, et increpet Dominus in te qui elegit Hierusalem. Numquid non iste torris est erutus de igne?"

3 Et Iesus erat indutus vestibus sordidis, et stabat ante faciem angeli, 4 qui respondit et ait ad eos qui stabant coram se, dicens, "Auferte vestimenta sordida ab eo." Et dixit ad eum, "Ecce: abstuli iniquitatem tuam et indui te mutatoriis." 5 Et dixit, "Ponite cidarim mundam super caput eius," et posuerunt cidarim mundam super caput eius et induerunt eum vestibus, et angelus Domini stabat.

6 Et contestabatur angelus Domini Iesum, dicens, 7 "Haec dicit Dominus exercituum: 'Si in viis meis ambulaveris et custodiam meam custodieris, tu quoque iudicabis domum meam et custodies atria mea, et dabo tibi ambulantes de his qui nunc hic adsistunt. 8 Audi, Iesu, sacerdos magne, tu et amici tui qui habitant coram te, quia viri portendentes sunt. Ecce enim: ego adducam servum meum, Orientem. 9 Quia ecce: lapis quem dedi coram Iesu; super lapidem unum

Chapter 3

In a vision Satan appeareth accusing the high priest. He is cleansed from his sins. Christ is promised, and great fruit from his passion.

And the Lord shewed me Joshua, the high priest, standing before the angel of the Lord, and Satan stood on his right hand to be his adversary. 2 And the Lord said to Satan, "The Lord rebuke thee, O Satan, and the Lord that chose Jerusalem rebuke thee. Is not this a brand plucked out of the fire?"

3 And Joshua was clothed with filthy garments, and he stood before the face of the angel, 4 who answered and said to them that stood before him, saying, "Take away the filthy garments from him." And he said to him, "Behold: I have taken away thy iniquity and have clothed thee with change of garments." 5 And he said, "Put a clean mitre upon his head," and they put a clean mitre upon his head and clothed him with garments, and the angel of the Lord stood.

6 And the angel of the Lord protested to Joshua, saying, 7 "Thus saith the Lord of hosts: 'If thou wilt walk in my ways and keep my charge, thou also shalt judge my house and shalt keep my courts, and I will give thee some of them that are now present here *to walk with thee.* 8 Hear, O Joshua, thou high priest, thou and thy friends that dwell before thee, for they are portending men. For behold: I will bring my servant, the Orient. 9 For behold: the stone that I have laid before Joshua; upon one stone there are seven eyes.

septem oculi sunt. Ecce: ego celabo sculpturam eius,' ait Dominus exercituum, 'et auferam iniquitatem terrae illius in die una. 10 In die illa,' dicit Dominus exercituum, 'vocabit vir amicum suum subter vineam et subter ficum.'"

Caput 4

Et reversus est angelus qui loquebatur in me, et suscitavit me quasi virum qui suscitatur de somno suo. 2 Et dixit ad me, "Quid tu vides?"

Et dixi, "Vidi, et ecce: candelabrum aureum totum et lampas eius super caput ipsius et septem lucernae eius super illud et septem infusoria lucernis quae erant super caput illius 3 et duae olivae super illud, una a dextris lampadis et una a sinistris eius." 4 Et respondi et aio ad angelum qui loquebatur in me, dicens, "Quid sunt haec, domine mi?"

5 Et respondit angelus qui loquebatur in me et dixit ad me, "Numquid nescis quid sunt haec?"

Et dixi, "Non, domine mi."

Behold: I will grave the graving thereof,' saith the Lord of hosts, 'and I will take away the iniquity of that land in one day. 10 In that day,' saith the Lord of hosts, 'every man shall call his friend under the vine and under the fig tree.'"

Chapter 4

The vision of the golden candlestick and seven lamps and of the two olive trees.

And the angel that spoke in me came again, and he waked me as a man that is wakened out of his sleep. 2 And he said to me, "What seest thou?"

And I said, "I have looked, and behold: a candlestick all of gold and its lamp upon the top of it and the seven lights thereof upon it and seven funnels for the lights that were upon the top thereof 3 and two olive trees over it, one upon the right side of the lamp and the other upon the left side thereof." 4 And I answered and said to the angel that spoke in me, saying, "What are these things, my lord?"

5 And the angel that spoke in me answered and said to me, "Knowest thou not what these things are?"

And I said, "No, my lord."

6 Et respondit et ait ad me, dicens, "Hoc est verbum Domini ad Zorobabel, dicens, '"Non in exercitu nec in robore, sed in spiritu meo," dicit Dominus exercituum. 7 Quis tu, mons magne coram Zorobabel? In planum, et educet lapidem primarium et exaequabit gratiam gratiae eius.'"

8 Et factum est verbum Domini ad me, dicens, 9 "Manus Zorobabel fundaverunt domum istam, et manus eius perficient eam, et scietis quia Dominus exercituum misit me ad vos. 10 Quis enim despexit dies parvos? Et laetabuntur et videbunt lapidem stagneum in manu Zorobabel. Septem isti oculi sunt Domini, qui discurrunt in universam terram."

11 Et respondi et dixi ad eum, "Quid sunt duae olivae istae ad dextram candelabri et ad sinistram eius?" 12 Et respondi secundo et dixi ad eum, "Quid sunt duo rami olivarum quae sunt iuxta duo rostra aurea in quibus sunt suffusoria ex auro?"

13 Et ait ad me, dicens, "Numquid nescis quid sunt haec?" Et dixi, "Non, domine mi."

14 Et dixit, "Isti sunt duo filii olei qui adsistunt Dominatori universae terrae."

6 And he answered and spoke to me, saying, "This is the word of the Lord to Zerubbabel, saying, '"Not with an army nor by might, but by my spirit," saith the Lord of hosts. 7 Who art thou, O great mountain before Zerubbabel? *Thou shalt become* a plain, and he shall bring out the chief stone and shall give equal grace to the grace thereof.'"

8 And the word of the Lord came to me, saying, 9 "The hands of Zerubbabel have laid the foundations of this house, and his hands shall finish it, and you shall know that the Lord of hosts hath sent me to you. 10 For who hath despised little days? And they shall rejoice and shall see the tin *plummet* in the hand of Zerubbabel. These are the seven eyes of the Lord, that run to and fro through the whole earth."

11 And I answered and said to him, "What are these two olive trees upon the right side of the candlestick and upon the left side thereof?" 12 And I answered again and said to him, "What are the two olive branches that are by the two golden beaks in which are the funnels of gold?"

13 And he spoke to me, saying, "Knowest thou not what these are?"

And I said, "No, my lord."

14 And he said, "These are two sons of oil who stand before the Lord of the whole earth."

Caput 5

Et conversus sum et levavi oculos meos, et vidi, et ecce: volumen volans.

2 Et dixit ad me, "Quid tu vides?"

Et dixi, "Ego video volumen volans; longitudo eius viginti cubitorum, et latitudo eius decem cubitorum."

3 Et dixit ad me, "Haec est maledictio quae egreditur super faciem omnis terrae, quia omnis fur sicut ibi scriptum est iudicabitur, et omnis iurans ex hoc similiter iudicabitur. 4 'Educam illud,' dicit Dominus exercituum, 'et veniet ad domum furis et ad domum iurantis in nomine meo mendaciter, et commorabitur in medio domus eius et consumet eam et ligna eius et lapides eius.'"

5 Et egressus est angelus qui loquebatur in me, et dixit ad me, "Leva oculos tuos, et vide quid est hoc quod egreditur."

6 Et dixi, "Quidnam est?"

Et ait, "Haec est amphora egrediens." Et dixit, "Haec est oculus eorum in universa terra." 7 Et ecce: talentum plumbi portabatur, et ecce: mulier una sedens in medio amphorae. 8 Et dixit, "Haec est impietas." Et proiecit eam in medio amphorae et misit massam plumbeam in os eius.

Chapter 5

The vision of the flying volume and of the woman in the vessel.

And I turned and lifted up my eyes, and I saw, and behold: a volume flying.

2 And he said to me, "What seest thou?"

And I said, "I see a volume flying; the length thereof is twenty cubits, and the breadth thereof ten cubits."

3 And he said to me, "This is the curse that goeth forth over the face of *the* earth, for every thief shall be judged as is there written, and every one that sweareth in like manner shall be judged by it. 4 'I will bring it forth,' saith the Lord of hosts, 'and it shall come to the house of the thief and to the house of him that sweareth falsely by my name, and it shall remain in the midst of his house and shall consume it with the timber thereof and the stones thereof.'"

5 And the angel went forth that spoke in me, and he said to me, "Lift up thy eyes, and see what this is that goeth forth."

6 And I said, "What is it?"

And he said, "This is a vessel going forth." And he said, "This is their eye in all the earth." 7 And behold: a talent of lead was carried, and behold: a woman sitting in the midst of the vessel. 8 And he said, "This is wickedness." And he cast her into the midst of the vessel and cast the weight of lead upon the mouth thereof.

9 Et levavi oculos meos et vidi, et ecce: duae mulieres egredientes, et spiritus in alis earum, et habebant alas quasi alas milvi, et levaverunt amphoram inter terram et caelum. 10 Et dixi ad angelum qui loquebatur in me, "Quo istae deferunt amphoram?"

11 Et dixit ad me, "Ut aedificetur ei domus in terra Sennaar, et stabiliatur et ponatur ibi super basem suam."

Caput 6

Et conversus sum et levavi oculos meos et vidi, et ecce: quattuor quadrigae egredientes de medio duorum montium, et montes montes aerei. 2 In quadriga prima equi rufi, et in quadriga secunda equi nigri, 3 et in quadriga tertia equi albi, et in quadriga quarta equi varii et fortes. 4 Et respondi et dixi ad angelum qui loquebatur in me, "Quid sunt haec, domine mi?"

5 Et respondit angelus et ait ad me, "Isti sunt quattuor venti caeli qui egrediuntur ut stent coram Dominatore omnis terrae."

9 And I lifted up my eyes and looked, and behold: there came out two women, and wind was in their wings, and they had wings like the wings of a kite, and they lifted up the vessel between the earth and the heaven. 10 And I said to the angel that spoke in me, "Whither do these carry the vessel?"

11 And he said to me, "That a house may be built for it in the land of Shinar, and that it may be established and set there upon its own basis."

Chapter 6

The vision of the four chariots. Crowns are ordered for Joshua, the high priest, as a type of Christ.

And I turned and lifted up my eyes and saw, and behold: four chariots came out from the midst of two mountains, and the mountains were mountains of brass. 2 In the first chariot were red horses, and in the second chariot black horses, 3 and in the third chariot white horses, and in the fourth chariot grisled horses and strong ones. 4 And I answered and said to the angel that spoke in me, "What are these, my lord?"

5 And the angel answered and said to me, "These are the four winds of the heaven which go forth to stand before the Lord of all the earth."

6 In qua erant equi nigri egrediebantur in terram aquilonis, et albi egressi sunt post eos, et varii egressi sunt ad terram austri, 7 qui autem erant robustissimi exierunt et quaerebant ire et discurrere per omnem terram. Et dixit, "Ite; perambulate terram," et perambulaverunt terram. 8 Et vocavit me et locutus est ad me, dicens, "Ecce: qui egrediuntur in terram aquilonis requiescere fecerunt spiritum meum in terra aquilonis."

9 Et factum est verbum Domini ad me, dicens, 10 "Sume a transmigratione, ab Oldai et a Tobia et ab Idaia, et venies tu in die illa et intrabis domum Iosiae, filii Sofoniae, qui venerunt de Babylone. 11 Et sumes argentum et aurum et facies coronas, et pones in capite Iesu, filii Iosedech, sacerdotis magni.

12 "Et loqueris ad eum, dicens, 'Haec ait Dominus exercituum, dicens, "Ecce, vir: Oriens nomen eius, et subter eum orietur et aedificabit templum Domino. 13 Et ipse extruet templum Domino, et ipse portabit gloriam et sedebit et dominabitur super solio suo, et erit sacerdos super solio suo, et consilium pacis erit inter duos illos. 14 Et coronae erunt Helem et Tobiae et Idaiae et Hen, filio Sofoniae, memoriale in templo Domini. 15 Et qui procul sunt venient et aedificabunt in templo Domini, et scietis quia Dominus exercituum misit me ad vos. Erit autem hoc si auditu audieritis vocem Domini, Dei vestri.""""

6 That in which were the black horses went forth into the land of the north, and the white went forth after them, and the grisled went forth to the land of the south, 7 and they that were most strong went out and sought to go and to run to and fro through all the earth. And he said, "Go; walk throughout the earth," and they walked throughout the earth. 8 And he called me and spoke to me, saying, "Behold: they that go forth into the land of the north have quieted my spirit in the land of the north."

9 And the word of the Lord came to me, saying, 10 "Take of *them of* the captivity, of Heldai and of Tobijah and of Jeda-iah, and thou shalt come in that day and shalt go into the house of Josiah, the son of Zephaniah, who came out of Babylon. 11 And thou shalt take gold and silver and shalt make crowns, and thou shalt set them on the head of Joshua, the son of Jehozadak, the high priest.

12 "And thou shalt speak to him, saying, 'Thus saith the Lord of hosts, saying: "Behold, a man: the Orient is his name, and under him shall he spring up and shall build a temple to the Lord. 13 Yea, he shall build a temple to the Lord, and he shall bear the glory and shall sit and rule upon his throne, and he shall be a priest upon his throne, and the counsel of peace shall be between them both. 14 And the crowns shall be to Helem and Tobijah and Jedaiah and to Hen, the son of Zephaniah, a memorial in the temple of the Lord. 15 And they that are far off shall come and shall build in the temple of the Lord, and you shall know that the Lord of hosts sent me to you. But this shall come to pass if hearing you will hear the voice of the Lord, your God.""'"

Caput 7

Et factum est in anno quarto Darii Regis factum est verbum Domini ad Zachariam in quarta mensis noni, qui est Casleu, 2 et miserunt ad domum Dei Sarasar et Rogomelech et viri qui erant cum eo ad deprecandam faciem Domini, 3 ut dicerent sacerdotibus domus Domini exercituum et prophetis, loquentes, "Numquid flendum mihi est in mense quinto, vel sanctificare me debeo sicuti feci iam multis annis?"

4 Et factum est verbum Domini exercituum ad me, dicens, 5 "Loquere ad omnem populum terrae et ad sacerdotes, dicens, 'Cum ieiunaretis et plangeretis in quinto et septimo per hos septuaginta annos, numquid ieiunium ieiunastis mihi? 6 Et cum comedistis et bibistis, numquid non vobis comedistis et vobismet ipsis bibistis? 7 Numquid non sunt verba quae locutus est Dominus in manu prophetarum priorum cum adhuc Hierusalem habitaretur et esset opulenta, ipsa et urbes in circuitu eius, et ad austrum et in campestribus habitaretur?'"

8 Et factum est verbum Domini ad Zachariam, dicens, 9 "Haec ait Dominus exercituum, dicens, 'Iudicium verum iudicate, et misericordiam et miserationes facite unusquisque cum fratre suo, 10 et viduam et pupillum et advenam et

Chapter 7

The people inquire concerning fasting. They are admonished to fast from sin.

And it came to pass in the fourth year of King Darius that the word of the Lord came to Zechariah in the fourth day of the ninth month, which is Chislev, 2 *when* Sharezer and Regem-melech and the men that were with him sent to the house of God to entreat the face of the Lord, 3 to speak to the priests of the house of the Lord of hosts and to the prophets, saying, "Must I weep in the fifth month, or must I sanctify myself as I have now done for many years?"

4 And the word of the Lord of hosts came to me, saying, 5 "Speak to all the people of the land and to the priests, saying, 'When you fasted and mourned in the fifth and the seventh *month* for these seventy years, did you keep a fast unto me? 6 And when you did eat and drink, did you not eat for yourselves and drink for yourselves? 7 Are not these the words which the Lord spoke by the hand of the former prophets when Jerusalem as yet was inhabited and was wealthy, both itself and the cities round about it, and there were inhabitants toward the south and in the plain?'"

8 And the word of the Lord came to Zechariah, saying, 9 "Thus saith the Lord of hosts, saying: 'Judge ye true judgment, and shew ye mercy and compassion every man to his brother, 10 and oppress not the widow and the fatherless and

pauperem nolite calumniari, et malum vir fratri suo non cogitet in corde suo.'"

11 Et noluerunt adtendere, et averterunt scapulam recedentem, et aures suas adgravaverunt ne audirent, 12 et cor suum posuerunt ut adamantem, ne audirent legem et verba quae misit Dominus exercituum in spiritu suo per manum prophetarum priorum, et facta est indignatio magna a Domino exercituum. 13 Et factum est sicut locutus est et non audierunt, "Sic clamabunt, et non exaudiam," dicit Dominus exercituum. 14 "Et dispersi eos per omnia regna quae nesciunt, et terra desolata est ab eis, eo quod non esset transiens et revertens, et posuerunt terram desiderabilem in desertum."

Caput 8

Et factum est verbum Domini exercituum, dicens, 2 "Haec dicit Dominus exercituum: 'Zelatus sum Sion zelo magno, et indignatione magna zelatus sum eam.' 3 Haec dicit Dominus exercituum: 'Reversus sum ad Sion, et habitabo in medio Hierusalem. Et vocabitur Hierusalem civitas

the stranger and the poor, and let not a man devise evil in his heart against his brother.'"

11 *But* they would not hearken, and they turned away the shoulder *to depart,* and they *stopped* their ears not to hear, 12 and they made their heart as the adamant stone, lest they should hear the law and the words which the Lord of hosts sent in his spirit by the hand of the former prophets, so a great indignation came from the Lord of hosts. 13 And it came to pass that as he spoke and they heard not, "So shall they cry, and I will not hear," saith the Lord of hosts. 14 "And I dispersed them throughout all kingdoms which they know not, and the land was left desolate behind them, so that no man passed through *or* returned, and they changed the delightful land into a wilderness."

Chapter 8

Joyful promises to Jerusalem fully verified in the church of Christ.

And the word of the Lord of hosts came *to me,* saying, 2 "Thus saith the Lord of hosts: 'I have been jealous for Zion with a great jealousy, and with a great indignation have I been jealous for her.' 3 Thus saith the Lord of hosts: 'I am returned to Zion, and I will dwell in the midst of Jerusalem. And Jerusalem shall be called the city of truth, and the

veritatis, et mons Domini exercituum, mons sanctificatus.' 4 Haec dicit Dominus exercituum: 'Adhuc habitabunt senes et anus in plateis Hierusalem, et viri baculus in manu eius prae multitudine dierum, 5 et plateae civitatis conplebuntur infantibus et puellis ludentibus in plateis eius.'

6 "Haec dicit Dominus exercituum: 'Si difficile videbitur in oculis reliquiarum populi huius in diebus illis, numquid in oculis meis difficile erit?' dicit Dominus exercituum. 7 Haec dicit Dominus exercituum: 'Ecce: ego salvabo populum meum de terra orientis et de terra occasus solis, 8 et adducam eos, et habitabunt in medio Hierusalem, et erunt mihi in populum, et ego ero eis in Deum in veritate et in iustitia.'

9 "Haec dicit Dominus exercituum: 'Confortentur manus vestrae, qui auditis in diebus his sermones istos per os prophetarum, in die qua fundata est domus Domini exercituum ut templum aedificaretur. 10 Siquidem ante dies illos merces hominum non erat, nec merces iumentorum erat, neque introeunti neque exeunti erat pax prae tribulatione, et dimisi omnes homines, unumquemque contra proximum suum.

11 "'Nunc autem non iuxta dies priores ego faciam reliquiis populi huius,' dicit Dominus exercituum. 12 'Sed semen pacis erit; vinea dabit fructum suum, et terra dabit germen suum, et caeli dabunt rorem suum, et possidere faciam reliquias populi huius universa haec. 13 Et erit sicut eratis maledictio in Gentibus, domus Iuda et domus Israhel, sic salvabo vos, et eritis benedictio. Nolite timere; confortentur manus vestrae.'

mountain of the Lord of hosts, the sanctified mountain.'
4 Thus saith the Lord of hosts: 'There shall yet old men and old women dwell in the streets of Jerusalem, and every *man with his* staff in his hand through multitude of days, 5 and the streets of the city shall be full of *boys* and girls playing in the streets thereof.'

6 "Thus saith the Lord of hosts: 'If it *seem* hard in the eyes of the remnant of this people in those days, shall it be hard in my eyes?' saith the Lord of hosts. 7 Thus saith the Lord of hosts: 'Behold: I will save my people from the land of the east and from the land of the going down of the sun, 8 and I will bring them, and they shall dwell in the midst of Jerusalem, and they shall be my people, and I will be their God in truth and in justice.'

9 "Thus saith the Lord of hosts: 'Let your hands be strengthened, you that hear in these days these words by the mouth of the prophets, in the day that the house of the Lord of hosts was founded that the temple might be built. 10 For before those days there was no hire for men, neither was there hire for beasts, neither was there peace to him that came in nor to him that went out because of the tribulation, and I let all men go, every one against his neighbour.

11 "'But now I will not deal with the remnant of this people according to the former days,' saith the Lord of hosts. 12 'But there shall be the seed of peace; the vine shall yield her fruit, and the earth shall give her increase, and the heavens shall give their dew, and I will cause the remnant of this people to possess all these things. 13 And it shall come to pass that as you were a curse among the Gentiles, O house of Judah and house of Israel, so will I save you, and you shall be a blessing. Fear not; let your hands be strengthened.'

14 "Quia haec dicit Dominus exercituum: 'Sicut cogitavi ut adfligerem vos cum ad iracundiam provocassent patres vestri me,' dicit Dominus, 15 'et non sum misertus, sic conversus cogitavi in diebus istis ut benefaciam domui Iuda et Hierusalem; nolite timere. 16 Haec sunt ergo verba quae facietis. Loquimini veritatem, unusquisque cum proximo suo; veritatem et iudicium pacis iudicate in portis vestris, 17 et unusquisque malum contra amicum suum ne cogitetis in cordibus vestris, et iuramentum mendax ne diligatis, omnia enim haec sunt quae odi,' dicit Dominus."

18 Et factum est verbum Domini exercituum ad me, dicens, 19 "Haec dicit Dominus exercituum: 'Ieiunium quarti et ieiunium quinti et ieiunium septimi et ieiunium decimi erit domui Iuda in gaudium et laetitiam et in sollemnitates praeclaras; veritatem tantum et pacem diligite.'

20 "Haec dicit Dominus exercituum: 'Usquequo veniant populi et habitent in civitatibus multis, 21 et vadant habitatores unus ad alterum, dicentes, "Eamus et deprecemur faciem Domini, et quaeramus Dominum exercituum," vadam etiam ego. 22 Et venient populi multi et gentes robustae ad quaerendum Dominum exercituum in Hierusalem et deprecandam faciem Domini.' 23 Haec dicit Dominus exercituum: 'In diebus illis, in quibus adprehendent decem homines ex omnibus linguis Gentium et adprehendent fimbriam viri Iudaei, dicentes, "Ibimus vobiscum, audivimus enim quoniam Deus vobiscum est."'"

14 "For thus saith the Lord of hosts: 'As I purposed to afflict you when your fathers had provoked me to wrath,' saith the Lord, 15 'and I had no mercy, so turning again I have thought in these days to do good to the house of Judah and Jerusalem; fear not. 16 These then are the things which you shall do. Speak ye truth, every one to his neighbour; judge ye truth and judgment of peace in your gates, 17 and let none of you imagine evil in your hearts against his friend, and love not a false oath, for all these are the things that I hate,' saith the Lord."

18 And the word of the Lord of hosts came to me, saying, 19 "Thus saith the Lord of hosts: 'The fast of the fourth *month* and the fast of the fifth and the fast of the seventh and the fast of the tenth shall be to the house of Judah joy and gladness and great solemnities; only love ye truth and peace.'

20 "Thus saith the Lord of hosts: 'Until people come and dwell in many cities, 21 and the inhabitants go one to another, saying, "Let us go and entreat the face of the Lord, and let us seek the Lord of hosts," I also will go. 22 And many peoples and strong nations shall come to seek the Lord of hosts in Jerusalem and to entreat the face of the Lord.' 23 Thus saith the Lord of hosts: 'In those days, wherein ten men of all languages of the Gentiles shall take hold and shall hold fast the skirt of one that is a Jew, saying, "We will go with you, for we have heard that God is with you."'"

Caput 9

Onus verbi Domini in terra Adrach et Damasci, requiei eius. Quia Domini est oculus hominis et omnium tribuum Israhel; 2 Emath quoque, in terminis eius, et Tyrus et Sidon, adsumpserunt quippe sibi sapientiam valde. 3 Et aedificavit Tyrus munitionem suam et coacervavit argentum quasi humum et aurum ut lutum platearum. 4 Ecce: Dominus possidebit eam et percutiet in mari fortitudinem eius, et haec igni devorabitur.

5 Videbit Ascalon et timebit, et Gaza, et dolebit nimis, et Accaron, quoniam confusa est spes eius. Et peribit rex de Gaza, et Ascalon non habitabitur. 6 Et sedebit separator in Azoto, et disperdam superbiam Philisthinorum. 7 Et auferam sanguinem eius de ore eius, et abominationes eius de medio dentium eius, et relinquetur etiam ipse Deo nostro,

Chapter 9

God will defend his church and bring over even her enemies to the faith. The meek coming of Christ to bring peace, to deliver the captives by his blood and to give us all good things.

The burden of the word of the Lord in the land of Hadrach and of Damascus, the rest thereof. For the eye of man and of all the tribes of Israel is the Lord's; 2 Hamath also, in the borders thereof, and Tyre and Sidon, for they have taken to themselves *to be exceeding wise.* 3 And Tyre hath built herself a stronghold and heaped together silver as earth and gold as the mire of the streets. 4 Behold: the Lord shall possess her and shall strike her strength in the sea, and she shall be devoured with fire.

5 Ashkelon shall see and shall fear, and Gaza, and shall be very sorrowful, and Ekron, because her hope is confounded. And the king shall perish from Gaza, and Ashkelon shall not be inhabited. 6 And the divider shall sit in Ashdod, and I will destroy the pride of the Philistines. 7 And I will take away his blood out of his mouth, and his abominations from between his teeth, and even he shall be left to our God, and

et erit quasi dux in Iuda, et Accaron quasi Iebuseus. 8 Et circumdabo domum meam ex his qui militant mihi, euntes et revertentes, et non transibit super eos ultra exactor, quia nunc vidi in oculis meis.

9 Exulta satis, filia Sion; iubila, filia Hierusalem. Ecce: rex tuus veniet tibi, iustus et salvator; ipse pauper et ascendens super asinum et super pullum, filium asinae. 10 Et disperdam quadrigam ex Ephraim et equum de Hierusalem, et dissipabitur arcus belli, et loquetur pacem Gentibus, et potestas eius a mari usque ad mare et a fluminibus usque ad fines terrae.

11 Tu quoque in sanguine testamenti tui emisisti vinctos tuos de lacu in quo non est aqua. 12 Convertimini ad munitionem, vincti spei; hodie quoque adnuntians duplicia reddam tibi, 13 quoniam extendi mihi Iudam quasi arcum; implevi Ephraim. Et suscitabo filios tuos, Sion, super filios tuos, Graecia, et ponam te quasi gladium fortium.

14 Et Dominus Deus super eos videbitur, et exibit ut fulgur iaculum eius, et Dominus Deus in tuba canet et vadet in turbine austri. 15 Dominus exercituum proteget eos, et devorabunt et subicient lapidibus fundae, et bibentes inebriabuntur quasi vino, et replebuntur ut fialae et quasi cornua altaris. 16 Et salvabit eos Dominus, Deus eorum, in die illa ut gregem populi sui, quia lapides sancti elevabuntur super terram eius. 17 Quid enim bonum eius est, et quid pulchrum eius, nisi frumentum electorum et vinum germinans virgines?

he shall be as a governor in Judah, and Ekron as a Jebusite. 8 And I will encompass my house with them that serve me in war, going and returning, and the oppressor shall no more pass through them, for now I have seen with my eyes.

9 Rejoice greatly, O daughter of Zion; shout for joy, O daughter of Jerusalem. Behold: thy king will come to thee, the just and saviour; he is poor and riding upon an ass and upon a colt, the foal of an ass. 10 And I will destroy the chariot out of Ephraim and the horse out of Jerusalem, and the bow for war shall be broken, and he shall speak peace to the Gentiles, and his power shall be from sea to sea and from the rivers even to the end of the earth.

11 Thou also by the blood of thy testament hast sent forth thy prisoners out of the pit wherein is no water. 12 Return to the stronghold, ye prisoners of hope; I will render thee double as I declare *today,* 13 because I have bent Judah for me as a bow; I have filled Ephraim. And I will raise up thy sons, O Zion, above thy sons, O Greece, and I will make thee as the sword of the mighty.

14 And the Lord God shall be seen over them, and his dart shall go forth as lightning, and the Lord God will sound the trumpet and go in the whirlwind of the south. 15 The Lord of hosts will protect them, and they shall devour and subdue with the stones of the sling, and drinking they shall be inebriated as it were with wine, and they shall be filled as bowls and as the horns of the altar. 16 And the Lord, their God, will save them in that day as the flock of his people, for holy stones shall be lifted up over his land. 17 For what is the good thing of him, and what is his beautiful thing, but the corn of the elect and wine springing forth virgins?

Caput 10

Petite a Domino pluviam in tempore serotino, et Dominus faciet nives et pluviam imbris dabit eis, singulis herbam in agro. 2 Quia simulacra locuta sunt inutile, et divini viderunt mendacium, et somniatores frustra locuti sunt; vane consolabantur. Idcirco abducti sunt quasi grex; adfligentur quia non est eis pastor.

3 Super pastores iratus est furor meus, et super hircos visitabo, quia visitavit Dominus exercituum gregem suum, domum Iuda, et posuit eos quasi equum gloriae suae in bello. 4 Ex ipso angulus, ex ipso paxillus, ex ipso arcus proelii, ex ipso egredietur omnis exactor simul. 5 Et erunt quasi fortes conculcantes lutum viarum in proelio, et bellabunt quia Dominus cum eis, et confundentur ascensores equorum.

6 "Et confortabo domum Iuda et domum Ioseph salvabo, et convertam eos quia miserebor eorum, et erunt sicut fuerunt quando non proieceram eos, ego enim Dominus, Deus eorum, et exaudiam eos. 7 Et erunt quasi fortes Ephraim, et laetabitur cor eorum quasi a vino, et filii eorum videbunt et laetabuntur, et exultabit cor eorum in Domino.

Chapter 10

God is to be sought to and not idols. The victories of his church which shall arise originally from the Jewish nation.

Ask ye of the Lord rain in the latter season, and the Lord will make snows and will give them showers of rain, to every one grass in the field. 2 For the idols have spoken what was unprofitable, and the diviners have seen a lie, and the dreamers have spoken vanity; they comforted in vain. Therefore they were led away as a flock; they shall be afflicted because they have no shepherd.

3 My wrath is kindled against the shepherds, and I will visit upon the buck-goats, for the Lord of hosts hath visited his flock, the house of Judah, and hath made them as the horse of his glory in the battle. 4 Out of him shall come forth the corner, out of him the pin, out of him the bow of battle, out of him every exacter together. 5 And they shall be as mighty men treading under foot the mire of the ways in battle, and they shall fight because the Lord is with them, and the riders of horses shall be confounded.

6 "And I will strengthen the house of Judah and save the house of Joseph, and I will bring them back again because I will have mercy on them, and they shall be as they were when I had cast them off, for I am the Lord, their God, and will hear them. 7 And they shall be as the valiant men of Ephraim, and their heart shall rejoice as through wine, and their children shall see and shall rejoice, and their heart shall be joyful in the Lord.

8 "Sibilabo eis, et congregabo illos quia redemi eos, et multiplicabo eos sicut ante fuerant multiplicati. 9 Et seminabo eos in populis, et de longe recordabuntur mei, et vivent cum filiis suis et revertentur. 10 Et reducam eos de terra Aegypti et de Assyriis congregabo eos et ad terram Galaad et Libani adducam eos, et non invenietur eis locus. 11 Et transibit in maris freto et percutiet in mari fluctus, et confundentur omnia profunda fluminis, et humiliabitur superbia Assur, et sceptrum Aegypti recedet. 12 Confortabo eos in Domino, et in nomine eius ambulabunt," dicit Dominus.

Caput 11

Aperi, Libane, portas tuas, et comedat ignis cedros tuas. 2 Ulula, abies, quia cecidit cedrus, quoniam magnifici vastati sunt. Ululate, quercus Basan, quoniam succisus est saltus munitus. 3 Vox ululatus pastorum, quia vastata est magnificentia eorum; vox rugitus leonum, quoniam vastata est superbia Iordanis.

8 "I will whistle for them, and I will gather them together because I have redeemed them, and I will multiply them as they were multiplied before. 9 And I will sow them among peoples, and from afar they shall remember me, and they shall live with their children and shall return. 10 And I will bring them back out of the land of Egypt and will gather them from among the Assyrians and will bring them to the land of Gilead and Lebanon, and place shall not be found for them. 11 And he shall pass over the strait of the sea and shall strike the waves in the sea, and all the depths of the river shall be confounded, and the pride of Assyria shall be humbled, and the sceptre of Egypt shall depart. 12 I will strengthen them in the Lord, and they shall walk in his name," saith the Lord.

Chapter 11

The destruction of Jerusalem and the temple. God's dealings with the Jews and their reprobation.

Open thy gates, O Lebanon, and let fire devour thy cedars. 2 Howl, thou fir tree, for the cedar is fallen, for the *mighty* are laid waste. Howl, ye oaks of Bashan, because the fenced forest is cut down. 3 The voice of the howling of the shepherds, because their glory is laid waste; the voice of the roaring of the lions, because the pride of the Jordan is spoiled.

4 Haec dicit Dominus, Deus meus: "Pasce pecora occisionis, 5 quae qui possederant occidebant et non dolebant, et vendebant ea, dicentes, 'Benedictus Dominus; divites facti sumus,' et pastores eorum non parcebant eis.

6 "Et ego non parcam ultra super habitantes terram," dicit Dominus. "Ecce: ego tradam homines, unumquemque in manu proximi sui et in manu regis sui, et concident terram, et non eruam de manu eorum."

7 Et pascam pecus occisionis propter hoc, O pauperes gregis. Et adsumpsi mihi duas virgas; unam vocavi Decorem, et alteram vocavi Funiculum, et pavi gregem. 8 Et succidi tres pastores in mense uno, et contracta est anima mea in eis, siquidem et anima eorum variavit in me.

9 Et dixi, "Non pascam vos. Quod moritur, moriatur, et quod succiditur, succidatur, et reliqui vorent unusquisque carnem proximi sui." 10 Et tuli virgam meam quae vocabatur Decus, et abscidi eam ut irritum facerem foedus meum quod percussi cum omnibus populis. 11 Et in irritum deductum est in die illa, et cognoverunt sic pauperes gregis qui custodiunt mihi quia verbum Domini est.

12 Et dixi ad eos, "Si bonum est in oculis vestris, adferte mercedem meam, et si non, quiescite." Et adpenderunt mercedem meam triginta argenteos.

13 Et dixit Dominus ad me, "Proice illud ad statuarium"— decorum pretium quo adpretiatus sum ab eis. Et tuli triginta argenteos, et proieci illos in domum Domini ad statuarium. 14 Et praecidi virgam meam secundam quae appellabatur Funiculus, ut dissolverem germanitatem inter Iudam et Israhel.

15 Et dixit Dominus ad me, "Adhuc sume tibi vasa pastoris

4 Thus saith the Lord, my God: "Feed the flock of the slaughter, 5 which they that possessed slew and repented not, and they sold them, saying, 'Blessed be the Lord; we are become rich,' and their shepherds spared them not.

6 "And I will no more spare the inhabitants of the land," saith the Lord. "Behold: I will deliver the men, every one into his neighbour's hand and into the hand of his king, and they shall destroy the land, and I will not deliver it out of their hand."

7 And I will feed the flock of slaughter for this, O ye poor of the flock. And I took unto me two rods; one I called Beauty, and the other I called a Cord, and I fed the flock. 8 And I cut off three shepherds in one month, and my soul was straitened in their regard, for their soul also varied in my regard.

9 And I said, "I will not feed you. That which dieth, let it die, and that which is cut off, let it be cut off, and let the rest devour every one the flesh of his neighbour." 10 And I took my rod that was called Beauty, and I cut it asunder to make void my covenant which I had made with all people. 11 And it was made void in that day, and so the poor of the flock that keep for me understood that it is the word of the Lord.

12 And I said to them, "If it be good in your eyes, bring hither my wages, and if not, be quiet." And they weighed for my wages thirty pieces of silver.

13 And the Lord said to me, "Cast it to the statuary"—a handsome price that I was prized at by them. And I took the thirty pieces of silver, and I cast them into the house of the Lord to the statuary. 14 And I cut off my second rod that was called a Cord, that I might break the brotherhood between Judah and Israel.

15 And the Lord said to me, "Take to thee yet the instru-

stulti, 16 quia ecce: ego suscitabo pastorem in terra qui derelicta non visitabit, dispersum non quaeret et contritum non
sanabit et id quod stat non enutriet, et carnes pinguium
comedet et ungulas eorum dissolvet. 17 O pastor et idolum
derelinquens gregem, gladius super brachium eius et super
oculum dextrum eius; brachium eius ariditate siccabitur, et
oculus dexter eius tenebrescens obscurabitur."

Caput 12

Onus verbi Domini super Israhel.

Dicit Dominus, extendens caelum et fundans terram et
fingens spiritum hominis in eo: 2 "Ecce: ego ponam Hierusalem superliminare crapulae omnibus populis in circuitu, sed
et Iuda erit in obsidione contra Hierusalem, 3 et erit in die
illa ponam Hierusalem lapidem oneris cunctis populis; omnes qui levabunt eam concisione lacerabuntur, et colligentur
adversum eam omnia regna terrae. 4 In die illa," dicit Dominus, "percutiam omnem equum in stuporem et ascensorem
eius in amentiam, et super domum Iuda aperiam oculos
meos et omnem equum populorum percutiam caecitate.

ments of a foolish shepherd, 16 for behold: I will raise up a shepherd in the land who shall not visit what is forsaken *nor* seek what is scattered nor heal what is broken, nor nourish that which standeth, and he shall eat the flesh of the fat ones and break their hoofs. 17 O shepherd and idol that forsaketh the flock, the sword upon his arm and upon his right eye; his arm shall *quite* wither away, and his right eye shall be *utterly* darkened."

Chapter 12

God shall protect his church against her persecutors. The mourning of Jerusalem.

The burden of the word of the Lord upon Israel.

Thus saith the Lord, who stretcheth forth the heavens and layeth the foundations of the earth and formeth the spirit of man in him: 2 "Behold: I will make Jerusalem a lintel of surfeiting to all the people round about, and Judah also shall be in the siege against Jerusalem, 3 and it shall come to pass in that day that I will make Jerusalem a burdensome stone to all people; all that shall lift it up shall be rent and torn, and all the kingdoms of the earth shall be gathered together against her. 4 In that day," saith the Lord, "I will strike every horse with astonishment and his rider with madness, and I will open my eyes upon the house of Judah and will strike every horse of the nations with blindness.

5 "Et dicent duces Iuda in corde suo, 'Confortentur mihi habitatores Hierusalem in Domino exercituum, Deo eorum.' 6 In die illa ponam duces Iuda sicut caminum ignis in lignis et sicut facem ignis in faeno, et devorabunt ad dextram et ad sinistram omnes populos in circuitu, et habitabitur Hierusalem rursum in loco suo in Hierusalem.

7 "Et salvabit Dominus tabernacula Iuda sicut in principio, ut non magnifice glorietur domus David et gloria habitantium Hierusalem contra Iudam. 8 In die illa proteget Dominus habitatores Hierusalem, et erit qui offenderit ex eis in die illa quasi David et domus David, quasi Dei, sicut angelus Domini in conspectu eorum. 9 Et erit in die illa quaeram conterere omnes gentes quae veniunt contra Hierusalem.

10 "Et effundam super domum David et super habitatores Hierusalem spiritum gratiae et precum, et aspicient ad me quem confixerunt, et plangent eum planctu quasi super unigenitum, et dolebunt super eum ut doleri solet in morte primogeniti. 11 In die illa magnus erit planctus in Hierusalem sicut planctus Adadremmon in campo Mageddon. 12 Et planget terra, familiae et familiae seorsum: familiae domus David seorsum et mulieres eorum seorsum, 13 familiae domus Nathan seorsum et mulieres eorum seorsum, familiae domus Levi seorsum et mulieres eorum seorsum, familiae Semei seorsum et mulieres eorum seorsum, 14 omnes familiae reliquae, familiae et familiae seorsum et mulieres eorum seorsum."

5 "And the governors of Judah shall say in their heart, 'Let the inhabitants of Jerusalem be strengthened for me in the Lord of hosts, their God.' 6 In that day I will make the governors of Judah like a furnace of fire amongst wood and as a firebrand amongst hay, and they shall devour all the people round about to the right hand and to the left, and Jerusalem shall be inhabited again in her own place in Jerusalem.

7 "And the Lord shall save the tabernacles of Judah as in the beginning, that the house of David and the glory of the inhabitants of Jerusalem may not boast *and magnify themselves* against Judah. 8 In that day shall the Lord protect the inhabitants of Jerusalem, and he that hath offended among them in that day shall be as David and the house of David, as that of God, as an angel of the Lord in their sight. 9 And it shall come to pass in that day that I will seek to destroy all the nations that come against Jerusalem.

10 "And I will pour out upon the house of David and upon the inhabitants of Jerusalem the spirit of grace and of prayers, and they shall look upon me whom they have pierced, and they shall mourn for him as one mourneth for an only son, and they shall grieve over him as the manner is to grieve for the death of the firstborn. 11 In that day there shall be a great lamentation in Jerusalem like the lamentation of Hadad-rimmon in the plain of Megiddo. 12 And the land shall mourn, families and families apart: the families of the house of David apart and their women apart, 13 the families of the house of Nathan apart and their women apart, the families of the house of Levi apart and their women apart, the families of Shimei apart and their women apart, 14 all the rest of the families, families and families apart and their women apart."

Caput 13

"In die illa erit fons patens domui David et habitantibus Hierusalem in ablutionem peccatoris et menstruatae. 2 Et erit in die illa," dicit Dominus exercituum, "disperdam nomina idolorum de terra, et non memorabuntur ultra, et pseudoprophetas et spiritum inmundum auferam de terra. 3 Et erit cum prophetaverit quispiam ultra, dicent ei pater eius et mater eius qui genuerunt eum, 'Non vives, quia mendacium locutus es in nomine Domini.' Et configent eum pater eius et mater eius, genitores eius, cum prophetaverit.

4 "Et erit in die illa confundentur prophetae, unusquisque ex visione sua cum prophetaverit, nec operientur pallio saccino ut mentiantur, 5 sed dicet, 'Non sum propheta; homo agricola ego sum, quoniam Adam exemplum meum ab adulescentia mea.'

6 "Et dicetur ei, 'Quid sunt plagae istae in medio manuum tuarum?'

"Et dicet, 'His plagatus sum in domo eorum qui diligebant me.'

7 "Framea, suscitare super pastorem meum et super virum coherentem mihi," dicit Dominus exercituum. "Percute

Chapter 13

The fountain of Christ. Idols and false prophets shall be extirpated. Christ shall suffer. His people shall be tried by fire.

"In that day there shall be a fountain open to the house of David and to the inhabitants of Jerusalem for the washing of the sinner and of the unclean woman. 2 And it shall come to pass in that day," saith the Lord of hosts, "that I will destroy the names of idols out of the earth, and they shall be remembered no more, and I will take away the false prophets and the unclean spirit out of the earth. 3 And it shall come to pass that when any man shall prophesy any more, his father and his mother that brought him *into the world* shall say to him, 'Thou shalt not live, because thou hast spoken a lie in the name of the Lord.' And his father and his mother, his parents, shall thrust him through when he shall prophesy.

4 "And it shall come to pass in that day that the prophets shall be confounded, every one by his own vision when he shall prophesy, neither shall they be clad with a garment of sackcloth to deceive, 5 but he shall say, 'I am no prophet; I am a husbandman, for Adam is my example from my youth.'

6 "And they shall say to him, 'What are these wounds in the midst of thy hands?'

"And he shall say, 'With these I was wounded in the house of them that loved me.'

7 "Awake, O sword, against my shepherd and against the man that cleaveth to me," saith the Lord of hosts. "Strike

pastorem, et dispergentur oves, et convertam manum meam ad parvulos. 8 Et erunt in omni terra," dicit Dominus, "partes duae in ea disperdentur et deficient, et tertia pars relinquetur in ea. 9 Et ducam tertiam partem per ignem et uram eos sicut uritur argentum, et probabo eos sicut probatur aurum. Ipse vocabit nomen meum, et ego exaudiam eum. Dicam, 'Populus meus es,' et ipse dicet, 'Dominus Deus meus.'"

Caput 14

Ecce: venient dies Domini, et dividentur spolia tua in medio tui.

2 Et congregabo omnes gentes ad Hierusalem in proelium, et capietur civitas, et vastabuntur domus, et mulieres violabuntur, et egredietur media pars civitatis in captivitatem, et reliquum populi non auferetur ex urbe. 3 Et egredietur Dominus et proeliabitur contra gentes illas sicut proeliatus est in die certaminis. 4 Et stabunt pedes eius in die illa super Montem Olivarum, qui est contra Hierusalem ad orientem, et scindetur Mons Olivarum ex media parte sui ad

the shepherd, and the sheep shall be scattered, and I will turn my hand to the little ones. 8 And there shall be in all the earth," saith the Lord, "two parts in it shall be *scattered* and shall perish, *but* the third part shall be left therein. 9 And I will bring the third part through the fire and will *refine* them as silver is *refined,* and I will try them as gold is tried. They shall call on my name, and I will hear them. I will say, 'Thou art my people,' and they shall say, 'The Lord is my God.'"

Chapter 14

After the persecutions of the church shall follow great prosperity. Persecutors shall be punished; so shall all that will not serve God in his church.

Behold: the days of the Lord shall come, and thy spoils shall be divided in the midst of thee.

2 And I will gather all nations to Jerusalem to battle, and the city shall be taken, and the houses shall be rifled, and the women shall be defiled, and half of the city shall go forth into captivity, and the rest of the people shall not be taken away out of the city. 3 Then the Lord shall go forth and shall fight against those nations as when he fought in the day of battle. 4 And his feet shall stand in that day upon the Mount of Olives, which is over against Jerusalem toward the east, and the Mount of Olives shall be divided *in the midst* thereof

orientem et ad occidentem praerupto grandi valde, et separabitur medium montis ad aquilonem, et medium eius ad meridiem. 5 Et fugietis ad vallem montium eorum, quoniam coniungetur vallis montium usque ad proximum, et fugietis sicut fugistis a facie terraemotus in diebus Oziae, regis Iuda, et veniet Dominus, Deus meus, omnesque sancti cum eo.

6 Et erit in die illa non erit lux, sed frigus et gelu. 7 Et erit dies una quae nota est Domino, non dies neque nox, et in tempore vesperae erit lux. 8 Et erit in die illa exibunt aquae vivae de Hierusalem: medium earum ad mare orientale et medium earum ad mare novissimum; in aestate et in hieme erunt. 9 Et erit Dominus rex super omnem terram; in die illa erit Dominus unus, et erit nomen eius unum.

10 Et revertetur omnis terra usque ad desertum, de colle Remmon ad austrum Hierusalem, et exaltabitur et habitabit in loco suo a porta Beniamin usque ad locum portae prioris et usque ad portam angulorum et a turre Ananehel usque ad torcularia regis. 11 Et habitabunt in ea, et anathema non erit amplius, sed sedebit Hierusalem secura.

12 Et haec erit plaga qua percutiet Dominus omnes gentes quae pugnaverunt adversus Hierusalem: tabescet caro uniuscuiusque stantis super pedes suos, et oculi eius contabescent in foraminibus suis, et lingua eorum contabescet in ore suo. 13 In die illa erit tumultus Domini magnus in eis, et

to the east and to the west with a very great opening, and half of the mountain shall be separated to the north, and half thereof to the south. 5 And you shall flee to the valley of those mountains, for the valley of the mountains shall be joined even to the next, and you shall flee as you fled from the face of the earthquake in the days of Uzziah, king of Judah, and the Lord, my God, shall come, and all the saints with him.

6 And it shall come to pass in that day that there shall be no light, but cold and frost. 7 And there shall be one day which is known to the Lord, not day nor night, and in the time of the evening there shall be light. 8 And it shall come to pass in that day that living waters shall go out from Jerusalem: half of them to the east sea, and half of them to the last sea; they shall be in summer and in winter. 9 And the Lord shall be king over all the earth; in that day there shall be one Lord, and his name shall be one.

10 And all the land shall return even to the desert, from the hill *to* Rimmon to the south of Jerusalem, and she shall be exalted and shall dwell in her own place from the gate of Benjamin even to the place of the former gate and even to the gate of the corners and from the tower of Hananel even to the king's winepresses. 11 And *people* shall dwell in it, and there shall be no more an anathema, but Jerusalem shall sit secure.

12 And this shall be the plague wherewith the Lord shall strike all nations that have fought against Jerusalem: the flesh of every one shall consume away while they stand upon their feet, and their eyes shall consume away in their holes, and their tongue shall consume away in their mouth. 13 In that day there shall be a great tumult from the Lord among

adprehendet vir manum proximi sui, et conseretur manus eius super manum proximi sui. 14 Sed et Iudas pugnabit adversus Hierusalem, et congregabuntur divitiae omnium gentium in circuitu: aurum et argentum et vestes multae satis. 15 Et sic erit ruina equi et muli et cameli et asini et omnium iumentorum quae fuerint in castris illis sicut ruina haec.

16 Et omnes qui reliqui fuerint de universis gentibus quae venerunt contra Hierusalem ascendent ab anno in annum ut adorent Regem, Dominum exercituum, et celebrent festivitatem tabernaculorum. 17 Et erit qui non ascenderit de familiis terrae ad Hierusalem ut adoret Regem, Dominum exercituum; non erit super eos imber. 18 Quod et si familia Aegypti non ascenderit et non venerit, nec super eos erit, sed erit ruina qua percutiet Dominus omnes gentes quae non ascenderint ad celebrandam festivitatem tabernaculorum. 19 Hoc erit peccatum Aegypti, et hoc peccatum omnium gentium quae non ascenderint ad celebrandam festivitatem tabernaculorum.

20 In die illa erit quod super frenum equi est sanctum Domino, et erunt lebetes in domo Domini quasi fialae coram altari. 21 Et erit omnis lebes in Hierusalem et Iuda sanctificatus Domino exercituum, et venient omnes immolantes et sument ex eis et coquent in eis, et non erit mercator ultra in domo Domini exercituum in die illo.

them, and a man shall take the hand of his neighbour, and his hand shall be clasped upon his neighbour's hand. 14 And even Judah shall fight against Jerusalem, and the riches of all nations round about shall be gathered together: gold and silver and garments in great abundance. 15 And the destruction of the horse and of the mule and of the camel and of the ass and of all the beasts that shall be in those tents shall be like this destruction.

16 And all they that shall be left of all nations that came against Jerusalem shall go up from year to year to adore the King, the Lord of hosts, and to keep the feast of tabernacles. 17 And it shall come to pass that he that shall not go up of the families of the land to Jerusalem to adore the King, the Lord of hosts; there shall be no rain upon them. 18 *And* if the family of Egypt go not up nor come, neither shall it be upon them, but there shall be destruction wherewith the Lord will strike all nations that will not go up to keep the feast of tabernacles. 19 This shall be the sin of Egypt, and this the sin of all nations that will not go up to keep the feast of tabernacles.

20 In that day that which is upon the bridle of the horse shall be holy to the Lord, and the caldrons in the house of the Lord shall be as the bowls before the altar. 21 And every caldron in Jerusalem and Judah shall be sanctified to the Lord of hosts, and all that sacrifice shall come and take of them and shall seethe in them, and the merchant shall be no more in the house of the Lord of hosts in that day.

MALACHI

Caput 1

Onus verbi Domini ad Israhel in manu Malachi.

2 "Dilexi vos," dicit Dominus, "et dixistis, 'In quo dilexisti nos?' Nonne frater erat Esau Iacob," dicit Dominus, "et dilexi Iacob, 3 Esau autem odio habui? Et posui montes eius in solitudinem et hereditatem eius in dracones deserti. 4 Quod si dixerit Idumea, 'Destructi sumus, sed revertentes aedificabimus quae destructa sunt,' haec dicit Dominus exercituum: 'Isti aedificabunt, et ego destruam, et vocabuntur termini impietatis et populus cui iratus est Dominus usque in aeternum. 5 Et oculi vestri videbunt, et vos dicetis, "Magnificetur Dominus super terminum Israhel."'

6 "'Filius honorat patrem, et servus dominum suum; si ergo pater ego sum, ubi est honor meus? Et si dominus ego

Chapter 1

God reproaches the Jews with their ingratitude and the priests for not offering pure sacrifices. He will accept of the sacrifice that shall be offered in every place among the Gentiles.

The burden of the word of the Lord to Israel by the hand of Malachi.

2 "I have loved you," saith the Lord, "and you have said, 'Wherein hast thou loved us?' Was not Esau brother to Jacob," saith the Lord, "and I have loved Jacob, 3 but have hated Esau? And I have made his mountains a wilderness and *given* his inheritance to the dragons of the desert. 4 But if Edom shall say, 'We are destroyed, but we will return and build up what hath been destroyed,' thus saith the Lord of hosts: 'They shall build up, and I will throw down, and they shall be called the borders of wickedness and the people with whom the Lord is angry for ever. 5 And your eyes shall see, and you shall say, "The Lord be magnified upon the border of Israel."'

6 "'The son honoureth the father, and the servant his master; if then I be a father, where is my honour? And if I be

sum, ubi est timor meus?' dicit Dominus exercituum ad vos, O sacerdotes, qui despicitis nomen meum et dixistis, 'In quo despeximus nomen tuum?' 7 Offertis super altare meum panem pollutum, et dicitis, 'In quo polluimus te?' In eo quod dicitis, 'Mensa Domini despecta est.' 8 Si offeratis caecum ad immolandum, nonne malum est? Et si offeratis claudum et languidum, nonne malum est? Offer illud duci tuo, si placuerit ei aut si susceperit faciem tuam," dicit Dominus exercituum.

9 "Et nunc deprecamini vultum Dei ut misereatur vestri (de manu enim vestra factum est hoc), si quo modo suscipiat facies vestras," dicit Dominus exercituum. 10 "Quis est in vobis qui claudat ostia et incendat altare meum gratuito? Non est mihi voluntas in vobis," dicit Dominus exercituum, "et munus non suscipiam de manu vestra. 11 Ab ortu enim solis usque ad occasum magnum est nomen meum in Gentibus, et in omni loco sacrificatur, et offertur nomini meo oblatio munda, quia magnum est nomen meum in Gentibus," dicit Dominus exercituum. 12 "Et vos polluistis illud in eo quod dicitis, 'Mensa Domini contaminata est, et quod superponitur contemptibile est cum igni qui illud devorat.' 13 Et dixistis, 'Ecce de labore,' et exsuflastis illud," dicit Dominus exercituum, "et intulistis de rapinis claudum et languidum et intulistis munus; numquid suscipiam illud de manu vestra?" dicit Dominus. 14 "Maledictus dolosus qui habet in grege suo masculum et votum faciens immolat debile Domino, quia Rex magnus ego," dicit Dominus exercituum, "et nomen meum horribile in Gentibus."

a master, where is my fear?' saith the Lord of hosts to you, O priests, that despise my name and have said, 'Wherein have we despised thy name?' 7 You offer polluted bread upon my altar, and you say, 'Wherein have we polluted thee?' In that you say, 'The table of the Lord is contemptible.' 8 If you offer the blind for sacrifice, is it not evil? And if you offer the lame and the sick, is it not evil? Offer it to thy prince, if he will be pleased with it or if he will regard thy face," saith the Lord of hosts.

9 "And now beseech ye the face of God that he may have mercy on you (for by your hand hath this been done), if by any means he will receive your faces," saith the Lord of hosts. 10 "Who is there among you that will shut the doors and will kindle the fire on my altar for nought? I have no pleasure in you," saith the Lord of hosts, "and I will not receive a gift of your hand. 11 For from the rising of the sun even to the going down my name is great among the Gentiles, and in every place there is sacrifice, and there is offered to my name a clean oblation, for my name is great among the Gentiles," saith the Lord of hosts. 12 "And you have profaned it in that you say, 'The table of the Lord is defiled, and that which is laid thereupon is contemptible with the fire that devoureth it.' 13 And you have said, 'Behold of our labour,' and you puffed it away," saith the Lord of hosts, "and you brought in of rapine the lame and the sick and brought in an offering; shall I accept it at your hands?" saith the Lord. 14 "Cursed is the deceitful man that hath in his flock a male and making a vow offereth in sacrifice that which is feeble to the Lord, for I am a great King," saith the Lord of hosts, "and my name is dreadful among the Gentiles."

Caput 2

"Et nunc ad vos mandatum hoc, O sacerdotes. 2 Si nolueritis audire et si nolueritis ponere super cor ut detis gloriam nomini meo," ait Dominus exercituum, "mittam in vos
egestatem et maledicam benedictionibus vestris, et maledicam illis quoniam non posuistis super cor. 3 Ecce: ego proiciam vobis brachium, et dispergam super vultum vestrum
stercus sollemnitatum vestrarum, et adsumet vos secum.

4 "Et scietis quia misi ad vos mandatum istud ut esset pactum meum cum Levi," dicit Dominus exercituum. 5 "Pactum
meum fuit cum eo vitae et pacis, et dedi ei timorem, et timuit me, et a facie nominis mei pavebat. 6 Lex veritatis fuit
in ore eius, et iniquitas non est inventa in labiis eius; in pace
et in aequitate ambulavit mecum et multos avertit ab iniquitate. 7 Labia enim sacerdotis custodient scientiam, et legem
requirent ex ore eius, quia angelus Domini exercituum est.
8 Vos autem recessistis de via et scandalizastis plurimos in
lege; irritum fecistis pactum Levi," dicit Dominus exercituum. 9 "Propter quod et ego dedi vos contemptibiles et
humiles omnibus populis, sicut non servastis vias meas et
accepistis faciem in lege."

Chapter 2

The priests are sharply reproved for neglecting their covenant. The evil of marrying with idolaters and too easily putting away their wives.

"And now, O ye priests, this commandment is to you. 2 If you will not hear and if you will not lay it to heart to give glory to my name," saith the Lord of hosts, "I will send poverty upon you and will curse your blessings, *yea* I will curse them because you have not laid it to heart. 3 Behold: I will cast the shoulder to you, and I will scatter upon your face the dung of your solemnities, and it shall take you away with it.

4 "And you shall know that I sent you this commandment that my covenant might be with Levi," saith the Lord of hosts. 5 "My covenant was with him of life and peace, and I gave him fear, and he feared me, and he was afraid before my name. 6 The law of truth was in his mouth, and iniquity was not found in his lips; he walked with me in peace and in equity and turned many away from iniquity. 7 For the lips of the priest shall keep knowledge, and they shall seek the law at his mouth, because he is the angel of the Lord of hosts. 8 But you have departed out of the way and have caused many to stumble at the law; you have made void the covenant of Levi," saith the Lord of hosts. 9 "Therefore have I also made you contemptible and base before all people, as you have not kept my ways and have accepted persons in the law."

10 Numquid non pater unus omnium nostrum? Numquid non Deus unus creavit nos? Quare ergo despicit unusquisque nostrum fratrem suum, violans pactum patrum nostrorum? 11 Transgressus est Iuda, et abominatio facta est in Israhel et in Hierusalem, quia contaminavit Iudas sanctificationem Domini, quam dilexit, et habuit filiam dei alieni. 12 Disperdet Dominus virum qui fecerit hoc, magistrum et discipulum, de tabernaculis Iacob, et offerentem munus Domino exercituum.

13 "Et hoc rursum fecistis: operiebatis lacrimis altare Domini, fletu et mugitu, ita ut ultra non respiciam ad sacrificium, nec accipiam placabile quid de manu vestra. 14 Et dixistis, 'Quam ob causam?' Quia Dominus testificatus est inter te et uxorem pubertatis tuae, quam tu despexisti, et haec particeps tua et uxor foederis tui. 15 Nonne unus fecit, et residuum spiritus eius est? Et quid unus quaerit nisi semen Dei? Custodite ergo spiritum vestrum, et uxorem adulescentiae tuae noli despicere. 16 Cum odio habueris, dimitte," dicit Dominus, Deus Israhel, "operiet autem iniquitas vestimentum eius," dicit Dominus exercituum. "Custodite spiritum vestrum, et nolite despicere."

17 Laborare fecistis Dominum in sermonibus vestris, et dixistis, "In quo eum fecimus laborare?" In eo quod dicitis, "Omnis qui facit malum bonus est in conspectu Domini, et tales ei placent, aut certe ubi est Deus iudicii?"

10 Have we not all one father? Hath not one God created us? Why then doth every one of us despise his brother, violating the covenant of our fathers? 11 Judah hath transgressed, and abomination hath been committed in Israel and in Jerusalem, for Judah hath profaned the holiness of the Lord, which he loved, and hath married the daughter of a strange god. 12 The Lord will cut off the man that hath done this, both the master and the scholar, out of the tabernacles of Jacob, and him that offereth an offering to the Lord of hosts.

13 "And this again have you done: you have covered the altar of the Lord with tears, with weeping and bellowing, so that I have no more a regard to sacrifice, neither do I accept any atonement at your hands. 14 And you have said, 'For what cause?' Because the Lord hath been witness between thee and the wife of thy youth, whom thou hast despised, *yet* she was thy partner and the wife of thy covenant. 15 Did not one make her, and she is the residue of his spirit? And what doth one seek but the seed of God? Keep then your spirit, and despise not the wife of thy youth. 16 When thou shalt hate her, put her away," saith the Lord, the God of Israel, "but iniquity shall cover his garment," saith the Lord of hosts. "Keep your spirit, and despise not."

17 You have wearied the Lord with your words, and you said, "Wherein have we wearied him?" In that you say, "Every one that doth evil is good in the sight of the Lord, and such please him, or surely where is the God of judgment?"

Caput 3

"Ecce: ego mitto angelum meum, et praeparabit viam ante faciem meam. Et statim veniet ad templum suum Dominator, quem vos quaeritis, et angelus testamenti, quem vos vultis. Ecce: venit," dicit Dominus exercituum.

2 Et quis poterit cogitare diem adventus eius? Et quis stabit ad videndum eum? Ipse enim quasi ignis conflans et quasi herba fullonum, 3 et sedebit conflans et emundans argentum, et purgabit filios Levi et colabit eos quasi aurum et quasi argentum, et erunt Domino offerentes sacrificia in iustitia. 4 Et placebit Domino sacrificium Iuda et Hierusalem sicut dies saeculi et sicut anni antiqui.

5 "Et accedam ad vos in iudicio et ero testis velox maleficis et adulteris et periuris et qui calumniantur mercedem mercennarii, viduas et pupillos, et opprimunt peregrinum nec timuerunt me," dicit Dominus exercituum. 6 "Ego enim Dominus, et non mutor, et vos, filii Iacob, non estis consumpti. 7 A diebus enim patrum vestrorum recessistis a legitimis meis et non custodistis; revertimini ad me, et revertar ad vos," dicit Dominus exercituum. "Et dixistis, 'In quo

Chapter 3

Christ shall come to his temple and purify the priesthood.
They that continue in their evil ways shall be punished but
true penitents shall receive a blessing.

"Behold: I send my angel, and he shall prepare the way before my face. And presently the Lord, whom you seek, and the angel of the testament, whom you desire, shall come to his temple. Behold: he cometh," saith the Lord of hosts.

2 And who shall be able to think of the day of his coming? And who shall stand to see him? For he is like a refining fire and like the fullers' herb, 3 and he shall sit refining and cleansing the silver, and he shall purify the sons of Levi and shall refine them as gold and as silver, and they shall offer sacrifices to the Lord in justice. 4 And the sacrifice of Judah and of Jerusalem shall please the Lord as *in* the days of old and *in* the ancient years.

5 "And I will come to you in judgment and will be a speedy witness against sorcerers and adulterers and false swearers and them that oppress the *hireling in his wages,* the widows and the fatherless, and oppress the stranger and have not feared me," saith the Lord of hosts. 6 "For I am the Lord, and I change not, and you, the sons of Jacob, are not consumed. 7 For from the days of your fathers you have departed from my ordinances and have not kept them; return to me, and I will return to you," saith the Lord of hosts. "And you have

revertemur?' 8 Si adfiget homo Deum? Quia vos configitis me. Et dixistis, 'In quo configimus te?' In decimis et in primitiis. 9 Et in penuria vos maledicti estis, et me vos configitis, gens tota. 10 Inferte omnem decimam in horreum, et sit cibus in domo mea, et probate me super hoc," dicit Dominus, "si non aperuero vobis cataractas caeli et effudero vobis benedictionem usque ad abundantiam. 11 Et increpabo pro vobis devorantem, et non corrumpet fructum terrae vestrae, nec erit sterilis vinea in agro," dicit Dominus exercituum. 12 "Et beatos vos dicent omnes gentes, eritis enim vos terra desiderabilis," dicit Dominus exercituum.

13 "Invaluerunt super me verba vestra," dicit Dominus. 14 "Et dixistis, 'Quid locuti sumus contra te?' Dixistis, 'Vanus est qui servit Deo, et quod emolumentum quia custodivimus praecepta eius et quia ambulavimus tristes coram Domino exercituum? 15 Ergo nunc beatos dicimus arrogantes, siquidem aedificati sunt facientes impietatem, et temptaverunt Deum et salvi facti sunt.'"

16 Tunc locuti sunt timentes Dominum unusquisque cum proximo suo, et adtendit Dominus et audivit, et scriptus est liber monumenti coram eo timentibus Dominum et cogitantibus nomen eius.

17 "Et erunt mihi," ait Dominus exercituum, "in die qua ego facio in peculium, et parcam eis sicut parcit vir filio suo servienti sibi. 18 Et convertemini et videbitis quid sit inter iustum et impium et inter servientem Deo et non servientem ei."

said, 'Wherein shall we return?' 8 Shall a man *afflict* God? For you *afflict* me. And you have said, 'Wherein do we *afflict* thee?' In tithes and in firstfruits. 9 And you are cursed with want, and you *afflict* me, *even* the whole nation of you. 10 Bring all the tithes into the storehouse *that* there may be meat in my house, and try me in this," saith the Lord, "if I open not unto you the flood-gates of heaven and pour you out a blessing even to abundance. 11 And I will rebuke for your sakes the devourer, and he shall not spoil the fruit of your land, neither shall the vine in the field be barren," saith the Lord of hosts. 12 "And all nations shall call you blessed, for you shall be a delightful land," saith the Lord of hosts.

13 "Your words have been *unsufferable* to me," saith the Lord. 14 "And you have said, 'What have we spoken against thee?' You have said, 'He laboureth in vain that serveth God, and what profit is it that we have kept his ordinances and that we have walked sorrowful before the Lord of hosts? 15 Wherefore now we call the proud people happy, for they that work wickedness are built up, and they have tempted God and are preserved.'"

16 Then they that feared the Lord spoke every one with his neighbour, and the Lord gave ear and heard it, and a book of remembrance was written before him for them that fear the Lord and think on his name.

17 "And they shall be my *special possession,"* saith the Lord of hosts, "in the day of my *doing,* and I will spare them as a man spareth his son that serveth him. 18 And you shall return and shall see the difference between the just and the wicked and between him that serveth God and him that serveth him not."

Caput 4

"Ecce enim: dies veniet succensa quasi caminus, et erunt omnes superbi et omnes facientes impietatem stipula, et inflammabit eos dies veniens," dicit Dominus exercituum, "quae non relinquet eis radicem et germen. 2 Et orietur vobis timentibus nomen meum sol iustitiae, et sanitas in pinnis eius, et egrediemini et salietis sicut vituli de armento. 3 Et calcabitis impios cum fuerint cinis sub planta pedum vestrorum in die qua ego facio," dicit Dominus exercituum. 4 "Mementote legis Mosi, servi mei, quam mandavi ei in Choreb ad omnem Israhel, praecepta et iudicia.

5 "Ecce: ego mittam vobis Heliam, prophetam, antequam veniat dies Domini magnus et horribilis. 6 Et convertet cor patrum ad filios et cor filiorum ad patres eorum, ne forte veniam et percutiam terram anathemate."

Chapter 4

The judgment of the wicked and reward of the just. An exhortation to observe the law. Elijah shall come for the conversion of the Jews.

"For behold: the day shall come kindled as a furnace, and all the proud and all that do wickedly shall be stubble, and the day that cometh shall set them on fire," saith the Lord of hosts. "It shall not leave them root nor branch. 2 *But* unto you that fear my name the sun of justice shall arise, and health in his wings, and you shall go forth and shall leap like calves of the herd. 3 And you shall tread down the wicked when they shall be ashes under the sole of your feet in the day that I do this," saith the Lord of hosts. 4 "Remember the law of Moses, my servant, which I commanded him in Horeb for all Israel, the precepts and judgments.

5 "Behold: I will send you Elijah, the prophet, before the coming of the great and dreadful day of the Lord. 6 And he shall turn the heart of the fathers to the children and the heart of the children to their fathers, *lest* I come and strike the earth with anathema."

1 MACCABEES

Caput 1

Et factum est postquam percussit Alexander, filius Philippi, Macedo, qui primus regnavit in Graecia, egressus de terra Cetthim Darium, regem Persarum et Medorum, 2 constituit proelia multa et omnium obtinuit munitiones et interfecit reges terrae, 3 et pertransiit usque ad fines terrae et accepit spolia multitudinis gentium, et siluit terra in conspectu eius. 4 Et congregavit virtutem et exercitum fortem nimis, et exaltatum est et elevatum cor eius. 5 Et obtinuit regiones gentium et tyrannos, et facti sunt illi in tributum. 6 Et post haec decidit in lectum et cognovit quia moreretur.

7 Et vocavit pueros suos, nobiles qui secum erant nutriti a iuventute, et divisit illis regnum suum cum adhuc viveret. 8 Et regnavit Alexander annis duodecim, et mortuus est. 9 Et obtinuerunt pueri eius regnum, unusquisque in loco suo, 10 et inposuerunt sibi omnes diademata post mortem eius, et filii eorum post eos annis multis, et multiplicata sunt mala in terra.

Chapter 1

The reign of Alexander and his successors. Antiochus rifles
and profanes the temple of God and persecutes unto death
all that will not forsake the law of God and the religion of
their fathers.

Now it came to pass after that Alexander, the son of
Philip, the Macedonian, who first reigned in Greece, coming out of the land of Kittim had overthrown Darius, king of
the Persians and Medes, 2 he fought many battles and took
the strongholds of all and slew the kings of the earth, 3 and
he went through even to the ends of the earth and took the
spoils of many nations, and the earth was quiet before him.
4 And he gathered a power and a very strong army, and his
heart was exalted and lifted up. 5 And he subdued countries
of nations and princes, and they became tributaries to him.
6 And after these things he fell down upon his bed and knew
that he should die.

7 And he called his servants, the nobles that were brought
up with him from his youth, and he divided his kingdom
among them while he was yet alive. 8 And Alexander reigned
twelve years, and he died. 9 And his servants *made themselves
kings,* every one in his place, 10 and they all put crowns upon
themselves after his death, and their sons after them many
years, and evils were multiplied in the earth.

11 Et exiit ex eis radix peccatrix, Antiochus Inlustris, filius Antiochi Regis, qui fuerat Romae obses, et regnavit in anno centesimo tricesimo et septimo regni Graecorum. 12 In diebus illis exierunt ex Israhel filii iniqui, et suaserunt multis, dicentes, "Eamus et disponamus testamentum cum gentibus quae circa nos sunt, quia ex quo recessimus ab eis invenerunt nos multa mala." 13 Et bonus visus est sermo in oculis eorum. 14 Et destinaverunt aliqui de populo et abierunt ad regem, et dedit illis potestatem ut facerent iustitiam gentium. 15 Et aedificaverunt gymnasium in Hierosolymis secundum leges nationum, 16 et fecerunt sibi praeputia et recesserunt a testamento sancto et iuncti sunt nationibus et venundati sunt ut facerent malum.

17 Et paratum est regnum in conspectu Antiochi, et coepit regnare in terra Aegypti, ut regnaret super duo regna. 18 Et intravit in Aegyptum in multitudine gravi, in curribus et elefantis et equitibus et copiosa navium multitudine, 19 et constituit bellum adversus Ptolomeum, regem Aegypti, et veritus est Ptolomeus a facie eius et fugit, et ceciderunt vulnerati multi. 20 Et conprehendit civitates munitas in terra Aegypti, et accepit spolia terrae Aegypti.

21 Et convertit Antiochus, postquam percussit Aegyptum in centesimo et quadragesimo et tertio anno, et ascendit ad Israhel. 22 Et ascendit Hierosolymam in multitudine gravi. 23 Et intravit in sanctificationem cum superbia et accepit altare aureum et candelabrum luminis et universa vasa eius et mensam propositionis et libatoria et fialas et mortariola

11 And there came out of them a wicked root, Antiochus the Illustrious, the son of King Antiochus, who had been a hostage at Rome, and he reigned in the hundred and thirty-seventh year of the kingdom of the Greeks. 12 In those days there went out of Israel wicked men, and they persuaded many, saying, "Let us go and make a covenant with the heathens that are round about us, for since we departed from them many evils have befallen us." 13 And the word seemed good in their eyes. 14 And some of the people determined to do this and went to the king, and he gave them license to do *after the ordinances* of the heathens. 15 And they built a place of exercise in Jerusalem according to the laws of the nations, 16 and they made themselves prepuces and departed from the holy covenant and joined themselves to the heathens and were sold to do evil.

17 And the kingdom was established before Antiochus, and he *had a mind* to reign over the land of Egypt, that he might reign over two kingdoms. 18 And he entered into Egypt with a great multitude, with chariots and elephants and horsemen and a great number of ships, 19 and he made war against Ptolemy, king of Egypt, *but* Ptolemy was afraid at his presence and fled, and many were wounded *unto death.* 20 And he took the strong cities in the land of Egypt, and he took the spoils of the land of Egypt.

21 And after Antiochus had ravaged Egypt in the hundred and forty-third year, he returned and went up against Israel. 22 And he went up to Jerusalem with a great multitude. 23 And he proudly entered into the sanctuary and took away the golden altar and the candlestick of light and all the vessels thereof and the table of proposition and the pouring vessels and the bowls and the little mortars of gold and the

aurea et velum et coronas et ornamentum aureum quod in facie templi erat, et comminuit omnia. 24 Et accepit argentum et aurum et vasa concupiscibilia, et accepit thesauros occultos quos invenit, et sublatis omnibus abiit in terram suam. 25 Et fecit caedem hominum et locutus est in superbia magna.

26 Et factus est planctus magnus in Israhel et in omni loco eorum. 27 Et ingemuerunt principes et seniores, et virgines et iuvenes infirmati sunt, et speciositas mulierum inmutata est. 28 Omnis maritus sumpsit lamentum, et quae sedebant in toro maritali lugebant. 29 Et commota est terra super habitantes in ea, et universa domus Iacob induit confusionem.

30 Et post duos annos dierum misit rex principem tributorum in civitates Iuda, et venit Hierusalem cum turba magna. 31 Et locutus est ad eos verba pacifica in dolo, et crediderunt ei. 32 Et inruit super civitatem repente et percussit eam plaga magna et perdidit populum multum ex Israhel. 33 Et accepit spolia civitatis et succendit eam igni et destruxit domos eius et muros eius in circuitu, 34 et captivas duxerunt mulieres et natos et pecora possederunt. 35 Et aedificaverunt civitatem David muro magno et firmo et turribus firmis et facta est illis in arcem, 36 et posuerunt illic gentem peccatricem, viros iniquos, et convaluerunt in ea, et posuerunt arma et escas et congregaverunt spolia Hierusalem 37 et reposuerunt illic, et facti sunt in laqueum magnum.

veil and the crowns and the golden ornament that was before the temple, and he broke them all in pieces. 24 And he took the silver and gold and the precious vessels, and he took the hidden treasures which he found, and when he had taken all away he departed into his own country. 25 And he made a great slaughter of men and spoke very proudly.

26 And there was great mourning in Israel and in every place *where they were.* 27 And the princes and the ancients mourned, and the virgins and the young men were made feeble, and the beauty of the women was changed. 28 Every bridegroom took up lamentation, and the *bride* that sat in the marriage bed mourned. 29 And the land was moved for the inhabitants thereof, and all the house of Jacob was covered with confusion.

30 And after two *full* years the king sent the chief *collector* of his tributes to the cities of Judah, and he came to Jerusalem with a great multitude. 31 And he spoke to them peaceable words in deceit, and they believed him. 32 And he fell upon the city suddenly and struck it with a great slaughter and destroyed much people in Israel. 33 And he took the spoils of the city and burnt it with fire and threw down the houses thereof and the walls thereof round about, 34 and they took the women captive and the children and the cattle they possessed. 35 And they built the city of David with a great and strong wall and with strong towers and made it a fortress for them, 36 and they placed there a sinful nation, wicked men, and they fortified *themselves* therein, and they stored up armour and victuals and gathered together the spoils of Jerusalem 37 and laid them up there, and they became a great snare.

38 Et factum est hoc ad insidias sanctificationi et in diabolum malum in Israhel. 39 Et effuderunt sanguinem innocentem per circuitum sanctificationis et contaminaverunt sanctificationem. 40 Et fugerunt habitatores Hierusalem propter eos, et facta est habitatio exterorum, et facta est extera semini suo, et nati eius reliquerunt eam. 41 Sanctificatio eius desolata est sicut solitudo; dies festi eius conversi sunt in luctum, sabbata eius in obprobrium, honores eius in nihilum. 42 Secundum gloriam eius multiplicata est ignominia eius, et sublimitas eius conversa est in luctum.

43 Et scripsit Rex Antiochus omni regno suo ut esset omnis populus unus et relinqueret unusquisque legem suam. 44 Et consenserunt omnes gentes secundum verbum Regis Antiochi. 45 Et multi ex Israhel consenserunt servituti eius, et sacrificaverunt idolis et coinquinaverunt sabbatum. 46 Et misit rex libros per manus nuntiorum in Hierusalem et in omnes civitates Iudae ut sequerentur legem gentium terrae 47 et prohiberent holocausta et sacrificia et placationes fieri in templo Dei 48 et prohiberent celebrari sabbatum et dies sollemnes. 49 Et iussit coinquinari sancta et sanctum populum Israhel. 50 Et iussit aedificari aras et templa et idola, et immolari carnes suillas et pecora communia, 51 et relinquere filios suos incircumcisos et coinquinari animas eorum in omnibus inmunditiis et abominationibus ita ut obliviscerentur legem et inmutarent omnes iustificationes Dei, 52 et quicumque non fecissent secundum verbum Regis Antiochi morerentur.

38 And this was *a place* to lie in wait against the sanctuary and an evil devil in Israel. 39 And they shed innocent blood round about the sanctuary and defiled the holy place. 40 And the inhabitants of Jerusalem fled away by reason of them, and the city was made the habitation of strangers, and she became a stranger to her own seed, and her children forsook her. 41 Her sanctuary was desolate like a wilderness; her festival days were turned into mourning, her sabbaths into reproach; her honours *were brought* to nothing. 42 Her dishonour was increased according to her glory, and her excellency was turned into mourning.

43 And King Antiochus wrote to all his kingdom that all the people should be one and every one should leave his own law. 44 And all nations consented according to the word of King Antiochus. 45 And many of Israel consented to his service, and they sacrificed to idols and profaned the sabbath. 46 And the king sent letters by the hands of messengers to Jerusalem and to all the cities of Judah that they should follow the law of the nations of the earth 47 and should forbid holocausts and sacrifices and atonements to be made in the temple of God 48 and should prohibit the sabbath and the festival days to be celebrated. 49 And he commanded the holy places to be profaned and the holy people of Israel. 50 And he commanded altars to be built and temples and idols, and swine's flesh to be immolated and *unclean* beasts, 51 and that they should leave their children uncircumcised and let their souls be defiled with all uncleannesses and abominations to the end that they should forget the law and should change all the justifications of God, 52 and that whosoever *would* not *do* according to the word of King Antiochus should be put to death.

53 Secundum omnia verba haec scripsit omni regno suo, et praeposuit principes populo qui haec fieri cogerent. 54 Et iusserunt civitatibus Iudae sacrificare. 55 Et congregati sunt multi de populo ad eos qui dereliquerant legem Domini, et fecerunt mala super terram, 56 et effugaverunt populum Israhel in abditis et in absconditis fugitivorum locis.

57 Die quintadecima mensis Casleu, quinto et quadragesimo centesimo anno, aedificavit Rex Antiochus abominandum idolum desolationis super altare Dei, et per universas civitates Iudae in circuitu aedificaverunt aras, 58 et ante ianuas domorum et in plateis incendebant tura et sacrificabant. 59 Et libros legis Dei conbuserunt igni, scindentes eos, 60 et apud quemcumque inveniebantur libri testamenti Domini et quicumque observabat legem Domini secundum edictum regis trucidabant eum. 61 In virtute sua faciebant haec populo Israhel qui inveniebatur in omni mense et mense in civitatibus.

62 Et quinta et vicesima die mensis sacrificabant super aram quae erat contra altare. 63 Et mulieres quae circumcidebant filios suos trucidabantur secundum iussum Regis Antiochi. 64 Et suspendebant pueros a cervicibus per universas domos eorum, et eos qui circumciderant eos trucidabant. 65 Et multi de populo Israhel definierunt apud se ut non manducarent inmunda, et elegerunt magis mori quam cibis coinquinari inmundis, 66 et noluerunt infringere legem Dei sanctam, et trucidati sunt. 67 Et facta est ira magna super populum valde.

⁵³ According to all these words he wrote to his whole kingdom, and he appointed rulers over the people that should force them to do these things. ⁵⁴ And they commanded the cities of Judah to sacrifice. ⁵⁵ Then many of the people were gathered to them that had forsaken the law of the Lord, and they committed evils in the land, ⁵⁶ and they drove away the people of Israel into lurking holes and into the secret places of fugitives.

⁵⁷ On the fifteenth day of the month Chislev, in the hundred and forty-fifth year, King Antiochus set up the abominable idol of desolation upon the altar of God, and they built altars throughout all the cities of Judah round about, ⁵⁸ and they burnt incense and sacrificed at the doors of the houses and in the streets. ⁵⁹ And they cut in pieces and burnt with fire the books of the law of God, ⁶⁰ and every one with whom the books of the testament of the Lord were found and whosoever observed the law of the Lord they put to death according to the edict of the king. ⁶¹ Thus by their power did they deal with the people of Israel that were found in the cities *month* after month.

⁶² And on the five and twentieth day of the month they sacrificed upon the altar of the idol that was over against the altar *of God.* ⁶³ Now the women that circumcised their children were slain according to the commandment of King Antiochus. ⁶⁴ And they hanged the children *about their* necks in all their houses, and those that had circumcised them they put to death. ⁶⁵ And many of the people of Israel determined with themselves that they would not eat unclean things, and they chose rather to die than to be defiled with unclean meats, ⁶⁶ and they would not break the holy law of God, and they were put to death. ⁶⁷ And there was very great wrath upon the people.

Caput 2

In illis diebus surrexit Matthathias, filius Iohannis, filii Simeonis, sacerdos ex filiis Ioarib, ab Hierusalem, et consedit in monte Modin. 2 Et habebat filios quinque: Iohannem, qui cognominabatur Gaddis, 3 et Simonem, qui cognominabatur Thasi, 4 et Iudam, qui vocabatur Macchabeus, 5 et Eleazarum, qui cognominabatur Abaron, et Ionathan, qui cognominabatur Apphus. 6 Hii viderunt mala quae fiebant in populo Iuda et in Hierusalem.

7 Et dixit Matthathias, "Vae mihi! Ut quid natus sum videre contritionem populi mei et contritionem civitatis sanctae et sedere illic cum datur in manibus inimicorum? 8 Sancta in manu extraneorum facta sunt; templum eius sicut homo ignobilis. 9 Vasa gloriae eius captiva abducta sunt; trucidati sunt senes eius in plateis, et iuvenes eius ceciderunt gladio inimicorum. 10 Quae gens non hereditavit regnum eius et non obtinuit spolia eius? 11 Omnis ornatus eius ablata est. Quae erat libera facta est ancilla. 12 Et ecce: sancta nostra et pulchritudo nostra et claritas nostra desolata est, et coinquinaverunt ea Gentes. 13 Quo ergo nobis adhuc vivere?" 14 Et scidit Matthathias et filii eius vestimenta sua, et operuerunt se ciliciis et planxerunt valde.

Chapter 2

The zeal and success of Mattathias. His exhortation to his
sons at his death.

In those days arose Mattathias, the son of John, the son of
Simeon, a priest of the sons of Joarib, from Jerusalem, and
he abode in the mountain of Modein. 2 And he had five sons:
John, who was surnamed Gaddi, 3 and Simon, who was surnamed Thassi, 4 and Judas, who was called Maccabeus, 5 and
Eleazar, who was surnamed Avaran, and Jonathan, who was
surnamed Apphus. 6 These saw the evils that were done in
the people of Judah and in Jerusalem.

7 And Mattathias said, "Woe is me! Wherefore was I born
to see the ruin of my people and the ruin of the holy city and
to dwell there when it is given into the hands of the enemies?
8 The holy places are come into the hands of strangers; her
temple is become as a man without honour. 9 The vessels of
her glory are carried away captive; her old men are murdered
in the streets, and her young men are fallen by the sword of
the enemies. 10 What nation hath not inherited her kingdom and gotten of her spoils? 11 All her ornaments are taken
away. She that was free is made a slave. 12 And behold: our
sanctuary and our beauty and our glory is laid waste, and the
Gentiles have defiled them. 13 To what end then should we
live any longer?" 14 And Mattathias and his sons rent their
garments, and they covered themselves with haircloth and
made great lamentation.

15 Et venerunt illuc qui missi erant a Rege Antiocho ut cogerent eos qui confugerant in civitatem Modin immolare et accendere tura et a lege Dei discedere. 16 Et multi de populo Israhel consentientes accesserunt ad eos, sed Matthathias et filii eius constanter steterunt. 17 Et respondentes qui missi erant ab Antiocho dixerunt Matthathiae, "Princeps et clarissimus et magnus es in hac civitate et ornatus filiis et fratribus. 18 Ergo accede prior, et fac iussum regis sicut fecerunt omnes gentes et viri Iuda et qui remanserunt in Hierusalem, et eris tu et filii tui inter amicos regis et amplificatus argento et auro et muneribus multis."

19 Et respondit Matthathias et dixit magna voce, "Et si omnes gentes Regi Antiocho oboediunt ut discedat unusquisque a servitute legis patrum suorum et consentiat mandatis eius, 20 ego et filii mei et fratres mei oboediemus legi patrum nostrorum. 21 Propitius sit nobis Deus! Non est nobis utile relinquere legem et iustitias Dei. 22 Non audibimus verba Regis Antiochi, nec sacrificabimus transgredientes legis nostrae mandata ut eamus altera via."

23 Et ut cessavit loqui verba haec, accessit quidam Iudaeus in omnium oculis sacrificare idolis super aram in civitate Modin secundum iussum regis. 24 Et vidit Matthathias et doluit, et contremuerunt renes eius, et accensus est furor eius secundum iudicium legis, et insiliens trucidavit eum super aram. 25 Sed et virum quem miserat Rex Antiochus, qui cogebat immolare, occidit in ipso tempore et aram

15 And they that were sent from King Antiochus came thither to compel them that were fled into the city of Modein to sacrifice and to burn incense and to depart from the law of God. 16 And many of the people of Israel consented and came to them, but Mattathias and his sons stood firm. 17 And they that were sent from Antiochus, answering, said to Mattathias, "Thou art a ruler and *an* honourable and great man in this city and adorned with sons and brethren. 18 Therefore come thou first, and *obey* the king's commandment as all nations have done and the men of Judah and they that remain in Jerusalem, and thou and thy sons shall be in the number of the king's friends and enriched with gold and silver and many presents."

19 Then Mattathias answered and said with a loud voice, "Although all nations obey King Antiochus so as to depart every man from the service of the law of his fathers and consent to his commandments, 20 I and my sons and my brethren will obey the law of our fathers. 21 God be merciful unto us! It is not profitable for us to forsake the law and the justices of God. 22 We will not hearken to the words of King Antiochus, neither will we sacrifice and transgress the commandments of our law to go another way."

23 Now as he left off speaking these words, there came a certain Jew in the sight of all to sacrifice to the idols upon the altar in the city of Modein according to the king's commandment. 24 And Mattathias saw and was grieved, and his reins trembled, and his wrath was kindled according to the judgment of the law, and running upon him he slew him upon the altar. 25 Moreover, the man whom King Antiochus had sent, who compelled them to sacrifice, he slew at the

destruxit 26 et zelatus est legem sicut fecit Finees Zambri, filio Salomi. 27 Et exclamavit Matthathias voce magna in civitate, dicens, "Omnis qui zelum habet legis statuens testamentum, exeat post me." 28 Et fugit ipse et filii eius in montes et reliquerunt quaecumque habebant in civitate. 29 Tunc descenderunt multi quaerentes iudicium et iustitiam in desertum, 30 et sederunt ibi, ipsi et filii eorum et mulieres eorum et pecora eorum, quoniam inundaverunt super eos mala.

31 Et renuntiatum est viris regis et exercitui qui erat in Hierusalem, in civitate David, quoniam discessissent viri quidam qui dissipaverunt mandatum regis in loca occulta in deserto et abissent post illos multi. 32 Et statim perrexerunt ad eos et constituerunt adversus eos proelium in die sabbatorum, 33 et dixerunt ad eos, "Resistitis et nunc adhuc? Exite, et facite secundum verbum Regis Antiochi, et vivetis."

34 Et dixerunt, "Non exibimus, neque faciemus verbum regis ut polluamus diem sabbatorum."

35 Et concitaverunt adversus eos proelium. 36 Et non responderunt eis, nec lapidem miserunt in eos nec oppilaverunt loca occulta, 37 dicentes, "Moriamur omnes in simplicitate nostra, et testes erunt super nos caelum et terra quod iniuste perditis nos." 38 Et intulerunt eis bellum sabbatis, et mortui sunt ipsi et uxores eorum et filii eorum et pecora eorum usque ad mille animas hominum.

39 Et cognovit Matthathias et amici eius, et luctum habuerunt super eos valde. 40 Et dixit vir proximo suo, "Si omnes fecerimus sicut fratres nostri fecerunt et non pugnaverimus

same time and pulled down the altar 26 and shewed zeal for the law as Phinehas did by Zimri, the son of Salu. 27 And Mattathias cried out in the city with a loud voice, saying, "Every one that hath zeal for the law and maintaineth the testament, let him follow me." 28 So he and his sons fled into the mountains and left all that they had in the city. 29 Then many that sought after judgment and justice went down into the desert, 30 and they abode there, they and their children and their wives and their cattle, because afflictions increased upon them.

31 And it was told to the king's men and to the army that was in Jerusalem, in the city of David, that certain men who had broken the king's commandment were gone away into the secret places in the wilderness and that many were gone after them. 32 And forthwith they went out towards them and made war against them on the sabbath day, 33 and they said to them, "Do you still *resist?* Come forth, and do according to the edict of King Antiochus, and you shall live."

34 And they said, "We will not come forth, neither will we *obey* the king's edict to profane the sabbath day."

35 And they made haste *to give* them battle. 36 *But* they answered them not, neither did they cast a stone at them nor stopped up the secret places, 37 saying, "Let us all die in our innocency, and heaven and earth shall be witnesses for us that you put us to death wrongfully." 38 So they gave them battle on the sabbath, and they were slain with their wives and their children and their cattle to the number of a thousand *persons.*

39 And Mattathias and his friends heard of it, and they mourned for them exceedingly. 40 And every man said to his neighbour, "If we shall all do as our brethren have done and

adversus gentes pro animabus nostris et iustificationibus nostris, nunc citius disperdent nos a terra." 41 Et cogitaverunt in illa die, dicentes, "Omnis homo quicumque venerit ad nos in bello die sabbatorum, pugnemus adversus eum, et non moriemur omnes sicut mortui sunt fratres nostri in occultis." 42 Tunc congregata est ad eos synagoga Asideorum, fortis viribus ex Israhel, omnis voluntarius in lege. 43 Et omnes qui fugiebant a malis additi sunt ad eos et facti sunt illis ad firmamentum. 44 Et collegerunt exercitum et percusserunt peccatores in ira sua et viros iniquos in indignatione sua, et ceteri fugerunt ad nationes ut evaderent. 45 Et circuivit Matthathias et amici eius, et destruxerunt aras, 46 et circumciderunt pueros incircumcisos quotquot invenerunt in finibus Israhel et in fortitudine. 47 Et persecuti sunt filios superbiae, et prosperatum est opus in manibus eorum, 48 et obtinuerunt legem de manibus gentium et de manibus regum, et non dederunt cornu peccatori.

49 Et adpropinquaverunt dies Matthathiae moriendi, et dixit filiis suis, "Nunc confortata est superbia et castigatio, et tempus eversionis et ira indignationis. 50 Nunc ergo, O filii, aemulatores estote legis, et date animas vestras pro testamento patrum vestrorum. 51 Et mementote operum patrum, quae fecerunt in generationibus suis, et accipietis gloriam magnam et nomen aeternum. 52 Abraham nonne in temptatione inventus est fidelis, et reputatum est ei ad iustitiam? 53 Ioseph in tempore angustiae suae custodivit mandatum, et factus est dominus Aegypti. 54 Finees, pater noster,

not fight against the heathens for our lives and our justifications, they will now quickly root us out of the earth." 41 And they determined in that day, saying, *"Whosoever* shall come up against us to fight on the sabbath day, we will fight against him, and we will not all die as our brethren that were slain in the secret places." 42 Then was assembled to them the congregation of the Hasideans, the *stoutest* of Israel, every one that had a good will for the law. 43 And all they that fled from the evils joined themselves to them and were a support to them. 44 And they gathered an army and slew the sinners in their wrath and the wicked men in their indignation, and the rest fled to the nations for safety. 45 And Mattathias and his friends went round about, and they threw down the altars, 46 and they circumcised all the children whom they found in the confines of Israel that were uncircumcised, and *they did* valiantly. 47 And they pursued after the children of pride, and the work prospered in their hands, 48 and they recovered the law out of the hands of the nations and out of the hands of the kings, and they yielded not the horn to the sinner.

49 Now the days drew near that Mattathias should die, and he said to his sons, "Now hath pride and chastisement gotten strength, and the time of destruction and the wrath of indignation. 50 Now therefore, O my sons, be ye zealous for the law, and give your lives for the covenant of your fathers. 51 And call to remembrance the works of the fathers, which they have done in their generations, and you shall receive great glory and an everlasting name. 52 Was not Abraham found faithful in temptation, and it was reputed to him unto justice? 53 Joseph in the time of his distress kept the commandment, and he was made lord of Egypt. 54 Phinehas,

zelando zelum Dei accepit testamentum sacerdotii aeterni. 55 Iesus dum implevit verbum factus est dux in Israhel. 56 Chaleb dum testificatur in ecclesia accepit hereditatem. 57 David in sua misericordia consecutus est sedem regni in saecula. 58 Helias dum zelat zelum legis receptus est in caelum. 59 Ananias et Azarias et Misahel credentes liberati sunt de flamma. 60 Danihel in sua simplicitate liberatus est de ore leonum.

61 "Et ita cogitate per generationem et generationem quia omnes qui sperant in eum non infirmantur. 62 Et a verbis viri peccatoris ne timueritis, quia gloria eius stercus et vermis est; 63 hodie extollitur, et cras non invenietur quia conversus est in terram suam et cogitatio eius periit. 64 Vos ergo, filii, confortamini, et viriliter agite in lege, quia in ipsa gloriosi eritis. 65 Et ecce: Simon, frater vester, scio quod vir consilii est; ipsum audite semper, et ipse vobis erit pater. 66 Et Iudas Macchabeus, fortis viribus a iuventute sua, sit vobis princeps militiae, et ipse aget bellum populi. 67 Et vos adducetis ad vos omnes factores legis, et vindicate vindictam populi vestri. 68 Retribuite retributionem Gentibus, et intendite in praeceptum legis." 69 Et benedixit eos et adpositus est ad patres suos. 70 Et defunctus est centesimo et quadragesimo et sexto anno, et sepultus est a filiis suis in sepulchris patrum suorum in Modin, et planxerunt eum omnis Israhel planctu magno.

our father, by being fervent in the zeal of God received the covenant of an everlasting priesthood. 55 Joshua whilst he fulfilled the word was made ruler in Israel. 56 Caleb *for* bearing witness *before* the congregation received an inheritance. 57 David by his mercy obtained the throne of an *everlasting* kingdom. 58 Elijah while he was full of zeal for the law was taken up into heaven. 59 Hananiah and Azariah and Mishael by believing were delivered out of the flame. 60 Daniel in his innocency was delivered out of the mouth of the lions.

61 "And thus consider through all generations that none that trust in him fail in strength. 62 And fear not the words of a sinful man, for his glory is dung and worms; 63 today he is lifted up, and tomorrow he shall not be found because he is returned into his earth and his thought is come to nothing. 64 You therefore, my sons, take courage, and behave manfully in the law, for by it you shall be glorious. 65 And behold: I know that your brother Simeon is a man of counsel; give ear to him always, and he shall be a father to you. 66 And Judas Maccabeus, who is valiant and strong from his youth up, let him be the leader of your army, and he shall manage the war of the people. 67 And you shall take to you all that observe the law, and revenge ye the wrong of your people. 68 Render to the Gentiles their reward, and take heed to the precepts of the law." 69 And he blessed them and was joined to his fathers. 70 And he died in the hundred and forty-sixth year, and he was buried by his sons in the sepulchres of his fathers in Modein, and all Israel mourned for him with great mourning.

Caput 3

Et surrexit Iudas, qui vocabatur Macchabeus, filius eius, pro eo. 2 Et adiuvabant eum omnes fratres eius et universi qui se coniunxerant patri eius, et proeliabantur proelium Israhel cum laetitia. 3 Et dilatavit gloriam populo suo et induit se loricam sicut gigans et succinxit se arma bellica sua in proeliis et protegebat castra gladio suo. 4 Similis factus est leoni in operibus suis et sicut catulus leonis rugiens in venatione. 5 Et persecutus est iniquos perscrutans eos, et qui conturbabant populum suum eos succendit flammis, 6 et repulsi sunt inimici eius prae timore eius, et omnes operarii iniquitatis conturbati sunt, et directa est salus in manu eius. 7 Et exacerbabat reges multos et laetificabat Iacob in operibus suis, et in saeculum memoria eius in benedictione. 8 Et perambulavit civitates Iuda et perdidit impios ex eis et avertit iram ab Israhel. 9 Et nominatus est usque ad novissimum terrae, et congregavit pereuntes.

10 Et congregavit Apollonius Gentes et a Samaria virtutem multam et magnam ad bellandum contra Israhel. 11 Et cognovit Iudas et exiit obviam illi, et percussit et occidit

Chapter 3

Judas Maccabeus succeeds his father and overthrows Apollonius and Seron. A great army is sent against him out of Syria. He prepares his people for battle by fasting and prayer.

Then his son Judas, called Maccabeus, rose up in his stead. 2 And all his brethren helped him and all they that had joined themselves to his father, and they fought with cheerfulness the battle of Israel. 3 And he *got* his people *great* honour and put on a breastplate as a giant and girt his warlike armour about him in battles and protected the camp with his sword. 4 In his acts he was like a lion and like a lion's whelp roaring for his prey. 5 And he pursued the wicked and sought them out, and them that troubled his people he burnt with fire, 6 and his enemies were driven away for fear of him, and all the workers of iniquity were troubled, and salvation *prospered* in his hand. 7 And he grieved many kings and made Jacob glad with his works, and his memory is blessed for ever. 8 And he went through the cities of Judah and destroyed the wicked out of them and turned away wrath from Israel. 9 And he was renowned even to the utmost part of the earth, and he gathered them that were perishing.

10 And Apollonius gathered together the Gentiles and a numerous and great army from Samaria to make war against Israel. 11 And Judas understood it and went forth to meet

illum, et ceciderunt vulnerati multi, et reliqui fugerunt. 12 Et accepit spolia eorum, et gladium Apollonii abstulit Iudas et erat pugnans in eo omnibus diebus.

13 Et audivit Seron, princeps exercitus Syriae, quod congregavit Iudas congregationem fidelium et ecclesiam secum, 14 et ait, "Faciam mihi nomen et glorificabor in regno et debellabo Iudam et eos qui cum ipso sunt qui spernebant verbum regis." 15 Et praeparavit se et ascenderunt cum eo castra impiorum, fortes auxiliarii, ut facerent vindictam in filios Israhel. 16 Et adpropinquaverunt usque ad Bethoron, et exivit Iudas obviam illi cum paucis.

17 Ut viderunt autem exercitum venientem sibi obviam, dixerunt Iudae, "Quomodo poterimus pauci pugnare contra multitudinem tantam et tam fortem? Et nos fatigati sumus ieiunio hodie."

18 Et ait Iudas, "Facile est concludi multos in manus paucorum, et non est differentia in conspectu Dei caeli liberare in multis et in paucis, 19 quia non in multitudine exercitus victoria belli, sed de caelo fortitudo est. 20 Ipsi veniunt ad nos in multitudine contumaci et superbia ut disperdant nos et uxores nostras et filios nostros et ut spolient nos. 21 Nos vero pugnabimus pro animabus nostris et legibus nostris, 22 et ipse Dominus conteret eos ante faciem nostram. Vos autem, ne timueritis eos."

him, and he overthrew him and killed him, and many fell down slain, and the rest fled away. 12 And he took their spoils, and Judas took the sword of Apollonius and fought with it all his *lifetime.*

13 And Seron, captain of the army of Syria, heard that Judas had assembled a company of the faithful and a congregation with him, 14 and he said, "I will get me a name and will be glorified in the kingdom and will overthrow Judas and those that are with him that have despised the edict of the king." 15 And he made himself ready, and the host of the wicked went up with him, strong succours, to be revenged of the children of Israel. 16 And they approached even as far as Beth-horon, and Judas went forth to meet him with a small company.

17 But when they saw the army coming to meet them they said to Judas, "How shall we being few be able to fight against so great a multitude and so strong? And we are *ready to* faint with fasting today."

18 And Judas said, "It is an easy matter for many to be shut up in the hands of a few, and there is no difference in the sight of the God of heaven to deliver with a great multitude or with a small company, 19 for the success of war is not in the multitude of the army, but strength *cometh* from heaven. 20 They come against us with an insolent multitude and with pride to destroy us and our wives and our children and to take our spoils. 21 But we will fight for our lives and our laws, 22 and the Lord himself will overthrow them before our face. But as for you, fear them not."

23 Ut cessavit autem loqui, insiluit in eos subito, et contritus est Seron et exercitus eius in conspectu ipsius, 24 et persecutus est eum in descensu Bethoron usque in campum, et ceciderunt ex eis octingenti viri, reliqui autem fugerunt in terram Philisthim. 25 Et cecidit timor Iudae ac fratrum eius et formido super omnes gentes in circuitu eorum. 26 Et pervenit ad regem nomen eius, et de proeliis Iudae narrabant omnes gentes.

27 Ut audivit autem Rex Antiochus sermones istos iratus est animo, et misit et congregavit exercitum universi regni sui, castra fortia valde. 28 Et aperuit aerarium suum et dedit stipendia exercitui in annum, et mandavit illis ut essent parati ad omnia. 29 Et vidit quod defecit pecunia de thesauris suis et tributa regionis modica propter dissensionem et plagam quam fecit in terra ut tolleret legitima quae erant a primis diebus, 30 et timuit ne non haberet ut semel et bis in sumptus et donativa, quae dederat ante larga manu, et abundaverat super reges qui ante eum fuerant. 31 Et consternatus erat animo valde et cogitavit ire in Persidem et accipere tributa regionum et congregare argentum multum.

32 Et reliquit Lysiam, hominem nobilem de genere regali, super negotia regia a flumine Eufrate usque ad flumen Aegypti 33 et ut nutriret Antiochum, filium suum, donec rediret. 34 Et tradidit ei medium exercitum et elefantos, et mandavit ei de omnibus quae volebat et de inhabitantibus Iudaeam et Hierusalem 35 et ut mitteret ad eos exercitum ad

23 And as soon as he had made an end of speaking, he rushed suddenly upon them, and Seron and his host were overthrown before him, 24 and he pursued him by the descent of Beth-horon even to the plain, and there fell of them eight hundred men, and the rest fled into the land of the Philistines. 25 And the fear of Judas and of his brethren and the dread *of them* fell upon all the nations round about them. 26 And his fame came to the king, and all nations told of the battles of Judas.

27 Now when King Antiochus heard these words he was angry in his mind, and he sent and gathered the forces of all his kingdom, an exceeding strong army. 28 And he opened his treasury and gave out pay to the army for a year, and he commanded them that they should be ready for all things. 29 And he perceived that the money of his treasures failed and that the tributes of the country were small because of the dissension and the evil that he had brought upon the land that he might take away the laws of old times, 30 and he feared that he should not have as *formerly enough* for charges and gifts, which he had given before with a liberal hand, *for* he had abounded more than the kings that had been before him. 31 And he was greatly perplexed in mind and purposed to go into Persia and to take tributes of the countries and to gather much money.

32 And he left Lysias, a nobleman of the blood royal, to oversee the affairs of the kingdom from the river Euphrates even to the river of Egypt 33 and to bring up his son Antiochus till he came again. 34 And he delivered to him half the army and the elephants, and he gave him charge concerning all that he would have done and concerning the inhabitants of Judea and Jerusalem 35 and that he should send an army

conterendam et extirpandam virtutem Israhel et reliquias Hierusalem et auferendam memoriam eorum de loco 36 et ut constitueret habitatores filios alienigenas in omnibus finibus eorum et sorte distribueret terram eorum. 37 Et rex adsumpsit partem exercitus residui et exivit ab Antiochia, civitate regni sui, anno centesimo et quadragesimo et septimo, et transfretavit Eufraten flumen et perambulabat superiores regiones.

38 Et elegit Lysias Ptolomeum, filium Dorimini, et Nicanorem et Gorgiam, viros potentes ex amicis regis, 39 et misit cum eis quadraginta milia virorum et septem milia equitum ut venirent in terram Iuda et disperderent eam secundum verbum regis. 40 Et processerunt cum universa virtute sua et venerunt et adplicuerunt Emmaum in terra campestri. 41 Et audierunt mercatores regionum nomen eorum, et acceperunt argentum et aurum multum valde et pueros, et venerunt in castra ut acciperent filios Israhel in servos, et additi sunt ad eos exercitus Syriae et terrae alienigenarum.

42 Et vidit Iudas et fratres eius quia multiplicata sunt mala et exercitus adplicabant ad fines eorum, et cognoverunt verba regis quae mandavit populo facere in interitum et consummationem. 43 Et dixerunt unusquisque ad proximum suum, "Erigamus deiectionem populi nostri, et pugnemus pro populo nostro et sanctis nostris." 44 Et congregatus est conventus ut essent parati in proelium et ut orarent et peterent misericordiam et miserationes.

45 Et Hierusalem non habitabatur sed erat sicut desertum; non erat qui ingrederetur et egrederetur de natis eius,

against them to destroy and root out the strength of Israel and the remnant of Jerusalem and to take away the memory of them from *that* place 36 and that he should settle *strangers* to dwell in all their coasts and divide their land by lot. 37 So the king took the half of the army that remained and went forth from Antioch, the *chief* city of his kingdom, in the hundred and forty-seventh year, and he passed over the river Euphrates and went through the higher countries.

38 Then Lysias chose Ptolemy, the son of Dorymenes, and Nicanor and Gorgias, mighty men of the king's friends, 39 and he sent with them forty thousand men and seven thousand horsemen to go into the land of Judah and to destroy it according to the king's orders. 40 So they went forth with all their power and came and pitched near Emmaus in the plain country. 41 And the merchants of the countries heard the fame of them, and they took silver and gold in abundance and servants, and they came into the camp to buy the children of Israel for slaves, and there were joined to them the forces of Syria and of the land of the strangers.

42 And Judas and his brethren saw that evils were multiplied and that the armies approached to their borders, and they knew the orders the king had given to destroy the people and utterly abolish them. 43 And they said every man to his neighbour, "Let us raise up the low condition of our people, and let us fight for our people and our sanctuary." 44 And the assembly was gathered that they might be ready for battle and that they might pray and ask mercy and compassion.

45 Now Jerusalem was not inhabited but was like a desert; there was none of her children that went in or out, and the

et sanctum conculcabatur, et filii alienigenarum erant in arce; ibi erat habitatio Gentium, et ablata est voluptas ab Iacob, et defecit ibi tibia et cithara.

46 Et congregati sunt et venerunt in Maspha contra Hierusalem, quia locus orationis erat in Maspha ante in Israhel. 47 Et ieiunaverunt illa die et induerunt se ciliciis et cinerem inposuerunt in capite suo, et disciderunt vestimenta sua, 48 et expanderunt libros legis, de quibus scrutabantur Gentes similitudinem simulacrorum suorum, 49 et adtulerunt ornamenta sacerdotalia et primitias et decimas et suscitaverunt Nazoreos qui impleverant dies, 50 et clamaverunt voce magna in caelum, dicentes, "Quid faciemus istis, et quo eos ducemus? 51 Et sancta tua conculcata sunt et contaminata sunt, et sacerdotes tui facti sunt in luctum et in humilitatem. 52 Et ecce: nationes convenerunt adversum nos ut nos disperdant; tu scis quae cogitant in nos. 53 Quomodo poterimus subsistere ante faciem illorum, nisi tu, Deus, adiuves nos?" 54 Et tubis exclamaverunt voce magna.

55 Et post haec constituit Iudas duces populi, tribunos et centuriones et pentecontarcos et decuriones. 56 Et dixit his qui aedificabant domos et sponsabant uxores et plantabant vineas et formidolosis ut redirent unusquisque in domum suam secundum legem. 57 Et moverunt castra et conlocaverunt ad austrum Emmaum. 58 Et ait Iudas, "Accingimini, et estote filii potentes, et estote parati in mane, ut pugnetis adversus nationes has quae convenerunt adversus nos

sanctuary was trodden down, and the children of strangers were in the castle; there was the habitation of the Gentiles, and joy was taken away from Jacob, and the pipe and harp ceased there.

46 And they assembled together and came to Mizpah over against Jerusalem, for in Mizpah was a place of prayer heretofore in Israel. 47 And they fasted that day and put on haircloth and put ashes upon their heads, and they rent their garments, 48 and they laid open the books of the law, in which the Gentiles searched for the likeness of their idols, 49 and they brought the priestly ornaments and the first-fruits and tithes and stirred up the Nazirites that had fulfilled their days, 50 and they cried with a loud voice toward heaven, saying, "What shall we do with these, and whither shall we carry them? 51 *For* thy holies are trodden down and are profaned, and thy priests are in mourning and are brought low. 52 And behold: the nations are come together against us to destroy us; thou knowest what they intend against us. 53 How shall we be able to stand before their face, unless thou, O God, help us?" 54 Then they *sounded* with trumpets *and* cried out with a loud voice.

55 And after *this* Judas appointed captains over the people, over thousands and over hundreds and over fifties and over tens. 56 And he said to them that were building houses *or* had betrothed wives *or* were planting vineyards *or* were fearful that they should return every man to his house according to the law. 57 So they removed the camp and pitched on the south side of Emmaus. 58 And Judas said, "Gird yourselves, and be valiant men, and be ready against the morning, that you may fight with these nations that are assembled against

disperdere nos et sancta nostra, 59 quoniam melius est nos mori in bello quam videre mala gentis nostrae et sanctorum. 60 Sicut autem fuerit voluntas in caelo, sic fiat."

Caput 4

Et adsumpsit Gorgias quinque milia virorum et mille equites electos, et moverunt castra nocte 2 ut adplicarent ad castra Iudaeorum et percuterent eos subito, et filii qui erant ex arce erant illis duces. 3 Et audivit Iudas et surrexit, ipse et potentes, percutere virtutem exercituum regis qui erant in Emmaum, 4 adhuc enim dispersus erat exercitus a castris. 5 Et venit Gorgias in castra Iudae noctu et neminem invenit, et quaerebat eos in montibus, quoniam dixit, "Fugiunt hii a nobis."

6 Et cum dies factus esset apparuit Iudas in campo cum tribus milibus virorum tantum, qui tegumenta et gladios non habebant. 7 Et viderunt castra Gentium valida et loricatos

us to destroy us and our sanctuary, 59 for it is better for us to die in battle than to see the evils of our nation and of the holies. 60 Nevertheless, as it shall be the will *of God* in heaven, so be it done."

Chapter 4

Judas routs the king's army. Gorgias flies before him. Lysias comes against him with a great army but is defeated. Judas cleanses the temple, sets up a new altar and fortifies the sanctuary.

Then Gorgias took five thousand men and a thousand of the *best* horsemen, and they removed *out of* the camp by night 2 that they might come upon the camp of the Jews and strike them suddenly, and the men that were of the castle were their guides. 3 And Judas heard of it and rose up, he and the valiant men, to attack the king's *forces* that were in Emmaus, 4 for as yet the army was dispersed from the camp. 5 And Gorgias came by night into the camp of Judas and found no man, and he sought them in the mountains, for he said, "These men flee from us."

6 And when it was day Judas shewed himself in the plain with three thousand men only, who neither had armour nor swords. 7 And they saw the camp of the Gentiles, that it was strong, and the men in breastplates and the horsemen round

et equitatus in circuitu eorum, et hii docti ad proelium. 8 Et ait Iudas viris qui secum erant, "Ne timueritis multitudinem eorum, et impetum eorum ne formidetis. 9 Mementote qualiter salvi facti sunt patres nostri in Mari Rubro cum sequeretur eos Pharao cum exercitu multo. 10 Et nunc clamemus in caelum, et miserebitur nostri Dominus et memor erit testamenti patrum nostrorum et conteret exercitum istum ante faciem nostram hodie, 11 et scient omnes gentes quia est qui redimat et liberet Israhel."

12 Et levaverunt alienigenae oculos suos et viderunt eos venientes ex adverso, 13 et exierunt de castris in proelium, et tuba cecinerunt hii qui erant cum Iuda. 14 Et congressi sunt, et contritae sunt Gentes et fugerunt in campum. 15 Novissimi autem omnes ceciderunt gladio, et persecuti sunt eos usque Gezeron et usque in campos Idumeae et Azoti et Iamniae, et ceciderunt ex illis usque ad tria milia virorum.

16 Et reversus est Iudas et exercitus eius sequens eum, 17 et dixit ad populum, "Non concupiscatis spolia, quia bellum contra nos est, 18 et Gorgias et exercitus eius in monte prope nos, sed state nunc contra inimicos nostros et expugnate eos, et sumetis postea spolia securi."

19 Et adhuc loquente Iuda haec, ecce: apparuit pars quaedam prospiciens de monte. 20 Et vidit Gorgias quod in fugam conversi sunt sui et succenderunt castra, fumus enim qui videbatur declarabat quod factum est. 21 Quibus illi conspectis timuerunt valde, aspicientes simul et Iudam et exercitum in campo paratum ad proelium. 22 Et fugerunt omnes in campum alienigenarum. 23 Et Iudas reversus est ad

about them, and these were trained up to war. 8 And Judas said to the men that were with him, "Fear ye not their multitude, neither be ye afraid of their assault. 9 Remember in what manner our fathers were saved in the Red Sea when Pharaoh pursued them with a great army. 10 And now let us cry to heaven, and the Lord will have mercy on us and will remember the covenant of our fathers and will destroy this army before our face this day, 11 and all nations shall know that there is one that redeemeth and delivereth Israel."

12 And the strangers lifted up their eyes and saw them coming against them, 13 and they went out of the camp to battle, and they that were with Judas sounded the trumpet. 14 And they joined battle, and the Gentiles were routed and fled into the plain. 15 But all the hindmost of them fell by the sword, and they pursued them as far as Gazara and even to the plains of Idumea and of Azotus and of Jamnia, and there fell of them to the number of three thousand men.

16 And Judas returned again with his army that followed him, 17 and he said to the people, "Be not greedy of the spoils, for there is war before us, 18 and Gorgias and his army are near us in the mountain, but stand ye now against our enemies and overthrow them, and you shall take the spoils afterwards with safety."

19 And as Judas was speaking these words, behold: part of them appeared looking forth from the mountain. 20 And Gorgias saw that his men were put to flight and that they *had* set fire to the camp, for the smoke that was seen declared what was done. 21 And when they had seen this they were seized with great fear, seeing at the same time *Judas* and his army in the plain ready to fight. 22 So they all fled away into the land of the strangers. 23 And Judas returned to

spolia castrorum, et acceperunt aurum multum et argentum et hyacinthum et purpuram marinam et opes magnas. 24 Et conversi hymnum canebant et benedicebant Deum in caelum, "quoniam bonus est, quoniam in saeculum misericordia eius." 25 Et facta est salus magna in Israhel in illa die.

26 Quicumque autem alienigenarum evaserunt venerunt et nuntiaverunt Lysiae universa quae acciderant. 27 Quibus auditis ille consternatus animo deficiebat, quod non qualia voluit talia contigerunt in Israhel et qualia mandavit rex. 28 Et sequenti anno congregavit Lysias virorum electorum sexaginta milia et equitum quinque milia ut debellaret eos. 29 Et venerunt in Iudaeam et castra posuerunt in Bethoron, et occurrit illis Iudas cum decem milibus viris. 30 Et viderunt exercitum fortem, et oravit et dixit, "Benedictus es, salvator Israhel, qui contrivisti impetum potentis in manu servi tui David et tradidisti castra alienigenarum in manu Ionathae, filii Saul, et armigeri eius. 31 Conclude exercitum istum in manu populi tui Israhel, et confundantur in exercitu suo et equitibus. 32 Da illis formidinem, et tabefac audaciam virtutis eorum, et commoveantur contritione sua. 33 Deice eos gladio diligentium te, et conlaudent te omnes qui noverunt nomen tuum in hymnis."

34 Et commiserunt proelium, et ceciderunt de exercitu Lysiae quinque milia virorum. 35 Videns autem Lysias suorum fugam et Iudaeorum audaciam et quod parati sunt aut vivere aut mori fortiter, abiit Antiochiam et elegit milites ut multiplicati rursus venirent in Iudaeam.

take the spoils of the camp, and they got much gold and silver and blue silk and purple of the sea and great riches. 24 And returning *home* they sung a hymn, and blessed God in heaven, "because he is good, because his mercy endureth for ever." 25 So Israel had a great deliverance that day.

26 And such of the strangers as escaped went and told Lysias all that had happened. 27 And when he heard these things he was amazed and *discouraged,* because things had not succeeded in Israel *according to his mind* and as the king had commanded. 28 So the year following Lysias gathered together threescore thousand chosen men and five thousand horsemen that he might subdue them. 29 And they came into Judea and pitched their tents in Beth-horon, and Judas met them with ten thousand men. 30 And they saw that the army was strong, and he prayed and said, "Blessed art thou, O saviour of Israel, who didst break the violence of the mighty by the hand of thy servant David and didst deliver up the camp of the strangers into the hands of Jonathan, the son of Saul, and of his armourbearer. 31 Shut up this army in the hands of thy people Israel, and let them be confounded in their host and their horsemen. 32 Strike them with fear, and cause the boldness of their strength to languish, and let them quake at their own destruction. 33 Cast them down with the sword of them that love thee, and let all that know thy name praise thee with hymns."

34 And they joined battle, and there fell of the army of Lysias five thousand men. 35 And when Lysias saw *that his men were put to flight* and *how bold* the Jews were and that they were ready either to live or to die manfully, he went to Antioch and chose soldiers that they might come again into Judea with greater numbers.

36 Dixit autem Iudas et fratres eius, "Ecce: contriti sunt inimici nostri; ascendamus nunc mundare sancta et renovare." 37 Et congregatus est omnis exercitus, et ascenderunt in Montem Sion. 38 Et viderunt sanctificationem desertam et altare profanatum et portas exustas et in atriis virgulta nata sicut in saltu vel in montibus et pastoforia diruta. 39 Et sciderunt vestimenta sua et planxerunt planctu magno et inposuerunt cinerem super caput suum, 40 et ceciderunt in faciem super terram, et exclamaverunt tubis signorum, et clamaverunt in caelum.

41 Tunc ordinavit Iudas viros ut pugnarent adversus eos qui erant in arce donec emundarent sancta. 42 Et elegit sacerdotes sine macula voluntatem habentes in lege Dei, 43 et mundaverunt sancta et tulerunt lapides contaminationis in locum inmundum. 44 Et cogitavit de altare holocaustorum quod profanatum erat, quid de eo faceret. 45 Et incidit illis consilium bonum ut destruerent illud ne forte esset illis in obprobrium quia contaminaverunt illud Gentes, et demoliti sunt illud. 46 Et reposuerunt lapides in monte domus in loco apto quoadusque veniret propheta et responderet de eis. 47 Et acceperunt lapides integros secundum legem et aedificaverunt altare novum secundum illud quod fuit prius, 48 et aedificaverunt sancta et quae intra domum erant intrinsecus, et aedem et atria sanctificaverunt. 49 Et fecerunt vasa sancta nova et intulerunt candelabrum et altare incensorum et mensam in templum. 50 Et incensum posuerunt super altare et accenderunt lucernas quae super candelabrum erant,

36 Then Judas and his brethren said, "Behold: our enemies are discomfited; let us go up now to cleanse the holy places and to repair them." 37 And all the army assembled together, and they went up into Mount Zion. 38 And they saw the sanctuary desolate and the altar profaned and the gates burnt and shrubs *growing* up in the courts as in a forest or on the mountains and the chambers joining to the temple thrown down. 39 And they rent their garments and made great lamentation and put ashes on their heads, 40 and they fell face down to the ground on their faces, and they sounded with the trumpets of alarm, and they cried towards heaven.

41 Then Judas appointed men to fight against them that were in the castle till they *had* cleansed the holy places. 42 And he chose priests without blemish whose will was set upon the law of God, 43 and they cleansed the holy places and took away the stones that had been defiled into an unclean place. 44 And he considered about the altar of holocausts that had been profaned, what he should do with it. 45 And a good counsel came *into their minds* to pull it down *lest* it should be a reproach to them because the Gentiles *had* defiled it, so they threw it down. 46 And they laid up the stones in the mountain of the *temple* in a convenient place till there should come a prophet and give answer concerning them. 47 Then they took whole stones according to the law and built a new altar according to the former, 48 and they built up the holy places and the things that were within the *temple,* and they sanctified the temple and the courts. 49 And they made new holy vessels and brought in the candlestick and the altar of incense and the table into the temple. 50 And they put incense upon the altar and lighted up the lamps that were upon the candlestick, and they gave light in the

et lucebant in templo. 51 Et posuerunt super mensam panes et adpenderunt vela et consummaverunt omnia opera quae fecerant.

52 Et ante matutinum surrexerunt quinta et vicesima die mensis noni (hic est mensis Casleu), centesimi quadragesimi octavi anni. 53 Et obtulerunt sacrificium secundum legem super altare holocaustorum novum quod fecerunt. 54 Secundum tempus et secundum diem in qua contaminaverunt illud gentes, in ipsa renovatum est in canticis et citharis et cinyris et in cymbalis. 55 Et cecidit omnis populus in faciem et adoraverunt et benedixerunt in caelum eum qui prosperavit eis.

56 Et fecerunt dedicationem altaris diebus octo, et obtulerunt holocausta cum laetitia et sacrificium salutaris et laudis. 57 Et ornaverunt faciem templi coronis aureis et scutulis, et dedicaverunt portas et pastoforia et inposuerunt eis ianuas. 58 Et facta est laetitia in populo magna valde, et aversum est obprobrium Gentium.

59 Et statuit Iudas et fratres eius et universa ecclesia Israhel ut agatur dies dedicationis altaris in temporibus suis ab anno in annum per dies octo a quinta et vicesima die mensis Casleu cum laetitia et gaudio. 60 Et aedificaverunt in tempore illo Montem Sion et per circuitum muros altos et turres firmas, nequando venirent Gentes et conculcarent eum sicut antea fecerunt. 61 Et conlocavit illic exercitum ut servarent eum, et munivit eum ad custodiendam Bethsuram, ut haberet populus munitionem contra faciem Idumeae.

temple. 51 And they set the loaves upon the table and hung up the veils and finished all the works that they had *begun to make.*

52 And they arose before the morning on the five and twentieth day of the ninth month *(which* is the month of Chislev), in the hundred and forty-eighth year. 53 And they offered sacrifice according to the law upon the new altar of holocausts which they *had* made. 54 According to the time and according to the day wherein the heathens *had* defiled it, in the same was it *dedicated* anew with canticles and harps and lutes and cymbals. 55 And all the people fell upon their faces and adored and blessed up to heaven him that *had* prospered them.

56 And they kept the dedication of the altar eight days, and they offered holocausts with joy and sacrifices of salvation and of praise. 57 And they adorned the front of the temple with crowns of gold and escutcheons, and they *renewed* the gates and the chambers and hanged doors upon them. 58 And there was exceeding great joy among the people, and the reproach of the Gentiles was turned away.

59 And Judas and his brethren and all the church of Israel decreed that the day of the dedication of the altar should be kept in its season from year to year for eight days from the five and twentieth day of the month of Chislev with joy and gladness. 60 They built up also at that time Mount Zion with high walls and strong towers round about, lest the Gentiles should at any time come and tread it down as they did before. 61 And he placed a garrison there to keep it, and he fortified it to secure Beth-zur, that the people might have a defence *against* Idumea.

Caput 5

Et factum est ut audierunt gentes in circuitu quia aedificatum est altare et sanctuarium sicut prius iratae sunt valde. 2 Et cogitabant tollere genus Iacob qui erant inter eos, et coeperunt occidere de populo et persequi. 3 Et debellabat Iudas filios Esau in Idumea et eos qui erant in Acrabattene, quia circumsedebant Israelitas, et percussit eos plaga magna. 4 Et recordatus est malitiam filiorum Bean, qui erant populo in laqueum et in scandalum insidiantes ei in via. 5 Et conclusi sunt ab eo in turribus, et adplicuit ad eos et anathematizavit eos et incendit turres eorum igni cum omnibus qui in eis erant. 6 Et transiit ad filios Ammon, et invenit manum fortem et populum copiosum, et Timotheum ducem ipsorum. 7 Et commisit cum eis proelia multa, et contriti sunt in conspectu eorum, et percussit eos, 8 et cepit Gazer civitatem et filias eius et reversus est in Iudaeam. 9 Et congregatae sunt Gentes quae sunt in Galaad adversus Israelitas

Chapter 5

Judas and his brethren attack the enemies of their country and deliver them that were distressed. Josephus and Azariah, attempting—contrary to order—to fight against their enemies, are defeated.

Now it came to pass when the nations round about heard that the altar and the sanctuary were built up as before that they were exceeding angry. 2 And they thought to destroy the generation of Jacob that were among them, and they began to kill some of the people and to persecute them. 3 Then Judas fought against the children of Esau in Idumea and them that were in Akrabattene, because they beset the Israelites around about, and he made a great slaughter of them. 4 And he remembered the malice of the children of Baean, who were a snare and a stumbling block to the people by lying in wait for them in the way. 5 And they were shut up by him in towers, and he set upon them and devoted them to *utter destruction* and burnt their towers with fire and all that were in them. 6 Then he passed over to the children of Ammon, *where* he found a mighty power and much people, and Timothy was their captain. 7 And he fought many battles with them, and they were discomfited in their sight, and he smote them, 8 and he took the city of Jazer and her *towns* and returned into Judea. 9 And the Gentiles that were in Gilead assembled themselves together against the Israelites

qui erant in finibus eorum ut tollerent eos, et fugerunt in Datheman munitionem.

10 Et miserunt litteras ad Iudam et fratres eius, dicentes, "Congregatae sunt adversum nos gentes per circuitum ut auferant nos, 11 et parant venire et occupare munitionem in quam confugimus, et Timotheus est dux exercitus eorum. 12 Nunc ergo veni, et eripe nos de manibus eorum, quia cecidit multitudo de nobis. 13 Et omnes fratres nostri qui erant in locis Tubin interfecti sunt, et captivas abduxerunt uxores eorum et natos et spolia, et peremerunt illic ferme mille viros." 14 Et adhuc epistulae legebantur, et ecce: alii nuntii venerunt de Galilea conscissis tunicis nuntiantes secundum verba haec, 15 dicentes convenisse adversum se a Ptolomaida et Tyro et Sidone et: "Repleta est omnis Galilea alienigenis ut nos consumant."

16 Ut audivit autem Iudas et populus sermones istos, convenit ecclesia magna cogitare quid facerent fratribus suis qui in tribulatione erant et expugnabantur ab eis. 17 Dixitque Iudas Simoni, fratri suo, "Elige tibi viros, et vade, et libera fratres tuos in Galilea, ego autem et frater meus Ionathas ibimus in Galaditin." 18 Et reliquit Iosepphum, filium Zacchariae, et Azariam duces populi cum residuo exercitu in Iudaea ad custodiendum, 19 et praecepit illis, dicens, "Praeestote populo huic, et nolite bellum committere adversus gentes donec revertamur." 20 Et partiti sunt Simoni viri tria milia ut iret in Galileam, Iudae autem octo milia in Galaditin.

that were in their quarters to destroy them, and they fled into the fortress of Dathema.

10 And they sent letters to Judas and his brethren, saying, "The heathens that are round about are gathered together against us to destroy us, 11 and they are preparing to come and to take the fortress into which we are fled, and Timothy is the captain of their host. 12 Now therefore come, and deliver us out of their hands, for many of us are slain. 13 And all our brethren that were in the places of Tob are killed, and they have carried away their wives and their children captives and *taken* their spoils, and they have slain there almost a thousand men." 14 And while they were yet reading *these* letters, *behold:* there came other messengers out of Galilee with their garments rent who related according to these words, 15 saying that they of Ptolemais and of Tyre and of Sidon were assembled against them and: "All Galilee is filled with strangers in order to consume us."

16 Now when Judas and the people heard these words, a great assembly met together to consider what they should do for their brethren that were in trouble and were assaulted by them. 17 And Judas said to Simon, his brother, "Choose thee men, and go, and deliver thy brethren in Galilee, and I and my brother Jonathan will go into the country of Gilead." 18 And he left Joseph, the son of Zacharias, and Azariah captains of the people with the remnant of the army in Judea to keep it, 19 and he commanded them, saying, "Take ye the charge of this people, *but* make no war against the heathens till we return." 20 Now three thousand men were allotted to Simon to go into Galilee, and eight thousand to Judas to go into the land of Gilead.

21 Et abiit Simon in Galileam et commisit proelia multa cum gentibus, et contritae sunt gentes a facie eius, et persecutus est eos usque ad portam Ptolomaidis. 22 Et ceciderunt de gentibus fere tria milia virorum, et accepit spolia eorum, 23 et sumpsit eos qui erant in Galilea et in Arbatis cum uxoribus et natis et omnibus quae erant illis, et adduxit in Iudaeam cum laetitia magna. 24 Et Iudas Macchabeus et Ionathas, frater eius, transierunt Iordanem et abierunt viam trium dierum per desertum. 25 Et occurrerunt eis Nabuthei et susceperunt eos pacifice et narraverunt eis omnia quae acciderant fratribus eorum in Galaditide 26 et quia multi ex eis conprehensi sunt in Barasa et Bosor et in Alimis et in Casfor et Mageth et Carnain, hae omnes civitates munitae et magnae. 27 Sed et in ceteris civitatibus Galaditidis tenentur conprehensi et in crastinum constituerunt admovere exercitum civitatibus his et conprehendere et tollere eos in una die. 28 Et convertit Iudas et exercitus eius viam in desertum Bosor repente et occupavit civitatem, et occidit omnem masculum in ore gladii et accepit omnia spolia eorum et succendit eam igni. 29 Et surrexerunt inde nocte et ibant usque ad munitionem.

30 Et factum est diluculo, cum adlevassent oculos suos, ecce: populus multus cuius non erat numerus portantes scalas et machinas ut conprehenderent munitionem et expugnarent eos. 31 Et vidit Iudas quia coepit bellum, et clamor belli ascendit ad caelum sicut tuba, et clamor magnus

21 And Simon went into Galilee and fought many battles with the heathens, and the heathens were discomfited before his face, and he pursued them even to the gate of Ptolemais. 22 And there fell of the heathens almost three thousand men, and he took the spoils of them, 23 and he took *with him* those that were in Galilee and in Arbatta with their wives and children and all that they had, and he brought them into Judea with great joy. 24 And Judas Maccabeus and Jonathan, his brother, passed over the Jordan and went three days' journey through the desert. 25 And the Nabateans met them and received them in a peaceable manner and told them all that happened to their brethren in the land of Gilead 26 and that many of them were shut up in Bozrah and in Bosor and in Alema and in Chaspho and in Maked and in Carnaim, all these strong and great cities. 27 Yea and that they were kept shut up in the rest of the cities of Gilead and that they *had* appointed to bring their army on the morrow near to these cities and to take them and to destroy them all in one day. 28 Then Judas and his army suddenly turned their march into the desert to Bosor and took the city, and he slew every male by the edge of the sword and took all their spoils and burnt it with fire. 29 And they removed from thence by night and went till they came to the fortress.

30 And it came to pass that early in the morning, when they lifted up their eyes, behold: there were *people* without number carrying ladders and engines to take the fortress and assault them. 31 And Judas saw that the fight was begun, and the cry of the battle went up to heaven like a trumpet,

de civitate, 32 et dixit exercitui suo, "Pugnate hodie pro fratribus vestris." 33 Et venit tribus ordinibus post eos, et exclamaverunt tubis et clamaverunt in oratione. 34 Et cognoverunt castra Timothei quia Macchabeus est, et refugerunt a facie eius, et percusserunt eos plaga magna, et ceciderunt ex eis in illa die fere octo milia virorum. 35 Et divertit Iudas in Maspha et expugnavit et cepit eam, et occidit omnem masculum eius et sumpsit spolia eius et succendit eam igni. 36 Inde perrexit et cepit Casbon et Mageth et Bosor et reliquas civitates Galaditidis. 37 Post haec autem verba congregavit Timotheus exercitum alium et castra posuit contra Rafon trans torrentem. 38 Et misit Iudas speculari exercitum, et renuntiaverunt ei, dicentes quia "Convenerunt ad eum omnes gentes quae in circuitu nostro sunt exercitus multus nimis, 39 et Arabas conduxerunt in auxilium sibi, et castra posuerunt trans torrentem, parati venire ad te in proelium." Et abiit Iudas obviam illis.

40 Et ait Timotheus principibus exercitus sui, "Cum adpropiaverit Iudas et exercitus eius ad torrentem aquae, si transierit ad nos prior non poterimus sustinere eum, quia potens poterit adversum nos. 41 Si vero timuerit transire et posuerit castra extra flumen, transfretemus ad eos et poterimus adversus illum."

42 Ut autem adpropinquavit Iudas ad torrentem aquae, statuit scribas populi secus torrentem et mandavit eis, dicens, "Neminem hominum reliqueritis, sed veniant omnes in proelium." 43 Et transfretavit ad illos prior et omnis

and a great cry out of the city, 32 and he said to his host, "Fight ye today for your brethren." 33 And he came with three companies behind them, and they sounded their trumpets and cried out in prayer. 34 And the host of Timothy understood that it was Maccabeus, and they fled away before his face, and they made a great slaughter of them, and there fell of them in that day almost eight thousand men. 35 And Judas turned aside to Mizpah and assaulted and took it, and he slew every male thereof and took the spoils thereof and burnt it with fire. 36 From thence he marched and took Chaspho and Maked and Bosor and the rest of the cities of Gilead. 37 But after this Timothy gathered another army and camped over against Raphon beyond the torrent. 38 And Judas sent *men* to view the army, and they brought him word, saying, "All the nations that are round about us are assembled unto him an army exceeding great, 39 and they have hired the Arabians to help them, and they have pitched their tents beyond the torrent, ready to come to fight against thee." And Judas went to meet them.

40 And Timothy said to the captains of his army, "When Judas and his army come near the torrent of water, if he pass over unto us first we shall not be able to withstand him, for he will certainly prevail over us. 41 But if he be afraid to pass over and camp *on the other side of* the river, we will pass over to them and shall prevail against him."

42 Now when Judas came near the torrent of water, he set the scribes of the people by the torrent and commanded them, saying, "*Suffer* no man *to stay behind,* but let all come to the battle." 43 And he passed over to them first and all the

populus post eum, et contritae sunt omnes gentes a facie eorum, et proiecerunt arma sua et fugerunt ad fanum quod erat in Carnain. 44 Et occupavit ipsam civitatem, et fanum succendit igni cum omnibus qui erant in ipso, et oppressa est Carnain et non potuit sustinere contra faciem Iudae. 45 Et congregavit Iudas universos Israhelitas qui erant in Galaditide a minimo usque ad maximum et uxores eorum et natos et exercitum magnum valde ut venirent in terram Iudae. 46 Et venerunt usque Efron. Et haec civitas magna in ingressu posita, munita valde, et non erat declinare ab ea dextra vel sinistra, sed per mediam iter erat. 47 Et incluserunt se qui erant in civitate et obstruxerunt portas lapidibus. Et misit ad eos Iudas verbis pacificis, 48 dicens, "Transeamus per terram vestram ut eamus in terram nostram, et nemo vobis nocebit; tantum pedibus transibimus." Et nolebant eis aperire. 49 Et praecepit Iudas praedicare in castris ut adplicarent, unusquisque in quo erat loco. 50 Et adplicuerunt se viri virtutis, et obpugnavit civitatem illam tota die et tota nocte, et tradita est civitas in manu eius. 51 Et peremerunt omnem masculum in ore gladii, et eradicavit eam et accepit spolia eius et transiit per totam civitatem super interfectos.

52 Et transgressi sunt Iordanem in campo magno contra faciem Bethsan. 53 Et erat Iudas congregans extremos, et exhortabatur populum per totam viam donec venirent in terram Iuda. 54 Et ascenderunt in Montem Sion cum laetitia et gaudio et obtulerunt holocausta quod nemo ex eis cecidisset donec reverterentur in pace.

people after him, and all the heathens were discomfited before them, and they threw away their weapons and fled to the temple that was in Carnaim. 44 And he took that city, and the temple he burnt with fire with all things that were therein, and Carnaim was subdued and could not stand against the face of Judas. 45 And Judas gathered together all the Israelites that were in the land of Gilead from the least even to the greatest and their wives and children and an army exceeding great to come into the land of Judah. 46 And they came as far as Ephron. Now this was a great city situate in the way, strongly fortified, and there was no means to turn from it on the right hand or on the left, but the way was through the midst of it. 47 And they that were in the city shut themselves in and stopped up the gates with stones. And Judas sent to them with peaceable words, 48 saying, "Let us pass through your land to go into our country, and no man shall hurt you; we will only pass through on foot." *But* they would not open to them. 49 Then Judas commanded proclamation to be made in the camp that they should make an assault, every man in the place where he was. 50 And the men of the army drew near, and he assaulted that city all the day and all the night, and the city was delivered into his hands. 51 And they slew every male with the edge of the sword, and he razed *the city* and took the spoils thereof and passed through all the city over them that were slain.

52 Then they passed over the Jordan *to* the great plain that is over against Beth-shan. 53 And Judas gathered together the hindmost, and he exhorted the people all the way through till they came into the land of Judah. 54 And they went up to Mount Zion with joy and gladness and offered holocausts because not one of them was slain till they had returned in peace.

55 Et in diebus quibus erat Iudas et Ionathas in terra Galaad, et Simon, frater eius, in Galilea contra faciem Ptolomaidis, 56 audivit Iosepphus, Zacchariae filius, et Azarias, princeps virtutis, res bene gestas et proelia quae facta sunt, 57 et dixit, "Faciamus et ipsi nobis nomen, et eamus pugnare adversum Gentes quae in circuitu nostro sunt." 58 Et praecepit his qui erant in exercitu suo, et abierunt Iamniam. 59 Et exivit Gorgias de civitate et viri eius obviam illis in pugnam. 60 Et fugati sunt Iosepphus et Azarias usque in fines Iudaeae, et ceciderunt illa die de populo Israhel ad duo milia viri, et facta est fuga magna in populo, 61 quia non audierunt Iudam et fratres eius, existimantes se fortiter facturos. 62 Ipsi autem non erant de semine virorum illorum per quos salus facta est in Israhel.

63 Et viri Iuda magnificati sunt valde in conspectu omnis Israhel et gentium omnium ubi audiebatur nomen eorum. 64 Et convenerunt ad eos fausta adclamantes. 65 Et exivit Iudas et fratres eius et expugnabant filios Esau in terra quae ad austrum est, et percussit Chebron et filias eius, et muros eius et turres succendit igni in circuitu. 66 Et movit castra ut iret in terram alienigenarum, et perambulabat Samariam. 67 In illa die ceciderunt sacerdotes in bello dum volunt fortiter facere, dum sine consilio exeunt in proelium. 68 Et declinavit Iudas in Azotum in terram alienigenarum, et diruit aras eorum, et sculptilia deorum ipsorum succendit igni, et cepit spolia civitatum et regressus est in terram Iuda.

55 Now in the days that Judas and Jonathan were in the land of Gilead, and Simon, his brother, in Galilee before Ptolemais, 56 Joseph, the son of Zechariah, and Azariah, captain of the soldiers, heard of the good success and the battles that were fought, 57 and he said, "Let us also get us a name, and let us go fight against the Gentiles that are round about us." 58 And he gave charge to them that were in his army, and they went towards Jamnia. 59 And Gorgias and his men went out of the city to *give* them battle. 60 And Joseph and Azariah were put to flight *and were pursued* unto the borders of Judea, and there fell on that day of the people of Israel about two thousand men, and there was a great overthrow of the people, 61 because they did not hearken to Judas and his brethren, thinking that they should do manfully. 62 But they were not of the seed of those men by whom salvation was brought to Israel.

63 And the men of Judah were magnified exceedingly in the sight of all Israel and of all the nations where their name was heard. 64 And people assembled to them with joyful acclamations. 65 Then Judas and his brethren went forth and attacked the children of Esau in the land toward the south, and he took Hebron and her *towns,* and he *burnt* the walls thereof and the towers all round it. 66 And he removed his camp to go into the land of the aliens, and he went through Samaria. 67 In that day *some* priests fell in battle; while desiring to do manfully *they* went out unadvisedly to fight. 68 And Judas turned to Azotus into the land of the strangers, and he threw down their altars, and he burnt the statues of their gods with fire, and he took the spoils of the cities and returned into the land of Judah.

Caput 6

Et Rex Antiochus perambulabat superiores regiones, et audivit esse civitatem Elymaidem in Perside nobilissimam et copiosam in argento et auro 2 templumque in ea locuples valde et illic velamina aurea et loricae et scuta, quae reliquit Alexander, Philippi, rex Macedo, qui regnavit primus in Graecia. 3 Et venit et quaerebat civitatem capere et praedare eam, et non potuit quoniam innotuit sermo his qui erant in civitate. 4 Et insurrexerunt in proelium, et fugit inde et abiit cum tristitia magna et reversus est in Babyloniam.

5 Et venit qui nuntiaret ei in Perside quia fugata sunt castra quae erant in terra Iuda 6 et quia abiit Lysias cum virtute forti in primis et fugatus est a facie Iudaeorum et invaluerunt armis et viribus et spoliis multis quae ceperunt de castris quae exciderunt 7 et quia diruerunt abominationem quam aedificaverat super altare quod erat in Hierusalem et sanctificationem sicut prius circumdederunt muris excelsis, sed et Bethsuram, civitatem suam.

Chapter 6

The fruitless repentance and death of Antiochus. His son
comes against Judas with a formidable army. He besieges
Zion but at last makes peace with the Jews.

Now King Antiochus was going through the higher countries, and he heard that the city of Elymais in Persia was greatly renowned and abounding in silver and gold 2 and that there was in it a temple exceeding rich and *coverings* of gold and breastplates and shields, which *King* Alexander, son of Philip, the *Macedonian,* that reigned first in Greece, *had* left there. 3 So he came and sought to take the city and to pillage it, *but* he was not able because the *design* was known to them that were in the city. 4 And they rose up against him in battle, and he fled away from thence and departed with great sadness and returned towards Babylonia.

5 And *whilst he was* in Persia there came one that told him *how* the armies that were in the land of Judah were put to flight 6 and that Lysias went with a very great power and was put to flight before the face of the Jews and that they were grown strong by the armour and power and *store of* spoils which they had gotten out of the camps which they had destroyed 7 and that they had thrown down the abomination which he had set up upon the altar in Jerusalem and that they had compassed about the sanctuary with high walls as before and Beth-zur also, his city.

8 Et factum est ut audivit rex sermones istos expavit et commotus est valde, et decidit in lectum et incidit in languorem prae tristitia, quia non factum est ei sicut cogitabat. 9 Et erat illic dies multos, quia renovata est in eo tristitia magna, et arbitratus est se mori. 10 Et vocavit omnes amicos suos et dixit illis, "Recessit somnus ab oculis meis, et concidi, et corrui corde prae sollicitudine. 11 Et dixi in corde meo, 'In quantam tribulationem deveni et in quos fluctus tristitiae, in qua nunc sum, qui iucundus eram et dilectus in potestate mea!' 12 Nunc vero reminiscor malorum quae feci in Hierusalem, unde et abstuli omnia spolia argentea et aurea quae erant in ea, et misi auferre habitantes Iudaeam sine causa. 13 Cognovi ergo quia propterea invenerunt me mala ista, et ecce: pereo tristitia magna in terra aliena."

14 Et vocavit Philippum, unum de amicis suis, et praeposuit eum super universum regnum suum. 15 Et dedit ei diadema et stolam suam et anulum, ut adduceret Antiochum, filium suum, et nutriret eum ut regnaret. 16 Et mortuus est illic Antiochus Rex anno centesimo quadragesimo nono. 17 Et cognovit Lysias quoniam mortuus est rex, et constituit regnare Antiochum, filium eius, quem nutrivit adulescentem, et vocavit nomen eius Eupator.

18 Et hii qui erant in arce concluserant Israhel in circuitu sanctorum, et quaerebant eis mala semper et firmamentum Gentium. 19 Et cogitavit Iudas disperdere eos, et convocavit universum populum ut obsiderent eos. 20 Et convenerunt simul et obsederunt eos anno centesimo quinquagesimo, et

8 And it came to pass when the king heard these words that he was struck with fear and exceedingly moved, and he laid himself down upon his bed and fell sick for grief, because it had not fallen out to him as he imagined. 9 And he remained there many days, for great grief *came more and more* upon him, and he made account that he should die. 10 And he called for all his friends and said to them, "Sleep is gone from my eyes, and I am fallen away, and my heart is cast down for anxiety. 11 And I said in my heart, 'Into how much tribulation am I come and into what floods of sorrow, wherein now I am, I that was pleasant and beloved in my power!' 12 But now I remember the evils that I have done in Jerusalem, from whence also I took away all the spoils of gold and of silver that were in it, and I sent to destroy the inhabitants of Judah without cause. 13 I know therefore that for this cause these evils have found me, and behold: I perish with great grief in a strange land."

14 Then he called Philip, one of his friends, and he made him regent over all his kingdom. 15 And he gave him the crown and his robe and his ring, that he should go to Antiochus, his son, and should bring him up *for the kingdom.* 16 So King Antiochus died there in the year one hundred and forty-nine. 17 And Lysias understood that the king was dead, and he set up Antiochus, his son, to reign, whom he brought up young, and he called his name Eupator.

18 Now they that were in the castle had shut up *the Israelites* round about the holy places, and they were continually seeking their hurt and *to strengthen* the Gentiles. 19 And Judas purposed to destroy them, and he called together all the people to besiege them. 20 And they came together and besieged them in the year one hundred and fifty, and they made

fecerunt ballistas et machinas. 21 Et exierunt quidam ex eis qui obsidebantur, et adiunxerunt se illis aliqui impii ex Israhel. 22 Et abierunt ad regem et dixerunt, "Quousque non facis iudicium et vindicas fratres nostros? 23 Nos decrevimus servire patri tuo et ambulare in praeceptis eius et obsequi edictis eius, 24 et filii populi nostri propter hoc abalienabantur se a nobis et quicumque inveniebantur ex nobis interficiebantur et hereditates nostrae diripiebantur. 25 Et non ad nos tantum extenderunt manum sed et in omnes fines nostros. 26 Et ecce: adplicuerunt hodie ad arcem in Hierusalem occupare eam, et munitionem in Bethsuram munierunt, 27 et nisi praeveneris eos velocius, maiora quam haec facient, nec poteris obtinere eos."

28 Et iratus est rex ut haec audivit, et convocavit omnes amicos suos et principes exercitus sui et eos qui super equites erant. 29 Sed et de regnis aliis et de insulis maritimis venerunt ad eum exercitus conducticii. 30 Et erat numerus exercitus eius centum milia peditum et viginti milia equitum et elefanti triginta duo docti ad proelium. 31 Et venerunt per Idumeam et adplicuerunt ad Bethsuram et pugnaverunt dies multos, et fecerunt machinas, et exierunt et succenderunt eas igni et pugnaverunt viriliter.

32 Et recessit Iudas ab arce et movit castra ad Bethzacaram contra castra regis. 33 Et surrexit rex ante lucem et concitavit exercitus in impetum contra viam Bethzacaram, et conparaverunt se exercitus in proelium, et tubis cecinerunt, 34 et elefantis ostenderunt sanguinem uvae et mori ad

battering-slings and engines. 21 And some of the besieged got out, and some wicked men of Israel joined themselves unto them. 22 And they went to the king and said, "How long dost thou *delay to* execute the judgment and to revenge our brethren? 23 We determined to serve thy father and to do according to his orders and obey his edicts, 24 and for this they of our nation are alienated from us and have slain as many of us as they could find and have spoiled our inheritances. 25 Neither have they put forth their hand against us only but also against all our borders. 26 And behold: they have approached this day to the castle *of* Jerusalem to take it, and they have fortified the stronghold *of* Beth-zur, 27 and unless thou speedily prevent them, they will do greater things than these, and thou shalt not be able to subdue them."

28 Now when the king heard this he was angry, and he called together all his friends and the captains of his army and them that were over the horsemen. 29 There came *also* to him from other realms and from the islands of the sea hired troops. 30 And the number of his army was an hundred thousand footmen and twenty thousand horsemen and thirty-two elephants trained to battle. 31 And they went through Idumea and approached to Beth-zur and fought many days, and they made engines, *but* they sallied forth and burnt them with fire and fought manfully.

32 And Judas departed from the castle and removed the camp to Beth-zechariah over against the king's camp. 33 And the king rose before it was light and made his troops *march on* fiercely towards the way of Beth-zechariah, and the armies made themselves ready for the battle, and they sounded the trumpets, 34 and they shewed the elephants the

acuendos eos in proelium. 35 Et diviserunt bestias per legiones, et adstiterunt singulis elefantis mille viri in loricis concatenatis et galeae aereae in capitibus eorum et quingenti equites ordinati unicuique bestiae electi erant. 36 Hii ante tempus ubicumque erat bestia ibi erant, et quocumque ibat ibant, et non discedebant ab ea. 37 Sed et turres ligneae super eos firmae protegentes super singulas bestias et super eas machinae et super singulas viri virtutis triginta duo, qui pugnabant desuper, et intus magister bestiae. 38 Et residuum equitatum hinc et inde statuit in duas partes tubis exercitum commovere et perurguere constipatos in legionibus eius. 39 Et ut refulsit sol in clypeos aureos et aereos, resplenduerunt montes ab eis, et resplenduerunt sicut lampades ignis. 40 Et distincta est pars exercitus regis per montes excelsos, et alia per loca humilia, et ibant caute et ordinate. 41 Et commovebantur omnes inhabitantes terram a voce multitudinis eorum et incessu turbae et conlisione armorum, erat enim exercitus magnus valde et fortis.

42 Et adpropiavit Iudas et exercitus eius in proelium, et ceciderunt de exercitu regis sescenti viri. 43 Et vidit Eleazar, filius Saura, unam de bestiis loricatam loricis regis, et erat eminens super ceteras bestias, et visum est ei quod in ea esset rex. 44 Et dedit se ut liberaret populum suum et adquireret sibi nomen aeternum. 45 Et cucurrit ad eam audaciter in medio legionis, interficiens a dextris et a sinistris, et

blood of grapes and mulberries to provoke them to fight. 35 And they distributed the beasts by the legions, and there stood by every elephant a thousand men in coats of mail and with helmets of brass on their heads and five hundred horsemen set in order were chosen for every beast. 36 These before the time wheresoever the beast was they were there, and whithersoever it went they went, and they departed not from it. 37 *And* upon the beast there were strong wooden towers which covered every one of them and engines upon them and upon every one thirty-two valiant men, who fought from above, and *an Indian to rule* the beast. 38 And the rest of the horsemen he placed on this side and on that side at the two wings with trumpets to stir up the army and to hasten them forward that stood thick together in the legions thereof. 39 Now when the sun shone upon the shields of gold and of brass, the mountains glittered therewith, and they shone like lamps of fire. 40 And part of the king's army was distinguished by the high mountains, and the other *part* by the low places, and they marched on warily and orderly. 41 And all the inhabitants of the land were moved at the noise of their multitude and the marching of the company and the rattling of the armour, for the army was exceeding great and strong.

42 And Judas and his army drew near for battle, and there fell of the king's army six hundred men. 43 And Eleazar, the son of Saura, saw one of the beasts harnessed with the king's harness, and it was higher than the other beasts, and it seemed to him that the king was on it. 44 And he exposed himself to deliver his people and to get himself an everlasting name. 45 And he ran up to it boldly in the midst of the legion, killing on the right hand and on the left, and they fell

cadebant ab eo huc et illuc. 46 Et ivit sub pedes elefanti et subposuit se ei et occidit eum, et cecidit in terram super ipsum, et mortuus est illic.

47 Et videntes virtutem regis et impetum exercitus eius deverterunt se ab eis. 48 Castra autem regis ascenderunt contra eos in Hierusalem, et adplicuerunt castra regis ad Iudaeam et Montem Sion. 49 Et fecit pacem cum his qui erant in Bethsura, et exierunt de civitate quia non erant eis ibi alimenta conclusis, quia sabbata erant terrae. 50 Et conprehendit rex Bethsuram, et constituit illic custodiam servare eam. 51 Et convertit castra ad locum sanctificationis dies multos, et statuit illic ballistas et machinas et ignis iacula et tormenta ad lapides iactandos et spicula et scorpios ad mittendas sagittas et fundibula. 52 Fecerunt autem et ipsi machinas adversus machinas eorum, et pugnaverunt dies multos. 53 Escae autem non erant in civitate eo quod septimus annus esset et qui remanserant in Iudaea de gentibus consumpserant reliquias eorum quae repositae fuerant. 54 Et remanserunt in sanctis viri pauci, quoniam obtinuerat eos fames et dispersi sunt, unusquisque in locum suum.

55 Et audivit Lysias quod Philippus, quem constituerat Rex Antiochus cum adhuc viveret ut nutriret Antiochum, filium suum, ut regnaret, 56 reversus esset a Perside et Media et exercitus qui abierat cum ipso et quia quaerebat suscipere regni negotia. 57 Et festinavit ire et dicere ad regem et duces exercitus, "Deficimus cotidie, et esca nobis modica est, et locus quem obsidemus est munitus, et incumbit nobis

by him on this side and that side. 46 And he went *between* the feet of the elephant and put himself under it and slew it, and it fell to the ground upon him, and he died there.

47 Then they, seeing the strength of the king and the fierceness of his army, turned away from them. 48 But the king's army went up against them to Jerusalem, and the king's army pitched their tents against Judea and Mount Zion. 49 And he made peace with them that were in Beth-zur, and they came forth out of the city because they had no victuals being shut up there, for it was the *year of rest* to the land. 50 And the king took Beth-zur, and he placed there a garrison to keep it. 51 And he turned his army against the *sanctuary* for many days, and he set up there battering-slings and engines and *instruments to cast* fire and engines to cast stones and javelins and pieces to shoot arrows and slings. 52 And they also made engines against their engines, and they fought for many days. 53 But there were no victuals in the city because it was the seventh year and such as had stayed in Judea of *them that came* from among the nations had eaten the residue of all that which had been stored up. 54 And there remained in the holy places *but a few,* for the famine had prevailed over them and they were dispersed, every man to his own place.

55 Now Lysias heard that Philip, whom King Antiochus while *he* lived had appointed to bring up his son Antiochus to be king, 56 was returned from Persia and Media with the army that went with him and that he sought to take upon him the affairs of the kingdom. 57 *Wherefore* he made haste to go and say to the king and to the captains of the army, "We decay daily, and our provision of victuals is small, and the place that we lay siege to is strong, and it lieth upon us to

ordinare de regno. 58 Nunc itaque demus dextras hominibus istis et faciamus cum illis pacem et cum omni gente eorum. 59 Et constituamus illis ut ambulent in legitimis suis sicut prius, propter legitima enim ipsorum quae despeximus irati sunt et fecerunt omnia haec."

60 Et placuit sermo in conspectu regis et principum, et misit ad eos pacem facere, et receperunt illam. 61 Et iuravit illis rex et principes, et exierunt de munitione. 62 Et intravit rex Montem Sion et vidit munitionem loci, et rupit citius iuramentum quod iuravit et mandavit destruere murum in gyro. 63 Et discessit festinanter et reversus est Antiochiam, et invenit Philippum dominantem civitati, et pugnavit adversus eum et occupavit civitatem.

Caput 7

Anno centesimo quinquagesimo primo, exiit Demetrius, Seleuci filius, ab urbe Roma et ascendit cum paucis viris in civitatem maritimam et regnavit illic. 2 Et factum est ut

take order for *the affairs of* the kingdom. 58 Now therefore let us come to an agreement with these men and make peace with them and with all their nation. 59 And let us covenant with them that they may live according to their own laws as before, for because of our despising their laws they have been provoked and have done all these things."

60 And the proposal was acceptable in the sight of the king and of the princes, and he sent to them to make peace, and they accepted of it. 61 And the king and the princes swore to them, and they came out of the stronghold. 62 Then the king entered into Mount Zion and saw the strength of the place, and he quickly broke the oath that he had taken and gave commandment to throw down the wall round about. 63 And he departed in haste and returned to Antioch, *where* he found Philip, master of the city, and he fought against him and took the city.

Chapter 7

Demetrius is made king and sends Bacchides and Alcimus, the priest, into Judea and after them Nicanor, who is slain by Judas with all his army.

In the hundred and fifty-first year, Demetrius, the son of Seleucus, departed from the city of Rome and came up with a few men into a city of the sea coast and reigned there. 2 And it came to pass as he entered into the house of

ingressus est in domum regni patrum suorum conprehendit exercitus Antiochum et Lysiam ut adduceret eos ad eum. 3 Et rex ei innotuit et ait, "Nolite mihi ostendere faciem eorum." 4 Et occidit eos exercitus, et sedit Demetrius super sedem regni sui. 5 Et venerunt ad eum viri iniqui et impii ex Israhel, et Alchimus dux eorum, qui volebat fieri sacerdos. 6 Et accusaverunt populum apud regem, dicentes, "Perdidit Iudas et fratres eius omnes amicos tuos, et nos disperdit de terra nostra. 7 Nunc ergo mitte virum cui credis, ut eat et videat exterminium omne quod fecit nobis et regionibus regis, et puniat omnes amicos eius et adiutores eorum."

8 Et elegit rex ex amicis suis Bacchidem, qui dominabatur trans flumen magnum in regno et fidelem regi, et misit eum 9 ut videret exterminium quod fecit Iudas, et Alchimum impium constituit in sacerdotium et mandavit ei facere ultionem in filios Israhel. 10 Et surrexerunt et venerunt cum exercitu magno in terram Iuda, et miserunt nuntios et locuti sunt ad Iudam et fratres eius verbis pacificis in dolo. 11 Et non intenderunt sermonibus eorum, viderunt enim quia venerunt cum exercitu magno.

12 Et convenerunt ad Alchimum et Bacchidem congregatio scribarum requirere quae iusta sunt, 13 et primi Asidei qui erant in filiis Israhel, et exquirebant ab eis pacem. 14 Dixerunt enim, "Homo sacerdos de semine Aaron venit; non decipiet nos." 15 Et locutus est cum eis verba pacifica, et

the kingdom of his fathers that the army seized upon Antiochus and Lysias to bring them unto him. 3 And *when* he knew *it he* said, *"Let me* not *see* their face." 4 So the army slew them, and Demetrius sat upon the throne of his kingdom. 5 And there came to him the wicked and ungodly men of Israel, and Alcimus was at the head of them, who desired to be made *high* priest. 6 And they accused the people to the king, saying, "Judas and his brethren have destroyed all thy friends, and he hath *driven* us out of our land. 7 Now therefore send *some* man whom thou trustest, *and let him* go and see all the havock he hath made amongst us and in the king's lands, and let him punish all his friends and their helpers."

8 Then the king chose Bacchides, *one* of his friends, that ruled beyond the great river in the kingdom and was faithful to the king, and he sent him 9 to see the havoc that Judas had made, and the wicked Alcimus he made *high priest* and commanded him to take revenge upon the children of Israel. 10 And they arose and came with a great army into the land of Judah, and they sent messengers and spoke to Judas and his brethren with peaceable words deceitfully. 11 *But* they gave no heed to their words, for they saw that they were come with a great army.

12 Then there assembled to Alcimus and Bacchides a company of the scribes to require things that are just, 13 and first the Hasideans that were among the children of Israel, and they sought peace of them. 14 For they said, "One that is a priest of the seed of Aaron is come; he will not deceive us." 15 And he spoke to them peaceably, and he swore to them,

iuravit illis, dicens, "Non inferemus vobis malum neque amicis vestris." 16 Et crediderunt ei. Et conprehendit ex eis sexaginta viros et occidit eos in una die secundum verbum quod scriptum est: 17 "Carnes sanctorum tuorum et sanguinem ipsorum effuderunt in circuitu Hierusalem, et non erat qui sepeliret."

18 Et incubuit timor et tremor in omnem populum, quia dixerunt, "Non est veritas et iudicium in eis, transgressi sunt enim constitutum et iusiurandum quod iuraverunt."

19 Et movit Bacchides castra ab Hierusalem et adplicuit in Bethzecha, et misit et conprehendit multos ex eis qui a se refugerant, et quosdam de populo mactavit et in puteum magnum proiecit. 20 Et commisit regionem Alchimo et reliquit cum eo auxilium in adiutorium ipsi. Et abiit Bacchides ad regem, 21 et satis agebat Alchimus pro principatu sacerdotii sui. 22 Et convenerunt ad eum omnes qui perturbabant populum suum, et obtinuerunt terram Iuda et fecerunt plagam magnam in Israhel.

23 Et vidit Iudas omnia mala quae fecit Alchimus et qui cum eo erant filiis Israhel, plus multo quam Gentes. 24 Et exiit in omnes fines Iudaeae in circuitu et fecit vindictam in viros desertores, et cessaverunt ultra exire in regionem. 25 Vidit autem Alchimus quod praevaluit Iudas et qui cum eo erant, et cognovit quia non potest sustinere eos, et regressus est ad regem et accusavit eos multis criminibus.

saying, "We will do you no harm nor your friends." 16 And they believed him. And he took *threescore* of them and slew them in one day according to the word that is written: 17 "The flesh of thy saints and the blood of them they have shed round about Jerusalem, and there was none to bury them."

18 Then fear and trembling fell upon all the people, for they said, "There is no truth nor justice among them, for they have broken the covenant and the oath which they made."

19 And Bacchides removed the camp from Jerusalem and pitched in Beth-zaith, and he sent and took many of them that were fled away from him, and some of the people he killed and threw them into a great pit. 20 Then he committed the country to Alcimus and left with him troops to help him. So Bacchides went away to the king, 21 *but* Alcimus did *what he could to maintain* his *chief* priesthood. 22 And *they* that disturbed *the* people resorted to him, and they got the land of Judah into their power and did much hurt in Israel.

23 And Judas saw all the evils that Alcimus and they that were with him did to the children of Israel, much more than the Gentiles. 24 And he went out into all the coasts of Judea round about and took vengeance upon the men that had revolted, and they ceased to go forth any more into the country. 25 And Alcimus saw that Judas and they that were with him prevailed, and he knew that he could not stand against them, and he went back to the king and accused them of many crimes.

26 Et misit rex Nicanorem, unum ex principibus suis nobilioribus, qui erat inimicitias exercens contra Israhel, et mandavit ei evertere populum. 27 Et venit Nicanor in Hierusalem cum exercitu magno, et misit ad Iudam et ad fratres eius cum dolo verbis pacificis, 28 dicens, "Non sit pugna inter me et vos; veniam cum viris paucis ut videam facies vestras cum pace." 29 Et venit ad Iudam, et salutaverunt se invicem pacifice, et hostes parati erant rapere Iudam. 30 Et innotuit sermo Iudae quoniam cum dolo venerat ad eum, et conterritus est ab eo et amplius noluit videre faciem eius. 31 Et cognovit Nicanor quoniam denudatum est consilium eius, et exivit obviam Iudae in pugnam iuxta Capharsalama. 32 Et ceciderunt de Nicanoris exercitu fere quinque milia viri, et fugerunt in civitatem David.

33 Et post haec verba ascendit Nicanor in Montem Sion, et exierunt de sacerdotibus populi salutare eum in pace et demonstrare ei holocaustomata quae offerebantur pro rege. 34 Et inridens sprevit eos et polluit, et locutus est superbe 35 et iuravit cum ira, dicens, "Nisi traditus fuerit Iudas et exercitus eius in manus meas, continuo cum regressus fuero in pace succendam domum istam." Et exiit cum ira magna.

36 Et intraverunt sacerdotes et steterunt ante faciem altaris et templi, et flentes dixerunt, 37 "Tu elegisti domum istam, Domine, ad invocandum nomen tuum in ea ut esset domus orationis et obsecrationis populo tuo. 38 Fac vindictam in homine isto et exercitu eius, et cadant gladio. Memento blasphemias eorum, et ne dederis eis ut permaneant."

26 And the king sent Nicanor, one of his *principal* lords, who *was a great enemy* to Israel, and he commanded him to destroy the people. 27 And Nicanor came to Jerusalem with a great army, and he sent to Judas and to his brethren deceitfully with friendly words, 28 saying, "Let there be no fighting between me and you; I will come with a few men to see your faces with peace." 29 And he came to Judas, and they saluted one another peaceably, and the enemies were prepared to take away Judas by force. 30 And the thing was known to Judas that he was come to him with deceit, and he was much afraid of him and would not see his face any more. 31 And Nicanor knew that his counsel was discovered, and he went out to fight against Judas near Caphar-salama. 32 And there fell of Nicanor's army almost five thousand men, and they fled into the city of David.

33 And after *this* Nicanor went up into Mount Zion, and some of the priests and the people came out to salute him peaceably and to shew him the holocausts that were offered for the king. 34 *But* he mocked them and despised them and abused them, and he spoke proudly 35 and swore in anger, saying, "Unless Judas and his army be delivered into my hands, as soon as ever I return in peace I will burn this house." And he went out in a great rage.

36 And the priests went in and stood before the face of the altar and the temple, and weeping they said, 37 "Thou, O Lord, hast chosen this house for thy name to be called upon therein that it might be a house of prayer and supplication for thy people. 38 Be avenged of this man and his army, and let them fall by the sword. Remember their blasphemies, and suffer them not to continue *any longer.*"

39 Et exiit Nicanor ab Hierusalem et castra adplicuit ad Bethoron, et occurrit illi exercitus Syriae. 40 Et Iudas adplicuit in Adarsa cum tribus milibus viris. Et oravit Iudas et dixit, 41 "Qui missi erant a Rege Sennacherib, Domine, quia blasphemaverunt te, exiit angelus et percussit ex eis centum octoginta quinque milia; 42 sic contere exercitum istum in conspectu nostro hodie, et sciant ceteri quia male locutus est super sancta tua, et iudica illum secundum malitiam illius."

43 Et commiserunt exercitus proelium tertiadecima die mensis Adar, et contrita sunt castra Nicanoris, et cecidit ipse primus in proelio. 44 Ut vidit autem exercitus eius quia cecidit Nicanor proiecerunt arma sua et fugerunt, 45 et persecuti sunt eos viam diei unius ab Adazer usquequo veniatur in Gazara, et tubis cecinerunt post eos cum significationibus. 46 Et exierunt de omnibus castellis Iudaeae in circuitu, et ventilabant eos cornibus, et convertebantur iterum ad eos, et ceciderunt omnes gladio, et non est relictus ex eis nec unus. 47 Et acceperunt spolia eorum in praedam, et caput Nicanoris amputaverunt et dexteram eius, quam extenderat superbe, et adtulerunt et suspenderunt contra Hierusalem. 48 Et laetatus est populus valde, et egerunt diem illam in laetitia magna. 49 Et constituit agi omnibus annis diem istam, tertiadecima mensis Adar. 50 Et siluit terra Iuda dies paucos.

39 Then Nicanor went out from Jerusalem and encamped near to Beth-horon, and an army of Syria joined him. 40 *But* Judas pitched in Adasa with three thousand men. And Judas prayed and said, 41 "O Lord, when they that were sent by King Sennacherib *blasphemed* thee, an angel went out and slew of them a hundred and eighty-five thousand; 42 *even* so destroy this army in our sight today, and let the rest know that he hath spoken ill against thy sanctuary, and judge thou him according to his wickedness."

43 And the armies joined battle on the thirteenth day of the month Adar, and the army of Nicanor was defeated, and he himself was first slain in the battle. 44 And when his army saw that Nicanor was slain they threw away their weapons and fled, 45 and they pursued after them one day's journey from Adasa even till ye come to Gazara, and they sounded the trumpets after them with signals. 46 And they went forth out of all the towns of Judea round about, and they pushed them with the horns, and they turned again to them, and they were all slain with the sword, and there was not left of them so much as one. 47 And they took the spoils of them for a booty, and they cut off Nicanor's head and his right hand, which he had proudly stretched out, and they brought it and hung it up over against Jerusalem. 48 And the people rejoiced exceedingly, and they spent that day with great joy. 49 And he ordained that this day should be kept every year, being the thirteenth of the month of Adar. 50 And the land of Judah was quiet for a *short time*.

Caput 8

Et audivit Iudas nomen Romanorum, quia sunt potentes viribus et adquiescunt ad omnia quae postulantur ab eis et quicumque accesserunt ad eos, statuerunt cum eis amicitias, et quia sunt potentes viribus. 2 Et audierunt proelia eorum et virtutes bonas quas fecerunt in Galatia, quia obtinuerunt eos et duxerunt sub tributum, 3 et quanta fecerunt in regione Hispaniae et quod in potestatem redegerunt metalla argenti et auri quae illic sunt et possederunt omnem locum consilio suo et patientia 4 locaque quae longe erant valde ab eis et reges qui supervenerant illis ab extremis terrae contriverunt et percusserunt eos plaga magna, ceteri autem dant eis tributum omnibus annis. 5 Et Philippum et Persen, Ceteorum regem, et ceteros qui adversus eos arma tulerant contriverunt in bello et obtinuerunt eos 6 et Antiochum, magnum regem Asiae, qui eis pugnam intulerat habens centum viginti elefantos et equitatum et currus et exercitum magnum valde, contritum ab eis 7 et quia ceperunt eum vivum et statuerunt ei ut daret ipse et qui regnarent post

Chapter 8

Judas hears of the great character of the Romans. He makes a league with them.

Now Judas heard of the fame of the Romans, that they are powerful *and strong* and willingly agree to all things that are requested of them and that whosoever have come to them, they have made amity with them, and that they are mighty in power. 2 And they heard of their battles and their noble acts which they *had* done in Galatia, *how* they conquered them and brought them under tribute, 3 and how great things they *had* done in the land of Spain and that they *had* brought *under* their power the mines of silver and of gold that are there and *had* gotten possession of all the place by their counsel and patience 4 and *had* conquered places that were very far off from them and kings that came against them from the ends of the earth and *had* overthrown them with great slaughter, and the rest pay them tribute every year. 5 And that they *had* defeated in battle Philip and Perses, the king of the Kitteans, and the rest that had borne arms against them and *had* conquered them 6 and *how* Antiochus, the great king of Asia, who went to fight against them having a hundred and twenty elephants with horsemen and chariots and a very great army, was routed by them 7 and *how* they took him alive and appointed to him that both he and they that should reign after him should pay a great tribute

eum tributum magnum et daret obsides et constitutum 8 et regionem Indorum et Lydos et Medos de optimis regionibus eorum, et acceptas eas ab illis dederunt Eumeni Regi. 9 Et quia qui erant apud Elladam voluerunt ire et tollere eos, et innotuit sermo his, 10 et miserunt ad eos ducem unum et pugnaverunt contra illos, et ceciderunt ex eis multi, et captivas duxerunt uxores eorum et filios et diripuerunt eos et terram eorum possederunt et destruxerunt muros eorum et in servitutem illos redegerunt usque in hunc diem. 11 Et residua regna et insulas quae aliquando restiterant illis exterminaverunt et in potestatem redegerunt. 12 Cum amicis autem suis et qui in ipsis requiem habebant conservaverunt amicitiam et obtinuerunt regna quae erant proxima et quae erant longe, quia quicumque audiebant nomen eorum timebant eos. 13 Quibus vero vellent auxilio esse ut regnarent regnabant, quos autem vellent, regno deturbabant, et exaltati sunt valde. 14 Et in omnibus istis nemo portabat diadema nec induebatur purpura ut magnificaretur in ea. 15 Et quia curiam fecerunt sibi et cotidie consulebant trecentos et viginti consilium agentes semper de multitudine, ut quae digna sunt gerant. 16 Et committunt uni homini magistratum suum per singulos annos dominari universae terrae suae, et omnes oboediunt uni, et non est invidia neque zelus inter eos. 17 Et elegit Iudas Eupolemum, filium Iohannis, filii Iacob, et Iasonem, filium Eleazari, et misit eos Romam constituere cum illis amicitiam et societatem. 18 Et ut auferrent ab eis

and that he should give hostages and that which was agreed upon 8 and the country of the Indians and *of* the Medes and *of* the Lydians, some of their best provinces, and those which they had taken from them they gave to King Eumenes. 9 And that they who were in Greece had a mind to go and to destroy them, and they had knowledge thereof, 10 and they sent a general against them and fought with them, and many of them were slain, and they carried away their wives and their children captives and spoiled them and took possession of their land and threw down their walls and brought them to be their servants unto this day. 11 And the other kingdoms and islands that at any time had resisted them they *had* destroyed and brought under their power. 12 But with their friends and such as relied upon them they kept amity and *had* conquered kingdoms that were near and that were far off, for all that heard their name were afraid of them. 13 *That* whom they had a mind to help to *a kingdom,* those reigned, and whom they would, they deposed from a kingdom, and they were greatly exalted. 14 And none of all these wore a crown or was clothed in purple to be magnified thereby. 15 And that they made themselves a senate-house and consulted daily three hundred and twenty men that sat in council always for the people, that they might do the things that were right. 16 And that they committed their government to one man every year to rule over all their country, and they all obey one, and there is no envy nor jealousy amongst them. 17 So Judas chose Eupolemus, the son of John, the son of Jacob, and Jason, the son of Eleazar, and he sent them to Rome to make *a league of* amity and confederacy with them. 18 And that they might take off from them

iugum Graecorum, quia viderunt quod in servitutem premerent regnum Israhel.

19 Et abierunt Romam, viam multam valde, et introierunt curiam et dixerunt, 20 "Iudas Macchabeus et fratres eius et populus Iudaeorum miserunt nos ad vos statuere vobiscum societatem et pacem et conscribere nos socios et amicos vestros." 21 Et placuit sermo in conspectu eorum. 22 Et hoc rescriptum est quod rescripserunt in tabulis aereis et miserunt in Hierusalem ut esset apud eos ibi memoriale pacis et societatis:

23 "Bene sit Romanis et genti Iudaeorum in mari et in terra in aeternum, gladiusque et hostis procul sit ab eis. 24 Quod si institerit bellum Romanis prius aut omnibus sociis eorum in omni dominatione eorum, 25 auxilium feret gens Iudaeorum prout tempus dictaverit corde pleno, 26 et proeliantibus non dabunt neque subministrabunt triticum, arma, pecuniam, naves, sicut placuit Romanis, et custodient mandata eorum nihil ab eis accipientes. 27 Similiter autem et si genti Iudaeorum prius acciderit bellum, adiuvabunt Romani ex animo prout eis tempus permiserit. 28 Et adiuvantibus non dabitur triticum, arma, pecunia, naves, sicut placuit Romanis, et custodient mandata eorum absque dolo. 29 Secundum haec verba constituerunt Romani populo Iudaeorum. 30 Quod si post haec verba hii aut illi addere vel demere ad haec aliquid voluerint, facient ex proposito suo, et

the yoke of the Grecians, for they saw that they oppressed the kingdom of Israel with servitude.

19 And they went to Rome, a very long journey, and they entered into the senate house and said, 20 "Judas Maccabeus and his brethren and the people of the Jews have sent us to you to make alliance and peace with you and that we may be registered your confederates and friends." 21 And the proposal was pleasing in their sight. 22 And this is the copy of the writing that they wrote back again *graven* in tables of brass and sent to Jerusalem that it might be with them there for a memorial of the peace and alliance:

23 "Good success be to the Romans and to the people of the Jews by sea and by land forever, and far be the sword and enemy from them. 24 But if there come first any war upon the Romans or any of their confederates in all their dominions, 25 the nation of the Jews shall help them according as the time shall direct with all their heart, 26 neither shall they give them whilst they are fighting *or* furnish them with wheat *or* arms *or* money *or* ships, as it hath seemed good to the Romans, and they shall obey their orders without taking anything of them. 27 In like manner *also* if war shall come first upon the nation of the Jews, the Romans shall help them *with all* their heart according as the time shall permit them. 28 And there shall not be given to them that come to their aid *either* wheat *or* arms *or* money *or* ships, as it hath seemed good to the Romans, and they shall observe their orders without deceit. 29 According to these articles did the Romans covenant with the people of the Jews. 30 And if after this one party or the other shall have a mind to add to these articles or take away anything, they may do it at their pleasure, and whatsoever they shall add or take away

quaecumque addiderint vel dempserint rata erunt. 31 Sed et de malis quae Demetrius, rex, fecit in eos scripsimus ei, dicentes, 'Quare gravasti iugum tuum super amicos nostros et socios, Iudaeos? 32 Si ergo iterum adierint nos adversum te, faciemus illis iudicium et pugnabimus tecum mari terraque.'"

Caput 9

Interea ut audivit Demetrius quia cecidit Nicanor et exercitus eius in proelio, adposuit Bacchidem et Alchimum rursum mittere in Iudaeam et dextrum cornu cum illis. 2 Et abierunt viam quae ducit in Galgala, et castra posuerunt in Masaloth, quae est in Arbellis, et occupaverunt eam et peremerunt animas hominum multas. 3 In mense primo anni centesimi et quinquagesimi secundi, adplicuerunt exercitum ad Hierusalem, 4 et surrexerunt et abierunt in Beream, viginti milia virorum et duo milia equitum.

shall be ratified. 31 Moreover concerning the evils that Demetrius, the king, hath done against them we have written to him, saying, 'Why hast thou made thy yoke heavy upon our friends and allies, the Jews? 32 If therefore they come again to us complaining of thee, we will do them justice and will make war against thee by sea and land.'"

Chapter 9

Bacchides is sent again into Judea. Judas fights against him with eight hundred men and is slain. Jonathan succeeds him and revenges the murder of his brother John. He fights against Bacchides. Alcimus dies miserably. Bacchides besieges Bethbasi. He is forced to raise the siege and leave the country.

In the meantime when Demetrius heard that Nicanor and his army were fallen in battle, he sent again Bacchides and Alcimus into Judea and the right wing of his army with them. 2 And they took the road that leadeth to Gilgal, and they camped in Mesaloth, which is in Arbela, and they made themselves masters of it and slew many *people.* 3 In the first month of the hundred and fifty-second year, they brought the army to Jerusalem, 4 and they arose and went to Berea *with* twenty thousand men and two thousand horsemen.

5 Et Iudas castra posuerat in Laisa, et tria milia viri cum eo electi, 6 et viderunt multitudinem exercitus, quia multi sunt, et timuerunt valde, et multi subtraxerunt se de castris, et non remanserunt ex eis nisi octingenti viri. 7 Et vidit Iudas quod defluxit exercitus suus et bellum perurguebat eum, et confractus est corde quia non habebat tempus congregandi eos, et dissolutus est. 8 Et dixit his qui residui erant, "Surgamus et eamus ad adversarios nostros, si poterimus pugnare adversus eos."

9 Et avertebant eum, dicentes, "Non poterimus, sed liberemus animas nostras modo et revertamur ad fratres nostros, et tunc pugnabimus adversus eos, nos autem pauci sumus."

10 Et ait Iudas, "Absit istam rem facere, ut fugiamus ab eis, et si adpropiavit tempus nostrum, moriamur in virtute propter fratres nostros, et non inferamus crimen gloriae nostrae." 11 Et movit exercitus de castris, et steterunt illis obviam. Et divisi sunt equites in duas partes, et fundibalarii et sagittarii praeibant exercitum, et primi certaminis omnes potentes. 12 Bacchides autem erat in dextro cornu, et proximavit legio ex duabus partibus, et clamabant tubis, 13 exclamaverunt autem et hii qui erant ex parte Iudae etiam ipsi, et commota est terra a voce exercituum, et commissum est proelium a mane usque ad vesperam.

14 Et vidit Iudas quia firmior est pars exercitus Bacchidis in dextris, et convenerunt cum ipso omnes constantes corde, 15 et contrita est dextra pars ab eis, et persecutus est eos usque ad montem Azoti. 16 Et qui in sinistro cornu erant

5 Now Judas had pitched his tents in Elasa, and three thousand chosen men with him, 6 and they saw the multitude of the army, that they were many, and they were seized with great fear, and many withdrew themselves out of the camp, and there remained of them no more than eight hundred men. 7 And Judas saw that his army slipped away and the battle pressed upon him, and his heart was cast down because he had not time to gather them together, and he was discouraged. 8 Then he said to them that remained, "Let us arise and go against our enemies, if we may be able to fight against them."

9 *But* they dissuaded him, saying, "We shall not be able, but let us save our lives now and return to our brethren, and then we will fight against them, *for* we are *but* few."

10 Then Judas said, "God forbid we should do this thing *and* flee away from them, but if our time be come, let us die manfully for our brethren, and let us not stain our glory." 11 And the army removed out of the camp, and they stood over against them. And the horsemen were divided into two troops, and the slingers and the archers went before the army, and they that were in the front were all men of valour. 12 And Bacchides was in the right wing, and the legion drew near on two sides, and they sounded the trumpets, 13 and they also that were on Judas's side, even they also cried out, and the earth shook at the noise of the armies, and the battle was fought from morning even unto the evening.

14 And Judas perceived that the stronger part of the army of Bacchides was on the right side, and all the stout of heart came together with him, 15 and the right wing was discomfited by them, and he pursued them even to the mount Azotus. 16 And they that were in the left wing saw that the

viderunt quod contritum est dextrum cornu, et secuti sunt post Iudam et eos qui cum ipso erant a tergo. 17 Et ingravatum est proelium, et ceciderunt vulnerati multi ex his et ex illis. 18 Et Iudas cecidit, et ceteri fugerunt.

19 Et Ionathas et Simon tulerunt Iudam, fratrem suum, et sepelierunt eum in sepulchro patrum suorum in civitate Modin. 20 Et fleverunt eum omnis populus Israhel planctu magno, et lugebant dies multos 21 et dixerunt, "Quomodo cecidit potens qui salvum faciebat populum Israhel!" 22 Et cetera verba Iudae bellorum et virtutum quas fecit et magnitudinis eius non sunt descripta, multa enim erant valde.

23 Et factum est post obitum Iudae emerserunt iniqui in omnibus finibus Israhel, et exorti sunt omnes qui operabantur iniquitatem. 24 In diebus illis facta est fames magna valde, et tradidit se Bacchidi omnis regio eorum cum ipsis. 25 Et elegit Bacchides impios viros et constituit eos dominos regionis, 26 et exquirebant et perscrutabantur amicos Iudae et adducebant eos ad Bacchidem, et vindicabat in illos et inludebat. 27 Et facta est tribulatio magna in Israhel qualis non fuit ex qua die non est visus propheta in Israhel.

28 Et congregati sunt omnes amici Iudae et dixerunt Ionathae, 29 "Ex quo frater tuus Iudas defunctus est vir similis ei non est qui exeat contra inimicos, Bacchidem et eos qui inimici sunt gentis nostrae. 30 Nunc itaque te elegimus hodie esse pro eo nobis principem et ducem ad bellandum bellum nostrum."

31 Et suscepit Ionathas tempore illo principatum et

right wing was discomfited, and they followed after Judas and them that were with him at their back. 17 And the battle was hard fought, and there fell many wounded of the one side and of the other. 18 And Judas was slain, and the rest fled away.

19 And Jonathan and Simon took Judas, their brother, and buried him in the sepulchre of their fathers in the city of Modein. 20 And all the people of Israel bewailed him with great lamentation, and they mourned *for him* many days 21 and said, "How is the mighty man fallen that saved the people of Israel!" 22 *But* the rest of the words of the wars of Judas and of the noble acts that he did and of his greatness are not written, for they were very many.

23 And it came to pass after the death of Judas that the wicked *began to put* forth *their heads* in all the confines of Israel, and all the workers of iniquity rose up. 24 In those days there was a very great famine, and they and all their country yielded to Bacchides. 25 And Bacchides chose the wicked men and made them lords of the country, 26 and they sought out and made diligent search after the friends of Judas and brought them to Bacchides, and he took vengeance of them and abused them. 27 And there was a great tribulation in Israel such as was not since the day that there was no prophet seen in Israel.

28 And all the friends of Judas came together and said to Jonathan, 29 "Since thy brother Judas died there is not a man like him to go forth against *our* enemies, Bacchides and them that are the enemies of our nation. 30 Now therefore we have chosen thee this day to be our prince and captain in his stead to fight our battles."

31 So Jonathan took upon him the government at that

surrexit loco Iudae, fratris sui, 32 et cognovit Bacchides et quaerebat eum occidere. 33 Et cognovit Ionathas et Simon, frater eius, et omnes qui cum eo erant, et fugerunt in desertum Thecuae, et consederunt ad aquam lacus Asphar, 34 et cognovit Bacchides, et die sabbatorum venit ipse et omnis exercitus eius trans Iordanem.

35 Et Ionathas misit fratrem suum, ducem populi, et rogavit Nabatheos, amicos suos, ut commodarent illis adparatum suum, qui erat copiosus. 36 Et exierunt filii Iambri ex Madaba et conprehenderunt Iohannem et omnia quae habebat et abierunt habentes ea. 37 Post haec verba renuntiatum est Ionathae et Simoni, fratri eius, quia filii Iambri faciunt nuptias magnas et ducunt sponsam ex Madaba, filiam unius de magnis principibus Chanaan, cum ambitione magna. 38 Et recordati sunt sanguinis Iohannis, fratris sui, et ascenderunt et absconderunt se sub tegumento montis. 39 Et levaverunt oculos suos et viderunt, et ecce: tumultus et adparatus multus, et sponsus processit, et amici eius et fratres eius obviam illis cum tympanis et musicis et armis multis. 40 Et surrexerunt ad eos ex insidiis et occiderunt eos, et ceciderunt multi vulnerati, et residui fugerunt in montes, et acceperunt omnia spolia eorum, 41 et conversae sunt nuptiae in luctum, et vox musicorum ipsorum in lamentum. 42 Et vindicaverunt vindictam sanguinis fratris sui, et reversi sunt ad ripam Iordanis.

time and rose up in the place of Judas, his brother, 32 and Bacchides had knowledge of it and sought to kill him. 33 And Jonathan and Simon, his brother, knew it, and all that were with them, and they fled into the desert of Tekoa, and they pitched by the water of the lake of Asphar, 34 and Bacchides understood it, and he came himself with all his army over the Jordan on the sabbath day.

35 And Jonathan sent his brother, a captain of the people, *to* desire the Nabateans, his friends, that they would lend them their equipage, which was copious. 36 And the children of Jambri came forth out of Medeba and took John and all that he had and went away with them. 37 After this it was told Jonathan and Simon, his brother, that the children of Jambri made a great marriage and were bringing the bride out of Medeba, the daughter of one of the great princes of Canaan, with great pomp. 38 And they remembered the blood of John, their brother, and they went up and hid themselves under the covert of the mountain. 39 And they lifted up their eyes and saw, and behold: a tumult and great preparation, and the bridegroom came forth, and his friends and his brethren to meet them with timbrels and musical instruments and many weapons. 40 And they rose up against them from the place where they lay in ambush and slew them, and there fell many wounded, and the rest fled into the mountains, and they took all their spoils, 41 and the marriage was turned into mourning, and the noise of their musical instruments into lamentation. 42 And they took revenge for the blood of their brother, and they returned to the bank of the Jordan.

43 Et audivit Bacchides, et venit die sabbatorum usque ad oram Iordanis in virtute magna. 44 Et dixit ad suos Ionathas, "Surgamus et pugnemus contra inimicos nostros, non est enim hodie sicut heri et nudius tertius. 45 Ecce enim: bellum ex adverso, aqua vero Iordanis hinc et inde, et ripae et paludes et saltus, et non est locus devertendi. 46 Nunc ergo clamate in caelum ut liberemini de manu inimicorum vestrorum." Et commissum est bellum. 47 Et extendit Ionathas manum suam percutere Bacchidem, et devertit ab eo retro. 48 Et desiluit Ionathas et qui cum eo erant in Iordanem et transnataverunt ad eos Iordanem. 49 Et ceciderunt de parte Bacchidis die illa mille viri, et reversi sunt in Hierusalem, 50 et aedificaverunt civitates munitas in Iudaea, munitionem quae erat in Hiericho et in Ammaum et in Bethoron et in Bethel et Tamnata et Phara et Thopo muris excelsis et portis et seris. 51 Et posuit custodiam in eis ut inimicitias exercerent in Israhel, 52 et munivit civitatem Bethsuram et Gazaram et arcem et posuit in eis auxilia et adparatum escarum, 53 et accepit filios principum regionis obsides et posuit eos in arce in Hierusalem in custodiam.

54 Et anno centesimo quinquagesimo tertio, mense secundo, praecepit Alchimus destrui muros domus sanctae interioris et destrui opera prophetarum, et coepit destruere. 55 In tempore illo percussus est Alchimus, et inpedita sunt opera illius, et obclusum est os eius, et dissolutus est paralysi, nec ultra loqui potuit verbum et mandare de domo sua. 56 Et mortuus est Alchimus in tempore illo cum tormento magno.

43 And Bacchides heard it, and he came on the sabbath day even to the bank of the Jordan with a great power. 44 And Jonathan said to his company, "Let us arise and fight against our enemies, for it is not now as yesterday and the day before. 45 For behold: the battle is before us, and the water of the Jordan on this side and on that side, and banks and marshes and woods, and there is no place for us to turn aside. 46 Now therefore cry ye to heaven that ye may be delivered from the hand of your enemies." And they joined battle. 47 And Jonathan stretched forth his hand to strike Bacchides, *but* he turned away from him backwards. 48 And Jonathan and they that were with him leapt into the Jordan and swam over the Jordan to them. 49 And there fell of Bacchides's side that day a thousand men, and they returned to Jerusalem, 50 and they built strong cities in Judea, the fortress that was in Jericho and in Emmaus and in Beth-horon and in Bethel and Timnath and Pharathon and Tephon with high walls and gates and bars. 51 And he placed garrisons in them that they might wage *war* against Israel, 52 and he fortified the city of Beth-zur and Gazara and the castle and set garrisons in them and provisions of victuals, 53 and he took the sons of the chief men of the country for hostages and put them in the castle in Jerusalem in custody.

54 Now in the year one hundred and fifty-three, the second month, Alcimus commanded the walls of the inner *court of the* sanctuary to be thrown down and the works of the prophets to be destroyed, and he began to destroy. 55 At that time Alcimus was struck, and his works were hindered, and his mouth was stopped, and he was taken with a palsy, *so that* he could no more speak a word nor give order concerning his house. 56 And Alcimus died at that time in great torment.

57 Et vidit Bacchides quoniam mortuus est Alchimus, et reversus est ad regem, et siluit terra annis duobus.

58 Et cogitaverunt omnes iniqui, dicentes, "Ecce: Ionathas et qui cum eo sunt in silentio habitant confidenter. Nunc ergo adducamus Bacchidem, et conprehendet eos omnes in una nocte." 59 Et abierunt et consilium ei dederunt. 60 Et surrexit ut veniret cum exercitu multo, et misit occulte epistulas sociis suis qui erant in Iudaea ut conprehenderent Ionathan et eos qui cum eo erant, sed non potuerunt, quia innotuit eis consilium eorum. 61 Et adprehendit de viris regionis qui principes erant malitiae quinquaginta viros et occidit eos.

62 Et secessit Ionathas et Simon et qui cum eo erant in Bethbessen, quae est in deserto, et exstruxit diruta eius, et firmaverunt eam. 63 Et cognovit Bacchides, et congregavit universam multitudinem suam et his qui de Iudaea erant denuntiavit. 64 Et venit et castra posuit desuper Bethbessen et obpugnavit eam dies multos et fecit machinas. 65 Et reliquit Ionathas Simonem, fratrem suum, in civitate et exiit in regionem et venit cum numero 66 et percussit Odaren et fratres eius et filios Phaseron in tabernaculis ipsorum, et coepit caedere et crescere in virtutibus. 67 Simon vero et qui cum ipso erant exierunt de civitate et succenderunt machinas. 68 Et pugnaverunt contra Bacchidem, et contritus est ab eis, et adflixerunt eum valde, quoniam consilium eius et congressus eius erat inanis. 69 Et iratus contra viros iniquos qui ei consilium dederant ut veniret in regionem ipsorum, multos ex eis occidit, ipse autem cogitavit cum reliquis abire in regionem suam.

57 And Bacchides saw that Alcimus was dead, and he returned to the king, and the land was quiet for two years.

58 And all the wicked *held a council,* saying, "Behold: Jonathan and they that are with him dwell at ease *and* without fear. Now therefore let us bring Bacchides hither, and he shall take them all in one night." 59 So they went and gave him counsel. 60 And he arose to come with a great army, and he sent secretly letters to his adherents that were in Judea to seize upon Jonathan and them that were with him, but they could not, for their design was known to them. 61 And he apprehended of the men of the country that were the principal authors of the mischief fifty men and slew them.

62 And Jonathan and Simon and they that were with him retired into Bethbasi, which is in the desert, and he repaired the breaches thereof, and they fortified it. 63 And *when* Bacchides knew it, *he* gathered together all his multitude and sent word to them that were of Judea. 64 And he came and camped above Bethbasi and fought against it many days and made engines. 65 *But* Jonathan left his brother Simon in the city and went forth into the country and came with a number *of men* 66 and struck Odares and his brethren and the children of Phasiron in their tents, and he began to slay and to increase in forces. 67 But Simon and they that were with him sallied out of the city and burnt the engines. 68 And they fought against Bacchides, and he was discomfited by them, and they afflicted him exceedingly, for his counsel and his enterprise was in vain. 69 And he was angry with the wicked men that had given him counsel to come into their country, and he slew many of them, and he purposed to return with the rest into their country.

70 Et cognovit Ionathas, et misit ad eum legatos conponere cum ipso pacem et reddere ei captivitatem. 71 Et libenter accepit et fecit secundum verba eius et iuravit nihil se ei facturum mali omnibus diebus vitae eius. 72 Et reddidit ei captivitatem quam prius erat praedatus de terra Iuda, et conversus abiit in terram suam, et non adposuit amplius venire in fines eius. 73 Et cessavit gladius ex Israhel, et habitavit Ionathas in Machmas, et coepit Ionathas ibi iudicare populum, et exterminavit impios ex Israhel.

Caput 10

Et anno centesimo sexagesimo ascendit Alexander, Antiochi filius, qui cognominatus est Nobilis, et occupavit Ptolomaidam, et receperunt eum, et regnavit illic. 2 Et audivit Demetrius Rex et congregavit exercitum valde copiosum et exivit obviam illi in proelium. 3 Et misit Demetrius ad Ionathan epistulam verbis pacificis ut magnificaret

⁷⁰ And Jonathan had knowledge of it, and he sent ambassadors to him to make peace with him and to restore to him the prisoners. ⁷¹ And he accepted it willingly and did according to his words and swore that he would do him no harm all the days of his life. ⁷² And he restored to him the prisoners which he before had taken out of the land of Judah, and he returned and went away into his own country, and he came no more into their borders. ⁷³ So the sword ceased from Israel, and Jonathan dwelt in Michmash, and Jonathan began there to judge the people, and he destroyed the wicked out of Israel.

Chapter 10

Alexander Balas sets himself up for king. Both he and Demetrius seek to make Jonathan their friend. Alexander kills Demetrius in battle and honours Jonathan. His victory over Apollonius.

Now in the hundred and sixtieth year Alexander, the son of Antiochus, surnamed the Illustrious, came up and took Ptolemais, and they received him, and he reigned there. 2 And King Demetrius heard of it and gathered together an exceeding great army and went forth against him to fight. 3 And Demetrius sent a letter to Jonathan with peaceable

eum. 4 Dixit enim, "Anticipemus pacem facere cum eo priusquam faciat cum Alexandro adversus nos. 5 Recordabitur enim omnium malorum quae fecimus in eum et in fratrem eius et in gentem eius." 6 Et dedit ei potestatem congregandi exercitum et fabricare arma et esse ipsum socium eius, et obsides qui erant in arce iussit tradi ei.

7 Et venit Ionathas in Hierusalem et legit epistulas in auditu omnis populi et eorum qui in arce erant. 8 Et timuerunt timore magno quoniam audierunt quod dedit ei rex potestatem congregandi exercitum. 9 Et traditi sunt Ionathae obsides, et reddidit eos parentibus suis. 10 Et habitavit Ionathas in Hierusalem et coepit aedificare et innovare civitatem. 11 Et dixit facientibus opera ut struerent muros et Montem Sion in circuitu lapidibus quadratis ad munitionem, et ita fecerunt. 12 Et fugerunt alienigenae qui erant in munitionibus quas aedificaverat Bacchides, 13 et reliquit unusquisque locum suum et abiit in terram suam; 14 tantum in Bethsura remanserunt aliqui ex his qui reliquerant legem et praecepta Dei, erat enim haec eis ad refugium.

15 Et audivit Alexander Rex promissa quae promisit Demetrius Ionathae, et narraverunt ei proelia et virtutes quas ipse fecit et fratres eius et labores quos laboraverunt. 16 Et ait, "Numquid inveniemus aliquem virum talem? Et nunc faciemus eum amicum et socium nostrum."

words to magnify him. 4 For he said, "Let us first make a peace with him before he make one with Alexander against us. 5 For he will remember all the evils that we have done against him and against his brother and against his nation." 6 And he gave him authority to gather together an army and to make arms and that he should be his confederate, and the hostages that were in the castle he commanded to be delivered to him.

7 And Jonathan came to Jerusalem and read the letters in the hearing of all the people and of them that were in the castle. 8 And they were struck with great fear because they heard that the king *had given* him authority to gather together an army. 9 And the hostages were delivered to Jonathan, and he restored them to their parents. 10 And Jonathan dwelt in Jerusalem and began to build and to repair the city. 11 And he ordered workmen to build the walls and Mount Zion round about with square stones for fortification, and so they did. 12 And the strangers that were in the strongholds which Bacchides had built fled away, 13 and every man left his place and departed into his own country; 14 only in Bethzur there remained some of them that had forsaken the law and the commandments of God, for this was a place of refuge for them.

15 And King Alexander heard of the promises that Demetrius *had* made Jonathan, and they told him of the battles and the worthy acts that he and his brethren *had done* and the labours that they *had* endured. 16 And he said, "Shall we find such another man? Now *therefore* we will make him our friend and our confederate."

17 Et scripsit epistulam et misit ei secundum haec verba, dicens:

18 "Rex Alexander fratri Ionathae salutem.

19 "Audivimus de te quod vir potens sis viribus et aptus es ut sis amicus noster, 20 et nunc constituimus te hodie summum sacerdotem gentis tuae et ut amicus regis voceris," (et misit ei purpuram et coronam auream) "et quae nostra sunt sentias nobiscum et conserves amicitias ad nos."

21 Et induit se Ionathas stola sancta septimo mense, anno centesimo sexagesimo, in die sollemni scenophegiae, et congregavit exercitum et fecit arma copiosa.

22 Et audivit Demetrius verba ista et contristatus est nimis et ait, 23 "Quid hoc fecimus quod praeoccupavit nos Alexander adprehendere amicitiam Iudaeorum ad munimen sui? 24 Scribam et ego illis verba deprecatoria et dignitates et dona, ut sint mecum in adiutorium."

25 Et scripsit eis in haec verba:

"Rex Demetrius genti Iudaeorum salutem.

26 "Quoniam servastis ad nos pactum et mansistis in amicitia nostra et non accessistis ad inimicos nostros, audivimus et gavisi sumus. 27 Et nunc perseverate adhuc conservare ad nos fidem, et retribuemus vobis bona pro his quae fecistis nobiscum, 28 et remittemus vobis praestationes multas et dabimus vobis donationes.

29 "Et nunc absolvo vos et omnes Iudaeos a tributis, et pretia salis indulgeo et coronas remitto et tertias seminis, 30 et dimidiam partem fructus ligni quod est portionis meae

17 So he wrote a letter and sent it to him according to these words, saying:

18 "King Alexander to his brother Jonathan, greeting.

19 "We have heard of thee that thou art a man *of great* power and fit to be our friend; 20 now *therefore* we make thee this day high priest of thy nation and that thou be called the king's friend," (and he sent him a purple robe and a crown of gold) "and that thou be of one mind with us in our affairs and keep friendship with us."

21 Then Jonathan put on the holy vestment in the seventh month, in the year one hundred and threescore, at the feast day of the tabernacles, and he gathered together an army and made a great number of arms.

22 And Demetrius heard these words and was exceeding sorry and said, 23 "What is this that we have done that Alexander hath prevented us to gain the friendship of the Jews to strengthen himself? 24 I also will write to them words of request and *offer* dignities and gifts, that they may be with me to aid me."

25 And he wrote to them in these words:

"King Demetrius to the nation of the Jews, greeting.

26 "Whereas you have kept covenant with us and have continued in our friendship and have not joined with our enemies, we have heard of it and are glad. 27 *Wherefore* now continue still to keep fidelity towards us, and we will reward you with good things for what you have done in our behalf, 28 and we will remit to you many charges and will give you gifts.

29 "And now I free you and all the Jews from tributes, and I release you from the customs of salt and remit the crowns and the thirds of the seed, 30 and the half of the fruit of trees

relinquo vobis ex hodierno die et deinceps, ne accipiatur a terra Iuda et a tribus civitatibus quae additae sunt illi ex Samaria et Galilea ex hodierna die et in totum tempus, 31 et Hierusalem sit sancta et libera cum finibus suis, et decimae et tributa ipsius sint.

32 "Remitto etiam potestatem arcis quae est in Hierusalem, et do eam summo sacerdoti ut constituat in ea viros quoscumque ipse elegerit qui custodiant eam. 33 Et omnem animam Iudaeorum quae captiva est a terra Iuda in omni regno meo relinquo liberam gratis, ut omnes a tributis resolvantur etiam pecorum suorum.

34 "Et omnes dies sollemnes et sabbata et neomeniae et dies decreti et tres dies ante diem sollemnem et tres dies post diem sollemnem sint omnes inmunitatis et remissionis omnibus Iudaeis qui sunt in regno meo, 35 et nemo habebit potestatem agere aliquid et movere negotia adversus aliquem eorum in omni causa.

36 "Et adscribantur ex Iudaeis in exercitu regis ad triginta milia virorum, et dabuntur illis copiae ut oportet omnibus exercitibus regis, et ex ipsis ordinabuntur qui sint in munitionibus regis magni, 37 et ex his constituentur supra negotia regni quae aguntur ex fide, et principes sint ex eis. Et ambulent in legibus suis sicut praecepit rex in terra Iuda.

38 "Et tres civitates quae additae sunt Iudaeae ex regione Samariae, cum Iudaea reputentur, ut sint sub uno et non oboediant aliae potestati nisi summi sacerdotis. 39 Ptolomaida et confines eius, quas dedi donum sanctis qui sunt

which is my share I leave to you from this day forward, so that it shall not be taken of the land of Judah and of the three cities that are added thereto out of Samaria and Galilee from this day forth and for ever, 31 and let Jerusalem be holy and free with the borders thereof, and let the tenths and tributes be for itself.

32 "I yield up also the power of the castle that is in Jerusalem, and I give it to the high priest to place therein such men as he shall choose to keep it. 33 And every soul of the Jews that hath been carried captive from the land of Judah in all my kingdom I set at liberty freely, that all be discharged from tributes even of their cattle.

34 "And I will that all the feasts and the sabbaths and the new moons and the days appointed and three days before the solemn day and three days after the solemn day be all days of immunity and freedom for all the Jews that are in my kingdom, 35 and no man shall have power to do anything *against them or* to molest *any* of them in any cause.

36 "And let there be enrolled in the king's army to the number of thirty thousand of the Jews, and allowance shall be made them as is due to all the king's forces, and certain of them shall be appointed to be in the fortresses of the great king, 37 and some of them shall be set over the affairs of the kingdom that are of trust, and let the governors be taken from among themselves. And let them walk in their own laws as the king hath commanded in the land of Judah.

38 "And the three cities that are added to Judea out of the country of Samaria, let them be accounted with Judea, that they may be under one and obey no other authority but that of the high priest. 39 Ptolemais and the confines thereof

in Hierusalem ad necessarios sumptus sanctorum. 40 Et ego do singulis annis quindecim milia siclorum argenti de rationibus regis, quae me contingunt, 41 et omne quod reliquum fuerit quod non reddiderant qui super negotia erant annis prioribus, ex hoc dabunt in opera domus. 42 Et super haec quinque milia siclorum argenti quae accipiebant de sanctorum ratione per singulos annos et haec ad sacerdotes pertineant qui ministerio funguntur. 43 Et quicumque fugerint in templum quod est in Hierosolymis et in omnibus finibus eius, obnoxii regi in omni negotio, dimittantur, et universa quae sunt eis in regno meo, libera habeant.

44 "Et ad aedificanda vel restauranda opera sanctorum sumptus dabuntur de ratione regis, 45 et ad extruendos muros Hierusalem et communiendos in circuitu sumptus dabuntur de ratione regis et ad construendos muros in Iudaea."

46 Ut audivit autem Ionathas et populus sermones istos, non crediderunt eis nec receperunt eos, quia recordati sunt malitiae magnae quam fecerat in Israhel, et tribulaverat eos valde. 47 Et conplacuit eis in Alexandrum quia ipse fuerat eis princeps sermonum pacis, et ipsi auxilium ferebant omnibus diebus.

48 Et congregavit Alexander Rex exercitum magnum et admovit castra ad Demetrium. 49 Et commiserunt proelium duo reges, et fugit exercitus Demetrii, et insecutus est eum Alexander et incubuit super eos. 50 Et invaluit proelium nimis donec occidit sol, et cecidit Demetrius in illa die.

I give as a *free* gift to the holy places that are in Jerusalem for the necessary charges of the holy things. 40 And I give every year fifteen thousand sicles of silver out of the king's accounts, of what belongs to me, 41 and all that is above which they that were over the affairs the years before had not paid, from this time they shall give it to the works of the house. 42 Moreover the five thousand sicles of silver which they received from the account of the holy places every year *shall* also belong to the priests that execute the ministry. 43 And whosoever shall flee into the temple that is in Jerusalem and in all the borders thereof, being indebted to the king for any matter, let them be set at liberty, and all that they have in my kingdom, let them have it free.

44 "For the building also or repairing the works of the holy places the charges shall be given out of the king's revenues; 45 for the building also of the walls of Jerusalem and the fortifying thereof round about the charges shall be given out of the king's account *as* also for the building of the walls in Judea."

46 Now when Jonathan and the people heard these words, they gave no credit to them nor received them, because they remembered the great evil that he had done in Israel, *for* he had afflicted them exceedingly. 47 And their inclinations were towards Alexander because he had been the chief promoter of *peace* in their regard, and him they *always* helped.

48 And King Alexander gathered together a great army and moved his camp near to Demetrius. 49 And the two kings joined battle, and the army of Demetrius fled away, and Alexander pursued after him and pressed them close. 50 And the battle was hard fought till the sun went down, and Demetrius was slain that day.

51 Et misit Alexander ad Ptolomeum, regem Aegypti, legatos secundum haec verba, dicens, 52 "Quoniam regressus sum in regnum meum et sedi in sede patrum meorum et obtinui principatum et contrivi Demetrium et possedi regionem nostram 53 et commisi cum eo pugnam, et contritus est ipse et castra eius a nobis, et sedimus in sede regni eius, 54 et nunc statuamus ad invicem amicitiam, et da mihi filiam tuam uxorem, et ero gener tuus, et dabo tibi dona et ipsi dignitatem."

55 Et respondit Ptolomeus Rex, dicens, "Felix dies in qua reversus es ad terram patrum tuorum et sedisti in sede regni eorum. 56 Et nunc faciam tibi quae scripsisti, sed occurre mihi Ptolomaidae, ut videamus nos invicem et spondeam tibi sicut dixisti."

57 Et exiit Ptolomeus de Aegypto, ipse et Cleopatra, filia eius, et venit Ptolomaidam anno centesimo sexagesimo secundo. 58 Et occurrit ei Alexander Rex, et dedit ei Cleopatram, filiam suam, et fecit nuptias eius Ptolomaidae sicut reges in magna gloria. 59 Et scripsit Rex Alexander Ionathae ut veniret obviam sibi. 60 Et abiit cum gloria Ptolomaidam, et occurrit ibi duobus regibus, et dedit illis argentum multum et aurum et dona, et invenit gratiam in conspectu eorum.

61 Et convenerunt adversus eum viri pestilentes ex Israhel, viri iniqui, interpellantes adversus eum, et non intendit ad eos rex. 62 Et iussit expoliari Ionathan vestimentis suis et

51 And Alexander sent ambassadors to Ptolemy, king of Egypt, with words to this effect, saying, 52 "Forasmuch as I am returned into my kingdom and am set in the throne of my ancestors and have gotten the dominion and have overthrown Demetrius and possessed our country 53 and have joined battle with him, and both he and his army have been destroyed by us, and we are placed in the throne of his kingdom, 54 now *therefore* let us make friendship one with another, and give me now thy daughter to wife, and I will be thy son-in-law, and I will give both *thee and her gifts worthy of thee.*"

55 And King Ptolemy answered, saying, "Happy is the day wherein thou didst return to the land of thy fathers and sattest in the throne of their kingdom. 56 And now I will do to thee as thou hast written, but meet me at Ptolemais, that we may see one another and I may give her to thee as thou hast said."

57 So Ptolemy went out of Egypt with Cleopatra, his daughter, and he came to Ptolemais in the hundred and sixty-second year. 58 And King Alexander met him, and he gave him his daughter Cleopatra, and he celebrated her marriage at Ptolemais with great glory after the manner of kings. 59 And King Alexander wrote to Jonathan that he should come *and* meet him. 60 And he went honourably to Ptolemais, and he met there the two kings, and he gave them much silver and gold and presents, and he found favour in their sight.

61 And some pestilent men of Israel, men *of a* wicked *life,* assembled themselves against him *to accuse* him, and the king gave no heed to them. 62 And he commanded that Jonathan's garments should be taken off and that he should be clothed

indui eum purpura, et ita fecerunt. Et conlocavit eum rex sedere secum, 63 dixitque principibus suis, "Exite cum eo in medium civitatis, et praedicate ut nemo interpellet adversus eum de ullo negotio nec quisquam ei molestus sit de ulla ratione." 64 Et factum est ut viderunt qui interpellabant gloriam eius quae praedicabatur et opertum eum purpura, fugerunt omnes. 65 Et magnificavit eum rex et scripsit eum inter primos amicos et posuit eum ducem et participem principatus. 66 Et reversus est Ionathas in Hierusalem cum pace et laetitia.

67 In anno centesimo sexagesimo quinto, venit Demetrius, filius Demetrii, a Creta in terram patrum suorum. 68 Et audivit Alexander Rex et contristatus est valde et reversus est Antiochiam. 69 Et constituit Demetrius Rex Apollonium ducem, qui praeerat Coelesyriae, et congregavit exercitum magnum et accessit ad Iamnia, et misit ad Ionathan, summum sacerdotem, 70 dicens, "Tu solus resistis nobis, ego autem factus sum in derisum et in obprobrium propterea quia tu potestatem adversum nos exerces in montibus. 71 Nunc ergo si confidis in virtutibus tuis, descende ad nos in campum, et conparemus illic invicem, quia mecum est virtus bellorum. 72 Interroga, et disce quis sum ego et ceteri qui auxilio sunt mihi, qui et dicunt quia non potest stare pes vester ante faciem nostram, quia bis in fugam conversi sunt patres tui in terra sua. 73 Et nunc quomodo poteris sustinere equitatum et exercitum tantum in campo, ubi non est lapis neque saxum neque locus fugiendi?"

74 Ut audivit autem Ionathas sermones Apollonii, motus est animo, et elegit decem milia virorum et exiit ab Hierusalem, et occurrit ei Simon, frater eius, in adiutorium. 75 Et adplicuerunt castra in Ioppen, et exclusit eum a civitate quia

with purple, and they did so. And the king made him sit by himself, 63 and he said to his princes, "Go out with him into the midst of the city, and make proclamation that no man complain against him of any matter and that no man trouble him for any manner of cause." 64 So *when* his accusers saw his glory proclaimed and him clothed with purple, they all fled away. 65 And the king magnified him and enrolled him amongst his chief friends and made him governor and partaker of his dominion. 66 And Jonathan returned into Jerusalem with peace and joy.

67 In the year one hundred and sixty-five, Demetrius, the son of Demetrius, came from Crete into the land of his fathers. 68 And King Alexander heard of it and was much troubled and returned to Antioch. 69 And King Demetrius made Apollonius his general, who was governor of Coelesyria, and he gathered together a great army and came to Jamnia, and he sent to Jonathan, the high priest, 70 saying, "Thou alone standest against us, and I am laughed at and reproached because thou shewest thy power against us in the mountains. 71 Now therefore if thou trustest in thy forces, come down to us into the plain, and there let us try one another, for with me is the strength of war. 72 Ask, and learn who I am and the rest that help me, who also say that your foot cannot stand before our face, for thy fathers have twice been put to flight in their own land. 73 And now how wilt thou be able to abide the horsemen and so great an army in the plain, where there is no stone nor rock nor place to flee to?"

74 Now when Jonathan heard the words of Apollonius, he was moved in his mind, and he chose ten thousand men and went out of Jerusalem, and Simon, his brother, met him to help him. 75 And they pitched their tents near Joppa, *but*

custodia Apollonii Ioppe erat, et obpugnavit eam. 76 Et exterriti, qui erant intra civitatem aperuerunt ei. Et obtinuit Ionathas Ioppen.

77 Et audivit Apollonius, et admovit tria milia equitum et exercitum multum. 78 Et abiit Azotum tamquam iter faciens, et statim exiit in campum, eo quod haberet multitudinem equitum et confideret in eis. Et insecutus est eum Ionathas in Azotum, et proelium commiserunt. 79 Et reliquit Apollonius in castris mille equites post eos occulte. 80 Et cognovit Ionathas quoniam sunt insidiae post se, et circuierunt castra eius et iecerunt iacula in populum a mane usque ad vesperam. 81 Populus autem stabat sicut praeceperat Ionathas, et laboraverunt equi eorum.

82 Et eiecit Simon exercitum suum et commisit contra legionem, equites enim fatigati erant, et contriti sunt ab eo et fugerunt. 83 Et qui dispersi sunt per campum fugerunt in Azotum et intraverunt in Bethdagon, idolium suum, ut ibi se liberarent. 84 Et succendit Ionathas Azotum et civitates quae erant in circuitu eius et accepit spolia eorum et templum Dagon, et omnes qui fugerunt in illud succendit igni. 85 Et fuerunt qui ceciderunt gladio cum his qui succensi sunt fere octo milia virorum.

86 Et movit inde Ionathas castra et adplicuit ea Ascalona, et exierunt de civitate obviam illi in magna gloria. 87 Et reversus est Ionathas in Hierusalem cum suis habentibus spolia multa. 88 Et factum est ut audivit Alexander, rex,

they shut him out of the city because a garrison of Apollonius was in Joppa, and he laid siege to it. 76 And they that were in the city, being affrighted, opened the gates to him. So Jonathan took Joppa.

77 And Apollonius heard of it, and he took three thousand horsemen and a great army. 78 And he went to Azotus as one that was making a journey, and immediately he went forth into the plain, because he had a great number of horsemen and he trusted in them. And Jonathan followed after him to Azotus, and they joined battle. 79 And Apollonius left privately in the camp a thousand horsemen behind them. 80 And Jonathan knew that there was an ambush behind him, and they surrounded his army and cast darts at the people from morning till evening. 81 But the people stood still as Jonathan had commanded them, and *so* their horses were fatigued.

82 Then Simon drew forth his army and attacked the legion, for the horsemen were wearied, and they were discomfited by him and fled. 83 And they that were scattered about the plain fled into Azotus and went into Beth-dagon, their idol's temple, there to save themselves. 84 *But* Jonathan set fire to Azotus and the cities that were around it and took the spoils of them and the temple of Dagon, and all them that were fled into it he burnt with fire. 85 So they that were slain by the sword with them that were burnt were almost eight thousand men.

86 And Jonathan removed his army from thence and camped against Askalon, and they went out of the city to meet him with great honour. 87 And Jonathan returned into Jerusalem with his people having many spoils. 88 And it came to pass when Alexander, the king, heard these words that he

sermones istos addidit adhuc glorificare Ionathan. 89 Et misit ei fibulam auream, sicuti est consuetudo dari cognatis regum. Et dedit ei Accaron et omnes fines eius in possessionem.

Caput 11

Et rex Aegypti congregavit exercitum sicut harena quae est circa oram maris et naves multas, et quaerebat obtinere regnum Alexandri dolo et addere illud regno suo. 2 Et exiit in Syriam verbis pacificis, et aperiebant ei civitates et occurrebant ei, quia mandaverat Alexander Rex exire ei obviam, eo quod socer suus esset. 3 Cum introiret autem civitatem Ptolomeus, ponebat custodias militum in singulis civitatibus. 4 Et ut adpropiavit Azoto, ostenderunt ei templum Dagon succensum igni et Azotum et cetera eius demolita et corpora proiecta et eorum qui caesi erant in bello tumulos,

honoured Jonathan yet more. 89 And he sent him a buckle of gold, as the custom is to be given to such as are of the royal blood. And he gave him Ekron and all the borders thereof in possession.

Chapter 11

Ptolemy invades the kingdom of Alexander; the latter is
slain, and the former dies soon after. Demetrius honours
Jonathan and is rescued by the Jews from his own subjects
in Antioch. Antiochus the younger favours Jonathan. His
exploits in divers places.

And the king of Egypt gathered together an army like the sand that lieth upon the sea shore and many ships, and he sought to get the kingdom of Alexander by deceit and join it to his own kingdom. 2 And he went out into Syria with peaceable words, and they opened to him the cities and met him, for King Alexander had ordered them to go forth to meet him, because he was his father-in-law. 3 Now when Ptolemy entered into the cities, he put garrisons of soldiers in every city. 4 And when he came near to Azotus, they shewed him the temple of Dagon that was burnt with fire and Azotus and the *suburbs* thereof that were destroyed and the bodies that were cast abroad and the graves of them that were slain in the battle, which they had made near the

quos fecerant secus viam. 5 Et narraverunt regi quia haec fecit Ionathas ut invidiam facerent ei, et tacuit rex.

6 Et occurrit Ionathas regi in Ioppen cum gloria, et invicem se salutaverunt, et dormierunt illic. 7 Et abiit Ionathas cum rege usque ad fluvium qui vocatur Eleutherus, et reversus est in Hierusalem.

8 Rex autem Ptolomeus obtinuit dominium civitatum usque Seleuciam maritimam, et cogitabat in Alexandrum consilia mala. 9 Et misit legatos ad Demetrium, dicens, "Veni; conponamus inter nos pactum, et dabo tibi filiam meam, quam habet Alexander, et regnabis in regno patris tui. 10 Paenitet enim me quod dederim illi filiam meam, quaesivit enim me occidere." 11 Et vituperavit eum propterea quod concupierat regnum eius. 12 Et abstulit filiam suam et dedit eam Demetrio et abalienavit se ab Alexandro, et manifestae factae sunt inimicitiae eius.

13 Et intravit Ptolomeus Antiochiam et inposuit duo diademata capiti suo, Aegypti et Asiae. 14 Alexander autem Rex erat in Cilicia illis temporibus quia rebellabant qui erant in locis illis. 15 Et audivit Alexander et venit ad eum in bellum, et produxit Ptolomeus Rex exercitum et occurrit ei in manu valida et fugavit eum. 16 Et fugit Alexander in Arabiam ut ibi protegeretur, Rex autem Ptolomeus exaltatus est. 17 Et abstulit Zabdiel, Arabs, caput Alexandri et misit Ptolomeo. 18 Et Rex Ptolomeus mortuus est in die tertia, et qui erant in munitionibus perierunt ab his qui erant intra castra. 19 Et regnavit Demetrius anno centesimo sexagesimo septimo.

way. 5 And they told the king that Jonathan *had done* these things to make him odious, *but* the king held his peace.

6 And Jonathan came to meet the king at Joppa with glory, and they saluted one another, and they lodged there. 7 And Jonathan went with the king as far as the river called Eleutherus, and he returned into Jerusalem.

8 And King Ptolemy got the dominion of the cities by the seaside even to Seleucia, and he devised evil designs against Alexander. 9 And he sent ambassadors to Demetrius, saying, "Come; let us make a league between us, and I will give thee my daughter, whom Alexander hath, and thou shalt reign in the kingdom of thy father. 10 For I repent that I have given him my daughter, for he hath sought to kill me." 11 And he slandered him because he coveted his kingdom. 12 And he took away his daughter and gave her to Demetrius and alienated himself from Alexander, and his enmities were made manifest.

13 And Ptolemy entered into Antioch and set two crowns upon his head, that of Egypt and that of Asia. 14 Now King Alexander was in Cilicia at that time because they that were in those places *had* rebelled. 15 And *when* Alexander heard of it *he* came to *give him* battle, and King Ptolemy brought forth his army and met him with a strong power and put him to flight. 16 And Alexander fled into Arabia, there to be protected, and King Ptolemy was exalted. 17 And Zabdiel, the Arabian, took off Alexander's head and sent it to Ptolemy. 18 And King Ptolemy died the third day *after,* and they that were in the strongholds were destroyed by them that were within the camp. 19 And Demetrius reigned in the hundred and sixty-seventh year.

20 In diebus illis congregavit Ionathas eos qui erant in Iudaea ut expugnarent arcem quae est in Hierusalem, et fecerunt contra eam machinas multas. 21 Et abierunt quidam qui oderant gentem suam viri iniqui ad Regem Demetrium et renuntiaverunt ei quod Ionathas obsideret arcem. 22 Et ut audivit iratus est, et statim venit Ptolomaidam et scripsit Ionathae ne obsideret arcem sed occurreret sibi ad conloquium festinato. 23 Ut audivit autem Ionathas iussit obsidere, et elegit de senioribus Israhel et de sacerdotibus et dedit se periculo. 24 Et accepit aurum et argentum et vestem et alia xenia multa et abiit ad regem Ptolomaidam, et invenit gratiam in conspectu eius. 25 Et interpellabant adversus eum quidam iniqui ex gente sua, 26 et fecit ei rex sicut fecerant ei qui ante ipsum fuerant, et exaltavit eum in conspectu omnium amicorum suorum. 27 Et statuit ei principatum sacerdotii et quaecumque alia habuit prius pretiosa, et fecit eum principem amicorum. 28 Et postulavit Ionathas a rege ut inmunem faceret Iudaeam et tres toparcias et Samariam et confines eius, et promisit ei talenta trecenta. 29 Et consensit rex, et scripsit Ionathae epistulas de his omnibus hunc modum continentes:

30 "Rex Demetrius Ionathae, fratri, salutem, et genti Iudaeorum.

31 "Exemplum epistulae quam scripsimus Lastheni, parenti nostro, de vobis misimus ad vos, ut sciretis.

20 In those days Jonathan gathered together them that were in Judea to take the castle that was in Jerusalem, and they made many engines of war against it. 21 Then some wicked men that hated their own nation went away to King Demetrius and told him that Jonathan was besieging the castle. 22 And when he heard it he was angry, and forthwith he came to Ptolemais and wrote to Jonathan that he should not besiege the castle but should come to him in haste *and* speak to him. 23 But when Jonathan heard this he bade them besiege it *still,* and he chose some of the ancients of Israel and of the priests and put himself in danger. 24 And he took gold and silver and raiment and many other presents and went to the king to Ptolemais, and he found favour in his sight. 25 And certain wicked men of his nation made complaints against him, 26 and the king treated him as his predecessors had done before, and he exalted him in the sight of all his friends. 27 And he confirmed him in the high priesthood, and all *the honours* he had before, and he made him the chief of his friends. 28 And Jonathan requested of the king that he would make Judea free from tribute and the three governments and Samaria and the confines thereof, and he promised him three hundred talents. 29 And the king consented, and he wrote letters to Jonathan of all these things to this effect:

30 "King Demetrius to his brother Jonathan and to the nation of the Jews, greeting.

31 "We *send* you *here* a copy of the letter which we have written to Lasthenes, our parent, concerning you, that you might know it.

32 "'Rex Demetrius Lastheni, parenti, salutem.

33 "'Genti Iudaeorum, amicis nostris et conservantibus quae iusta sunt apud nos, decrevimus benefacere, propter benignitatem ipsorum quam erga nos habent. 34 Statuimus ergo illis omnes fines Iudaeae et tres civitates, Apherema, Lydan et Ramathan, quae additae sunt Iudaeae ex Samaria, et omnes confines earum sequestrari omnibus sacrificantibus in Hierosolymis pro his quae ab eis rex accipiebat per singulos annos et pro fructibus terrae et pomorum. 35 Et alia quae ad nos pertinebant decimarum et tributorum, ex hoc tempore remittimus eis, et areas salinarum et coronas quae nobis deferebantur. 36 Omnia ipsis concedimus, et nihil horum irritum erit ex hoc et in omne tempus. 37 Nunc ergo curate facere horum exemplum, et detur Ionathae et ponatur in monte sancto in loco celebri.'"

38 Et videns Demetrius Rex quod siluit terra in conspectu suo et nihil ei resistit, dimisit totum exercitum suum, unumquemque in locum suum, excepto peregrino exercitu quem contraxit ab insulis gentium. Et inimici erant ei omnes exercitus patrum eius.

39 Tryfon autem erat quidam, partium Alexandri prius, et vidit quoniam omnis exercitus murmurabat contra Demetrium, et iit ad Emalcuhel, Arabem, qui nutriebat Antiochum, filium Alexandri. 40 Et adsidebat ei ut traderet eum

32 "'King Demetrius to Lasthenes, his parent, greeting.

33 "'We have determined to do good to the nation of the Jews, who are our friends and keep the things that are just with us, for their good will which they bear towards us. 34 We have ratified therefore unto them all the borders of Judea and the three cities, Aphairema, Lydda and Ramatha, which are added to Judea out of Samaria, and all their confines to be set apart to all them that sacrifice in Jerusalem instead of the *payments* which the king received of them every year and for the fruits of the land and of the trees. 35 And as for other things that belonged to us of the tithes and of the tributes, from this time we discharge them of them, the salt pans also and the crowns that were presented to us. 36 We give all to them, and nothing hereof shall be revoked from this time forth and for ever. 37 Now therefore see that thou make a copy of these things, and let it be given to Jonathan and set upon the holy mountain in a conspicuous place.'"

38 And King Demetrius, seeing that the land was quiet before him and nothing resisted him, sent away all his forces, every man to his own place, except the foreign army which he had drawn together from the islands of the nations. So all the troops of his fathers hated him.

39 Now there was one Trypho, who had been of Alexander's party before, *who, seeing* that all the army murmured against Demetrius, *went* to Imalkue, the Arabian, who brought up Antiochus, the son of Alexander. 40 And he

ipsi ut regnaret loco patris sui, et enuntiavit ei quanta fecit Demetrius et inimicitias exercituum eius adversum illum. Et mansit illic diebus multis.

41 Et misit Ionathas ad Demetrium Regem ut eiceret eos qui in arce erant in Hierusalem et qui in praesidiis erant, quia inpugnabant Israhel. 42 Et misit Demetrius ad Ionathan, dicens, "Non haec tantum faciam tibi et genti tuae, sed gloria inlustrabo te et gentem tuam cum fuerit oportunum. 43 Nunc ergo recte feceris si miseris in auxilium mihi viros, quia discessit omnis exercitus meus." 44 Et misit ei Ionathas tria milia virorum fortium Antiochiam, et venerunt ad regem, et delectatus est rex in adventu eorum.

45 Et convenerunt qui erant de civitate, centum viginti milia virorum, et volebant interficere regem. 46 Et fugit rex in aulam, et occupaverunt qui erant de civitate itinera civitatis et coeperunt pugnare. 47 Et vocavit rex Iudaeos in auxilium, et convenerunt omnes simul ad eum, et dispersi sunt omnes per civitatem. 48 Et occiderunt in illa die centum milia hominum, et succenderunt civitatem et ceperunt spolia multa in illa die et liberaverunt regem. 49 Et viderunt qui erant de civitate quod obtinuissent Iudaei civitatem sicut volebant, et infirmati sunt mente sua et clamaverunt ad regem cum precibus, dicentes, 50 "Da nobis dextras, et cessent Iudaei obpugnare nos et civitatem." 51 Et proiecerunt arma sua et fecerunt pacem, et glorificati sunt Iudaei in conspectu

pressed him much to deliver him to him that he might be king in his father's place, and he told him all that Demetrius *had done* and *how* his soldiers hated him. And he remained there many days.

41 And Jonathan sent to King Demetrius, *desiring* that he would cast out them that were in the castle in Jerusalem and those that were in the strongholds, because they fought against Israel. 42 And Demetrius sent to Jonathan, saying, "I will not only do this for thee and for thy people, but I will greatly honour thee and thy nation when opportunity shall serve. 43 Now therefore thou shalt do well if thou send me men to help me, for all my army is gone from me." 44 And Jonathan sent him three thousand valiant men to Antioch, and they came to the king, and the king was very glad of their coming.

45 And they that were of the city assembled themselves together *to the number of* a hundred and twenty thousand men and would have killed the king. 46 And the king fled into the palace, and they of the city kept the passages of the city and began to fight. 47 And the king called the Jews to his assistance, and they came to him all at once, and they all dispersed themselves through the city. 48 And they slew in that day a hundred thousand men, and they set fire to the city and got many spoils that day and delivered the king. 49 And they that were of the city saw that the Jews had got the city as they would, and they were discouraged in their minds and cried to the king, making supplication and saying, 50 "Grant us peace, and let the Jews cease from assaulting us and the city." 51 And they threw down their arms and made peace,

regis et in conspectu omnium qui erant in regno eius et nominati sunt in regno et regressi sunt in Hierusalem habentes spolia multa.

52 Et sedit Demetrius Rex in sede regni sui, et siluit terra in conspectu eius. 53 Et mentitus est omnia quaecumque dixit et alienavit se ab Ionatha et non retribuit ei secundum beneficia quae sibi tribuerat et vexabat eum valde.

54 Post haec autem reversus est Tryfon et Antiochus cum eo, puer adulescens, et regnavit et inposuit sibi diadema. 55 Et congregati sunt ad eum omnes exercitus quos disperserat Demetrius, et pugnaverunt contra eum, et fugit et terga vertit. 56 Et accepit Tryfon bestias et obtinuit Antiochiam. 57 Et scripsit Antiochus adulescens Ionathae, dicens, "Constituo tibi sacerdotium, et constituo te super quattuor civitates, ut sis de amicis regis." 58 Et misit illi vasa aurea in ministerium, et dedit ei potestatem bibendi in auro et esse in purpura et habere fibulam auream, 59 et Simonem, fratrem eius, constituit ducem a terminis Tyri usque ad fines Aegypti.

60 Et exiit Ionathas et perambulabat trans flumen civitates, et congregatus est ad eum omnis exercitus Syriae in auxilium, et venit Ascalona, et occurrerunt ei de civitate honorifice. 61 Et abiit inde Gazam, et concluserunt se qui erant Gazae, et obsedit eam et succendit quae erant in circuitu civitatis et praedatus est ea. 62 Et rogaverunt Gazenses Ionathan, et dedit illis dextram, et accepit filios eorum obsides

and the Jews were glorified in the sight of the king and in the sight of all that were in his realm and were renowned throughout the kingdom and returned to Jerusalem with many spoils.

52 So King Demetrius sat in the throne of his kingdom, and the land was quiet before him. 53 And he falsified all whatsoever he had said and alienated himself from Jonathan and did not reward him according to the benefits he had received from him *but* gave him great trouble.

54 And after this Trypho returned and with him Antiochus, the young boy, *who* was made king and put on the diadem. 55 And there assembled unto him all the bands which Demetrius had sent away, and they fought against *Demetrius, who* turned his back and fled. 56 And Trypho took the elephants and made himself master of Antioch. 57 And young Antiochus wrote to Jonathan, saying, "I confirm thee in the *high* priesthood, and I appoint thee *ruler* over the four cities *and* to be one of the king's friends." 58 And he sent him vessels of gold for his service, and he gave him leave to drink in gold and to be *clothed* in purple and to wear a golden buckle, 59 and he made his brother Simon governor from the borders of Tyre even to the confines of Egypt.

60 Then Jonathan went forth and passed through the cities beyond the river, and all the forces of Syria gathered themselves to him to help him, and he came to Askalon, and they met him honourably out of the city. 61 And he went from thence to Gaza, and they that were in Gaza shut him out, and he besieged it and burnt *all the suburbs* round *about* and took the spoils. 62 And the men of Gaza made supplication to Jonathan, and he gave them the right hand, and he

et misit illos in Hierusalem, et perambulavit regionem usque Damascum.

63 Et audivit Ionathas quia praevaricati sunt principes Demetrii in Cades, quae est in Galilea, cum exercitu multo, volentes eum removere a negotio regni, 64 et occurrit illis, fratrem autem suum Simonem reliquit intra provinciam. 65 Et adplicuit Simon ad Bethsuram et expugnabat eam diebus multis et conclusit eos. 66 Et postulaverunt ab eo dextras accipere, et dedit illis, et eiecit eos inde et cepit civitatem et posuit in ea praesidium.

67 Et Ionathas et castra eius adplicuerunt ad aquam Gennesar, et ante lucem vigilaverunt in campo Asor. 68 Et ecce: castra alienigenarum occurrebant ei in campo, et tendebant ei insidias in montibus, ipse autem occurrit ex adverso. 69 Insidiae vero exsurrexerunt de locis suis et commiserunt proelium. 70 Et fugerunt qui erant ex parte Ionathae omnes, et nemo relictus est ex eis nisi Matthathias, filius Absolomi, et Iudas, filius Chalfi, princeps militiae exercitus. 71 Et scidit Ionathas vestimenta sua et posuit terram in capite suo et oravit. 72 Et reversus est Ionathas ad eos in proelium, et convertit eos in fugam, et pugnaverunt. 73 Et viderunt qui fugiebant partis illius, et reversi sunt ad eum, et insequebantur cum eo usque Cades ad castra sua, et pervenerunt usque illuc. 74 Et ceciderunt de alienigenis in die illa tria milia virorum, et regressus est Ionathas in Hierusalem.

took their sons for hostages and sent them to Jerusalem, and he went through the country as far as Damascus.

63 And Jonathan heard that the generals of Demetrius were come treacherously to Kadesh, which is in Galilee, with a great army, purposing to remove him from the affairs of the kingdom, 64 and he went against them, but left his brother Simon in the country. 65 And Simon encamped against Beth-zur and assaulted it many days and shut them up. 66 And they desired him to make peace, and he granted it them, and he cast them out from thence and took the city and placed a garrison in it.

67 And Jonathan and his army encamped by the water of Gennesaret, and before it was light they were ready in the plain of Hazor. 68 And behold: the army of the strangers met him in the plain, and they laid an ambush for him in the mountains, but he went out against them. 69 And they that lay in ambush arose out of their places and joined battle. 70 And all that were on Jonathan's side fled, and none was left of them but Mattathias, the son of Absalom, and Judas, the son of Chalphi, chief captain of the army. 71 And Jonathan rent his garments and cast earth upon his head and prayed. 72 And Jonathan turned again to them to battle, and he put them to flight, and they fought. 73 And they of his part that fled saw this, and they turned again to him, and they *all* with him pursued *the enemies* even to Kadesh to their own camp, and they came even thither. 74 And there fell of the aliens in that day three thousand men, and Jonathan returned to Jerusalem.

Caput 12

Et vidit Ionathas quia tempus eum iuvat; elegit viros et misit eos Romam statuere et renovare cum eis amicitiam, 2 et ad Spartiatas et ad alia loca misit epistulas secundum eandem formam. 3 Et abierunt Romam et intraverunt in curiam et dixerunt, "Ionathas, summus sacerdos, et gens Iudaeorum miserunt nos ut renovaremus amicitiam et societatem secundum pristinam." 4 Et dederunt illis epistulas ad ipsos per loca ut deducerent eos in terram Iuda cum pace.

5 Et hoc exemplum epistularum quas scripsit Ionathas Spartiatis:

6 "Ionathas, summus sacerdos, et seniores gentis et sacerdotes et reliquus populus Iudaeorum Spartiatis, fratribus, salutem.

7 "Iam pridem missae erant epistulae ad Onian, summum sacerdotem, ab Ario, qui regnabat apud vos, quoniam estis fratres nostri, sicut rescriptum continet quod subiectum est. 8 Et suscepit Onias virum qui fuerat missus cum honore et accepit epistulas, in quibus significabatur de societate et amicitia. 9 Nos, cum nullo horum indigeremus

Chapter 12

Jonathan renews his league with the Romans and Lacedaemonians. The forces of Demetrius flee away from him. He is
deceived and made prisoner by Trypho.

And Jonathan saw that the time served him, *and* he chose
certain men and sent them to Rome to confirm and to renew the amity with them, 2 and he sent letters to the Spartans and to other places according to the same form. 3 And
they went to Rome and entered into the senate house and
said, "Jonathan, the high priest, and the nation of the Jews
have sent us to renew the amity and alliance as it was before." 4 And they gave them letters to their governors in
every place to conduct them into the land of Judah with
peace.

5 And this is a copy of the letters which Jonathan wrote to
the Spartans:

6 "Jonathan, the high priest, and the ancients of the nation and the priests and the rest of the people of the Jews to
the Spartans, their brethren, greeting.

7 "There were letters sent long ago to Onias, the high
priest, from Arius, who reigned *then* among you, *to signify*
that you are our brethren, as the copy here underwritten
doth specify. 8 And Onias received the ambassador with
honour and received the letters, wherein there was mention
made of the alliance and amity. 9 We, though we needed

habentes solacio sanctos libros qui sunt in manibus nostris, 10 maluimus mittere ad vos renovare fraternitatem et amicitiam, ne forte alieni efficiamur a vobis, multa enim tempora transierunt ex quo misistis ad nos. 11 Nos ergo in omni tempore sine intermissione in diebus sollemnibus et ceteris quibus oportet memores sumus vestri in sacrificiis quae offerimus et in observationibus, sicut fas est et decet meminisse fratrum. 12 Laetamur itaque de gloria vestra.

13 "Nos autem circumdederunt multae tribulationes et multa proelia, et inpugnaverunt nos reges qui sunt in circuitu nostro. 14 Noluimus ergo vobis molesti esse neque ceteris sociis et amicis nostris in his proeliis. 15 Habuimus enim de caelo auxilium, et liberati sumus nos, et humiliati sunt inimici nostri.

16 "Elegimus itaque Numenium, Antiochi filium, et Antipatrem, Iasonis filium, et misimus ad Romanos renovare cum eis amicitiam et societatem pristinam. 17 Mandavimus itaque eis ut veniant etiam ad vos et salutent vos et reddant vobis epistulas nostras de innovatione fraternitatis nostrae. 18 Et nunc bene facietis respondentes nobis ad haec."

19 Et hoc rescriptum epistularum quod miserat Oniae:

20 "Arius, rex Spartiatarum, Oniae, sacerdoti magno, salutem.

21 "Inventum est in scriptura de Spartiatis et Iudaeis quoniam sunt fratres et quia sunt de genere Abraham. 22 Et nunc ex quo haec cognovimus, bene facitis scribentes nobis de pace vestra. 23 Sed et nos rescripsimus vobis pecora nostra et

none of these things, having for our comfort the holy books that are in our hands, 10 chose rather to send to you to renew the brotherhood and friendship, *lest* we should become strangers to you *altogether,* for there is a long time passed since you sent to us. 11 We therefore at all times without ceasing both in our festivals and other days wherein it is convenient remember you in the sacrifices that we offer and in our observances, as it is meet and becoming to remember brethren. 12 And we rejoice at your glory.

13 "But we have had many troubles and wars on every side, and the kings that are round about us have fought against us. 14 But we would not be troublesome to you nor the rest of our allies and friends in these wars. 15 For we have had help from heaven, and we have been delivered, and our enemies are humbled.

16 "We have chosen therefore Numenius, the son of Antiochus, and Antipater, the son of Jason, and have sent them to the Romans to renew with them the former amity and alliance. 17 And we have commanded them to go also to you and to salute you and to deliver you our letters concerning the renewing of our brotherhood. 18 And now you shall do well to give us an answer hereto."

19 And this is the copy of the letter which he had sent to Onias:

20 "Arius, king of the Spartans, to Onias, the high priest, greeting.

21 "It is found in writing concerning the Spartans and the Jews that they are brethren and that they are of the stock of Abraham. 22 And now since this is come to our knowledge, you do well to write to us of your prosperity. 23 And we also have written back to you that our cattle and our

possessiones nostrae vestrae sunt, et vestra nostra. Mandavimus itaque haec nuntiari vobis."

24 Et audivit Ionathas quoniam regressi sunt principes Demetrii cum exercitu multo supra quam prius pugnare adversus eum. 25 Et exiit ab Hierusalem et occurrit eis in Amathite regione, non enim dederat eis spatium ut ingrederentur regionem eius. 26 Et misit speculatores in castra eorum, et reversi renuntiaverunt quia constituunt supervenire illis nocte. 27 Cum occidisset autem sol, praecepit Ionathas suis vigilare et esse in armis paratos ad pugnam tota nocte, et posuit custodes per circuitum castrorum. 28 Et audierunt adversarii quia paratus est Ionathas cum suis in bello, et timuerunt et formidaverunt corde suo, et accenderunt focos in castris suis. 29 Ionathas autem et qui cum eo erant non cognoverunt usque mane, videbant autem lumina ardentia. 30 Et secutus est eos Ionathas et non conprehendit eos, transierant enim flumen Eleutherum.

31 Et divertit Ionathas ad Arabas qui vocantur Zabadei, et percussit eos et accepit spolia eorum. 32 Et iunxit et venit Damascum et perambulavit omnem regionem illam. 33 Simon autem exiit et venit usque ad Ascalona et ad proxima praesidia, et declinavit in Ioppen et occupavit eam 34 (audivit enim quod vellent praesidium tradere partibus Demetrii), et posuit ibi custodes ut custodirent eam.

35 Et reversus est Ionathas et convocavit seniores populi, et cogitavit cum eis aedificare praesidia in Iudaea 36 et aedificare muros in Hierusalem et exaltare altitudinem magnam

possessions are yours, and yours ours. We therefore have commanded that these things should be told you."

24 Now Jonathan heard that the generals of Demetrius were come again with a greater army than before to fight against him. 25 So he went out from Jerusalem and met them in the land of Hamath, for he *gave* them no time to enter into his country. 26 And he sent spies into their camp, and they came back and brought him word that they designed to come upon them in the night. 27 And when the sun was set, Jonathan commanded his men to watch and to be in arms all night long ready to fight, and he set sentinels round about the camp. 28 And the enemies heard that Jonathan and his men were ready for battle, and they were struck with fear and dread in their heart, and they kindled fires in their camp. 29 But Jonathan and they that were with him knew it not till the morning, *for* they saw the lights burning. 30 And Jonathan pursued after them *but* overtook them not, for they had passed the river Eleutherus.

31 And Jonathan turned upon the Arabians that are called Zabadeans, and he defeated them and took the spoils of them. 32 And he went forward and came to Damascus and passed through all that country. 33 Simon also went forth and came as far as Askalon and the neighbouring fortresses, and he turned aside to Joppa and took possession of it 34 (for he heard that they designed to deliver the hold to them that took part with Demetrius), and he put a garrison there to keep it.

35 And Jonathan came back and called together the ancients of the people, and he took a resolution with them to build fortresses in Judea 36 and to build up walls in Jerusalem and raise a *mount* between the castle and the city to

inter medium arcis et civitatis ut separaret eam a civitate ut esset ipsa singulariter et neque emant neque vendant. 37 Et convenerunt ut aedificarent civitatem, et cecidit murus qui erat super torrentem ab ortu solis, et reparavit eum qui vocatur Caphetetha; 38 et Simon aedificavit Adiada in Sephela et munivit eam et inposuit portas et seras.

39 Et cum cogitasset Tryfon regnare Asiae et adsumere diadema et extendere manum in Antiochum Regem, 40 timens ne forte non permitteret eum Ionathas sed pugnaret adversus eum, quaerebat conprehendere eum et occidere. Et exsurgens abiit in Bethsan. 41 Et exiit Ionathas obviam illi cum quadraginta milibus virorum electorum in proelium et venit Bethsan. 42 Et vidit Tryfon quia venit Ionathas cum exercitu multo ut extenderet in eum manus et timuit 43 et excepit eum cum honore et commendavit eum omnibus amicis suis et dedit ei munera, et praecepit exercitibus suis ut oboedirent ei sicut sibi.

44 Et dixit Ionathae, "Ut quid vexasti universum populum, cum bellum nobis non sit? 45 Et nunc remitte eos in domos suas, elige autem tibi viros paucos qui tecum sint, et veni mecum Ptolomaidam, et tradam illam tibi et reliqua praesidia et exercitum et universos praepositos negotii, et conversus abibo, propterea enim veni."

46 Et credidit ei et fecit Ionathas sicut dixit et dimisit exercitum, et abierunt in terram Iudam; 47 retinuit autem secum tria milia virorum, ex quibus remisit in Galileam duo milia, mille autem cum eo venerunt. 48 Ut intravit autem Ionathas Ptolomaidam, cluserunt portas civitatis Ptolomenses

separate it from the city that so it might *have no communication* and that they might neither buy nor sell. 37 And they came together to build up the city, *for* the wall that was upon the brook towards the east was broken down, and he repaired that which is called Chaphenatha; 38 and Simon built Adida in Shephelah and fortified it and set up gates and bars.

39 Now when Trypho had conceived a design to make himself king of Asia and to take the crown and to stretch out his hand against King Antiochus, 40 fearing *lest* Jonathan would not suffer him but would fight against him, he sought to seize upon him and to kill him. So he rose up and came to Beth-shan. 41 And Jonathan went out to meet him with forty thousand men chosen for battle and came to Beth-shan. 42 Now *when* Trypho saw that Jonathan came with a great army, *he durst not* stretch forth his hand against *him* 43 *but* received him with honour and commended him to all his friends and gave him presents, and he commanded his troops to obey him as himself.

44 And he said to Jonathan, "Why hast thou troubled all the people, whereas we have no war? 45 Now *therefore* send them back to their own houses, and choose thee a few men that may be with thee, and come with me to Ptolemais, and I will deliver it to thee and the rest of the strongholds and the army and all that have any charge, and I will return and go away, for this is the cause of my coming."

46 And Jonathan believed him and did as he said and sent away his army, and they departed into the land of Judah; 47 but he kept with him three thousand men, of whom he sent two thousand into Galilee, and one thousand went with him. 48 Now as soon as Jonathan entered into Ptolemais, they of Ptolemais shut the gates of the city, and took

et conprehenderunt eum, et omnes qui cum eo intraverant gladio interfecerunt.

⁴⁹ Et misit Tryfon exercitum et equites in Galileam et in campum magnum ut perderent omnes socios Ionathae. ⁵⁰ At illi, cum cognovissent quia conprehensus est Ionathas et periit et omnes qui cum eo erant, hortati sunt semet ipsos et exierunt parati in proelium. ⁵¹ Et videntes hii qui insecuti fuerant quia pro anima res est illis, reversi sunt. ⁵² Illi autem venerunt omnes cum pace in terram Iuda. Et planxerunt Ionathan et eos qui cum eo fuerant valde, et luxit Israhel luctu magno.

⁵³ Et quaesierunt omnes gentes quae erant in circuitu eorum perdere eos. Dixerunt enim, ⁵⁴ "Non habent principem et adiuvantem; nunc ergo expugnemus illos et tollamus de hominibus memoriam eorum."

Caput 13

Et audivit Simon quod congregavit Tryfon exercitum copiosum ut veniret in terram Iuda et adtereret eam. ² Videns quia in tremore populus est et in timore, ascendit

him, and all them that came in with him they slew with the sword.

⁴⁹ Then Trypho sent an army and horsemen into Galilee and into the great plain to destroy all Jonathan's company. ⁵⁰ But they, when they understood that Jonathan and all that were with him were taken and slain, encouraged one another and went out ready for battle. ⁵¹ Then they that had come after them, seeing that *they* stood *for* their lives, returned back. ⁵² *Whereupon* they all came peaceably into the land of Judah. And they bewailed Jonathan and them that had been with him exceedingly, and Israel mourned with great lamentation.

⁵³ Then all the heathens that were round about them sought to destroy them. For they said, ⁵⁴ "They have no prince nor any to help them; now therefore let us make war upon them and take away the memory of them from amongst men."

Chapter 13

Simon is made captain-general in the room of his brother. Jonathan is slain by Trypho. Simon is favoured by Demetrius. He taketh Gaza and the castle of Jerusalem.

Now Simon heard that Trypho was gathering together a very great army to invade the land of Judah and to destroy it. ² *And* seeing that the people was in dread and in fear, he

Hierusalem et congregavit populum 3 et adhortans dixit, "Vos scitis quanta ego et fratres mei et domus patris mei fecimus pro legibus et pro sanctis proelia et angustias quales vidimus, 4 horum gratia perierunt fratres mei omnes propter Israhel, et relictus sum ego solus. 5 Et nunc non mihi contingat parcere animae meae in omni tempore tribulationis, non enim melior sum fratribus meis. 6 Vindicabo itaque gentem meam et sancta natos quoque nostros et uxores, quia congregatae sunt universae gentes conterere nos inimicitiae gratia."

7 Et accensus est spiritus populi simul ut audivit sermones istos. 8 Et responderunt voce magna, dicentes, "Tu es dux noster loco Iudae et Ionathae, fratris tui. 9 Pugna proelium nostrum, et omnia quaecumque dixeris nobis faciemus." 10 Et congregans omnes viros bellatores adceleravit consummare omnes muros Hierusalem, et munivit eam in gyro. 11 Et misit Ionathan, filium Absalomi, et cum eo exercitum novum in Ioppen, et eiectis his qui erant in ea remansit illic ipse.

12 Et movit Tryfon a Ptolomaida cum exercitu multo ut veniret in terram Iuda, et Ionathas cum eo in custodia. 13 Simon autem adplicuit in Addus contra faciem campi. 14 Et ut cognovit Tryfon quia surrexit Simon in loco fratris sui Ionathae et quia commissurus esset cum eo proelium, misit ad eum legatos, 15 dicens, "Pro argento quod debebat frater tuus Ionathas in ratione regis propter negotia quae habuit, detinuimus eum. 16 Et nunc mitte argenti talenta centum et duos filios eius obsides, ut non dimissus fugiat a nobis, et remittemus eum."

went up to Jerusalem and assembled the people 3 and exhorted them, saying, "You know what great battles I and my brethren and the house of my father have fought for the laws and the sanctuary and the distresses that we have seen, 4 by reason whereof all my brethren have lost their lives for Israel's sake, and I am left alone. 5 And now far be it from me to spare my life in any time of trouble, for I am not better than my brethren. 6 I will avenge then my nation and the sanctuary and our children and wives, for all the heathens are gathered together to destroy us out of mere malice."

7 And the spirit of the people was enkindled as soon as they heard these words. 8 And they answered with a loud voice, saying, "Thou art our leader in the place of Judas and Jonathan, thy brother. 9 Fight thou our battles, and we will do whatsoever thou shalt say to us." 10 So gathering together all the men of war he made haste to finish all the walls of Jerusalem, and he fortified it round about. 11 And he sent Jonathan, the son of Absalom, and with him a new army into Joppa, and he cast out them that were in it and himself remained there.

12 And Trypho removed from Ptolemais with a great army to invade the land of Judah, and Jonathan was with him in custody. 13 But Simon pitched in Adida over against the plain. 14 And when Trypho understood that Simon was risen up in the place of his brother Jonathan and that he meant to join battle with him, he sent messengers to him, 15 saying, "We have detained thy brother Jonathan for the money that he owed in the king's account by reason of the affairs which he had the management of. 16 *But* now send a hundred talents of silver and his two sons for hostages, that when he is set at liberty he may not revolt from us, and we will release him."

17 Et cognovit Simon quia cum dolo loqueretur secum; iussit tamen dari argentum et pueros, ne inimicitiam magnam sumeret ad Israhel populum, dicentem, 18 "Quia non misit argentum et pueros, propterea periit." 19 Et misit pueros et centum talenta, et mentitus est et non dimisit Ionathan.

20 Et post haec venit Tryfon intra regionem ut contereret eam, et gyraverunt per viam quae ducit Ador, et Simon et castra eius ambulabant in omnem locum quocumque ibant. 21 Qui autem in arce erant miserunt ad Tryfonem legatos ut festinaret venire per desertum et mitteret illis alimonias. 22 Et paravit Tryfon omnem equitatum ut veniret illa nocte, erat autem nix valde multa, et non venit in Galaditin. 23 Et cum adpropiasset Baschama, occidit Ionathan et filios eius illic. 24 Et convertit Tryfon et abiit in terram suam.

25 Et misit Simon et accepit ossa Ionathae, fratris sui, et sepelivit ea in Modin civitate patrum eius. 26 Et planxerunt eum omnis Israhel planctu magno, et luxerunt eum dies multos. 27 Et aedificavit Simon super sepulchrum patris sui et fratrum suorum aedificium altum visu, lapide polito retro et ante, 28 et statuit septem pyromidas, unam contra unam, patri et matri et quattuor fratribus, 29 et his circumposuit columnas magnas, et super columnas arma ad memoriam aeternam, et iuxta arma naves sculptas quae viderentur ab omnibus navigantibus mare. 30 Hoc est sepulchrum quod fecit in Modin usque in hunc diem.

17 Now Simon knew that he spoke deceitfully to him; nevertheless he ordered the money and the children to be sent, lest he should bring upon himself a great hatred of the people of Israel, who might have said, 18 "Because he sent not the money and the children, therefore is he lost." 19 So he sent the children and the hundred talents, and he lied and did not let Jonathan go.

20 And after this Trypho entered within the country to destroy it, and they went about by the way that leadeth to Adora, and Simon and his army marched to every place whithersoever they went. 21 And they that were in the castle sent messengers to Trypho that he should make haste to come through the desert and send them victuals. 22 And Trypho made ready all his horsemen to come that night, but there fell a very great snow, and he came not into the country of Gilead. 23 And when he approached to Baskama, he slew Jonathan and his sons there. 24 And Trypho returned and went into his own country.

25 And Simon sent and took the bones of Jonathan, his brother, and buried them in Modein in the city of his fathers. 26 And all Israel bewailed him with great lamentation, and they mourned for him many days. 27 And Simon built over the sepulchre of his father and of his brethren a building lofty to the sight, of polished stone behind and before, 28 and he set up seven pyramids, one against another, for his father and his mother and his four brethren, 29 and round about these he set great pillars, and upon the pillars arms for a perpetual memory, and by the arms ships carved which might be seen by all that sailed on the sea. 30 This is the sepulchre that he made in Modein even unto this day.

31 Tryfon autem, cum iter faceret cum Antiocho Rege adulescente, dolo occidit eum. 32 Et regnavit loco eius et inposuit sibi diadema Asiae et fecit plagam magnam in terra.

33 Et aedificavit Simon praesidia Iudaeae, muniens ea turribus excelsis et muris magnis et portis et seris, et posuit alimenta in munitionibus. 34 Et elegit Simon viros et misit ad Demetrium Regem ut faceret remissionem regioni, quia actus omnes Tryfonis per direptionem fuerant gesti. 35 Et Demetrius Rex ad verba ista respondit ei et scripsit epistulam talem:

36 "Rex Demetrius Simoni, summo sacerdoti et amico regum, et senioribus et genti Iudaeorum salutem.

37 "Coronam auream et bahem quam misistis suscepimus, et parati sumus facere vobiscum pacem magnam et scribere praepositis regis remittere vobis quae indulsimus. 38 Quaecumque enim constituimus vobis constant. Munitiones quas aedificastis sint vobis. 39 Remittimus quoque ignorantias et peccata usque in hodiernum diem et coronam quam debebatis, et si quid aliud erat tributarium in Hierusalem, iam non sit tributarium. 40 Et si qui ex vobis apti sunt conscribi inter nostros, conscribantur, et sit inter nos pax."

41 Anno centesimo septuagesimo ablatum est iugum Gentium ab Israhel. 42 Et coepit populus Israhel scribere in tabulis et gestis publicis, "Anno primo sub Simone, summo sacerdote, magno duce et principe Iudaeorum."

31 But Trypho, when he was upon a journey with the young King Antiochus, treacherously slew him. 32 And he reigned in his place and put on the crown of Asia and brought great evils upon the land.

33 And Simon built up the strongholds of Judea, fortifying them with high towers and great walls and gates and bars, and he stored up victuals in the fortresses. 34 And Simon chose men and sent to King Demetrius to the end that he should grant an immunity to the land, for all that Trypho did was to spoil. 35 And King Demetrius in answer to this *request wrote* a letter in this manner:

36 "King Demetrius to Simon, the high priest and friend of kings, and to the ancients and to the nation of the Jews, greeting.

37 "The golden crown and the palm which you sent we have received, and we are ready to make a firm peace with you and to write to the king's chief officers to release you the things that we have released. 38 For all that we have decreed in your favour *shall* stand in force. The strongholds that you have built *shall* be your own. 39 And as for any oversight or fault committed unto this day, we forgive it and the crown which you owed, and if any other thing were taxed in Jerusalem, now let it not be taxed. 40 And if any of you be fit to be enrolled among ours, let them be enrolled, and let there be peace between us."

41 In the year one hundred and seventy the yoke of the Gentiles was taken off from Israel. 42 And the people of Israel began to write in the instruments and public records, "The first year under Simon, the high priest, the great captain and prince of the Jews."

43 In illis diebus Simon adplicuit ad Gazam et circumdedit eam castris, et fecit machinas et adplicuit ad civitatem, et percussit turrem unam et conprehendit eam. 44 Et eruperunt qui erant intra machinam in civitatem, et factus est motus magnus in civitate. 45 Et ascenderunt qui erant in civitate cum uxoribus et filiis supra murum scissis tunicis suis, et clamaverunt voce magna, postulantes a Simone dextras sibi dari.

46 Et dixerunt, "Non nobis reddas secundum malitias nostras sed secundum misericordias tuas." 47 Et flexus Simon non debellavit eos; eiecit tamen eos de civitate et emundavit aedes in quibus fuerant simulacra, et tunc intravit in eam cum hymnis benedicens Dominum. 48 Et eiecta ex ea omni inmunditia conlocavit in ea viros qui legem facerent, et munivit eam et fecit sibi habitationem.

49 Qui autem erant in arce Hierusalem prohibebantur egredi et ingredi in regionem et emere ac vendere, et esurierunt valde, et multi ex eis fame perierunt. 50 Et clamaverunt ad Simonem ut dextras acciperent, et dedit illis, et eiecit eos inde et mundavit arcem a contaminationibus.

51 Et intraverunt in eam tertia et vicesima die secundi mensis, anno centesimo septuagesimo primo, cum laude et ramis palmarum et cinyris et cymbalis et nablis et hymnis et canticis quia contritus est inimicus magnus ex Israhel. 52 Et constituit ut omnibus annis agerentur dies hii cum laetitia. 53 Et munivit montem templi qui erat secus arcem, et habitavit

43 In those days Simon besieged Gaza and camped round about it, and he made engines and set them to the city, and he struck one tower and took it. 44 And they that were within the engine leaped into the city, and there was a great uproar in the city. 45 And they that were in the city went up with their wives and children upon the wall with their garments rent, and they cried with a loud voice, beseeching Simon to grant them peace.

46 And they said, "Deal not with us according to our evil deeds but according to thy mercy." 47 And Simon being moved did not destroy them, but yet he cast them out of the city and cleansed the houses wherein there had been idols, and then he entered into it with hymns blessing the Lord. 48 And having cast out of it all uncleanness he placed in it men that should observe the law, and he fortified it and made it his habitation.

49 But they that were in the castle of Jerusalem were hindered from going out and coming into the country and from buying and selling, and they were straitened with hunger, and many of them perished through famine. 50 And they cried to Simon for peace, and he granted it to them, and he cast them out from thence and cleansed the castle from uncleannesses.

51 And they entered into it the three and twentieth day of the second month, in the year one hundred and seventy-one, with thanksgiving and branches of palm trees and harps and cymbals and psalteries and hymns and canticles because the great enemy was destroyed out of Israel. 52 And he ordained that these days should be kept every year with gladness. 53 And he fortified the mountain of the temple that was near the castle, and he dwelt there himself and they that were

ibi ipse et qui cum eo erant. 54 Et vidit Simon Iohannem, filium suum, quod fortis proelii vir esset, et posuit eum ducem virtutum universarum, et habitavit in Gazaris.

Caput 14

Anno centesimo septuagesimo secundo, congregavit Rex Demetrius exercitum suum et abiit in Mediam ad contrahenda sibi auxilia ut expugnaret Tryfonem. 2 Et audivit Arsaces, rex Persidis et Mediae, quia intravit Demetrius confines suos, et misit unum de principibus suis ut conprehenderet eum vivum et adduceret eum ad se. 3 Et abiit et percussit castra Demetrii et conprehendit eum et duxit eum ad Arsacen, et posuit eum in custodiam.

4 Et siluit omnis terra Iuda omnibus diebus Simonis, et quaesivit bona genti suae, et placuit illis potestas eius et gloria eius omnibus diebus. 5 Et cum omni gloria sua accepit Ioppen in portum et fecit introitum in insulis maris. 6 Et dilatavit fines gentis suae et obtinuit regionem. 7 Et congregavit

with him. 54 And Simon saw that John, his son, was a valiant man for war, and he made him captain of all the forces, and he dwelt in Gazara.

Chapter 14

Demetrius is taken by the king of Persia. Judea flourishes under the government of Simon.

In the year one hundred and seventy-two, King Demetrius assembled his army and went into Media to get him succours to fight against Trypho. 2 And Arsaces, the king of Persia and Media, heard that Demetrius was entered within his borders, and he sent one of his princes to take him alive and bring him to him. 3 And he went and defeated the army of Demetrius and took him and brought him to Arsaces, and he put him into custody.

4 And all the land of Judah was at rest all the days of Simon, and he sought the good of his nation, and his power and his glory pleased them well all his days. 5 And with all his glory he took Joppa for a haven and made an entrance to the isles of the sea. 6 And he enlarged the bounds of his nation and made himself master of the country. 7 And he gathered

captivitatem multam et dominatus est Gazarae et Bethsurae et arci et abstulit inmunditias ex ea, et non erat qui resisteret ei.

8 Et unusquisque colebat terram suam cum pace, et terra Iuda dabat fructus suos, et ligna camporum fructum suum. 9 Seniores in plateis sedebant omnes et de bonis terrae tractabant, et iuvenes induebant se gloriam et stolas belli. 10 Et civitatibus tribuebat alimonias, et constituebat eas ut essent vasa munitionis, quoadusque nominatum est nomen gloriae eius usque ad extremum terrae. 11 Fecit pacem super terram, et laetatus est Israhel laetitia magna.

12 Et sedit unusquisque sub vite sua et sub ficulnea sua, et non erat qui eos terreret. 13 Defecit inpugnans eos super terram; reges contriti sunt in diebus illis. 14 Et confirmavit omnes humiles populi sui, et legem exquisivit et abstulit omnem iniquum et malum. 15 Sancta glorificavit et multiplicavit vasa sanctorum.

16 Et auditum est Romae quia defunctus esset Ionathas et usque in Spartiatas, et contristati sunt valde. 17 Ut audierunt autem quod Simon, frater eius, factus esset summus sacerdos loco eius et ipse obtineret omnem regionem et civitates in ea, 18 scripserunt ad eum in tabulis aereis ut renovarent amicitias et societatem quam fecerant cum Iuda et cum Ionatha, fratribus eius. 19 Et lectae sunt in conspectu ecclesiae in Hierusalem. Et hoc exemplum epistularum quas miserunt Spartiatae:

together a great number of captives and had the dominion of Gazara and of Beth-zur and of the castle and took away all uncleanness out of it, and there was none that resisted him.

8 And every man tilled his land with peace, and the land of Judah yielded her increase, and the trees of the fields their fruit. 9 The ancient men sat all in the streets and treated together of the good things of the land, and the young men put on them glory and the robes of war. 10 And he provided victuals for the cities, and he appointed that they should be furnished with ammunition, so that the fame of his glory was renowned even to the end of the earth. 11 He made peace in the land, and Israel rejoiced with great joy.

12 And every man sat under his vine and under his fig tree, and there was none to make them afraid. 13 There was none left in the land to fight against them; kings were discomfited in those days. 14 And he strengthened all those of his people that were brought low, and he sought the law and took away every unjust and wicked man. 15 He glorified the sanctuary and multiplied the vessels of the holy places.

16 And it was heard at Rome and as far as Sparta that Jonathan was dead, and they were very sorry. 17 But when they heard that Simon, his brother, was made high priest in his place and was possessed of all the country and the cities therein, 18 they wrote to him in tables of brass to renew the friendship and alliance which they had made with Judas and with Jonathan, his brethren. 19 And they were read before the assembly in Jerusalem. And this is the copy of the letters that the Spartans sent:

20 "Spartianorum principes et civitates Simoni, sacerdoti magno, et senioribus et sacerdotibus et reliquo populo Iudaeorum, fratribus, salutem.

21 "Legati qui missi sunt ad populum nostrum nuntiaverunt nobis de vestra gloria et honore ac laetitia, et gavisi sumus in introitu eorum. 22 Et scripsimus quae ab ipsis erant dicta in conciliis populi sic:

"'Numenius, Antiochi, et Antipater, Iasonis filius, legati Iudaeorum, venerunt ad nos renovantes nobiscum amicitiam pristinam. 23 Et placuit populo excipere viros gloriose et ponere exemplum sermonum eorum in segregatis populi libris ut sit ad memoriam populo Spartiatarum, exemplum autem horum scripsimus Simoni, magno sacerdoti.'"

24 Post haec autem misit Simon Numenium Romam habentem clypeum aureum magnum pondus minarum mille ad statuendam cum eis societatem. Cum audisset autem populus Romanus 25 sermones istos, dixerunt, "Quam gratiarum actionem reddemus Simoni et filiis eius? 26 Restituit enim ipse fratres suos et expugnavit inimicos Israhel ab eis." Et statuerunt ei libertatem et descripserunt in tabulis aereis et posuerunt in titulis in Monte Sion.

27 Et hoc est exemplum scripturae:

"Octava decima die mensis Elul, anno centesimo septuagesimo secundo, anno tertio sub Simone, sacerdote magno, in Asaramel, 28 in conventu magno sacerdotum et populi et principum gentis et seniorum regionis, nota facta sunt haec.

"Quoniam frequenter facta sunt proelia in regione nostra, 29 Simon autem, Matthathiae filius ex filiis Iarib, et fratres

20 "The princes and the cities of the Spartans to Simon, the high priest, and to the ancients and the priests and the rest of the people of the Jews, their brethren, greeting.

21 "The ambassadors that were sent to our people have told us of your glory and honour and joy, and we rejoice at their coming. 22 And we registered what was said by them in the councils of the people in this manner:

"'Numenius, the son of Antiochus, and Antipater, the son of Jason, ambassadors of the Jews, came to us to renew the former friendship with us. 23 And it pleased the people to receive the men honourably and to put a copy of their words in the public records to be a memorial to the people of the Spartans, and we have written a copy of them to Simon, the high priest.'"

24 And after this Simon sent Numenius to Rome with a great shield of gold of the weight of a thousand pounds to confirm the league with them. And when the people of Rome had heard 25 these words, they said, "What thanks shall we give to Simon and his sons? 26 For he hath restored his brethren and hath driven away in fight the enemies of Israel from them." And they decreed him liberty and registered it in tables of brass and set it upon pillars in Mount Zion.

27 And this is a copy of the writing:

"The eighteenth day of the month Elul, in the year one hundred and seventy-two, being the third year under Simon, the high priest, at Asaramel, 28 in a great assembly of the priests and of the people and the princes of the nation and the ancients of the country, these things were notified.

"Forasmuch as there have often been wars in our country, 29 and Simon, the son of Mattathias of the children of Joarib,

eius dederunt se periculo et restiterunt adversariis gentis suae ut starent sancta ipsorum et lex et gloria magna glorificaverunt gentem suam.

30 "Et congregavit Ionathas gentem suam et factus est illis sacerdos magnus, et adpositus est ad populum suum. 31 Et voluerunt inimici eorum calcare et adterere regionem ipsorum et extendere manus in sancta eorum.

32 "Tunc restitit Simon et pugnavit pro gente sua et erogavit multas pecunias et armavit viros virtutis gentis suae et dedit eis stipendia, 33 et munivit civitates Iudaeae et Bethsuram, quae erat in finibus Iudaeae, ubi erant arma hostium antea, et posuit illic praesidium viros Iudaeos. 34 Et Ioppen munivit, quae erat ad mare, et Gazaram, quae est in finibus Azoti, in qua hostes antea habitabant, et conlocavit illic Iudaeos et quaecumque apta erant ad correptionem eorum posuit in eis.

35 "Et vidit populus actum Simonis et gloriam quam cogitabat facere genti suae et posuerunt eum ducem suum et principem sacerdotum, eo quod ipse fecerat haec omnia et iustitiam et fidem quam conservavit genti suae et exquisivit omni modo exaltare populum suum.

36 "Et in diebus eius prosperatum est in manibus eius, ut tollerentur gentes de regione ipsorum et qui in civitate David erant in Hierusalem in arce, de qua procedebant et contaminabant omnia quae in circuitu sanctorum sunt et inferebant plagam magnam castitati. 37 Et conlocavit in ea viros Iudaeos ad tutamentum regionis et civitatis, et exaltavit muros Hierusalem.

and his brethren have put themselves in danger and have resisted the enemies of their nation for the maintenance of their holy places and the law and have raised their nation to great glory.

30 "And Jonathan gathered together his nation and was made their high priest, and he was laid to his people. 31 And their enemies desired to tread down and destroy their country and to stretch forth their hands against their holy places.

32 "Then Simon resisted and fought for his nation and laid out much of his money and armed the valiant men of his nation and gave them wages, 33 and he fortified the cities of Judea and Beth-zur, that *lieth* in the borders of Judea, where the armour of the enemies was before, and he placed there a garrison of Jews. 34 And he fortified Joppa, which *lieth* by the sea, and Gazara, which bordereth upon Azotus, wherein the enemies dwelt before, and he placed Jews there and furnished them with all things convenient for their reparation.

35 "And the people, seeing the acts of Simon and to what glory he meant to bring his nation, made him their prince and high priest, because he had done all these things and for the justice and faith which he kept to his nation and for that he sought by all means to advance his people.

36 "And in his days things prospered in his hands, so that the heathens were taken away out of their country and they also that were in the city of David in Jerusalem in the castle, out of which they issued forth and profaned all places round about the sanctuary and did much evil to its purity. 37 And he placed therein Jews for the defence of the country and of the city, and he raised up the walls of Jerusalem.

38 "Et Rex Demetrius statuit illi summum sacerdotium. 39 Secundum haec fecit eum amicum suum et glorificavit eum gloria magna. 40 Audivit enim quod appellati sunt Iudaei a Romanis amici et socii et fratres et quia susceperunt legatos Simonis gloriose 41 et quia Iudaei et sacerdotes eorum consenserunt esse eum ducem suum et summum sacerdotem in aeternum, donec surgat propheta fidelis, 42 et ut sit super eos dux et ut cura esset illi pro sanctis et ut constitueret praepositos super opera eorum et super regionem et super arma et super praesidia. 43 Et cura sit illi de sanctis et ut audiatur ab omnibus et ut scribantur in nomine eius omnes conscriptiones in regione et ut operiatur purpura et auro 44 et ne liceat ulli ex populo et ex sacerdotibus irritum facere aliquid horum et contradicere his quae ab eo dicuntur aut convocare conventum in regione sine ipso et vestiri purpura et uti fibula aurea. 45 Qui autem fecerit extra haec aut irritum fecerit aliquid horum reus erit."

46 Et conplacuit omni populo statuere Simonem et facere secundum verba ista. 47 Et suscepit Simon et placuit ei ut summo sacerdotio fungeretur et esset dux et princeps gentis Iudaeorum et sacerdotum et praeesset omnibus. 48 Et scripturam istam dixerunt ponere in tabulis aereis et ponere eas in peribolo sanctorum in loco celebri, 49 exemplum autem eorum ponere in aerario ut habeat Simon et filii eius.

38 "And King Demetrius confirmed him in the high priest-hood. 39 According to these things he made him his friend and glorified him with great glory. 40 For he *had* heard that the Romans *had* called the Jews their friends and confeder-ates and brethren and that they *had* received Simon's ambas-sadors with honour 41 and that the Jews and their priests *had* consented that he should be their prince and high priest for ever, till there should arise a faithful prophet, 42 and that he should be chief over them and that he should have the charge of the sanctuary and that he should appoint rulers over their works and over the country and over the armour and over the strongholds. 43 And that he should have care of the holy places and that he should be obeyed by all and that all the writings in the country should be made in his name and that he should be clothed with purple and gold 44 and that it should not be lawful for any of the people or of the priests to disannul any of these things or to gainsay his words or to call together an assembly in the country without him or to be clothed with purple or to wear a buckle of gold. 45 And whosoever shall do otherwise or shall make void any of these things shall be punished."

46 And it pleased all the people to establish Simon and to do according to these words. 47 And Simon accepted thereof and was well pleased to execute the office of the high priest-hood and to be captain and prince of the nation of the Jews and of the priests and to be chief over all. 48 And they com-manded that this writing should be put in tables of brass and that they should be set up within the compass of the sanctu-ary in a conspicuous place 49 and that a copy thereof should be put in the treasury that Simon and his sons may have it.

Caput 15

Et misit Rex Antiochus, filius Demetrii, epistulas ab insulis maris Simoni, sacerdoti et principi gentis Iudaeorum, et universae genti, 2 et erant continentes hunc modum:

"Rex Antiochus Simoni, sacerdoti magno, et genti Iudaeorum salutem.

3 "Quoniam quidem pestilentes obtinuerunt regnum patrum nostrorum, volo autem vindicare regnum et restituere illud sicut erat antea, et electam feci multitudinem exercitus et feci naves bellicas, 4 volo autem procedere per regionem ut ulciscar in eos qui corruperunt regionem nostram et qui desolaverunt civitates multas in regno meo, 5 nunc ergo statuo tibi omnes oblationes quas remiserunt tibi ante me omnes reges et quaecumque alia dona remiserunt tibi, 6 et permitto tibi facere percussuram proprii nomismatis in regione tua, 7 Hierusalem autem sanctam esse et liberam, et omnia arma quae fabricata sunt et praesidia quae struxisti quae tenes, maneant tibi. 8 Et omne debitum regis et quae futura sunt regi ex hoc et in totum tempus remittuntur tibi.

Chapter 15

Antiochus, son of Demetrius, honours Simon. The Romans
write to divers nations in favour of the Jews. Antiochus
quarrels with Simon and sends troops to annoy him.

And King Antiochus, the son of Demetrius, sent letters
from the isles of the sea to Simon, the priest and prince of
the nation of the Jews, and to all the people, 2 and the contents were these:

"King Antiochus to Simon, the high priest, and to the nation of the Jews, greeting.

3 "Forasmuch as certain pestilent men have usurped the
kingdom of our fathers, and my purpose is to challenge the
kingdom and to restore it to its former estate, and I have
chosen a great army and have built ships of war, 4 and I design to go through the country that I may take revenge of
them that have destroyed our country and that have made
many cities desolate in my realm, 5 now therefore I confirm
unto thee all the oblations which all the kings before me remitted to thee and what other gifts soever they remitted to
thee, 6 and I give thee leave to coin thy own money in thy
country, 7 and let Jerusalem be holy and free, and all the armour that hath been made and the fortresses which thou
hast built and which thou keepest in thy hands, let them
remain to thee. 8 And all that is due to the king and what
should be the king's hereafter from this present and for ever

9 Cum autem obtinuerimus regnum nostrum glorificabimus te et gentem tuam et templum gloria magna ita ut manifestetur gloria vestra in universa terra."

10 Anno centesimo septuagesimo quarto, exiit Antiochus in terram patrum suorum, et convenerunt ad eum omnes exercitus, ita ut pauci relicti essent cum Tryfone. 11 Et insecutus est eum Antiochus Rex, et venit Doram fugiens per maritimam. 12 Sciebat enim quod congregata sunt in eum mala et reliquit eum exercitus. 13 Et adplicuit Antiochus super Doram cum centum viginti milibus virorum belligeratorum et octo milibus equitum, 14 et circuivit civitatem, et naves a mari accesserunt, et vexabant civitatem a terra et mari et neminem sinebant ingredi vel egredi.

15 Venit autem Numenius et qui cum eo fuerant ab urbe Roma habentes epistulas regibus et regionibus scriptas, in quibus continebantur haec:

16 "Lucius, consul Romanorum, Ptolomeo Regi salutem.

17 "Legati Iudaeorum venerunt ad nos, amici nostri, renovantes pristinam amicitiam et societatem, missi a Simone, principe sacerdotum, et populo Iudaeorum. 18 Adtulerunt autem et clypeum aureum minarum mille. 19 Placuit itaque nobis scribere regibus et regionibus ut non inferant illis mala neque inpugnent eos et civitates eorum et regiones eorum et ut non ferant auxilium pugnantibus adversus eos. 20 Visum est autem nobis accipere ab eis clypeum. 21 Si qui ergo pestilentes refugerunt de regione ipsorum ad vos, tradite eos

is forgiven thee. 9 And when we shall have recovered our kingdom we will glorify thee and thy nation and the temple with great glory so that your glory shall be made manifest in all the earth."

10 In the year one hundred and seventy-four, Antiochus entered into the land of his fathers, and all the forces assembled to him, so that few were left with Trypho. 11 And King Antiochus pursued after him, and he fled along by the sea coast and came to Dor. 12 For he perceived that evils were gathered together upon him and his troops *had* forsaken him. 13 And Antiochus camped above Dor with a hundred and twenty thousand men of war and eight thousand horsemen, 14 and he invested the city, and the ships drew near by sea, and they annoyed the city by land and by sea and suffered none to come in or to go out.

15 And Numenius and they that had been with him came from the city of Rome having letters written to the kings and countries, the contents whereof were these:

16 "Lucius, the consul of the Romans, to King Ptolemy, greeting.

17 "The ambassadors of the Jews, our friends, came to us to renew the former friendship and alliance, being sent from Simon, the high priest, and the people of the Jews. 18 And they brought also a shield of gold of a thousand pounds. 19 It hath seemed good therefore to us to write to the kings and countries that they should do them no harm nor fight against them, *their* cities *or* countries and that they should give no aid to them that fight against them. 20 And it hath seemed good to us to receive the shield of them. 21 If therefore any pestilent men are fled out of their country to you,

Simoni, principi sacerdotum, ut vindicet in eos secundum legem suam."

22 Haec eadem scripta sunt Demetrio Regi et Attalo et Ariarathi et Arsaci. 23 Et in omnes regiones et Lampsaco et Spartiatis et in Delum et in Myndum et in Sicyonem et in Cariam et in Samum et in Pamphiliam et in Lyciam et Alicarnassum et in Choo et in Siden et in Aradon et Rhodum et Faselida et Gortinam et Cnidum et Cyprum et Cyrenen. 24 Exemplum autem eorum scripserunt Simoni, principi sacerdotum, et populo Iudaeorum.

25 Antiochus autem Rex adplicuit castra in Dora secundo, admovens ei semper manus et machinas faciens, et conclusit Tryfonem ne procederet. 26 Et misit ad eum Simon duo milia virorum electorum in auxilium et argentum et aurum et vasa copiosa. 27 Et noluit ea accipere sed inrupit omnia quae pactus est cum eo antea et alienavit se ab eo.

28 Et misit ad eum Athenobium, unum de amicis suis, ut tractaret cum ipso, dicens, "Vos tenetis Ioppen et Gazaram et arcem quae est in Hierusalem, civitates regni mei; 29 fines earum desolastis, et fecistis plagam magnam in terra et dominati estis per loca multa in regno meo. 30 Nunc ergo tradite civitates quas occupastis et tributa locorum quibus dominati estis extra fines Iudaeae. 31 Sin autem, date pro illis quingenta talenta argenti, et exterminii quod exterminastis et tributorum civitatium alia talenta quingenta; sin autem, veniemus et expugnabimus vos."

deliver them to Simon, the high priest, that he may punish them according to their law."

22 These same things were written to King Demetrius and to Attalus and to Ariarathes and to Arsaces, 23 And to all the countries and to Lampsacus and to the Spartans and to Delos and Myndus and Sicyon and Caria and Samos and Pamphylia and Lycia and Halicarnassus and Cos and Side and Aradus and Rhodes and Phaselis and Gortyna and Cnidus and Cyprus and Cyrene. 24 And they wrote a copy thereof to Simon, the high priest, and to the people of the Jews.

25 But King Antiochus moved his camp to Dor the second time, assaulting it continually and making engines, and shut up Trypho that he could not go out. 26 And Simon sent to him two thousand chosen men to aid him, silver also and gold and abundance of furniture. 27 And he would not receive them but broke all the covenant that he had made with him before and alienated himself from him.

28 And he sent to him Athenobius, one of his friends, to treat with him, saying, "You hold Joppa and Gazara and the castle that is in Jerusalem, which are cities of my kingdom; 29 their borders you have wasted, and you have made great havoc in the land and have got the dominion of many places in my kingdom. 30 Now therefore deliver up the cities that you have taken and the tributes of the places whereof you have gotten the dominion without the borders of Judea. 31 But if not, give me for them five hundred talents of silver, and for the havoc that you have made and the tributes of the cities other five hundred talents, or else we will come and fight against you."

32 Et venit Athenobius, amicus regis, in Hierusalem et vidit gloriam Simonis et claritatem in auro et argento et adparatum copiosum, et obstipuit et rettulit ei verba regis.

33 Et respondit ei Simon et dixit ei, "Neque alienam terram sumpsimus, neque aliena detinemus, sed hereditatem patrum nostrorum, quae ab inimicis nostris iniuste aliquo tempore possessa est. 34 Nos vero tempus habentes vindicamus hereditatem patrum nostrorum. 35 Nam de Ioppe et Gazara quae expostulas, ipsi faciebant in populo plagam magnam et in regione nostra; horum damus talenta centum."

Et non respondit ei Athenobius verbum, 36 reversus autem cum ira ad regem, renuntiavit ei verba ista et gloriam Simonis et universa quae vidit, et iratus est rex ira magna. 37 Tryfon autem fugit navi in Orthosiada.

38 Et constituit rex Cendebeum ducem maritimum et exercitum equitum et peditum dedit illi. 39 Et mandavit illi movere castra contra faciem Iudaeae, et mandavit ei aedificare Caedronem et obstruere portas civitatis et debellare populum. Rex autem persequebatur Tryfonem.

40 Et pervenit Cendebeus Iamniam et coepit inritare plebem et conculcare Iudaeam et captivare populum et interficere et aedificare Caedronem. 41 Et conlocavit illic equites et exercitum ut egressi perambularent viam Iudaeae sicut constituit ei rex.

32 So Athenobius, the king's friend, came to Jerusalem and saw the glory of Simon and his magnificence in gold and silver and his great equipage, and he was astonished and told him the king's words.

33 And Simon answered him and said to him, "We have neither taken other men's land, neither do we hold that which is other men's, but the inheritance of our fathers, which was for some time unjustly possessed by our enemies. 34 But we having opportunity claim the inheritance of our fathers. 35 And as to thy complaints concerning Joppa and Gazara, they did great harm to the people and to our country; *yet* for these we *will* give a hundred talents."

And Athenobius answered him not a word, 36 but returning in a rage to the king, made report to him of these words and of the glory of Simon and of all that he had seen, and the king was exceeding angry. 37 And Trypho fled away by ship to Orthosia.

38 And the king appointed Cendebeus captain of the sea coast and gave him an army of footmen and horsemen. 39 And he commanded him to march with his army towards Judea, and he commanded him to build up Kedron and to fortify the gates of the city and to war against the people. But the king himself pursued after Trypho.

40 And Cendebeus came to Jamnia and began to provoke the people and to ravage Judea and to take the people prisoners and to kill and to build Kedron. 41 And he placed there horsemen and an army that they might issue forth and make incursions upon the ways of Judea as the king had commanded him.

Caput 16

Et ascendit Iohannis de Gazaris et nuntiavit Simoni, patri suo, quae fecit Cendebeus in populo ipsorum. 2 Et vocavit Simon duos filios suos seniores, Iudam et Iohannem, et ait illis, "Ego et fratres mei et domus patris mei expugnavimus hostes Israhel ab adulescentia usque in hunc diem, et prosperatum est in manibus nostris liberare Israhel aliquotiens. 3 Nunc autem senui, sed estote loco meo, et fratres mei, et egressi pugnate pro gente nostra, auxilium vero de caelo vobiscum sit."

4 Et elegit de regione viginti milia virorum belligeratorum et equites, et profecti sunt ad Cendebeum, et dormierunt in Modin. 5 Et surrexerunt mane et abierunt in campum, et ecce: exercitus copiosus in obviam illis peditum et equitum, et fluvius torrens erat inter medium ipsorum.

6 Et admovit castra contra faciem eorum ipse et populus eius, et vidit populum trepidantem ad transfretandum torrentem, et transfretavit primus, et viderunt eum viri et transierunt post eum. 7 Et divisit populum et equites in medio peditum, erat autem equitatus adversariorum copiosus nimis. 8 Et exclamaverunt sacris tubis, et in fugam conversus

Chapter 16

The sons of Simon defeat the troops of Antiochus. Simon
with two of his sons are treacherously murdered by Ptolemy,
his son-in-law.

Then John came up from Gazara and told Simon, his father, what Cendebeus *had done* against their people. 2 And
Simon called his two eldest sons, Judas and John, and said to
them, "I and my brethren and my father's house have fought
against the enemies of Israel from our youth even to this
day, and things have prospered so well in our hands that we
have delivered Israel oftentimes. 3 And now I am old, but be
you instead of me, and my brethren, and go out, and fight
for our nation, and the help from heaven be with you."

4 Then he chose out of the country twenty thousand
fighting men and horsemen, and they went forth against
Cendebeus, and they rested in Modein. 5 And they arose in
the morning and went into the plain, and behold: a very
great army of footmen and horsemen came against them,
and there was a running river between them.

6 And he and his people pitched their camp over against
them, and he saw that the people were afraid to go over the
river, so he went over first; then the men seeing him passed
over after him. 7 And he divided the people and set the
horsemen in the midst of the footmen, but the horsemen of
the enemies were very numerous. 8 And they sounded the

est Cendebeus et castra eius, et ceciderunt ex eis multi vulnerati, residui autem fugerunt in munitionem.

9 Tunc vulneratus est Iudas, frater Iohannis, Iohannes autem insecutus est eos donec venit Caedronem, quam aedificavit; 10 et fugerunt usque ad turres quae erant in agris Azoti, et succendit eas igni. Et ceciderunt ex illis duo milia virorum, et reversus est in Iudaeam in pace.

11 Et Ptolomeus, filius Abobi, constitutus erat dux in campo Hiericho, et habebat argentum et aurum multum, 12 erat enim gener summi sacerdotis. 13 Et exaltatum est cor eius, et volebat obtinere regionem, et cogitabat dolum adversus Simonem et filios eius ut tolleret eos. 14 Simon autem, perambulans civitates quae erant in regione Iudaeae et sollicitudinem gerens earum, descendit in Hiericho, ipse et Matthathias, filius eius, et Iudas, anno centesimo septuagesimo septimo, mense undecimo (hic est mensis Sabath). 15 Et suscepit eos filius Abobi in munitiunculam quae vocatur Doch cum dolo, quam aedificavit, et fecit eis convivium magnum et abscondit illic viros. 16 Et cum inebriatus esset Simon et filii eius, surrexit Ptolomeus cum suis et sumpserunt arma sua et intraverunt in convivium et occiderunt eum et duos filios eius et quosdam pueros eius. 17 Et fecit deceptionem magnam in Israhel et reddidit mala pro bonis.

18 Et scripsit haec Ptolomeus et misit regi ut mitteret ei exercitum in auxilium, et traderet ei regionem et civitates

holy trumpets, and Cendebeus and his army were put to flight, and there fell many of them wounded, and the rest fled into the stronghold.

9 At that time Judas, John's brother, was wounded, but John pursued after them till he came to Kedron, which he had built; 10 and they fled even to the towers that were in the fields of Azotus, and he burnt them with fire. And there fell of them two thousand men, and he returned into Judea in peace.

11 Now Ptolemy, the son of Abubus, was appointed captain in the plain of Jericho, and he had abundance of silver and gold, 12 for he was son-in-law of the high priest. 13 And his heart was lifted up, and he designed to make himself master of the country, and he purposed treachery against Simon and his sons to destroy them. 14 Now Simon, as he was going through the cities that were in the country of Judea and taking care for the good ordering of them, went down to Jericho, he and Mattathias *and* Judas, his *sons,* in the year one hundred and seventy-seven, the eleventh month (the same is the month Shebat). 15 And the son of Abubus received them deceitfully into a little fortress that is called Dok, which he had built, and he made them a great feast and hid men there. 16 And when Simon and his sons had drunk plentifully, Ptolemy and his men rose up and took their weapons and entered into the banqueting place and slew him and his two sons and some of his servants. 17 And he committed a great treachery in Israel and rendered evil for good.

18 And Ptolemy wrote these things and sent to the king that he should send him an army to aid him, and he would

eorum et tributa. 19 Et misit alios in Gazaram tollere Iohannem, et tribunis misit epistulas ut venirent ad se, et daret eis argentum et aurum et dona. 20 Et alios misit occupare Hierusalem et montem templi.

21 Et praecurrens quidam nuntiavit Iohanni in Gazara quia periit pater eius et fratres eius et quia "misit te quoque interfici." 22 Ut audivit autem vehementer expavit, et conprehendit viros qui venerant perdere eum, et occidit eos, cognovit enim quia quaerebant eum perdere.

23 Et cetera sermonum Iohannis et bellorum eius et bonarum virtutum quibus fortiter gessit et aedificii murorum quos struxit et rerum gestarum eius, 24 ecce: haec scripta sunt in libro dierum sacerdotii eius ex quo factus est princeps sacerdotum post patrem suum.

deliver him the country and their cities and tributes. 19 And he sent others to Gazara to kill John, and to the tribunes he sent letters to come to him, and that he would give them silver and gold and gifts. 20 And he sent others to take Jerusalem and the mountain of the temple.

21 Now one running before told John in Gazara that his father and his brethren were slain and that "he hath sent men to kill thee also." 22 But when he heard it he was exceedingly afraid, and he apprehended the men that came to kill him, and he put them to death, for he knew that they sought to take him away.

23 And as concerning the rest of the acts of John and his wars and the worthy deeds which he bravely achieved and the building of the walls which he made and the things that he did, 24 behold: these are written in the book of the days of his priesthood from the time he was made high priest after his father.

2 MACCABEES

Caput 1

"Fratribus, qui sunt per Aegyptum Iudaeis, salutem dicunt fratres, qui sunt in Hierosolymis Iudaei et qui in regione Iudaeae, et pacem bonam.

2 "Benefaciat vobis Deus et meminerit testamenti sui quod locutus est ad Abraham et Isaac et Iacob, servos suos fideles, 3 et det vobis cor omnibus ut colatis eum et faciatis eius voluntatem corde magno et animo volente. 4 Adaperiat cor vestrum in lege sua et in praeceptis suis et faciat pacem. 5 Exaudiat orationes vestras et reconcilietur vobis nec vos deserat in tempore malo. 6 Et nunc hic sumus orantes pro vobis.

7 "Regnante Demetrio, anno centesimo sexagesimo nono, nos Iudaei scripsimus vobis in tribulatione et impetu qui supervenit nobis in istis annis ex quo recessit Iason a sancta terra et a regno. 8 Portam succenderunt et effuderunt sanguinem innocentem, et oravimus ad Dominum et exauditi

Chapter 1

Letters of the Jews of Jerusalem to them that were in Egypt.
They give thanks for their delivery from Antiochus and exhort their brethren to keep the feast of the dedication of
the altar and of the miraculous fire.

"To the brethren, the Jews that are throughout Egypt,
the brethren, the Jews that are in Jerusalem and in the land
of Judea, send health and good peace.

2 "May God be gracious to you and remember his covenant that he *made with* Abraham and Isaac and Jacob, his
faithful servants, 3 and give you all a heart to worship him
and to do his will with a great heart and a willing mind. 4 May
he open your heart in his law and in his commandments and
send you peace. 5 May he hear your prayers and be reconciled
unto you and never forsake you in the evil time. 6 And now
here we are praying for you.

7 "When Demetrius reigned, in the year one hundred and
sixty-nine, we Jews wrote to you in the trouble and violence
that came upon us in those years after Jason withdrew himself from the holy land and from the kingdom. 8 They burnt
the gate and shed innocent blood; then we prayed to the
Lord and were heard, and we offered sacrifices and fine

sumus, et obtulimus sacrificium et similaginem et accendimus lucernas et proposuimus panes. 9 Et nunc frequentate dies Scenophegiae mensis Casleu."

10 "Anno centesimo octogesimo octavo, populus qui est Hierosolymis et in Iudaea senatusque et Iudas Aristobolo, magistro Ptolomei Regis, qui est de genere christorum sacerdotum, et his qui in Aegypto sunt Iudaeis, salutem et sanitatem.

11 "De magnis periculis a Deo liberati, magnifice gratias agimus ipsi, utpote qui adversus talem regem dimicavimus. 12 Ipse enim ebullire fecit de Perside eos qui pugnaverunt contra nos et sanctum civitatem. 13 Nam cum in Perside esset dux ipse et cum ipso inmensus exercitus, cecidit in templo Naneae, consilio deceptus sacerdotum Naneae. 14 Etenim cum ea habitaturus venit ad locum Antiochus et amici eius et ut acciperet pecunias multas dotis nomine. 15 Cumque proposuissent eas sacerdotes Naneae et ipse cum paucis ingressus esset intra ambitum fani, clauserunt templum 16 cum intrasset Antiochus, apertoque occulto aditu templi, mittentes lapides percusserunt ducem et eos qui cum eo erant et diviserunt membratim, et capitibus amputatis foras proiecerunt. 17 Per omnia benedictus Deus, qui tradidit impios.

18 "Facturi igitur quinta et vicesima die mensis Casleu purificationem templi, necessarium duximus significare vobis ut vos quoque agatis diem Scenophegiae et diem ignis qui

flour and lighted the lamps and set forth the loaves. 9 And now celebrate ye the days of Scenopegia in the month of Chislev."

10 "In the year one hundred and eighty-eight, the people that is at Jerusalem and in Judea and the senate and Judas to Aristobulus, the preceptor of King Ptolemy, who is of the stock of the anointed priests, and to the Jews that are in Egypt, health and welfare.

11 "Having been delivered by God out of great dangers, we give him great thanks, forasmuch as we have been in war with such a king. 12 For he made numbers of men swarm out of Persia that have fought against us and the holy city. 13 For when the leader himself was in Persia and with him a very great army, he fell in the temple of Nanea, being deceived by the counsel of the priests of Nanea. 14 For Antiochus with his friends came to the place as though he would *marry* her and that he might receive great sums of money under the title of a dowry. 15 And when the priests of Nanea had set *it* forth and he with a small company had entered into the compass of the temple, they shut the temple 16 when Antiochus was come in, and opening a secret entrance of the temple, they cast stones and slew the leader and them that were with him and hewed them in pieces, and cutting off their heads they threw them forth. 17 Blessed be God in all things, who hath delivered up the wicked.

18 "Therefore, whereas we purpose to keep the purification of the temple on the five and twentieth day of the month of Chislev, we thought it necessary to signify it to you that you also may keep the day of Scenopegia and the day of

datus est quando Neemias, aedificato templo et altari, obtulit sacrificia.

19 "Nam cum in Persidem ducerentur patres nostri, sacerdotes qui tunc Dei cultores erant acceptum ignem de altario occulte absconderunt in valle ubi erat puteus altus et siccus, et in eo contutati sunt eum ita ut omnibus ignotus esset locus. 20 Cum praeterissent autem multi anni et placuit Deo ut mitteretur Neemias a rege Persidis, nepotes sacerdotum illorum qui absconderant misit ad requirendum ignem, et sicut narraverunt nobis, non invenerunt ignem, sed aquam crassam.

21 "Et iussit eos haurire et adferre sibi, et sacrificia quae inposita erant iussit sacerdos Neemias aspargi aqua ipsa, et ligna et quae erant superposita. 22 Utque hoc factum est et tempus adfuit quo sol refulsit, qui prius erat in nubilo, accensus est ignis magnus ita ut omnes mirarentur. 23 Orationem autem faciebant omnes sacerdotes dum consummaretur sacrificium, Ionatha inchoante, ceteris autem respondentibus. 24 Et Neemiae erat oratio hunc habens modum: 'Domine Deus, omnium creator, terribilis et fortis, iustus et misericors, qui solus es rex bonus, 25 solus praestans, solus iustus et omnipotens et aeternus, qui liberas Israhel de omni malo, qui fecisti patres electos et sanctificasti eos, 26 accipe sacrificium pro universo populo tuo Israhel, et custodi partem tuam, et sanctifica. 27 Congrega dispersionem nostram; libera eos qui serviunt Gentibus, et contemptos et abominatos respice, ut sciant Gentes quod tu es Deus noster. 28 Adflige opprimentes nos et contumeliam facientes in superbia. 29 Constitue populum tuum in loco

the fire that was given when Nehemiah offered sacrifice after the temple and the altar was built.

19 "For when our fathers were led into Persia, the priests that then were worshippers of God took privately the fire from the altar and hid it in a valley where there was a deep pit without water, and there they kept it safe so that the place was unknown to all men. 20 But when many years had passed and it pleased God that Nehemiah should be sent by the king of Persia, he sent some of the posterity of those priests that had hid it to seek for the fire, and as they told us, they found no fire, but thick water.

21 "Then he bade them draw it up and bring it to him, and the priest Nehemiah commanded the sacrifices that were laid on to be sprinkled with the same water, both the wood and the things that were laid upon it. 22 And when this was done and the time came that the sun shone out, which before was in a cloud, there was a great fire kindled so that all wondered. 23 And all the priests made prayer while the sacrifice was consuming, Jonathan beginning and the rest answering. 24 And the prayer of Nehemiah was after this manner: 'O Lord God, creator of all things, dreadful and strong, just and merciful, who alone art the good king, 25 who alone art gracious, who alone art just and almighty and eternal, who deliverest Israel from all evil, who didst choose the fathers and didst sanctify them, 26 receive the sacrifice for all thy people Israel, and preserve thy own portion, and sanctify it. 27 Gather together our scattered people; deliver them that are slaves to the Gentiles, and look upon them that are despised and abhorred, that the Gentiles may know that thou art our God. 28 Punish them that oppress us and that treat us injuriously with pride. 29 Establish thy people

sancto tuo, sicut dixit Moses.' 30 Sacerdotes autem psalle-
bant hymnos usquequo consumptum esset sacrificium.

31 "Cum autem consummatum fuisset sacrificium, ex residua aqua Neemias iussit lapides maiores perfundi. 32 Quod
ut factum est, flamma ex eis accensa est, sed ex lumine quod
refulsit ab altari consumpta est.

33 "Ut vero manifestata est res, renuntiatum est regi Persarum quod in loco in quo ignem absconderant hii qui trans-
lati erant sacerdotes aqua apparuit, de qua Neemias et qui
cum eo erant purificaverunt sacrificia. 34 Considerans autem
rex et rem diligenter examinans, fecit ei templum ut probaret quod factum erat. 35 Et cum probasset, sacerdotibus donavit multa bona et alia atque alia munera, et accipiens manu
sua tribuebat eis. 36 Appellavit autem Neemias hunc locum
Nepthar, quod interpretatur 'Purificatio.' Vocatur autem
apud plures Nephi."

Caput 2

"Invenitur autem in descriptionibus Hieremiae, prophetae, quod iussit accipere ignem eos qui transmigrabantur,
ut significatum est, et ut mandavit transmigratis, 2 et dedit

in thy holy place, as Moses hath spoken.' 30 And the priests sung hymns till the sacrifice was consumed.

31 "And when the sacrifice was consumed, Nehemiah commanded the water that was left to be poured out upon the great stones. 32 Which being done, there was kindled a flame from them, but it was consumed by the light that shined from the altar.

33 "And when this matter became public, it was told to the king of Persia that in the place where the priests that were led away had hid the fire there appeared water, with which Nehemiah and they that were with him *had* purified the sacrifices. 34 And the king, considering and diligently examining the matter, made a temple for it that he might prove what had happened. 35 And when he had proved it, he gave the priests many goods and divers presents, and he took and distributed them to them with his own hand. 36 And Nehemiah called this place Nephthar, which is interpreted 'Purification.' But many call it Nephi."

Chapter 2

A continuation of the second letter. Of Jeremiah's hiding
the ark at the time of the captivity. The author's preface.

"Now it is found in the descriptions of Jeremiah, the prophet, that he commanded them that went into captivity to take the fire, as it hath been signified, and how he gave charge to them that were carried away into captivity, 2 and

illis legem ne obliviscerentur praecepta Domini et ut non exerrarent mentibus, videntes simulacra aurea et argentea et ornamenta eorum. 3 Et alia huiuscemodi dicens hortabatur ne legem amoverent a corde suo.

4 "Erat autem in ipsa scriptura quomodo tabernaculum et arcam iussit propheta, divino responso ad se facto, comitari secum usquequo exiit in montem in quo Moses ascendit et vidit Dei hereditatem. 5 Et veniens ibi Hieremias invenit locum speluncae, et tabernaculum et arcam et altare incensi intulit illuc, et ostium obstruxit.

6 "Et accesserunt quidam simul qui sequebantur ut notarent sibi locum, et non potuerunt invenire. 7 Ut autem cognovit Hieremias, culpans illos dixit quod, 'Ignotus erit locus donec congreget Deus congregationem populi et propitius fiat. 8 Et tunc Dominus ostendet haec, et apparebit maiestas Domini, et nubes erit sicut et Mosi manifestabatur, et sicut cum Salomon petiit ut locus sanctificaretur magno Deo manifestabat haec.' 9 Magnifice etenim sapientiam tractabat, et ut sapientiam habens obtulit sacrificium dedicationis et consummationis templi. 10 Sicut et Moses orabat ad Dominum et descendit ignis de caelo et consumpsit holocaustum, sic et Salomon oravit, et descendit ignis de caelo et consumpsit holocaustum.

11 "Et dixit Moses, 'Eo quod non sit comestum quod erat pro peccato, consumptum est.' 12 Similiter et Salomon octo diebus celebravit dedicationem.

how he gave them the law that they should not forget the commandments of the Lord and that they should not err in their minds, seeing the idols of gold and silver and the ornaments of them. 3 And with other such like speeches he exhorted them that they would not remove the law from their heart.

4 "It was also contained in the same writing how the prophet, *being warned by God,* commanded that the tabernacle and the ark should accompany him till he came forth to the mountain where Moses went up and saw the inheritance of God. 5 And when Jeremiah came thither he found a hollow cave, and he carried in thither the tabernacle and the ark and the altar of incense, and *so* stopped the door.

6 "Then some of them *that* followed him came up to mark the place, *but* they could not find it. 7 And when Jeremiah perceived it, he blamed them, *saying,* 'The place shall be unknown till God gather together the congregation of the people and receive them to mercy. 8 And then the Lord will shew these things, and the majesty of the Lord shall appear, and there shall be a cloud as it was also shewed to Moses, and as he shewed it when Solomon prayed that the place might be sanctified to the great God.' 9 For he treated wisdom in a magnificent manner, and like a wise man he offered the sacrifice of the dedication and of the finishing of the temple. 10 And as Moses prayed to the Lord and fire came down from heaven and consumed the holocaust, so Solomon also prayed, and fire came down from heaven and consumed the holocaust.

11 "And Moses said, 'Because the sin-offering was not eaten, it was consumed.' 12 So Solomon also celebrated the dedication eight days.

13 "Inferebantur autem in descriptionibus et commentariis Neemiae haec eadem et ut construens bibliothecam congregavit de regionibus libros et prophetarum et David et epistulas regum et de donariis. 14 Similiter autem et Iudas ea quae deciderant per bellum quod nobis acciderat congregavit omnia, et sunt apud nos. 15 Si ergo desideratis haec, mittite qui perferant vobis.

16 "Acturi itaque purificationem scripsimus vobis, bene igitur facietis si egeritis hos dies. 17 Deus autem, qui liberavit populum suum et reddidit hereditatem omnibus et regnum et sacerdotium et sanctificationem 18 sicut promisit in lege, speramus quod cito nostri miserebitur et congregabit de sub caelo in locum sanctum. 19 Eripuit enim nos de magnis periculis et locum purgavit."

20 De Iuda vero Macchabeo et fratribus eius et de templi magni purificatione et de arae dedicatione, 21 sed et de proeliis quae pertinent ad Antiochum Nobilem et filium eius Eupatorem, 22 et de inluminationibus quae de caelo factae sunt ad eos qui pro Iudaeis fortiter fecerunt ita ut universam regionem, cum pauci essent, vindicarent et barbaram multitudinem fugarent 23 et famosissimum in toto orbe templum recuperarent et civitatem liberarent et leges quae abolitae erant restituerentur, Domino cum omni tranquillitate propitio facto illis.

13 "And these same things were set down in the memoirs and commentaries of Nehemiah and how he made a library and gathered together out of the countries the books both of the prophets and of David and the epistles of the kings and concerning the holy gifts. 14 And in like manner Judas also gathered together all such things as were lost by the war we had, and they are in our possession. 15 Wherefore if you want these things, send some that may fetch them to you.

16 "As we are then about to celebrate the purification we have written unto you, and you shall do well if you keep the same days. 17 And we hope that God, who hath delivered his people and hath rendered to all the inheritance and the kingdom and the priesthood and the sanctuary 18 as he promised in the law, will shortly have mercy upon us and will gather us together from every land under heaven into the holy place. 19 For he hath delivered us out of great perils and hath cleansed the place."

20 Now as concerning Judas Maccabeus and his brethren and the purification of the great temple and the dedication of the altar, 21 as also the wars against Antiochus the Illustrious and his son Eupator, 22 and the manifestations that came from heaven to them that behaved themselves manfully on the behalf of the Jews so that, being but a few, they made themselves masters of the whole country and put to flight the barbarous multitude 23 and recovered again the most renowned temple in all the world and delivered the city and restored the laws that were abolished, the Lord with all clemency shewing mercy to them.

24 Itemque ab Iasone Cyreneo quinque libris conprehensa temptavimus nos uno volumine breviare. 25 Considerantes enim multitudinem librorum et difficultatem volentibus adgredi narrationes historiarum propter multitudinem rerum, 26 curavimus volentibus quidem legere ut esset animi oblectatio, studiosis vero ut facilius possint memoriae commendare, omnibus autem legentibus utilitas conferatur. 27 Et nobis quidem ipsis, qui opus hoc breviandi causa suscepimus non facilem laborem, immo vero negotium plenum vigiliarum et sudoris adsumpsimus. 28 Sicut hii qui praeparant convivium et quaerunt aliorum voluntati parere, propter multorum gratiam libenter laborem sustinemus, 29 veritatem quidem de singulis auctoribus concedentes, ipsi autem secundum datam formam, brevitati studentes. 30 Sicut enim novae domus architecto de universa structura curandum est, ei vero qui pingere curat quae apta sunt ad ornatum exquirenda sunt, ita aestimandum est et in nobis. 31 Etenim intellectum colligere et ordinare sermonem et curiosius partes singulas quasque disquaerere historiae congruit auctori, 32 brevitatem vero dictionis sectari et exsecutiones rerum vitare brevianti concedendum est. 33 Hinc igitur narrationem incipiemus; de praefatione tantum dixisse sufficiat, stultum etenim est ante historiam effluere, in ipsa autem historia succingi.

24 And all such things as have been comprised in five books by Jason of Cyrene we have attempted to abridge in one book. 25 For considering the multitude of books and the difficulty that they find that desire to undertake the narrations of histories because of the multitude of the matter, 26 we have taken care for those indeed that are willing to read that it might be a pleasure of mind, and for the studious that they may more easily commit to memory, and that all that read might receive profit. 27 And as to ourselves indeed, in undertaking this work of abridging we have taken in hand no easy task, yea rather a business full of watching and sweat. 28 But as they that prepare a feast and seek to satisfy the will of others, for the sake of many we willingly undergo the labour, 29 leaving to the authors the exact handling of every particular, and as for ourselves, according to the plan proposed, studying to be brief. 30 For as the master builder of a new house must have care of the whole building, but he that taketh care to paint it must seek out fit things for the adorning of it, so must it be judged *for* us. 31 For to collect all that is to be known, *to* put the discourse in order and curiously to discuss every particular point is the duty of the author of a history, 32 but to pursue brevity of speech and to avoid nice declarations of things is to be granted to him that maketh an abridgment. 33 Here then we will begin the narration; let this be enough by way of a preface, for it is a foolish thing to make a long prologue and to be short in the story itself.

Caput 3

Igitur cum sancta civitas habitaretur in omni pace, leges etiam adhuc optime custodirentur propter Oniae, pontificis, pietatem et animos odio habentes mala, 2 fiebat ut et ipsi reges et principes locum summo honore dignum ducerent et templum maximis muneribus inlustrarent, 3 ita ut Seleucus, Asiae rex, de reditibus suis praestaret omnes sumptus ad ministerium sacrificiorum pertinentes.

4 Simon autem de tribu Beniamin, praepositus templi constitutus, contendebat obsistente sibi principe sacerdotum iniquum aliquid in civitate moliri. 5 Et cum vincere Onian non posset venit ad Apollonium, Tharseae filium, qui illo tempore erat dux Coelesyriae et Foenicis, 6 et nuntiavit ei pecuniis innumerabilibus plenum esse aerarium Hierosolymis et communes copias inmensas esse quae non pertinent ad rationem sacrificiorum, esse autem possibile sub potestate regis cadere universa. 7 Cumque rettulisset Apollonius ad regem de pecuniis quae delatae erant, ille accitum Heliodorum, qui erat super negotia eius, misit cum mandatis ut

Chapter 3

Heliodorus is sent by King Seleucus to take away the treasures deposited in the temple. He is struck by God and healed by the prayers of the high priest.

Therefore when the holy city was inhabited with all peace and the laws as yet were very well kept because of the godliness of Onias, the high priest, and the hatred his soul had for evil, 2 it came to pass that even the kings themselves and the princes esteemed the place worthy of the highest honour and glorified the temple with very great gifts, 3 so that Seleucus, king of Asia, allowed out of his revenues all the charges belonging to the ministry of the sacrifices.

4 But *one* Simon of the tribe of Benjamin, who was appointed overseer of the temple, strove in opposition to the high priest to bring about some unjust thing in the city. 5 And when he could not overcome Onias he went to Apollonius, the son of Tharseas, who at that time was governor of Coelesyria and Phoenicia, 6 and told him that the treasury in Jerusalem was full of immense sums of money and the common store was infinite which did not belong to the account of the sacrifices and that it was possible *to bring* all into the king's hands. 7 Now when Apollonius had given the king notice concerning the money that he was told of, he called for Heliodorus, who had the charge over his affairs, and sent him with commission to bring him the foresaid

praedictam pecuniam transportaret. 8 Statimque Heliodorus iter est adgressus, specie quidem quasi per Coelesyriam et Foenicen civitates esset peragraturus, re autem vera regis propositum perfecturus.

9 Sed cum venisset Hierosolymam et benigne a summo sacerdote in civitate esset exceptus, narravit de dato indicio pecuniarum et cuius rei gratia adesset aperuit, interrogabat autem si vere haec ita essent. 10 Tunc summus sacerdos ostendit deposita esse haec et victualia viduarum ac pupillorum, 11 quaedam vero esse Hircani, Tobiae, viri valde eminentis, in his quae detulerat impius Simon, universa autem argenti talenta quadringenta esse et auri ducenta; 12 decipi vero eos qui credidissent loco et templo quod per universum mundum honoratur pro sui veneratione et sanctitate inpossibile omnino esse.

13 At ille, pro his quae habebat in mandatis a rege, dicebat omni genere regi ea esse deferenda. 14 Constituta autem die intrabat de his Heliodorus ordinaturus, non modica vero per universam civitatem erat trepidatio. 15 Sacerdotes autem ante altare cum sacerdotalibus stolis iactaverunt se et invocabant de caelo eum qui de depositis legem posuit, ut his qui deposuerant ea salva custodiret.

16 Iam vero qui videret summi sacerdotis vultum mente vulnerabatur, facies enim et color inmutatus declarabat internum animi dolorem. 17 Circumfusa enim erat viro maestitia quaedam et horror corporis, per quae manifestus aspicientibus dolor cordis eius efficiebatur. 18 Alii etiam gregatim

money. 8 So Heliodorus forthwith began his journey, under a colour of visiting the cities of Coelesyria and Phoenicia, but indeed to fulfil the king's purpose.

9 *And* when he was come to Jerusalem and had been courteously received in the city by the high priest, he told him what information had been given concerning the money and declared the cause for which he was come and asked if these things were so indeed. 10 Then the high priest told him that these were sums deposited and provisions for the subsistence of the widows and the fatherless, 11 and that some part of that which wicked Simon had given intelligence of belonged to Hyrcanus, son of Tobias, a man of great dignity, and that the whole was four hundred talents of silver and two hundred of gold; 12 but that to deceive them who had trusted to the place and temple which is honoured throughout the whole world for the reverence and holiness of it was a thing which could not by any means be done.

13 But he, by reason of the orders he had received from the king, said that by all means *the money* must be carried to the king. 14 So on the day he had appointed Heliodorus entered in to order this matter, but there was no small terror throughout the whole city. 15 And the priests prostrated themselves before the altar in their priests' vestments and called upon him from heaven who made the law concerning things given to be kept, that he would preserve them safe for them that had deposited them.

16 Now *whosoever* saw the countenance of the high priest was wounded in heart, for his face and the changing of his colour declared the inward sorrow of his mind. 17 For *the man was so compassed with sadness* and horror of the body *that* it *was* manifest to them that beheld him *what* sorrow he had in his heart. 18 Others also came flocking together out of

de domibus confluebant publica supplicatione obsecrantes pro eo quod in contemptum locus esset venturus. 19 Accinctaeque mulieres ciliciis pectus per plateas confluebant. Sed et virgines quae conclusae erant procurrebant ad Onian, aliae autem ad muros, quaedam vero per fenestras aspiciebant, 20 universae autem protendentes manus in caelum deprecabantur. 21 Erat enim misera commixtae multitudinis et magni sacerdotis in agone constituti expectatio. 22 Et hii quidem invocabant omnipotentem Deum ut credita sibi his qui crediderant cum omni integritate conservarentur. 23 Heliodorus autem quod decreverat perficiebat, eodem loco ipse cum satellitibus circa aerarium praesens. 24 Sed spiritus omnipotentis Dei magnam fecit suae ostensionis evidentiam, ita ut omnes qui ausi fuerant parere ei, ruentes Dei virtute, in dissolutionem et formidinem converterentur.

25 Apparuit enim illis quidam equus terribilem habens sessorem, optimis operimentis adornatus, isque cum impetu Heliodoro priores calces elisit, qui autem ei sedebat videbatur arma habere aurea. 26 Alii etiam apparuerunt duo iuvenes virtute decori, optimi gloria speciosique amictu, qui circumsteterunt eum et ex utraque parte flagellabant sine intermissione multis plagis verberantes. 27 Subito autem Heliodorus concidit in terram, eumque multa caligine circumfusum rapuerunt atque in sella gestatoria positum eiecerunt. 28 Et is qui cum multis cursoribus et satellitibus praedictum ingressus est aerarium portabatur, nullo sibi auxilium ferente, manifesta cognita Dei virtute. 29 Et ille quidem per divinam virtutem iacebat mutus atque omni spe et salute privatus. 30 Hii autem Dominum benedicebant quia magnificavit

their houses praying and making public supplication because the place was like to come into contempt. 19 And the
women, girded with haircloth about their breasts, came together in the streets. And the virgins also that were shut up
came forth, *some* to Onias and some to the walls, and others
looked out of the windows, 20 and all, holding up their hands
towards heaven, made supplication. 21 For the expectation
of the mixed multitude and of the high priest who was in an
agony *would have moved any one to pity.* 22 And these indeed
called upon almighty God to preserve the things that had
been committed to them *safe and sure* for those that had
committed them. 23 But Heliodorus executed that which he
had resolved on, himself being present in the same place
with his guard about the treasury. 24 But the spirit of the almighty God gave a great evidence of his presence, so that all
that had presumed to obey him, falling down by the power
of God, were struck with fainting and dread.

25 For there appeared to them a horse with a terrible rider
upon him, adorned with a very rich covering, and he *ran*
fiercely *and* struck Heliodorus with his forefeet, and he that
sat upon him seemed to have armour of gold. 26 Moreover
there appeared two other young men, beautiful and strong,
bright and glorious and in comely apparel, who stood by him
on either side and scourged him without ceasing with many
stripes. 27 And Heliodorus suddenly fell to the ground, and
they took him up covered with great darkness, and having
put him into a litter they carried him out. 28 So he that came
with many servants and all his guard into the aforesaid treasury was carried out, no one being able to help him, the
manifest power of God being known. 29 And he indeed by
the power of God lay speechless and without all hope *of recovery.* 30 But they praised the Lord because he *had* glorified

locum suum, et templum quod paulo ante timore ac tumultu erat plenum apparente omnipotente Domino gaudio et laetitia impletum est.

31 Tunc vero ex amicis Heliodori quidam rogabant confestim Onian ut invocaret Altissimum ut vitam donaret ei qui in supremo spiritu erat constitutus. 32 Considerans autem summus sacerdos ne forte rex suspicaretur malitiam aliquam ex Iudaeis circa Heliodorum consummatam, obtulit pro salute viri hostiam salutarem. 33 Cumque summus sacerdos exoraret, idem iuvenes eisdem vestibus amicti adstantes Heliodoro dixerunt, "Oniae, sacerdoti, gratias age, nam propter eum tibi Dominus vitam donavit. 34 Tu autem, a Deo flagellatus, nuntia omnibus magnalia Dei et potestatem." Et his dictis non conparuerunt.

35 Heliodorus autem, hostia Deo oblata et votis magnis promissis ei qui vivere illi concessit et Oniae gratias agens, recepto exercitu, repedabat ad regem. 36 Testabatur autem omnibus ea quae sub oculis suis viderat opera magni Dei. 37 Cum autem rex interrogasset Heliodorum quis esset aptus adhuc semel Hierosolymam mitti, ait, 38 "Si quem habes hostem aut regni tui insidiatorem, mitte illuc, et flagellatum eum recipies, si tamen evaserit, eo quod in loco vere sit Dei quaedam virtus. 39 Nam ipse qui habet in caelis habitationem visitator et adiutor est loci illius, et venientes ad malefaciendum percutit ac perdit."

40 Igitur de Heliodoro et aerarii custodia ita se res habet.

his place, and the temple that a little before was full of fear and trouble when the almighty Lord appeared was filled with joy and gladness.

31 *Then* some of the friends of Heliodorus forthwith begged of Onias that he would call upon the Most High to grant him his life who was *ready to give up the ghost.* 32 So the high priest, considering that the king might perhaps suspect that some mischief had been done to Heliodorus by the Jews, offered a sacrifice of health for the recovery of the man. 33 And when the high priest was praying, the same young men in the same clothing stood by Heliodorus and said to him, "Give thanks to Onias, the priest, because for his sake the Lord hath granted thee life. 34 And thou, having been scourged by God, declare unto all men the great works and the power of God." And having spoken thus they appeared no more.

35 So Heliodorus, after he had offered a sacrifice to God and made great vows to him that had granted him life and given thanks to Onias, taking his troops with him, returned to the king. 36 And he testified to all men the works of the great God which he had seen with his own eyes. 37 And when the king *asked* Heliodorus who might be a fit man to be sent yet once more to Jerusalem, he said, 38 "If thou hast any enemy or traitor to thy kingdom, send him thither, and thou shalt receive him again scourged, if so be he escape, for there is undoubtedly in *that* place a certain power of God. 39 For he that hath his dwelling in the heavens is the visitor and protector of that place, and he striketh and destroyeth them that come to do evil to it."

40 And the things concerning Heliodorus and the keeping of the treasury fell out in this manner.

Caput 4

Simon autem praedictus, pecuniarum et patriae delator, male loquebatur de Onia, tamquam ipse Heliodorum instigasset ad haec et ipse fuisset incentor malorum, 2 provisoremque civitatis ac defensorem gentis suae et aemulatorem legis Dei audebat insidiatorem regni dicere. 3 Sed cum inimicitiae in tantum procederent ut etiam per quosdam Simonis necessarios homicidia fierent, 4 considerans Onias periculum contentionis et Apollonium insanire, utpote ducem Coelesyriae et Foenicis, ad augendam malitiam Simonis, ad regem se contulit, 5 non ut civium accusator sed communem utilitatem apud semet ipsum universae multitudinis considerans. 6 Videbat enim sine regali providentia inpossibile esse pacem rebus dari nec Simonem posse cessare ab stultitia sua.

7 Sed post Seleuci vitae excessum, cum suscepisset regnum Antiochus, qui Nobilis appellabatur, ambiebat Iason, frater Oniae, summum sacerdotium, 8 adito rege, promittens ei argenti talenta trecenta sexaginta et ex reditibus aliis

Chapter 4

Onias has recourse to the king. The ambition and wickedness of Jason and Menelaus. Onias is treacherously murdered.

But Simon, of whom we spoke before, who was the betrayer of the money and of his country, spoke ill of Onias, as though he had incited Heliodorus to do these things and had been the promoter of evils, 2 and he presumed to call him a traitor to the kingdom who provided for the city and defended his nation and was zealous for the law of God. 3 But when the enmities proceeded so far that murders also were committed by some of Simon's friends, 4 Onias, considering the danger of this contention and that Apollonius, who was the governor of Coelesyria and Phoenicia, was outrageous, which increased the malice of Simon, went to the king, 5 not to be an accuser of his countrymen but with a view to the common good of all the people. 6 For he saw that, except the king took care, it was impossible that matters should be settled in peace or that Simon would cease from his folly.

7 But after the death of Seleucus, when Antiochus, who was called the Illustrious, had taken possession of the kingdom, Jason, the brother of Onias, ambitiously sought the high priesthood 8 and went to the king, promising him three hundred and sixty talents of silver and out of other revenues

talenta octoginta. 9 Super haec promittebat et alia centum quinquaginta si potestati eius concederetur gymnasium et ephoebian sibi constituere et eos qui in Hierosolymis erant Antiochenos scribere.

10 Quod cum rex annuisset, et obtinuisset principatum, statim ad gentilem ritum contribules suos transferre coepit. 11 Et amotis his quae humanitatis causa Iudaeis a regibus fuerant constituta per Iohannem, patrem Eupolemi, qui apud Romanos de amicitia et societate functus est legatione, legitima civium iura destituens prava instituta sancibat. 12 Etenim ausus est sub ipsa arce gymnasium constituere et optimos quosque ephoeborum in lupanaribus ponere. 13 Erat autem hoc non initium sed incrementum quoddam et profectus gentilis et alienigenae conversationis propter impii et non sacerdotis, Iasonis, nefarium et inauditum scelus, 14 ita ut sacerdotes iam non circa altaris officia dediti essent, sed contempto templo et sacrificiis neglectis, festinarent participes fieri palestrae et praebitionis eius iniustae et in exercitiis disci. 15 Et patrios quidem honores nihil habentes, Graecas glorias optimas arbitrabantur, 16 quarum gratia periculosa eos contentio habebat et eorum instituta aemulabantur, ac per omnia his consimiles esse cupiebant quos hostes et peremptores habuerant. 17 In leges enim divinas impie agere inpune non cedit, sed hoc sequens tempus declarabit.

18 Cum autem quinquennalis agon Tyro celebraretur et rex praesens esset, 19 misit Iason facinorosus ab Hierosolymis viros peccatores portantes argenti didragmas trecentas

fourscore talents. 9 Besides this he promised also a hundred and fifty more if he might have license to set him up a place for exercise and a place for youth and to entitle them that were at Jerusalem Antiochians.

10 Which when the king had granted, and he had gotten the rule into his hands, forthwith he began to bring over his countrymen to the fashion of the heathens. 11 And abolishing those things which had been decreed of special favour by the kings in behalf of the Jews by the means of John, the father of *that* Eupolemus, who went ambassador to Rome to make amity and alliance, he disannulled the lawful ordinances of the citizens and brought in fashions that were perverse. 12 For he had the boldness to set up under the very castle a place of exercise and to put all the choicest youths in brothel houses. 13 Now this was not the beginning but an *increase* and progress of heathenish and foreign manners through the abominable and unheard-of wickedness of Jason, that impious wretch and no priest, 14 insomuch that the priests were not now occupied about the offices of the altar, but despising the temple and neglecting the sacrifices, hastened to be partakers of the games and of the unlawful allowance thereof and of the exercise of the discus. 15 And setting nought by the honours of their fathers, they esteemed the Grecian glories for the best, 16 for the sake of which they incurred a dangerous contention and followed earnestly their ordinances, and in all things they coveted to be like them who were their enemies and murderers. 17 For acting wickedly against the laws of God doth not pass unpunished, but this the time following will declare.

18 Now when the game that was used every fifth year was kept at Tyre, *the* king being present, 19 the wicked Jason sent from Jerusalem sinful men *to* carry three hundred didrachmas

in sacrificium Herculis, quas postulaverunt hii qui adporta-verant ne in sacrificiis erogarentur, quia non oporteret, sed in alios sumptus eas deputari. 20 Itaque haec oblata sunt qui-dem ab eo qui misit in sacrificium Herculis, propter prae-sentes autem datae sunt in fabricam navium triremium.

21 Misso autem in Aegyptum Apollonio, Mnesthei filio, propter primates Ptolomei Filometoris Regis, cum cogno-visset Antiochus alienum se a negotiis regni effectum, pro-priis utilitatibus consulens profectus inde venit Ioppen et inde Hierosolymam, 22 et magnifice ab Iasone et civitate susceptus cum facularum luminibus et laudibus ingressus est, et inde in Foenicen exercitum convertit.

23 Et post triennii tempus misit Iason Menelaum, supra-dicti Simonis fratrem, portantem pecunias regi et de nego-tiis necessariis responsa perlaturum. 24 At ille, commendatus regi, cum magnificasset faciem potestatis eius, in semet ip-sum retorsit summum sacerdotium, superponens Iasoni ta-lenta argenti trecenta. 25 Acceptisque a rege mandatis, venit nihil quidem dignum habens sacerdotio, animos vero crude-lis tyranni et ferae beluae iram gerens.

26 Et Iason quidem, qui proprium fratrem circumscripse-rat, ipse deceptus profugus in Ammaniten expulsus est re-gionem. 27 Menelaus autem principatum quidem obtinuit, de pecuniis vero regi promissis nihil agebat cum exactionem faceret Sostratus, qui arci erat praepositus. 28 Nam ad hunc exactio vectigalium pertinebat, quam ob causam utrique ad

of silver for the sacrifice of Hercules, *but* the bearers thereof desired it might not be bestowed on the sacrifices, because it was not necessary, but might be deputed for other charges. 20 So *the money* was appointed by him that sent it to the sacrifice of Hercules, but because of them that carried it was employed for the making of galleys.

21 Now when Apollonius, the son of Mnestheus, was sent into Egypt *to treat with* the nobles of *King* Philometor, *and* Antiochus understood that he was wholly excluded from the affairs of the kingdom, consulting his own interest he departed thence and came to Joppa and from thence to Jerusalem, 22 *where* he was received in a magnificent manner by Jason and the city and came in with torch-lights and with praises, and from thence he returned with his army into Phoenicia.

23 *Three* years afterwards Jason sent Menelaus, brother of the aforesaid Simon, *to* carry money to the king and to bring answers from him concerning certain necessary affairs. 24 But he, being recommended to the king, when he had magnified the appearance of his power, got the high priesthood for himself by offering more than Jason by three hundred talents of silver. 25 So, having received the king's mandate, he returned bringing nothing worthy of the *high* priesthood, but having the mind of a cruel tyrant and the rage of a savage beast.

26 Then Jason, who had undermined his own brother, being himself undermined was driven out a fugitive into the country of the Ammonites. 27 So Menelaus got the principality, but as for the money he had promised to the king he *took no care* when Sostratus, the governor of the castle, called for it. 28 For to him appertained the gathering of the taxes,

regem sunt evocati. 29 Et Menelaus amotus est a sacerdotio, succedente Lysimacho, fratre suo, Sostratus autem praelatus est Cypriis.

30 Et cum haec agerentur, contigit Tarsenses et Mallotas seditionem movere, eo quod Antiochidi, concubinae regis, dono essent dati. 31 Festinanter itaque rex venit sedare illos, relicto suffecto uno ex comitibus suis, Andronico. 32 Ratus autem Menelaus accepisse se tempus oportunum, aurea quaedam vasa e templo furatus, donavit Andronico, et alia vendiderat Tyri et per vicinas civitates. 33 Quod cum certissime cognovisset Onias, arguebat eum ipse, in loco tuto se continens Antiochiae secus Dafnen. 34 Unde Menelaus, accedens ad Andronicum, rogabat ut Onian interficeret, qui cum venisset ad Onian et datis dextris cum iureiurando (quamvis esset ei suspectus) suasisset de asylo procedere, statim eum peremit, non veritus iustitiam. 35 Ob quam causam non solum Iudaei sed aliae quoque nationes indignabantur et moleste ferebant de nece tanti viri iniusta.

36 Sed regressum regem de Ciliciae locis, adierunt Iudaei apud Antiochiam simul et Graeci conquerentes de iniqua nece Oniae. 37 Contristatus itaque animo Antiochus propter Onian et flexus ad misericordiam, lacrimas fudit, recordatus defuncti sobrietatem et modestiam. 38 Accensisque animis, Andronicum purpura exutum circumduci per totam civitatem iubet, et in eodem loco in quo in Onian impietatem

wherefore they were both called before the king. 29 And Menelaus was removed from the priesthood, Lysimachus, his brother, succeeding, and Sostratus was made governor of the Cyprians.

30 *When* these things were in doing, it fell out that they of Tarsus and Mallus raised a sedition, because they were given for a gift to Antiochis, the king's concubine. 31 The king therefore went in all haste to appease them, leaving Andronicus, one of his nobles, for his deputy. 32 Then Menelaus, supposing that he had found a convenient time, having stolen certain vessels of gold out of the temple, gave them to Andronicus, and others he had sold at Tyre and in the neighbouring cities. 33 Which when Onias understood most certainly, he reproved him, keeping himself in a safe place at Antioch beside Daphne. 34 Whereupon Menelaus, coming to Andronicus, desired him to kill Onias, and *he went* to Onias and gave him his right hand with an oath and (though he were suspected by him) *persuaded* him to come forth out of the sanctuary *and* immediately slew him without any regard to justice. 35 For which cause not only the Jews but also the other nations conceived indignation and were much grieved for the unjust murder of so great a man.

36 *And* when the king was come back from the places of Cilicia, the Jews that were at Antioch and also the Greeks went to him complaining of the unjust murder of Onias. 37 Antiochus therefore was grieved in his mind for Onias, and being moved to pity, shed tears, remembering the sobriety and modesty of the deceased. 38 And being inflamed *to anger,* he *commanded* Andronicus to be stripped of his purple and to be led about through all the city, and that in the same place wherein he had committed the impiety against Onias,

commiserat, sacrilegum vita privari, Domino illi dignam retribuente poenam.

39 Multis autem sacrilegiis in templo a Lysimacho commissis Menelai consilio et divulgata fama, congregata est multitudo adversus Lysimachum, multo iam auro exportato. 40 Turbis autem insurgentibus et animis ira repletis, Lysimachus, armatis fere tribus milibus, iniquis manibus uti coepit, duce quodam Tyranno, aetate pariter et dementia provecto. 41 Sed ut intellexerunt conatum Lysimachi, alii lapides, alii fustes validos arripere, quidam vero cinerem in Lysimachum iacere. 42 Et multi quidem vulnerati, quidam autem et prostrati, omnes vero in fugam versi sunt, ipsum etiam sacrilegum, secus aerarium interfecerunt.

43 De his ergo coepit iudicium adversus Menelaum agitari. 44 Et cum venisset rex Tyrum, ad ipsum negotium detulerunt missi viri tres a senioribus. 45 Et cum superaretur Menelaus, promisit Ptolomeo multas pecunias dare ad suadendum regi. 46 Itaque Ptolomeus in quodam atrio positum quasi refrigerandi gratia regem adiit et a sententia deduxit. 47 Et Menelaum, quidem universae malitiae reum, criminibus absolvit, miseros autem, qui etiam si apud Scytas causam dixissent innocentes iudicarentur, hos morte damnavit. 48 Cito ergo iniustam poenam dederunt qui pro civitate et populo et sacris vasis causam prosecuti sunt. 49 Quam ob rem Tyrii quoque indignati erga sepulturam eorum liberalissimi

the sacrilegious wretch should be put to death, the Lord repaying him his deserved punishment.

39 Now when many sacrileges had been committed by Lysimachus in the temple by the counsel of Menelaus and the rumour of it was spread abroad, the multitude gathered themselves together against Lysimachus, a great quantity of gold being already carried away. 40 *Wherefore,* the multitude making an insurrection and their minds being filled with anger, Lysimachus armed about three thousand men and began to use violence, one Tyrannus being captain, a man far gone both in age and in madness. 41 But when they perceived the attempt of Lysimachus, some caught up stones, some strong clubs, and some threw ashes upon Lysimachus. 42 And many of them were wounded, and some struck down to the ground, but all were put to flight, and as for the sacrilegious fellow himself, they slew him beside the treasury.

43 Now concerning these matters an accusation was laid against Menelaus. 44 And when the king was come to Tyre, three men were sent from the ancients to plead the cause before him. 45 *But* Menelaus, *being* convicted, promised Ptolemy to give him much money to persuade the king to favour him. 46 So Ptolemy went to the king in a certain court where he was, as it were, to cool himself, and brought him *to be of another mind.* 47 So Menelaus, who was guilty of all the evil, was acquitted by him of the accusations, and those poor men, who if they had pleaded their cause even before Scythians should have been judged innocent, were condemned to death. 48 Thus they that prosecuted the cause for the city and for the people and the sacred vessels did soon suffer unjust punishment. 49 Wherefore even the Tyrians being moved with indignation were *liberal* towards their

extiterunt. 50 Menelaus autem propter eorum qui in poten-
tia erant avaritiam permanebat in potestate, crescens in malitia ad insidias civium.

Caput 5

Eodem tempore Antiochus secundam profectionem paravit in Aegyptum. 2 Contigit autem per universam Hierosolymorum civitatem videri diebus quadraginta per aera equites discurrentes auratas stolas habentes et hastis quasi
cohortes armatas 3 et cursus equorum per ordines digestos
et congressiones fieri comminus et scutorum motus et ga-
leatorum multitudinem gladiis destrictis et telorum iactus
et aureorum armorum splendorem omnisque generis lorica-
rum. 4 Quapropter omnes rogabant in bonum monstra converti.

5 Sed cum falsus rumor exisset tamquam vita excessisset
Antiochus, adsumptis Iason non minus mille viris, repente
adgressus est civitatem, et civibus ad murum convolantibus,
ad ultimum adprehensa civitate, Menelaus fugit in arcem.
6 Iason vero non parcebat in caede civibus suis nec cogitabat
prosperitatem adversus cognatos malum esse maximum,

burial. 50 And *so* through the covetousness of them that were in power Menelaus continued in authority, increasing in malice to the betraying of the citizens.

Chapter 5

Wonderful signs are seen in the air. Jason's wickedness and end. Antiochus takes Jerusalem and plunders the temple.

At the same time Antiochus prepared for a second journey into Egypt. 2 And it came to pass that through the whole city of Jerusalem for the space of forty days there were seen horsemen running in the air in gilded raiment and armed with spears like bands of soldiers 3 and horses set in order by ranks running *one against another* with the shakings of shields and a multitude of men in helmets with drawn swords and casting of darts and glittering of golden armour and of harnesses of all sorts. 4 Wherefore all men prayed that these prodigies might turn to good.

5 *Now* when there was gone forth a false rumour as though Antiochus had been dead, Jason, taking with him no fewer than a thousand men, suddenly assaulted the city, and though the citizens ran together to the wall, the city at length was taken, and Menelaus fled into the castle. 6 But Jason slew his countrymen without mercy, *not considering* that prosperity against one's own kindred is a very great evil,

arbitrans hostium et non civium se tropea capturum. 7 Et principatum quidem non obtinuit, finem vero insidiarum suarum confusionem accepit et profugus iterum abiit in Ammaniten. 8 Ad ultimum, in exitium sui conclusus ab Areta, Arabum tyranno, fugiens de civitate in civitatem, omnibus odiosus ut refuga legum et execrabilis ut patriae et civium hostis, in Aegyptum extrusus est, 9 et qui multos de patria sua expulerat peregre periit, Lacedemonas profectus quasi pro cognatione ibi refugium habiturus. 10 Et qui insepultos abiecerat multos ipse et inlamentatus et insepultus abicitur, sepultura neque peregrina usus neque patrio sepulchro participans.

11 His itaque gestis, suspicatus est rex societatem deserturos Iudaeos, et ob hoc profectus ex Aegypto efferatis animis, civitatem quidem armis cepit, 12 iussit autem militibus interficere nec parcere occursantibus et per domos ascendentes trucidare. 13 Fiebant ergo caedes iuvenum ac seniorum et mulierum et natorum exterminia virginumque et parvulorum neces. 14 Erant autem toto triduo octoginta milia interfecti; quadraginta milia vincti, non minus autem venundati.

15 Sed nec ista sufficiunt. Ausus est etiam intrare templum, universa terra sanctius, Menelao ductore, qui legum et patriae fuit proditor. 16 Et scelestis manibus sumens sancta vasa quae ab aliis regibus et civitatibus erant posita ad ornatum loci et gloriam, contrectabat indigne et contaminabat. 17 Ita alienatus mente Antiochus non considerabat

thinking *they had been enemies,* and not *citizens, whom he conquered.* 7 *Yet* he did not get the principality but received confusion at the end *for the reward* of his treachery and fled again into the country of the Ammonites. 8 At the last, having been shut up by Aretas, the king of the Arabians, in order for his destruction, flying from city to city, hated by all men as a forsaker of the laws and execrable as an enemy of his country and countrymen, he was thrust out into Egypt, 9 and he that had driven many out of their country perished in a strange land, going to Lacedaemon as if for kindred sake he should have refuge there. 10 *But* he that had cast out many unburied was himself cast forth both unlamented and unburied, neither having foreign burial nor being partaker of the sepulchre of his fathers.

11 Now when these things were done, the king suspected that the Jews would forsake the alliance, whereupon departing out of Egypt with a furious mind, he took the city by force of arms, 12 and commanded the soldiers to kill and not to spare any that came in their way and to go up into the houses to slay. 13 Thus there was a slaughter of young and *old,* a destruction of women and children and killing of virgins and infants. 14 And there were slain in the space of three whole days fourscore thousand; forty thousand were made prisoners, and as many sold.

15 But this was not enough. He presumed also to enter into the temple, the most holy in all the world, Menelaus, that traitor to the laws and to his country, being his guide. 16 And taking in his wicked hands the holy vessels which were given by other kings and cities for the ornament and the glory of the place, he unworthily handled and profaned them. 17 Thus Antiochus, going astray in mind, did not

quod propter peccata habitantium civitatem modicum Deus fuerat iratus, propter quod et accidit circa locum despectio. 18 Alioquin, nisi contigisset eos multis peccatis esse involutos, sicut Heliodorus, qui missus est a Seleuco Rege ad expoliandum aerarium, etiam hic statim adveniens flagellatus et repulsus utique fuisset ab audacia. 19 Verum non propter locum gentem sed propter gentem locum Deus elegit. 20 Ideoque et ipse locus particeps factus est populi malorum, postea autem fiet socius bonorum, et qui derelictus in ira Dei omnipotentis, iterum in magni Domini reconciliatione cum summa gloria exaltabitur.

21 Igitur Antiochus, mille et octingentis ablatis de templo talentis, velociter Antiochiam regressus est, existimans se prae superbia terram ad navigandum, pelagus vero ad iter agendum deducturum propter mentis elationem. 22 Reliquit autem et praepositos ad adfligendam gentem: Hierosolymis quidem Philippum, genere Frigem, moribus crudeliorem eo ipso a quo constitutus est, 23 in Garizin autem Andronicum et Menelaum, qui gravius quam ceteri inminebant civibus. 24 Cumque adpositus esset contra Iudaeos, misit odiosum principem Apollonium cum exercitu viginti et duobus milibus, praecipiens ei omnes perfectae aetatis interficere, mulieres ac iuvenes vendere. 25 Qui cum venisset Hierosolymam pacem simulans, quievit usque ad sanctum diem sabbati, et tunc, feriatis Iudaeis, arma capere suis praecepit. 26 Omnesque qui ad spectaculum processerant trucidavit, et civitatem cum armatis discurrens ingentem multitudinem peremit.

consider that God was angry for a while because of the sins of the inhabitants of the city, and therefore this contempt had happened to the place. 18 Otherwise, had they not been involved in many sins, as Heliodorus, who was sent by King Seleucus to rob the treasury, so this man also, as soon as he had come, had been forthwith scourged and put back from his presumption. 19 But God did not choose the people for the place's sake but the place for the people's sake. 20 And therefore the place also itself was made partaker of the evils of the people, but afterward shall *communicate in* the good things thereof, and as it was forsaken in the wrath of almighty God, shall be exalted again with great glory when the great Lord shall be reconciled.

21 So when Antiochus had taken away out of the temple a thousand and eight hundred talents, he went back in all haste to Antioch, thinking through pride that he might now make the land navigable and the sea passable on foot; such was the haughtiness of his mind. 22 *He* left also governors to afflict the people: at Jerusalem, Philip, a Phrygian by birth, *but* in manners more barbarous than he that set him there, 23 and in Gerizim Andronicus and Menelaus, who bore a more heavy hand upon the citizens than the rest. 24 And whereas he was set against the Jews, he sent that hateful prince Apollonius with an army of two and twenty thousand men, commanding him to kill all that were of perfect age *and* to sell the women and the *younger sort.* 25 Who when he was come to Jerusalem pretending peace, rested till the holy day of the sabbath, and then, the Jews keeping holiday, he commanded his men to take arms. 26 And he slew all that were come forth to see, and running through the city with armed men he destroyed a very great multitude.

27 Iudas autem Macchabeus, qui decimus fuerat, secesserat in desertum locum ibique inter feras vitam in montibus cum suis agebat, et faeni cibo vescentes demorabantur, ne participes essent coinquinationis.

Caput 6

Sed non post multum temporis, misit rex senem quendam Antiochenum qui conpelleret Iudaeos ut se transferrent a patriis et Dei legibus, 2 contaminare etiam quod in Hierosolymis erat templum et cognominare Iovis Olympii et in Garizin, prout erant hii qui locum inhabitabant, Iovis Hospitalis.

3 Pessima autem et universis gravis malorum erat incursio. 4 Nam templum luxuria et comesationibus Gentium erat plenum et scortantium cum meretricibus. Sacratisque aedibus mulieres se ultro ingerebant, intro ferentes ea quae non licebat. 5 Altare etiam plenum erat inlicitis quae legibus prohibebantur. 6 Neque autem sabbata custodiebantur, neque dies sollemnes patrii servabantur, nec simpliciter se quisquam Iudaeum esse confitebatur. 7 Ducebantur autem

27 But Judas Maccabeus, who was the tenth, had withdrawn himself into a desert place and there lived amongst wild beasts in the mountains with his company, and they continued feeding on herbs, that they might not be partakers of the pollution.

Chapter 6

Antiochus commands the law to be abolished, sets up an idol in the temple and persecutes the faithful. The martyrdom of Eleazar.

But not long after, the king sent a certain old man of Antioch to compel the Jews to depart from the laws of their fathers and of God, 2 and to defile the temple that was in Jerusalem and to call it the temple of Jupiter Olympius and that in Gerizim of Jupiter Hospitalis, according as they were that inhabited the place.

3 And very bad was this invasion of evils and grievous to all. 4 For the temple was full of the riot and revellings of the Gentiles and of men lying with lewd women. And women thrust themselves of their accord into the holy places and brought in things that were not lawful. 5 The altar also was filled with unlawful things which were forbidden by the laws. 6 And neither were the sabbaths kept, nor the solemn days of the fathers observed, neither did any man plainly profess himself to be a Jew. 7 But they were led by bitter

cum amara necessitate in die natalis regis ad sacrificia, et cum Liberi sacra celebrarentur, cogebantur hedera coronati Libero circumire.

8 Decretum autem exiit in proximas Gentilium civitates, suggerentibus Ptolomeis, ut pari modo et ipsi adversus Iudaeos agerent ut sacrificarent, 9 eos autem qui nollent transire ad instituta Gentium interficerent; erat ergo videre miseriam. 10 Duae enim mulieres delatae sunt natos suos circumcidisse, quas, infantibus ad ubera suspensis cum publice per civitatem circumduxissent, per muros praecipitaverunt. 11 Alii vero ad proximas coeuntes speluncas et latenter sabbati diem celebrantes, cum indicati essent Philippo, flammis succensi sunt, eo quod verebantur propter religionem et observantiam manu sibimet auxilium ferre.

12 Obsecro autem eos qui hunc librum lecturi sunt ne abhorrescant propter adversos casus sed reputent ea quae acciderunt non ad interitum sed ad correptionem generis esse nostri. 13 Etenim multo tempore non sinere peccatoribus ex sententia agere sed statim ultiones adhibere magni beneficii est indicium. 14 Non enim sicut in aliis nationibus Dominus patienter expectat, ut eas cum iudicii dies venerit in plenitudine peccatorum puniat, 15 ita et in nobis statuit ut peccatis nostris in finem devolutis, ita demum in nos vindicet. 16 Propter quod numquam quidem a nobis misericordiam suam amovet, corripiens vero in adversis populum suum non derelinquit. 17 Sed haec nobis ad commonitionem legentium dicta sint paucis. Iam autem veniendum est ad narrationem.

constraint on the king's birthday to the sacrifices, and when the feast of Bacchus was kept, they were compelled to go about crowned with ivy in honour of Bacchus.

8 And there went out a decree into the neighbouring cities of the Gentiles, by the suggestion of the Ptolemeans, that they also should act in like manner against the Jews, to oblige them to sacrifice, 9 and whosoever would not conform themselves to the ways of the Gentiles should be put to death; then was misery to be seen. 10 For two women were accused to have circumcised their children, whom, when they had openly led about through the city with the infants hanging at their breasts, they threw down headlong from the walls. 11 And others that had met together in caves that were near and were keeping the sabbath day privately, being discovered by Philip, were burnt with fire, because they made a conscience to help themselves with their hands by reason of the religious observance *of the day.*

12 Now I beseech those that shall read this book that they be not shocked at these calamities but that they consider the things that happened not as being for the destruction but for the correction of our nation. 13 For it is a token of great goodness when sinners are not suffered to go on in their ways for a long time but are presently punished. 14 For not as with other nations, whom the Lord patiently expecteth, that when the day of judgment shall come he may punish them in the fulness of their sins, 15 doth he also deal with us so as to suffer our sins to come to their height and then take vengeance on us. 16 *And* therefore he never withdraweth his mercy from us, but though he chastise his people with adversity he forsaketh them not. 17 But let this suffice in a few words for a warning to the readers. And now we must come to the narration.

18 Igitur Eleazarus, unus de primoribus scribarum, vir aetate provectus et vultu decorus, aperto ore hians conpellebatur carnem porcinam manducare. 19 At ille, gloriosissimam mortem magis quam odibilem vitam amplectens, voluntarie praeibat ad supplicium. 20 Intuens autem quemadmodum oporteret accedere, patienter sustinens, destinavit non admittere inlicita propter vitae amorem. 21 Hii autem qui adstabant, iniqua miseratione commoti propter antiquam viri amicitiam, tollentes eum secreto rogabant adferri carnes quibus vesci ei licebat, ut simularetur manducasse sicut rex imperaverat de sacrificii carnibus, 22 ut hoc facto a morte liberaretur, et propter veterem viri amicitiam hanc in eo faciebant humanitatem.

23 At ille cogitare coepit aetatis ac senectutis suae eminentiam dignam et ingenitae nobilitatis canitiem atque a puero optimae conversationis actus, et secundum sanctae et a Deo conditae legis constituta respondit cito, dicens praemitti se velle in infernum. 24 "Non enim aetati nostrae dignum est," inquit, "fingere, ut multi adulescentium arbitrantes Eleazarum nonaginta annorum transisse ad vitam alienigenarum, 25 et ipsi propter meam simulationem et propter modicum corruptibilis vitae tempus decipiantur, et per hoc maculam atque execrationem meae senectuti conquiram. 26 Nam et si in praesenti tempore suppliciis hominum eripiar, sed manum Omnipotentis neque vivens neque defunctus effugiam. 27 Quam ob rem fortiter vita excedendo senectute quidem dignus apparebo, 28 adulescentibus autem exemplum forte relinquam, si prompto animo ac fortiter

18 *Eleazar,* one of the chief of the scribes, a man advanced in years and of a comely countenance, was pressed to open his *mouth* to eat swine's flesh. 19 But he, choosing rather a most glorious death than a hateful life, went forward voluntarily to the torment. 20 And considering in what manner he was come to it, patiently bearing, he determined not to do any unlawful things for the love of life. 21 But they that stood by, being moved with wicked pity for the old friendship they had with the man, taking him aside desired that flesh might be brought which it was lawful for him to eat, that he might make as if he had eaten as the king had commanded of the flesh of the sacrifice, 22 that by so doing he might be delivered from death, and for the sake of their old friendship with the man they did him this courtesy.

23 But he began to consider the *dignity* of his age and his ancient years and the *inbred honour of his* grey head and his *good life and* conversation from a child, and he answered without delay according to the ordinances of the holy law made by God, saying that he would rather be sent into the other world. 24 "For it doth not become our age," said he, "to dissemble, whereby many young persons might think that Eleazar at the age of fourscore and ten years was gone over to the life of the heathens, 25 and so they through my dissimulation and for a little time of a corruptible life should be deceived, and hereby I should bring a stain and a curse upon my old age. 26 For though for the present time I should be delivered from the punishments of men, yet should I not escape the hand of the Almighty neither alive nor dead. 27 Wherefore, by departing manfully out of this life, I shall shew myself worthy of my old age, 28 and I shall leave an example of fortitude to young men, if with a ready mind and

pro gravissimis et sanctissimis legibus honesta morte per-
fungar." His dictis confestim ad supplicium trahebatur.
29 Hii autem qui eum ducebant et paulo ante fuerant mitio-
res in iram versi sunt propter sermones ab eo dictos, quos illi
per arrogantiam prolatos arbitrabantur. 30 Sed cum plagis
perimeretur, ingemuit et dixit, "Domine, qui habes sanctam
scientiam, manifeste scis tu quia cum a morte possem liberari, duros corporis sustineo dolores, secundum animam
vero propter timorem tuum libenter haec patior."

31 Et iste quidem hoc modo vita decessit, non solum iuvenibus sed et universae genti memoriam mortis suae ad exemplum virtutis et fortitudinis derelinquens.

Caput 7

Contigit autem et septem fratres una cum matre sua ad-
prehensos conpelli a rege edere contra fas carnes porcinas,
flagris et taureis cruciatos. 2 Unus autem ex illis, qui erat primus, sic ait: "Quid quaeris et quid vis discere a nobis? Parati
sumus mori magis quam patrias Dei leges praevaricari."

constancy I suffer an honourable death for the most venerable and most holy laws." And having spoken thus, he was forthwith carried to execution. 29 And they that led him and had been a little before more mild were changed to wrath for the words he had spoken, which they thought were uttered out of arrogancy. 30 But when he was now ready to die with the stripes, he groaned and said, "O Lord, who hast the holy knowledge, thou knowest manifestly that whereas I might be delivered from death, I suffer grevious pains in body, but in soul am well content to suffer these things because I fear thee."

31 *Thus* did this man die, leaving not only to young men but also to the whole nation the memory of his death for an example of virtue and fortitude.

Chapter 7

The glorious martyrdom of the seven brethren and their mother.

*I*t came to pass also that seven brethren together with their mother were apprehended and compelled by the king to eat swine's flesh against the law, *for which end* they were tormented with whips and scourges. 2 But one of them, who was the eldest, said thus: "What wouldst thou ask or learn of us? We are ready to die rather than to transgress the laws of God received from our fathers."

3 Iratus itaque rex iussit sartagines et ollas aeneas succendi, quibus statim succensis, 4 iussit ei qui prior fuerat locutus amputari linguam et, cute capitis abstracta, summas quoque manus ei et pedes praecidi, ceteris eius fratribus et matre inspicientibus. 5 Et cum iam per omnia inutilis factus esset, iussit ignem admoveri et adhuc spirantem torreri in sartagine, in qua cum diu cruciaretur, ceteri una cum matre invicem se hortabantur mori fortiter, 6 dicentes, "Dominus Deus aspiciet veritatem et consolabitur in nobis, quemadmodum in protestatione cantici declaravit Moses: 'Et in servis suis consolabitur.'"

7 Mortuo itaque primo illo hoc modo, sequentem deducebant ad inludendum, et cute capitis eius cum capillis detracta interrogabant si manducaret priusquam toto corpore per membra singula puniretur. 8 At ille respondens patria voce dixit, "Non faciam." Propter quod et iste, sequenti loco, primi tormenta suscepit, 9 et in ultimo spiritu constitutus, sic ait: "Tu quidem, scelestissime, in praesenti vita nos perdis, sed Rex mundi defunctos nos pro suis legibus in aeternae vitae resurrectione suscitabit."

10 Post hunc tertius inluditur, et linguam postulatus cito protulit et manus constanter extendit 11 et cum fiducia ait, "E caelo ista possideo, sed propter Dei leges nunc haec ipsa despicio, quoniam ab ipso me ea recepturum spero,"

3 Then the king, being angry, commanded frying pans and brazen cauldrons to be made hot, which forthwith being heated, 4 he commanded to cut out the tongue of him that had spoken first, and, the skin of his head being drawn off, to chop off also the extremities of his hands and feet, the rest of his brethren and his mother looking on. 5 And when he was now maimed in all parts, he commanded him, being yet *alive,* to be brought to the fire and to be fried in the frying-pan, *and* while he was suffering therein long torments, the rest together with the mother exhorted one another to die manfully, 6 saying, "The Lord God will look upon the truth and will take pleasure in us, as Moses declared in the profession of the canticle: 'And in his servants he will take pleasure.'"

7 So when the first was dead after this manner, they brought the next to make him a mocking-stock, and when they had pulled off the skin of his head with the hair they asked him if he would eat before he were punished throughout the whole body in every limb. 8 But he answered in his own language and said, "I will not do it." Wherefore he also, in the next place, received the torments of the first, 9 and when he was at the last gasp, he said thus: "Thou indeed, O most wicked man, destroyest us out of this present life, but the King of the world will raise us up who die for his laws in the resurrection of eternal life."

10 After him the third was made a mocking-stock, and when he was required he quickly put forth his tongue and courageously stretched out his hands 11 and said with confidence, "These I have from heaven, but for the laws of God I now despise them, because I hope to receive them again

12 ita ut rex et qui cum ipso erant mirarentur adulescentis animum, quod tamquam nihilum duceret cruciatus.

13 Et hoc ita defuncto quartum similiter vexabant torquentes. 14 Et cum iam esset ad mortem sic ait: "Potius est, ab hominibus morti datos, spem expectare a Deo iterum ab ipso resuscitandos, tibi enim resurrectio ad vitam non erit."

15 Et cum admovissent quintum, vexabant eum. At ille, respiciens in eum, 16 dixit, "Potestatem inter homines habens, cum sis corruptibilis, facis quod vis; noli autem putare genus nostrum a Deo esse derelictum. 17 Tu autem patienter sustine, et videbis magnam potestatem ipsius, qualiter te et semen tuum torquebit."

18 Post hunc ducebant sextum, et is mori incipiens sic ait: "Noli frustra errare, nos enim propter nosmet ipsos haec patimur, peccantes in Deum nostrum, et digna admiratione facta sunt in nobis; 19 tu autem ne existimes tibi inpune futurum, quod contra Deum pugnare temptaveris."

20 Supra modum autem mater mirabilis et bonorum memoria digna, quae pereuntes septem filios sub unius diei tempore conspiciens bono animo ferebat propter spem quam in Deum habebat, 21 singulos illorum hortabatur patria voce fortiter, repleta sapientia et femineae cogitationi masculinum animum inserens, 22 dixit ad eos, "Nescio qualiter in utero meo apparuistis, neque enim ego spiritum et animam donavi vobis et vitam, et singulorum membra non ego ipsa conpegi. 23 Sed enim mundi creator, qui formavit hominis nativitatem quique omnium invenit originem, et

from him," 12 so that the king and they that were with him wondered at the young man's courage, because he esteemed the torments as nothing.

13 And after he was thus dead they tormented the fourth in the like manner. 14 And when he was now ready to die he spoke thus: "It is better, being put to death by men, to look for hope from God to be raised up again by him, for as to thee, thou shalt have no resurrection unto life."

15 And when they had brought the fifth, they tormented him. But he, looking upon *the king,* 16 said, "Whereas thou hast power among men, though thou art corruptible, thou dost what thou wilt; but think not that our nation is forsaken by God. 17 But stay patiently *a while,* and thou shalt see his great power, in what manner he will torment thee and thy seed."

18 After him they brought the sixth, and he *being ready* to die spoke thus: "Be not deceived without cause, for we suffer these things for ourselves, having sinned against our God, and things worthy of admiration are done to us; 19 but do not think that thou shalt escape unpunished, for that thou hast attempted to fight against God."

20 Now the mother was to be admired above measure and worthy to be remembered by good men, who beheld seven sons slain in the space of one day and bore it with a good courage for the hope that she had in God, 21 *and* she bravely exhorted every one of them in her own language, being filled with wisdom and joining a man's heart to a woman's thought, 22 she said to them, "I know not how you were formed in my womb, for I neither gave you breath nor soul nor life, neither did I frame the limbs of every one of you. 23 *But* the creator of the world, that formed the nativity of man and

spiritum vobis iterum cum misericordia reddet et vitam, sicut nunc vosmet ipsos despicitis propter leges eius."

24 Antiochus autem contemni se arbitratus simul et exprobrantis voce despecta, cum adhuc adulescentior superesset, non solum verbis hortabatur sed et iuramento adfirmabat divitem se et beatum facturum et translatum a patriis legibus amicum habiturum et res necessarias ei praebiturum. 25 Sed ad ista cum adulescens nequaquam inclinaretur, vocavit rex matrem et suadebat ei ut adulescenti fieret in salutem. 26 Cum autem multis eam verbis esset hortatus, promisit suasuram se filio suo. 27 Itaque inclinata ad illum, inridens crudelem tyrannum, ait patria voce, "Fili mi, miserere mei, quae te in utero novem mensibus portavi et lac triennio dedi et alui et in aetatem istam perduxi. 28 Peto, nate, ut aspicias ad caelum et terram et ad omnia quae in eis sunt, et intellegas quia ex nihilo fecit illa Deus et hominum genus. 29 Ita fiet ut non timeas carnificem istum, sed dignus fratribus tuis effectus particeps, suscipe mortem, ut in illa miseratione cum fratribus tuis te recipiam."

30 Cum haec illa adhuc diceret, ait adulescens, "Quem sustinetis? Non oboedio praecepto regis sed praecepto legis, quae data est nobis per Mosen. 31 Tu vero, qui inventor omnis malitiae factus es in Hebraeos, non effugies manum Dei. 32 Nos enim pro peccatis nostris haec patimur. 33 Et si nobis propter increpationem et correptionem Dominus, Deus noster, modicum iratus est, sed iterum reconciliabitur servis suis. 34 Tu autem, O sceleste et omnium hominum

that found out the origin of all, he will restore to you again in his mercy both breath and life, as now you despise yourselves for the sake of his laws."

24 Now Antiochus, thinking himself despised and withal despising the voice of the upbraider, when the youngest was yet alive, did not only exhort him by words but also assured him with an oath that he would make him a rich and a happy man and if he would turn from the laws of his fathers would take him for a friend and furnish him with things necessary. 25 But when the young man was not moved with these things, the king called the mother and counselled her to deal with the young man to save his life. 26 And when he had exhorted her with many words, she promised that she would counsel her son. 27 So bending herself towards him, mocking the cruel tyrant, she said in her own language, "My son, have pity upon me, that bore thee nine months in my womb and gave thee suck three years and nourished thee and brought thee up unto this age. 28 I beseech thee, my son, look upon heaven and earth and all that is in them, and consider that God made them out of nothing and mankind also. 29 So *thou* shalt not fear this tormentor, but being made a worthy partner with thy brethren, receive death, that in that mercy I may receive thee again with thy brethren."

30 While she was yet speaking these words, the young man said, "For whom do you stay? I will not obey the commandment of the king but the commandment of the law, which was given us by Moses. 31 But thou, that hast been the author of all mischief against the Hebrews, shalt not escape the hand of God. 32 For we suffer thus for our sins. 33 And though the Lord, our God, is angry with us a little while for our chastisement and correction, yet he will be reconciled again to his servants. 34 But thou, O wicked and of all men

flagitiosissime, noli frustra extolli vanis spebus, in servos eius inflammatus. 35 Nondum enim omnipotentis Dei et omnia inspicientis iudicium effugisti. 36 Nam fratres mei, modico nunc dolore sustentato, sub testamento aeternae vitae effecti sunt, tu vero iudicio Dei iustas superbiae tuae poenas solves. 37 Ego autem sicut et fratres mei animam et corpus meum trado pro patriis legibus, invocans Deum maturius genti nostrae propitium fieri teque cum tormentis et verberibus confiteri quod ipse est Deus solus. 38 In me vero et in fratribus meis desinet Omnipotentis ira, quae super omne genus nostrum iuste superducta est."

39 Tunc rex accensus ira in hunc super omnes crudelius desaeviit, indigne ferens derisum se. 40 Et hic itaque mundus obiit, per omnia in Domino confidens. 41 Novissime autem post filios et mater consumpta est. 42 Igitur de sacrificiis et de nimiis crudelitatibus satis dictum est.

Caput 8

Iudas vero Macchabeus et qui cum illo erant introibant latenter in castella, et convocantes cognatos et eos qui permanserunt in Iudaismo adsumentes, eduxerunt ad se sex

most flagitious, be not lifted up without cause with vain hopes, whilst thou art raging against his servants. 35 For thou hast not yet escaped the judgment of the almighty God, who beholdeth all things. 36 For my brethren, having now undergone a short pain, are under the covenant of eternal life, but thou by the judgment of God shalt receive just punishment for thy pride. 37 But I *like* my brethren offer up my life and my body for the laws of our fathers, calling upon God to be speedily merciful to our nation and that thou by torments and stripes mayst confess that he alone is God. 38 But in me and in my brethren the wrath of the Almighty, which hath justly been brought upon all our nation, shall cease."

39 Then the king being incensed with anger raged against him more cruelly than all the rest, taking it grievously that he was mocked. 40 So this man also died undefiled, wholly trusting in the Lord. 41 And last of all after the sons the mother also was consumed. 42 *But* now there is enough said of the sacrifices and of the excessive cruelties.

Chapter 8

Judas Maccabeus, gathering an army, gains divers victories.

But Judas Maccabeus and they that were with him went privately into the towns, and calling together their kinsmen and *friends and* taking unto them such as continued in the Jews' religion, they *assembled* six thousand men.

milia viros. 2 Et invocabant Dominum ut respiceret in populum qui ab omnibus calcabatur et misereretur templo quod contaminabatur ab impiis, 3 misereretur etiam exterminio civitatis, quae esset ilico conplananda, et vocem sanguinis ad se clamantis audiret, 4 memoraretur quoque iniquissimas mortes innocentium parvulorum et blasphemias nomini suo inlatas et indignaretur super his.

5 At Macchabeus congregata multitudine intolerabilis gentibus efficiebatur, ira enim Domini in misericordiam conversa est. 6 Et superveniens castellis et civitatibus inprovisus succendebat eas, et oportuna loca occupans, non paucas hostium strages dabat, 7 maxime autem noctibus ad huiuscemodi excursus ferebatur. Et fama virtutis eius ubique diffundebatur.

8 Videns autem Philippus paulatim virum ad profectum venire ac frequentius res ei prospere cedere, ad Ptolomeum, ducem Coelesyriae et Foenicis, scripsit ut auxilium ferret regis negotiis. 9 At ille velociter misit Nicanorem, Patrocli, de primoribus amicum, datis ei de permixtis gentibus armatis non minus viginti milibus, ut universum Iudaeorum genus deleret, adiuncto ei et Gorgia, viro militari et in bellicis rebus experientissimo. 10 Constituit autem Nicanor ut regi tributum quod Romanis erat dandum duo milia talentum de captivitate Iudaeorum suppleret 11 statimque ad maritimas misit civitates, convocans ad coemptionem Iudaicorum mancipiorum, promittens se nonaginta mancipia talento

2 And they called upon the Lord that he would look upon his people that was trodden down by all and would have pity on the temple that was defiled by the wicked, 3 that he would have pity also upon the *city that was destroyed,* that was ready to be made even with the ground, and would hear the voice of the blood that cried to him, 4 that he would remember also the most unjust deaths of innocent children and the blasphemies offered to his name and would shew his indignation on this occasion.

5 Now when Maccabeus had gathered a multitude he could not be withstood by the heathens, for the wrath of the Lord was turned into mercy. 6 So coming unawares upon the towns and cities he set them on fire, and taking possession of the most commodious place, he made no small slaughter of the enemies, 7 and especially in the nights he went upon these expeditions. And the fame of his valour was spread abroad everywhere.

8 Then Philip, seeing that the man gained ground by little and little and that things for the most part succeeded prosperously with him, wrote to Ptolemy, the governor of Coelesyria and Phoenicia, to send aid to the king's affairs. 9 And he with all speed sent Nicanor, the son of Patroclus, one of his special friends, giving him no fewer than twenty thousand armed men of different nations, to root out the whole race of the Jews, joining also with him Gorgias, a good soldier and of great experience in matters of war. 10 And Nicanor purposed to raise for the king the tribute of two thousand talents that was to be given to the Romans by making so much money of the captive Jews, 11 *wherefore* he sent immediately to the cities upon the sea coast *to* invite men together to buy up the Jewish slaves, promising that *they*

distracturum, non respiciens ad vindictam quae eum ab Omnipotente esset consecutura.

12 Iudas autem ubi conperit indicavit his qui secum erant Iudaeis Nicanoris adventum. 13 Ex quibus quidam, formidantes et non credentes Dei iustitiae, in fugam vertebantur, 14 alii vero, si quid eis supererat, vendebant simulque Dominum deprecabantur ut eriperet eos ab impio Nicanore, qui eos priusquam comminus veniret vendiderat, 15 et si non propter eos, propter testamentum tamen quod erat ad patres eorum et propter invocationem sancti et magnifici nominis eius super ipsos.

16 Convocatis autem Macchabeus septem milibus qui cum ipso erant rogabat ne hostibus reconciliarentur neque metuerent inique venientium adversum se hostium multitudinem sed fortiter contenderent, 17 ante oculos habentes contumeliam quae loco sancto ab his iniuste esset inlata itemque et ludibrio habitae civitatis iniuriam, adhuc etiam veterum instituta convulsa. 18 "Nam illi quidem armis confidunt," ait, "simul et audacia, nos autem in omnipotente Domino, qui potest et venientes adversus nos et universum mundum uno nutu delere, confidimus." 19 Admonuit autem eos et de auxiliis Dei quae facta sunt erga parentes et quod sub Sennacherib centum octoginta quinque milia perierunt 20 et de proelio quod eis adversus Galatas fuit in Babylonia, ut omnes ubi ad rem ventum est, Macedonibus sociis haesitantibus, ipsi sex milia soli peremerunt centum viginti milia propter auxilium illis datum e caelo, et beneficia pro his plurima consecuti sunt.

21 His verbis constantes effecti sunt et pro legibus et

should *have* ninety slaves for one talent, not reflecting on the vengeance which was to follow him from the Almighty.

12 Now when Judas found that Nicanor was coming he imparted to the Jews that were with him *that the enemy was at hand.* 13 *And* some of them, being afraid and distrusting the justice of God, fled away, 14 *others* sold *all that they had left* and withal besought the Lord that he would deliver them from the wicked Nicanor, who had sold them before he came near them, 15 and if not for their sakes, yet for the covenant that he had made with their fathers and for the sake of his holy and glorious name that was invoked upon them.

16 But Maccabeus, calling together seven thousand that were with him, exhorted them not to be reconciled to the enemies nor to fear the multitude of the enemies who came wrongfully against them but to fight manfully, 17 setting before their eyes the injury they had unjustly done the holy place and also the injury they had done to the city, which had been shamefully abused, besides their destroying the ordinances of the fathers. 18 "For," said he, "they trust in their weapons and in their boldness, but we trust in the almighty Lord, who at a beck can utterly destroy both them that come against us and the whole world." 19 Moreover he put them in mind also of the helps their fathers had received from God and how under Sennacherib a hundred and eighty-five thousand had been destroyed 20 and of the battle that they had fought against the Galatians in Babylonia, how they, being in all but six thousand, when it came to the point and the Macedonians their companions were at a stand, slew a hundred and twenty thousand because of the help they had from heaven, and for this they received many favours.

21 With these words they were greatly encouraged and

patria mori parati. 22 Constituit itaque fratres suos duces utrique ordini, Simonem et Iosepphum et Ionathan, subiectis unicuique millenis et quingentenis. 23 Ad hoc etiam ab Ezra lecto illis sancto libro et dato signo "adiutorii Dei," in prima acie ipse dux commisit cum Nicanore. 24 Et facto sibi adiutore Omnipotente, interfecerunt super novem milia hominum, maiorem autem partem exercitus Nicanoris vulneribus debilem factam fugere conpulerunt. 25 Pecuniis vero eorum qui ad emptionem ipsorum venerant sublatis, ipsos usquequaque persecuti sunt.

26 Sed reverterunt hora conclusi, nam erat ante sabbatum, quam ob causam non perseveraverunt insequentes. 27 Arma autem ipsorum et spolia congregantes, sabbatum agebant, benedicentes Dominum, qui liberavit eos in isto die, misericordiae initium stillans in eos. 28 Post sabbatum vero debilibus et orfanis et viduis diviserunt spolia, et residua ipsi cum suis habuere. 29 His itaque gestis et communiter ab omnibus facta obsecratione, misericordem Dominum postulabant ut in finem servis suis reconciliaretur.

30 Et ex his qui cum Timotheo et Bacchide erant contra se contendentes super viginti milia interfecerunt, et munitiones excelsas obtinuerunt, et plures praedas diviserunt, aequam portionem debilibus, pupillis et viduis, sed et senioribus facientes. 31 Et cum arma eorum collegissent diligenter, omnia conposuerunt in locis oportunis, residua vero spolia Hierosolymam detulerunt. 32 Et Phylarchen, qui cum Timotheo erat, interfecerunt, virum scelestum qui in

disposed even to die for the laws and their country. 22 So he appointed his brethren captains over each division of his army, Simon and Joseph and Jonathan, giving to each one fifteen hundred men. 23 And after the holy book had been read to them by Ezra and he had given them for a watchword "the help of God," himself leading the first band he joined battle with Nicanor. 24 And the Almighty being their helper, they slew above nine thousand men, and having wounded and disabled the greater part of Nicanor's army they obliged them to fly. 25 And they took the money of them that came to buy them, and they pursued them on every side.

26 But they came back for want of time, for it was the day before the sabbath, and therefore they did not continue the pursuit. 27 But when they had gathered together their arms and their spoils, they kept the sabbath, blessing the Lord, who had delivered them that day, distilling the beginning of mercy upon them. 28 Then after the sabbath they divided the spoils to the feeble and the orphans and the widows, and the rest they took for themselves and their servants. 29 *When* this was done, and they had all made a common supplication, they besought the merciful Lord to be reconciled to his servants unto the end.

30 *Moreover* they slew above twenty thousand of them that were with Timothy and Bacchides who fought them, and they made themselves masters of the high strongholds, and they divided amongst them many spoils, giving equal portions to the feeble, the fatherless and the widows, yea and the aged also. 31 And when they had carefully gathered together their arms, they laid them all up in convenient places, and the residue of their spoils they carried to Jerusalem. 32 They slew also Philarches, who was with Timothy, a

multis Iudaeos adflixerat. 33 Et cum epinicia agerent in Hierosolymis, eum qui sacras ianuas incenderat, id est Calliste-
nen, cum in quoddam domicilium refugisset, incenderunt,
digna ei mercede pro impietatibus suis reddita.

34 Facinorosissimus autem Nicanor, qui mille negotiantes
ad Iudaeorum venditionem adduxerat, 35 humiliatus auxilio
Domini ab his quos nullos existimaverat, deposita veste gloriae, per mediterranea fugiens, solus venit Antiochiam, sum-
mam infelicitatem de interitu sui exercitus consecutus. 36 Et
qui promiserat Romanis se tributum restituere de captivitate Hierosolymorum praedicabat nunc protectorem Deum
habere Iudaeos et ob ipsum invulnerabiles esse, eo quod sequerentur leges ab ipso constitutas.

Caput 9

Eodem tempore Antiochus inhoneste revertebatur de
Perside. 2 Intraverat enim in eam quae dicitur Persipolis et
temptavit expoliare templum et civitatem opprimere, sed

wicked man who had many ways afflicted the Jews. 33 And when they kept the feast of the victory at Jerusalem, they burnt Callisthenes, that had set fire to the holy gates, who had taken refuge in a certain house, rendering to him a worthy reward for his impieties.

34 But as for that most wicked man, Nicanor, who had brought a thousand merchants to the sale of the Jews, 35 being through the help of the Lord brought down by them of whom he had made no account, laying aside his garment of glory, fleeing through the midland country, he came alone to Antioch, being rendered very unhappy by the destruction of his army. 36 And he that had promised to levy the tribute for the Romans by the means of the captives of Jerusalem now professed that the Jews had God for their protector and therefore they could not be hurt, because they followed the laws appointed by him.

Chapter 9

The wretched end and fruitless repentance of King Antiochus.

At that time Antiochus returned with dishonour out of Persia. 2 For he had entered into the *city* called Persepolis and attempted to rob the temple and to oppress the city, but

multitudine ad arma concurrente in fugam versi sunt, et ita contigit ut Antiochus post fugam turpiter rediret.

3 Et cum venisset circa Ecbatanam, recognovit quae erga Nicanorem et Timotheum gesta sunt. 4 Elatus autem in ira arbitrabatur se iniuriam illorum qui se fugaverant posse in Iudaeos retorquere. Ideoque iussit agitari currum suum sine intermissione agens iter, caelesti eum iudicio perurguente, quod ita superbe locutus est venturum se Hierosolymam et congeriem sepulchri Iudaeorum eam facturum.

5 Sed qui universa conspicit, Dominus, Deus Israhel, percussit eum insanabili et invisibili plaga. Ut enim finivit hunc ipsum sermonem, adprehendit eum dolor dirus viscerum, et amara internorum tormenta, 6 et quidem satis iuste, quippe qui multis et novis cruciatibus aliorum torserat viscera, licet ille nullo modo a sua malitia cessaret. 7 Super hoc autem, superbia repletus, ignem spirans animo in Iudaeos et praecipiens adcelerari negotium, contigit illum impetu euntem de curru cadere et gravi corporis conlisione membra vexari. 8 Isque qui sibi videbatur etiam fluctibus maris imperare, supra humanum modum superbia repletus, et montium altitudines in statera adpendere nunc, humiliatus ad terram, in gestatorio portabatur, manifestam Dei virtutem in semet ipso contestans, 9 ita ut de corpore impii vermes scaturrirent, ac viventes in doloribus carnes eius effluerent, odore etiam illius et fetore exercitus gravaretur. 10 Et qui paulo

the multitude running together to arms put them to flight, and so it fell out that Antiochus, being put to flight, returned with disgrace.

3 Now when he was come about Ecbatana, he received the news of what had happened to Nicanor and Timothy. 4 And swelling with anger he thought to revenge upon the Jews the injury done by them that had put him to flight. And therefore he commanded his chariot to be driven without stopping in his journey, the judgment of heaven urging him forward, because he had spoken so proudly that he would come to Jerusalem and make it a common burying place of the Jews.

5 But the Lord, the God of Israel, that seeth all things, struck him with an incurable and an invisible plague. For as soon as he had ended these words, a dreadful pain in his bowels came upon him, and bitter torments of the inner parts, 6 and indeed very justly, seeing he had tormented the bowels of others with many and new torments, albeit he by no means ceased from his malice. 7 Moreover, being filled with pride, breathing out fire in his rage against the Jews and commanding the matter to be hastened, it happened as he was going with violence that he fell from the chariot *so that* his limbs were much pained by a grievous bruising of the body. 8 *Thus* he that seemed to himself to command even the waves of the sea, being proud above the condition of man, and to weigh the heights of the mountains in a balance now, being cast down to the ground, was carried in a litter, bearing witness to the manifest power of God in himself, 9 so that worms swarmed out of the body of this man, and whilst *he* lived in *sorrow and* pain, his flesh fell off, and the filthiness of his smell was noisome to the army. 10 And the man

ante sidera caeli contingere se arbitrabatur, eum nemo poterat propter intolerantiam fetoris portare.

11 Hinc igitur coepit, ex gravi superbia deductus, ad agnitionem sui venire, divina admonitus plaga, per momenta singula doloribus suis augmenta capientibus. 12 Et cum nec ipse iam fetorem suum ferre posset, ita ait: "Iustum est subditum esse Deo et mortalem non paria Deo sentire." 13 Orabat autem hic scelestus Dominum, a quo non esset misericordiam consecuturus. 14 Et civitatem ad quam festinans veniebat ut eam ad solum deduceret et sepulchrum congestorum faceret nunc optat liberam reddere. 15 Et Iudaeos, quos nec sepultura quidem se dignos habiturum sed avibus ac feris diripiendos traditurum et cum parvulis exterminaturum dixerat, aequales nunc Atheniensibus facturum pollicetur. 16 Templum etiam sanctum, quod prius expoliaverat, optimis donis ornaturum et sancta vasa multiplicaturum et pertinentes ad sacrificia sumptus de reditibus suis praestaturum. 17 Super haec et Iudaeum se futurum et omnem locum terrae perambulaturum et praedicaturum Dei potestatem.

18 Sed non cessantibus doloribus (supervenerat enim in eum iustum Dei iudicium), desperans scripsit ad Iudaeos in modum deprecationis epistulam haec continentem:

19 "Optimis civibus, Iudaeis, plurimam salutem et bene valere et esse felices rex et princeps, Antiochus. 20 Si bene valetis et filii vestri et ex sententia vobis cuncta sunt, maximas agimus gratias.

that thought a little before he could reach to the stars of heaven, no man could endure to carry for the intolerable stench.

11 And by this means, being brought from his great pride, he began to come to the knowledge of himself, being admonished by the scourge of God, his pains increasing every moment. 12 And when he himself could not now abide his own stench, he spoke thus: "It is just to be subject to God and that a mortal man should not equal himself to God." 13 Then this wicked man prayed to the Lord, of whom he was not like to obtain mercy. 14 And the city to which he was going in haste to lay it even with the ground and to make it a common burying-place he now desireth to make free. 15 And the Jews, whom he said he would not account worthy to be so much as buried but would give them up to be devoured by the birds and wild beasts and would utterly destroy them with their children, he now promiseth to make equal with the Athenians. 16 The holy temple also, which before he had spoiled, he promiseth to adorn with goodly gifts and to multiply the holy vessels and to allow out of his revenues the charges pertaining to the sacrifices. 17 *Yea* also that he would become a Jew himself and would go through every place of the earth and declare the power of God.

18 But his pains not ceasing (for the just judgment of God was come upon him), despairing *of life* he wrote to the Jews in the manner of a supplication a letter in these words:

19 "To his very good subjects, the Jews, Antiochus, king and ruler, wisheth much health and welfare and happiness. 20 If you and your children are well and if all matters go with you to your mind, we give very great thanks.

21 "Et ego in infirmitate constitutus, vestri autem benigne memor, regressus de Persidis locis et infirmitate gravi adprehensus, necessarium duxi pro communi utilitate curam habere, 22 non desperans memet ipsum sed spem multam habens effugiendi infirmitatem. 23 Respiciens autem quod et pater meus, quibus temporibus in locis superioribus ducebat exercitum, ostendit qui post se susciperet principatum, 24 ut si quid contrarium accideret aut difficile nuntiaretur, scientes hii qui in regionibus erant cui esset rerum summa derelicta non turbarentur. 25 Ad haec, considerans de proximo potentes quosque et vicinos temporibus insidiantes et eventum expectantes, designavi filium meum Antiochus regem, quem saepe recurrens in superiora regna multis vestrum commendabam, et scripsi ad eum quae subiecta sunt.

26 "Oro itaque vos et peto memores beneficiorum publice et privatim ut unusquisque conservet fidem ad me et ad filium meum. 27 Confido enim eum modeste et humane acturum et sequentem propositum meum et communem vobis fore."

28 Igitur homicida et blasphemus, pessime percussus, et ut ipse alios tractaverat, peregre in montibus miserabili obitu vita functus est. 29 Transferebat autem corpus Philippus, conlactaneus eius, qui metuens filium Antiochi ad Ptolomeum Filometora in Aegyptum abiit.

21 *"As* for me, being infirm, but yet kindly remembering you, returning out of the places of Persia and being taken with a grievous disease, I thought it necessary to take care for the common good, 22 not distrusting my *life* but having great hope to escape the sickness. 23 But considering that my father also, at what time he led an army into the higher countries, appointed who should reign after him, 24 to the end that if any thing contrary to expectation should fall out or any bad tidings should be brought, they that were in the countries, knowing to whom the whole government was left, might not be troubled. 25 Moreover, considering that neighbouring princes and borderers wait for opportunities and expect what shall be the event, I have appointed my son Antiochus king, whom I often recommended to many of you when I went into the higher provinces, and I have written to him what I have joined here below.

26 "I pray you therefore and request of you that remembering favours both public and private you will every man of you continue to be faithful to me and to my son. 27 For I trust that he will behave with moderation and humanity and following my intentions *will* be gracious unto you."

28 Thus the murderer and blasphemer, being grievously struck, as himself had treated others, died a miserable death in a strange country among the mountains. 29 But Philip, that was brought up with him, carried away his body, and out of fear of the son of Antiochus went into Egypt to Ptolemy Philometor.

Caput 10

Macchabeus autem et qui cum illo erant Domino se protegente templum quidem et civitatem recepit. ²Aras autem quas alienigenae per plateas extruxerant itemque delubra demolitus est. ³Et purgato templo aliud altare fecerunt, et de ignitis lapidibus igne concepto obtulerunt sacrificia post biennium et incensum et lucernas et panes propositionis posuerunt. ⁴Quibus gestis rogabant Dominum, prostrati in terram, ne amplius malis talibus inciderent, sed et si quando peccassent, ut ab ipso mitius corriperentur et non blasphemis ac barbaris hominibus traderentur.

⁵Qua die autem templum ab alienigenis pollutum fuerat, contigit eadem die purificationem fieri, vicesima et quinta mensis qui fuit Casleu. ⁶Et cum laetitia diebus octo egerunt in modum tabernaculorum, recordantes quod ante modicum temporis diem sollemnem tabernaculorum in montibus et in speluncis more bestiarum egerant. ⁷Propter quod tyrsos et ramos virides et palmas praeferebant ei qui prosperavit mundari locum suum. ⁸Et decreverunt communi

Chapter 10

The purification of the temple and city. Other exploits of
Judas. His victory over Timothy.

But Maccabeus and they that were with him by the protection of the Lord recovered the temple and the city again.
2 But he threw down the altars which the heathens had set
up in the streets as also the temples *of the idols.* 3 And having purified the temple they made another altar, and taking
fire out of the fiery stones they offered sacrifices after two
years and set forth incense and lamps and the loaves of proposition. 4 And when they had done these things they besought the Lord, lying prostrate on the ground, that they
might no more fall into such evils, but if they should at
any time sin, that they might be chastised by him more
gently and not be delivered up to barbarians and blasphemous men.

5 Now upon the same day that the temple had been polluted by the strangers, on the very same day it *was cleansed
again, to wit,* on the five and twentieth day of the month *of*
Chislev. 6 And they kept eight days with joy after the manner
of the feast of the tabernacles, remembering that not long
before they had kept the feast of the tabernacles when they
were in the mountains and in dens like wild beasts. 7 Therefore they *now* carried boughs and green branches and palms
for him that had given them good success in cleansing his
place. 8 And they ordained by a common statute and decree

praecepto et decreto universae genti Iudaeorum omnibus annis agere dies istos.

9 Et Antiochi quidem, qui appellatus est Nobilis, vitae excessus ita se habuit.

10 Nunc autem de Eupatore, Antiochi filio impii, quae gesta sunt narrabimus, breviantes mala quae in bellis gesta sunt. 11 Hic enim suscepto regno constituit super negotia regni Lysiam quendam, Foenicis et Syriae militiae principem. 12 Nam Ptolomeus, qui dicebatur Macer, iusti tenax erga Iudaeos esse instituit et praecipue propter iniquitatem quae facta erat in eos et pacifice agere cum eis. 13 Sed ob hoc accusatus ab amicis apud Eupatorem, cum frequenter proditor audiret eo quod Cyprum, creditam sibi a Filometore, deseruisset, et ad Antiochum Nobilem translatus etiam ab eo recessisset, veneno vitam finivit.

14 Gorgias autem, cum esset dux locorum, adsumptis advenis frequenter Iudaeos debellabat. 15 Iudaei vero qui tenebant oportunas munitiones fugatos ab Hierosolymis suscipiebant et bellare temptabant. 16 Hii vero qui erant cum Macchabeo, per orationes Dominum rogantes ut esset sibi adiutor, impetum fecerunt in munitiones Idumeorum 17 multaque vi insistentes loca obtinuerunt, occurrentes interemerunt et omnes simul non minus viginti milibus trucidaverunt. 18 Quidam autem cum confugissent in duas turres valde munitas, omnem adparatum ad repugnandum habentes, 19 Macchabeus ad eorum expugnationem relicto Simone et Ioseppho itemque Zaccheo eisque qui cum ipsis erant

that all the nation of the Jews should keep those days every year.

9 And *this was the end* of Antiochus, that was called the Illustrious.

10 But now we will relate the acts of Eupator, the son of that wicked Antiochus, abridging the account of the evils that happened in the wars. 11 For when he was come to the crown he appointed over the affairs of his realm one Lysias, general of the army of Phoenicia and Syria. 12 For Ptolemy, that was called Macer, was determined to be strictly just to the Jews and especially by reason of the wrong that had been done them and to deal peaceably with them. 13 But being accused for this to Eupator by his friends and being oftentimes called traitor because he had left Cyprus, which Philometor had committed to him, and coming over to Antiochus the Illustrious had revolted also from him, he put an end to his life by poison.

14 But Gorgias, who was governor of the holds, taking with him the strangers often fought against the Jews. 15 And the Jews that occupied the most commodious holds received those that were driven out of Jerusalem and attempted to make war. 16 Then they that were with Maccabeus, beseeching the Lord by prayers to be their helper, made a strong attack upon the strongholds of the Idumeans 17 and assaulting them with great force won the holds, killed them that came in the way and slew altogether no fewer than twenty thousand. 18 And whereas some were fled into two very strong towers, having all manner of provision to sustain a siege, 19 Maccabeus left Simon and Joseph and Zacheus and them

satis multis ipse ad eas quae amplius perurguebant pugnas conversus est. 20 Hii vero qui cum Simone erant, cupiditate ducti, a quibusdam qui in turribus erant suasi sunt pecunia et septuaginta milibus didragmis acceptis dimiserunt quosdam effugere.

21 Cum autem Macchabeo nuntiatum esset quod factum est, congregatis principibus populi accusavit quod pecunia fratres vendidissent, adversariis eorum dimissis. 22 Hos igitur proditores factos interfecit et confestim duas turres occupavit. 23 Armis autem ac manibus omnia prospere agendo, in duabus munitionibus plus quam viginti milia peremit.

24 At Timotheus, qui prius a Iudaeis fuerat superatus, convocato exercitu peregrinae multitudinis et congregato equitatu Asiano, advenit quasi armis Iudaeam capturus. 25 Macchabeus autem et qui cum ipso erant, adpropiante illo, deprecabantur Dominum, caput terra aspergentes lumbosque ciliciis praecincti, 26 ad altaris crepidinem provoluti ut sibi propitius inimicis autem eorum esset inimicus et adversariis adversaretur, sicut lex dicit. 27 Et ita post orationem sumptis armis, longius de civitate procedentes, et proximi hostibus effecti resederunt. 28 Primo autem solis ortu utrique commiserunt, isti quidem victoriae et prosperitatis sponsorem cum virtute Dominum habentes, illi autem ducem belli animum habebant.

that were with them in sufficient number to besiege them and departed to those expeditions which urged more. 20 Now they that were with Simon, being led with covetousness, were persuaded for the sake of money by some that were in the towers and taking seventy thousand didrachmas let some of them escape.

21 But when it was told Maccabeus what was done, he assembled the rulers of the people and accused those men that they had sold their brethren for money, having let their adversaries escape. 22 So he put these traitors to death and forthwith took the two towers. 23 And having good success in arms and in all things he took in hand, he slew more than twenty thousand in the two holds.

24 But Timothy, who before had been overcome by the Jews, having called together a multitude of foreign troops and assembled horsemen out of Asia, came as though he would take Judea by force of arms. 25 But Maccabeus and they that were with him, when he drew near, prayed to the Lord, sprinkling earth upon their heads and girding their loins with haircloth 26 and lying prostrate at the foot of the altar *besought him* to be merciful to them and to be an enemy to their enemies and an adversary to their adversaries, as the law saith. 27 And so after prayer taking their arms, they went forth further from the city, and when they were come very near the enemies they rested. 28 But as soon as the sun was risen both sides joined battle, the one part having with their valour the Lord for a surety of victory and success, but the other side making their rage their leader in battle.

29 Sed cum vehemens pugna esset, apparuerunt adversariis de caelo viri quinque in equis, frenis aureis decori, ducatum Iudaeis praestantes, 30 ex quibus duo Macchabeum medium habentes armis suis circumseptum incolomem conservabant, in adversarios autem tela et fulmina iaciebant, ex quo et caecitate confusi et repleti perturbatione cadebant. 31 Interfecti sunt autem viginti milia quingenti et equites sescenti.

32 Timotheus autem confugit in Gazara, praesidium munitum, cui praeerat Caereas. 33 Macchabeus autem et qui cum eo erant laetantes obsederunt praesidium diebus quattuor. 34 At hii qui intus erant, loci firmitate confisi, super modum maledicebant et sermones nefandos iactabant. 35 Sed cum dies quinta inlucesceret, viginti iuvenes ex his qui cum Macchabeo erant, accensi animis propter blasphemiam, viriliter accesserunt ad murum et feroci animo incedentes ascendebant. 36 Sed et alii similiter ascendentes turres portasque succendere adgressi atque ipsos maledicos vivos concremare. 37 Per continuum autem biduum praesidio vastato, Timotheum occultantem se in quodam reppertum loco peremerunt, et fratrem illius, Caerean, et Apollofanem occiderunt. 38 Quibus gestis in hymnis et confessionibus benedicebant Dominum, qui magna fecit in Israhel et victoriam illi dedit.

29 But when they were in the heat of the engagement, there appeared to the enemies from heaven five men upon horses, comely with golden bridles, conducting the Jews, 30 two of whom took Maccabeus between them and covered him on every side with their arms and kept him safe, but cast darts and fireballs against the enemy, so that they fell down being both confounded with blindness and filled with trouble. 31 And there were slain twenty thousand five hundred and six hundred horsemen.

32 But Timothy fled into Gazara, a stronghold, where Chaereas was governor. 33 Then Maccabeus and they that were with him cheerfully laid siege to the fortress four days. 34 But they that were within, trusting to the strength of the place, blasphemed exceedingly and cast forth abominable words. 35 But when the fifth day appeared, twenty young men of them that were with Maccabeus, inflamed in their minds because of the blasphemy, approached manfully to the wall and pushing forward with fierce courage got up upon it. 36 Moreover others also getting up after them went to set fire to the towers and the gates and to burn the blasphemers alive. 37 And having for two days together pillaged and sacked the fortress, they killed Timothy, who was found hid in a certain place; they slew also his brother, Chaereas, and Apollophanes. 38 And when this was done, they blessed the Lord with hymns and thanksgiving, who had done great things in Israel and given them the victory.

Caput 11

Sed parvo post tempore, Lysias, procurator regis et propinquus ac negotiorum praepositus, graviter ferens de his
quae acciderant, 2 congregatis octoginta milibus et equitatu
universo veniebat adversus Iudaeos, existimans se civitatem
quidem captam Gentibus habitaculum facturum, 3 templum
vero in pecuniae quaestum sicut cetera delubra Gentium habiturum et per singulos annos venale sacerdotium, 4 nus-
quam recogitans Dei potestatem sed mente effrenatus in
multitudine peditum et in milibus equitum et in octoginta
elefantis confidebat. 5 Ingressus autem Iudaeam et adpro-
pians Bethsurae, quod erat in angusto loco, ab Hierosolyma
intervallo quinque stadiorum, illud praesidium expugnabat.

6 Ut autem Macchabeus et qui cum eo erant cognoverunt
expugnari praesidia, cum fletu et lacrimis rogabant Dominum et omnis turba simul ut bonum angelum mitteret ad
salutem Israhel. 7 Et ipse primus Macchabeus sumptis armis
ceteros adhortatus est simul secum periculum subire et ferre
auxilium fratribus suis. 8 Cumque pariter prompto animo
procederent, Hierosolymis apparuit praecedens eos eques

Chapter 11

Lysias is overthrown by Judas. He sues for peace.

A short time after this, Lysias, the king's lieutenant and cousin and who had chief charge over all the affairs, being greatly displeased with what had happened, 2 gathered together fourscore thousand men and all the horsemen and came against the Jews, thinking to take the city and make it a habitation of the Gentiles 3 and to make a gain of the temple as of the other temples of the Gentiles and to set the *high* priesthood to sale every year, 4 never considering the power of God but puffed up in mind and trusting in the multitude of his foot soldiers and the thousands of his horsemen and his fourscore elephants. 5 So he came into Judea, and approaching to Beth-zur, which was in a narrow place, the space of five furlongs from Jerusalem, he laid siege to that fortress.

6 But when Maccabeus and they that were with him understood that the strongholds were besieged, they and all the people besought the Lord with lamentations and tears that he would send a good angel to save Israel. 7 Then Maccabeus himself first taking his arms, exhorted the rest to expose themselves together with him to the danger and to succour their brethren. 8 And when they were going forth together with a willing mind, there appeared at Jerusalem a horseman going before them in white clothing, with golden

in veste candida, armis aureis, hastam vibrans. 9 Tum simul omnes benedixerunt misericordem Dominum et convaluerunt animis, non solum homines sed et bestias ferocissimas et muros ferreos parati penetrare. 10 Ibant igitur prompti, de caelo habentes adiutorem et miserantem super eos Dominum. 11 Leonum autem more impetu inruentes hostibus prostraverunt ex eis undecim milia peditum et equitum mille sescentos, 12 universos autem in fugam verterunt, plures vero ex eis vulnerati nudi evaserunt, sed et ipse Lysias turpiter fugiens evasit. 13 Et quia non insensatus erat, secum ipse reputans factam erga se diminutionem et intellegens invictos esse Hebraeos, omnipotentis Dei auxilio nitentes, misit ad eos 14 promisitque consensurum se omnibus quae iusta sunt et regem conpulsurum amicum fieri.

15 Annuit autem Macchabeus precibus Lysiae, in omnibus utilitati consulens, et quaecumque Macchabeus scripsit Lysiae de Iudaeis ea rex concessit. 16 Nam erant scriptae Iudaeis epistulae a Lysia quidem hunc modum continentes:

"Lysias populo Iudaeorum salutem.

17 "Iohannes et Abessalom, qui missi sunt a vobis, tradentes scripta, postulabant ut ea quae per illos significabantur implerem. 18 Quaecumque igitur regi potuerunt perferri exposui, et quae res permittebat concessi. 19 Si igitur in negotiis fidem conservaveritis, etiam deinceps bonorum vobis causa esse temptabo. 20 De ceteris autem per singula verbo mandavi et istis et his qui a me missi sunt conloqui

armour, shaking a spear. 9 Then they all together blessed the merciful Lord and took great courage, being ready to break through not only men but also the fiercest beasts and walls of iron. 10 So they went on courageously, having a helper from heaven and the Lord, who shewed mercy to them. 11 And rushing violently upon the enemy like lions they slew of them eleven thousand footmen and one thousand six hundred horsemen 12 and put all the rest to flight, and many of them being wounded escaped naked, yea and Lysias himself fled away shamefully and escaped. 13 And as he was a man of understanding, considering with himself the loss he had suffered and perceiving that the Hebrews could not be overcome because they relied upon the help of the almighty God, he sent to them 14 and promised that he would agree to all things that are just and that he would persuade the king to be their friend.

15 Then Maccabeus consented to the request of Lysias, providing for the common good in all things, and whatsoever Maccabeus wrote to Lysias concerning the Jews the king allowed of. 16 For there were letters written to the Jews from Lysias to this effect:

"Lysias to the people of the Jews, greeting.

17 "John and Absalom, who were sent from you, delivering your writings, requested that I would accomplish those things which were signified by them. 18 Therefore whatsoever things could be reported to the king I have represented to him, and *he hath* granted as much as the matter permitted. 19 If therefore you will keep yourselves loyal in affairs, hereafter also I will endeavour to be a means of your good. 20 But as concerning other particulars I have given orders by word both to these and to them that are sent by

vobiscum. 21 Bene valete. Anno centesimo quadragesimo octavo, Dioscori die mensis vicesima et quarta."

22 Regis autem epistula ista continebat:

"Rex Antiochus Lysiae, fratri, salutem.

23 "Patre nostro inter deos translato, nos volentes eos qui sunt in regno nostro sine tumultu agere et rebus suis adhibere diligentiam, 24 audivimus Iudaeos non consensisse patri meo ut transferrentur ad ritum Graecorum sed tenere velle suum institutum ac propterea postulare a nobis concedi sibi legitima sua. 25 Volentes igitur hanc quoque gentem quietam esse, statuentes iudicavimus templum restitui illis ut agerent secundum maiorum suorum consuetudinem. 26 Bene igitur feceris si miseris ad eos et dextram dederis, ut cognita nostra voluntate bono animo sint et utilitatibus propriis deserviant."

27 Ad Iudaeos autem regis epistula talis erat:

"Rex Antiochus senatui Iudaeorum et ceteris Iudaeis salutem. 28 Si valetis, sic estis ut volumus, sed et ipsi bene valemus.

29 "Adiit nos Menelaus dicens velle vos descendere ad vestros qui sunt apud nos. 30 His igitur qui commeant usque ad diem tricesimum mensis Xandici damus dextras securitatis, 31 ut Iudaei utantur cibis et legibus suis sicut et prius et nemo eorum ullo modo molestiam patiatur de his quae per ignorantiam gesta sunt. 32 Misimus autem et Menelaum, qui

me to commune with you. 21 Fare ye well. In the year one hundred and forty-eight, the four and twentieth day of the month of Dioscorus."

22 But the king's letter contained these words:

"King Antiochus to Lysias, his brother, greeting.

23 "Our father being translated amongst the gods, we are desirous that they that are in our realm should live *quietly* and apply *themselves diligently* to their own concerns, 24 *and* we have heard that the Jews would not consent to my father to turn to the rites of the Greeks but that they would keep to their own manner of living and therefore that they request us to allow them to live after their own laws. 25 *Wherefore* being desirous that this nation also should be at rest, we have ordained and decreed that the temple should be restored to them *and* that they may live according to the custom of their ancestors. 26 Thou shalt do well therefore to send to them and grant them peace, that our pleasure being known they may be of good comfort and look to their own affairs."

27 But the king's letter to the Jews was in this manner:

"King Antiochus to the senate of the Jews and to the rest of the Jews, greeting. 28 If you are well, you are as we desire; *we* ourselves also are well.

29 "Menelaus came to us saying that you desired to come down to your countrymen that are with us. 30 We grant therefore a safe conduct to all that come and go until the thirtieth day of the month of Xanthicus, 31 that the Jews may use their own kind of meats and their own laws as before and that none of them any manner of ways be molested for things which have been done by ignorance. 32 And we

vos adloquatur. 33 Valete. Anno centesimo quadragesimo octavo, Xandici mensis quintadecima die."

34 Miserunt autem etiam Romani epistulam ita se habentem:

"Quintus Memmius et Titus Manilius, legati Romanorum, populo Iudaeorum salutem.

35 "De his quae Lysias, cognatus regis, concessit vobis, et nos concessimus. 36 De quibus autem ad regem iudicavit referendum, confestim aliquem mittite diligentius inter vos conferentes ut decernamus sicut congruit vobis, nos enim Antiochiam accedimus. 37 Ideoque festinate rescribere, ut nos quoque sciamus cuius estis voluntatis. 38 Bene valete. Anno centesimo quadragesimo octavo, quintadecima die mensis Xandici."

Caput 12

His factis pactionibus, Lysias pergebat ad regem, Iudaei autem agriculturae operam dabant. 2 Sed hii qui resederant, Timotheus et Apollonius, Gennaei filius, sed et Hieronimus et Demofon, super hos et Nicanor, Cypriarches, non

have sent also Menelaus to speak to you. 33 Fare ye well. In the year one hundred and forty-eight, the fifteenth day of the month of Xanthicus."

34 *The* Romans also sent them a letter to this effect:

"Quintus Memmius and Titus Manilius, ambassadors of the Romans, to the people of the Jews, greeting.

35 *Whatsoever* Lysias, the king's cousin, hath granted you, we also have granted. 36 But touching such things as he thought should be referred to the king, after you have diligently conferred among yourselves send some one forthwith that we may decree as it is convenient for you, for we are going to Antioch. 37 And therefore make haste to write back, that we may know of what mind you are. 38 Fare ye well. In the year one hundred and forty-eight, the fifteenth day of the month of Xanthicus."

Chapter 12

The Jews are still molested by their neighbours. Judas gains divers victories over them. He orders sacrifice and prayers for the dead.

When these covenants were made, Lysias went to the king, and the Jews gave themselves to husbandry. 2 But they that were behind, namely Timothy and Apollonius, the son of Gennaeus, also Hieronymus and Demophon and besides them Nicanor, the governor of Cyprus, would not suffer

sinebant eos in silentio agere et quiete. 3 Ioppitae vero tale quoddam flagitium perpetrarunt: rogaverunt Iudaeos cum quibus habitabant ascendere scaphas quas paraverant cum uxoribus et filiis, quasi nullis inimicitiis inter eos subiacentibus. 4 Secundum commune itaque decretum civitatis et ipsis adquiescentibus pacisque causa nihil suspectum habentibus, cum in altum processissent, submerserunt non minus ducentos.

5 Quam crudelitatem Iudas in suae gentis homines factam ut cognovit, praecepit viris qui erant cum ipso, et invocato iusto iudice, Deo, 6 venit adversus interfectores fratrum et portum quidem noctu succendit, scaphas exusit, eos autem qui ab igne refugerant gladio peremit. 7 Et cum haec ita egisset, discessit quasi iterum reversurus et universos Ioppitas eradicaturus. 8 Sed cum cognovisset et eos qui erant Iamniae velle pari modo facere habitantibus secum Iudaeis, 9 Iamnitis quoque nocte supervenit et portum cum navibus succendit ita ut lumen ignis appareret Hierosolymis ab stadiis ducentis quadraginta.

10 Inde cum iam abissent novem stadiis et iter facerent ad Timotheum, commiserunt cum eo Arabes quinque milia viri et equites quingenti. 11 Cumque pugna valida fieret et auxilio Dei prospere cessisset, residui victi Arabes petebant a Iuda dextram sibi dari, promittentes se pascua daturos et in ceteris profuturos. 12 Iudas autem, arbitratus vere in multis eos utiles, promisit pacem, dextrisque acceptis discessere ad tabernacula sua.

them to live in peace and to be quiet. 3 The men of Joppa also were guilty of this kind of wickedness: they desired the Jews who dwelt among them to go with their wives and children into the boats which they had prepared, as though they had no enmity to them. 4 *Which when they* had consented to according to the common decree of the city, *suspecting* nothing because of the peace, when they were gone forth into the deep, they drowned no fewer than two hundred of them.

5 *But* as soon as Judas heard of this cruelty done to his countrymen, he commanded the men that were with him, and after having called upon God, the just judge, 6 he came against those murderers of his brethren and set the haven on fire in the night, burnt the boats and slew with the sword them that escaped from the fire. 7 And when he had done these things in this manner, he departed as if he would return again and root out all the Joppites. 8 But when he understood that the men of Jamnia also designed to do in like manner to the Jews that dwelt among them, 9 he came upon the Jamnites also by night and set the haven on fire with the ships so that the light of the fire was seen at Jerusalem two hundred and forty furlongs off.

10 *And* when they were now gone from thence nine furlongs and were marching towards Timothy, five thousand footmen and five hundred horsemen of the Arabians set upon them.11 And after *a* hard fight, *in which* by the help of God they got the victory, the rest of the Arabians being overcome besought Judas for peace, promising to give him pastures and to assist him in other things. 12 And Judas, thinking that they might be profitable indeed in many things, promised them peace, and after having joined hands they departed to their tents.

13 Adgressus est autem et civitatem quandam firmam pontibus murisque circumseptam, quae a turbis habitabatur gentium promiscuarum, cui nomen Caspin. 14 Hii vero qui intus erant, confidentes in stabilitate murorum et adparatu alimoniarum, remissius agebant maledictis lacessentes Iudam ac blasphemantes et loquentes quae fas non est. 15 Macchabeus autem invocato magno mundi Principe, qui sine arietibus et machinis temporibus Iesu praecipitavit Hiericho, inruit ferociter muris. 16 Et capta civitate per Domini voluntatem, innumerabiles caedes fecit, ita ut adiacens stagnum stadiorum duorum latitudinis sanguine infectum fluere videretur.

17 Inde discesserunt stadia septingenta quinquaginta et venerunt in Characa ad eos qui dicuntur Tubianei Iudaeos. 18 Et Timotheum quidem in illis locis non conprehenderunt, nulloque negotio perfecto regressus est, relicto in quodam loco firmissimo praesidio. 19 Dositheus autem et Sosipater, qui erant duces cum Macchabeo, peremerunt a Timotheo relictos in praesidio decem milia viros. 20 At Macchabeus, ordinatis circum se sex milibus et constitutis per cohortes, adversus Timotheum processit habentem secum centum viginti milia peditum equitumque duo milia quingentos. 21 Cognito autem Iudae adventu, Timotheus praemisit mulieres et filios et reliquum adparatum in praesidium quod Carnion dicitur, erat enim inexpugnabile et accessu difficile propter locorum angustias. 22 Cumque cohors Iudae prima apparuisset, timor hostibus incussus est ex praesentia Dei, qui universa conspicit, et in fugam versi sunt alius ab

13 *He* also laid siege to a certain strong city encompassed with bridges and walls and inhabited by multitudes of different nations, the name of which is Caspin. 14 But they that were within it, trusting in the strength of the walls and the provision of victuals, behaved in a more negligent manner and provoked Judas with railing and blaspheming and uttering such words as were not to be spoken. 15 But Maccabeus, calling upon the great Lord of the world, who without any rams or engines of war threw down the walls of Jericho in the time of Joshua, fiercely assaulted the walls. 16 And having taken the city by the will of the Lord, he made an unspeakable slaughter, so that a pool adjoining of two furlongs broad seemed to run with the blood *of the slain.*

17 From thence they departed seven hundred and fifty furlongs and came to Charax to the Jews that are called Toubianites. 18 *But* as for Timothy, they found him not in those places, *for before he had* dispatched *any* thing he went back, having left a very strong garrison in a certain hold. 19 But Dositheus and Sosipater, who were captains with Maccabeus, slew them that were left by Timothy in the hold to the number of ten thousand men. 20 And Maccabeus, having set in order about him six thousand men and divided them by bands, went forth against Timothy, who had with him a hundred and twenty thousand footmen and two thousand five hundred horsemen. 21 Now when Timothy had knowledge of the coming of Judas, he sent the women and children and the other baggage before him into a fortress called Carnaim, for it was impregnable and hard to come at by reason of the straitness of the places. 22 *But* when the first band of Judas came in sight, the enemies were struck with fear by the presence of God, who seeth all things, and they were put to flight

alio, ita ut magis a suis deicerentur et gladiorum suorum ictibus debilitarentur. 23 Iudas autem vehementer instabat puniens profanos, et prostravit ex eis triginta milia virorum. 24 Ipse vero Timotheus incidit in partes Dosithei et Sosipatris, et multis precibus postulabat ut vivus dimitteretur, eo quod multorum ex Iudaeis parentes haberet ac fratres, quos morte eius decipi eveniret. 25 Et cum fidem dedisset restituturum se eos secundum constitutum, inlaesum eum dimiserunt propter fratrum salutem.

26 Iudas autem egressus est a Carnio, interfectis viginti quinque milibus. 27 Post horum fugam et necem, movit exercitum ad Efron, civitatem munitam, in qua multitudo diversarum gentium habitabat, et robusti iuvenes pro muris consistentes fortiter repugnabant, in hac autem machinae multae et telorum erat adparatus. 28 Sed cum Omnipotentem invocassent, qui potestate sua vires hostium confringit, ceperunt civitatem et ex eis qui intus erant viginti quinque milia prostraverunt.

29 Inde ad civitatem Scytarum abierunt, quae ab Hierosolymis sescentis stadiis aberat. 30 Contestantibus autem his qui apud Scytopolitas erant Iudaeis quod benigne ab eis haberentur, etiam temporibus infelicitatis quod modeste secum egerint, 31 gratias agentes eis, et exhortati etiam de cetero erga genus suum benignos esse, venerunt Hierosolymam, die sollemni septimanarum instante.

one from another, so that they were *often* thrown down by their own companions and wounded with the strokes of their own swords. 23 But Judas was vehemently earnest in punishing the profane, of whom he slew thirty thousand men. 24 And Timothy himself fell into the hands of the band of Dositheus and Sosipater, and with many prayers he besought them to let him go with his life, because he had the parents and brethren of many of the Jews, who by his death might happen to be deceived. 25 And when he had given his faith that he would restore them according to the agreement, they let him go without hurt for the saving of their brethren.

26 Then Judas went away *to* Carnaim, *where* he slew five and twenty thousand persons. 27 *And* after he had put to flight and destroyed these, he removed his army to Ephron, a strong city, wherein there dwelt a multitude of divers nations, and stout young men standing upon the walls made a vigorous resistance, and in this place there were many engines of war and a provision of darts. 28 But when they had invocated the Almighty, who with his power breaketh the strength of the enemies, they took the city and slew five and twenty thousand of them that were within.

29 From thence they departed to Scythopolis, which lieth six hundred furlongs from Jerusalem. 30 But the Jews that were among the Scythopolitans testifying that they were used kindly by them and that even in the times of their adversity they had treated them with humanity, 31 they gave them thanks, *exhorting* them to be still friendly to their nation, *and so* they came to Jerusalem, the *feast* of the weeks being at hand.

32 Et post Pentecosten abierunt contra Gorgiam, praepositum Idumeae. 33 Exivit autem cum peditibus tribus milibus et equitibus quadringentis. 34 Quibus congressis contigit paucos ruere Iudaeorum. 35 Dositheus vero, quidam de Bachenoris eques, vir fortis, Gorgiam tenebat, et cum vellet illum capere vivum, eques quidam de Thracibus inruit in eum umerumque eius amputavit, atque ita Gorgias effugit in Maresa.

36 At illis qui cum Esdrin erant diutius pugnantibus et fatigatis, invocavit Dominum Iudas adiutorem et ducem belli fieri; 37 incipiens voce patria et cum hymnis clamorem extollens, fugam Gorgiae militibus incussit. 38 Iudas autem collecto exercitu venit in civitatem Odollam, et cum septima dies superveniret, secundum consuetudinem purificati in eodem loco sabbatum egerunt.

39 Et sequenti die venit cum suis Iudas ut corpora prostratorum tolleret et cum parentibus poneret in sepulchris paternis. 40 Invenerunt autem sub tunicis interfectorum de donariis idolorum quae apud Iamnian fuerunt, a quibus lex prohibet Iudaeos, omnibus ergo manifestum factum est ob hanc causam eos corruisse. 41 Omnes itaque benedixerunt iustum iudicium Domini, qui occulta fecerat manifesta. 42 Atque ita ad preces conversi rogaverunt ut id quod factum erat delictum oblivioni traderetur. At vero fortissimus Iudas hortabatur populum conservare se sine peccatis, sub oculis videntes quae facta sint pro peccatis eorum qui prostrati sunt. 43 Et facta conlatione, duodecim milia dragmas argenti

32 And after Pentecost they marched against Gorgias, the governor of Idumea. 33 And he came out with three thousand footmen and four hundred horsemen. 34 And when they had joined battle it happened that a few of the Jews were slain. 35 But Dositheus, a horseman, one of Bacenor's band, a valiant man, took hold of Gorgias, and when he would have taken him alive, a certain horseman of the Thracians came upon him and cut off his shoulder, and so Gorgias escaped to Marisa.

36 But when they that were with Esdris had fought long and were weary, Judas called upon the Lord to be their helper and leader of the battle; 37 *then,* beginning in his own language and singing hymns with a loud voice, he put Gorgias's soldiers to flight. 38 So Judas having gathered together his army came into the city Adullam, and when the seventh day came, they purified themselves according to the custom and kept the sabbath in the same place.

39 And the day following Judas came with his company to take away the bodies of them that were slain and to bury them with their kinsmen in the sepulchres of their fathers. 40 And they found under the coats of the slain some of the donaries of the idols *of* Jamnia, which the law forbiddeth to the Jews, so that all plainly saw that for this cause they were slain. 41 Then they all blessed the just judgment of the Lord, who had discovered the things that were hidden. 42 And so betaking themselves to prayers they besought him that the sin which had been committed might be forgotten. But the most valiant Judas exhorted the people to keep themselves from sin, forasmuch as they saw before their eyes what had happened because of the sins of those that were slain. 43 And making a gathering, he sent twelve thousand drachms of

misit Hierosolymam offerri pro peccato sacrificium, bene et religiose de resurrectione cogitans 44 (nisi enim eos qui ceciderant resurrecturos speraret, superfluum videretur et vanum orare pro mortuis), 45 et quia considerabat quod hii qui cum pietate dormitionem acceperant optimam haberent repositam gratiam. 46 Sancta ergo et salubris est cogitatio pro defunctis exorare, ut a peccatis solvantur.

Caput 13

Anno centesimo quadragesimo nono, cognovit Iudas Antiochum Eupatorem venire cum multitudine adversus Iudaeam 2 et cum eo Lysiam, procuratorem et praepositum negotiorum, secum habentem peditum centum decem milia et equitum quinque milia et elefantos viginti duos currus cum falcibus trecentos. 3 Commiscuit autem se illis et Menelaus et cum multa fallacia deprecabatur Antiochum non pro patriae salute sed sperans se constitui in principatum. 4 Sed Rex regum suscitavit animos Antiochi in peccatorem, et suggerente Lysia hunc esse causam omnium malorum,

silver to Jerusalem for sacrifice to be offered for the *sins of the dead,* thinking well and religiously concerning the resurrection 44 (for if he had not hoped that they that were slain should rise again, it would have seemed superfluous and vain to pray for the dead), 45 and because he considered that they who had fallen asleep with godliness had great grace laid up for them. 46 It is therefore a holy and wholesome thought to pray for the dead, that they may be loosed from sins.

Chapter 13

Antiochus and Lysias again invade Judea. Menelaus is put to death. The king's great army is worsted twice. The peace is renewed.

In the year one hundred and forty-nine, Judas understood that Antiochus Eupator was coming with a multitude against Judea 2 and with him Lysias, the regent, *who* had charge over the affairs *of the realm,* having with him a hundred and ten thousand footmen, *five* thousand horsemen, *twenty-two* elephants *and* three hundred chariots armed with hooks. 3 *Menelaus* also joined himself with them and with great deceitfulness besought Antiochus not for the welfare of his country but in hopes that he should be appointed chief ruler. 4 But the King of kings stirred up the mind of Antiochus against the sinner, and upon Lysias suggesting that he was the cause

iussit (ut eis est consuetudo) apprehensum in eodem loco necari.

5 Erat autem in eodem loco turris quinquaginta cubitorum, aggestum undique habens cineris; haec prospectum habebat in praeceps. 6 Inde in cinerem deici iussit sacrilegum, omnibus eum propellentibus ad interitum 7 Et tali lege praevaricatorem legis contigit mori nec terrae dari Menelaum. 8 Et quidem satis iuste, nam quia multa erga aram Dei delicta commisit, cuius ignis et cinis erat sanctus, ipse in cineris morte damnatus est.

9 Sed rex, mente effrenatus, veniebat nequiorem se patre suo Iudaeis ostensurus. 10 Quibus Iudas cognitis, praecepit populo ut die ac nocte Dominum invocarent, quo sicut semper et nunc adiuvaret eos, 11 quippe qui lege et patria sanctoque templo privari vererentur, ac populum qui nuper paululum respirasset ne sineret blasphemis rursum nationibus subdi. 12 Omnibus itaque id simul facientibus et petentibus a Domino misericordiam cum fletu et ieiuniis, per triduum continuum prostratis, hortatus est eos Iudas ut se praepararent.

13 Ipse vero cum senioribus cogitavit, priusquam rex admoveret exercitum ad Iudaeam et obtineret civitatem, exire et Domini iudicio committere exitum rei. 14 Dans itaque potestatem omnium Deo, mundi creatori, et hortatus suos ut fortiter dimicarent et usque ad mortem pro legibus,

of all the evils, he commanded (as the custom is with them) that he should be apprehended and put to death in the same place.

5 Now there was in that place a tower fifty cubits high having a heap of ashes on every side; this had a prospect steep down. 6 From thence he commanded the sacrilegious wretch to be thrown down into the ashes, all men thrusting him forward unto death. 7 And by such a law it happened that Menelaus, the transgressor of the law, was put to death not having so much as burial in the earth. 8 And indeed very justly, for insomuch as he had committed many sins against the altar of God, the fire and ashes of which were holy, he was condemned to die in ashes.

9 But the king, with his mind full of rage, came on to shew himself worse to the Jews than his father was. 10 Which when Judas understood, he commanded the people to call upon the Lord day and night, that as he had always done, so now also he would help them, 11 because they were afraid to be deprived of the law and of their country and of the holy temple, and that he would not suffer the people that had of late taken breath for a little while to be again in subjection to blasphemous nations. 12 So when they had all done this together and had craved mercy of the Lord with weeping and fasting, lying prostrate on the ground for three days continually, Judas exhorted them to make themselves ready.

13 But he with the ancients determined, before the king should bring his army into Judea and make himself master of the city, to go out and to commit the event of the thing to the judgment of the Lord. 14 So committing *all* to God, the creator of the world, and having exhorted his people to fight manfully and to stand up even to death for the laws, the

templo, civitate, patria et civibus starent, circa Modin exercitum constituit. 15 Et dato signo suis "Dei victoriae," iuvenibus fortissimis electis nocte adgressus aulam regiam in castris interfecit viros quattuor milia et maximum elefantorum cum his qui superpositi erant, 16 summoque metu ac perturbatione hostium castra replentes, rebus prospere gestis abierunt. 17 Hoc autem factum est die inlucescente, adiuvante eum Domini protectione.

18 Sed rex, accepto gustu audaciae Iudaeorum, arte difficultatem locorum temptabat. 19 Et Bethsurae, quod erat Iudaeorum praesidium munitum, castra admovebat, sed fugabatur; inpingebat; minuebatur. 20 His autem qui intus erant Iudas necessaria mittebat. 21 Enuntiavit autem mysteria hostibus Rhodocus, quidam de Iudaico exercitu, qui requisitus, conprehensus, est et conclusus. 22 Iterum rex sermonem habuit ad eos qui erant in Bethsuris, dextram dedit, accepit, abiit. 23 Commisit cum Iuda; superatus est. Ut autem cognovit rebellasse Philippum Antiochiae, qui relictus erat super negotia, mente consternatus, Iudaeos deprecans subditusque eis, iurat de omnibus quibus iustum visum est et reconciliatus obtulit sacrificium, honorificavit templum et munera posuit. 24 Macchabeum amplexus est et fecit eum ab Ptolomaide usque ad Gerrenos ducem et principem. 25 Ut autem venit Ptolomaidam, graviter ferebant Ptolomenses,

temple, the city, their country and citizens, he placed his army about Modein. 15 And having given his company for a watchword "the victory of God," with most valiant chosen young men he set upon the king's quarter by night and slew four thousand men in the camp and the greatest of the elephants with them that had been upon him, 16 and having filled the camp of the enemies with exceeding great fear and tumult, they went off with good success. 17 Now this was done at the break of day by the protection and help of the Lord.

18 But the king, having taken a taste of the hardiness of the Jews, attempted *to take the strong places* by policy. 19 And he marched with his army to Beth-zur, which was a stronghold of the Jews, but he was repulsed; he failed; he lost his men. 20 Now Judas sent necessaries to them that were within. 21 But Rhodocus, one of the Jews' army, disclosed the secrets to the enemies, so he was sought out, and taken up, and put in prison. 22 Again the king treated with them that were in Beth-zur, gave his right hand, took theirs *and* went away. 23 He fought with Judas *and* was overcome. And when he understood that Philip, who had been left over the affairs, had rebelled at Antioch, he was in a consternation of mind, and entreating the Jews and yielding to them, he swore to all things that seemed reasonable and being reconciled, offered sacrifices, honoured the temple and left gifts. 24 He embraced Maccabeus and made him governor and prince from Ptolemais unto the Gerrenians. 25 But when he was come to Ptolemais, the *men of that city* were much

amicitiae conventionem, indignantes ne forte foedus inrumperent. 26 Tunc ascendit Lysias tribunal et exposuit rationem et populum sedavit regressusque est Antiochiam. Et hoc modo regis profectio et reditus processit.

Caput 14

Sed post triennii tempus, cognovit Iudas et qui cum eo erant Demetrium, Seleuci, cum multitudine valida et navibus per portum Tripolis ascendisse ad loca oportuna 2 et tenuisse regiones adversus Antiochum et eius ducem, Lysiam.

3 Alchimus autem quidam, qui summus sacerdos fuerat sed voluntarie coinquinatus est temporibus commixtionis, considerans nullo modo sibi esse salutem neque accessum ad altare, 4 venit ad Regem Demetrium centesimo quinquagesimo anno, offerens ei auream coronam et palmam, super haec et tallos qui templi esse videbantur. Et ipsa quidem die siluit. 5 Tempus autem oportunum dementiae suae nanctus,

displeased with the conditions of the peace, being angry for *fear* they should break the covenant. 26 Then Lysias went up to the judgment seat and set forth the reason and appeased the people and returned to Antioch. And thus matters went with regard to the king's coming and his return.

Chapter 14

Demetrius challenges the kingdom. Alcimus applies to him to be made high priest. Nicanor is sent into Judea. His dealings with Judas. His threats. The history of Razis.

But after the space of three years, Judas and they that were with him understood that Demetrius, the son of Seleucus, was come up with a great power and a navy by the haven of Tripolis to places proper for his purpose 2 and had made himself master of the countries against Antiochus and his general, Lysias.

3 Now one Alcimus, who had been chief priest but had wilfully defiled himself in the time of mingling with the heathens, seeing that there was no safety for him nor access to the altar, 4 came to King Demetrius in the year one hundred and fifty, presenting unto him a crown of gold and a palm and besides these some boughs which seemed to belong to the temple. And that day indeed he held his peace. 5 But having gotten a convenient time to further his madness, be-

convocatus a Demetrio ad consilium et interrogatus quibus rebus et consiliis Iudaei niterentur, 6 respondit ipsi:

"Qui dicuntur Asidei Iudaeorum, quibus praeest Iudas Macchabeus, bella nutriunt et seditiones movent nec patiuntur regnum esse quietum. 7 Nam et ego defraudatus parentum (gloria dico autem summo sacerdotio) huc veni, 8 primo quidem utilitatibus regis fidem servans, secundo autem etiam civibus consulens, nam illorum pravitate universum genus nostrum non minime vexatur. 9 Sed his singulis, oro, rex, cognitis, et regioni et generi secundum pervulgatam omnibus humanitatem tuam prospice, 10 nam quamdiu superest Iudas inpossibile est pacem esse negotiis."

11 Talibus autem ab hoc dictis, et ceteri amici, hostiliter se habentes adversus Iudam, inflammaverunt Demetrium. 12 Qui statim Nicanorem, praepositum elefantorum, ducem misit in Iudaeam, 13 datis mandatis ut ipsum quidem Iudam caperet, eos vero qui cum illo erant dispergeret et constitueret Alchimum maximi templi summum sacerdotem. 14 Tunc Gentes quae de Iudaea fugerant Iudam gregatim se Nicanori miscebant, miserias et clades Iudaeorum prosperitates rerum suarum existimantes.

15 Audito itaque Iudaei Nicanoris adventu et conventu nationum conspersi terra, rogabant eum qui populum suum constituit ut in aeternum custodiret quique suam portionem

ing called to counsel by Demetrius and asked what the Jews relied upon and what were their counsels, 6 he answered thereunto:

"They among the Jews that are called Hasideans, of whom Judas Maccabeus is captain, nourish wars and raise seditions and will not suffer the realm to be in peace. 7 For I also being deprived of my ancestors' glory (I mean of the high priesthood) am now come hither, 8 principally indeed out of fidelity to the king's interests, but in the next place also to provide for the good of my countrymen, for all our nation suffereth much from the evil proceedings of those men. 9 Wherefore, O king, seeing thou knowest all these things, take care, I beseech thee, both of the country and of our nation according to thy humanity, which is known to all men, 10 for as long as Judas liveth it is not possible that the state should be quiet."

11 Now when this man had spoken to this effect, the rest also of the king's friends, who were enemies of Judas, incensed Demetrius against him. 12 And forthwith he sent Nicanor, the commander over the elephants, governor into Judea, 13 giving him in charge to take Judas himself and disperse all them that were with him and to make Alcimus the high priest of the great temple. 14 Then the Gentiles who had fled out of Judea from Judas came to Nicanor by flocks, thinking the miseries and calamities of the Jews to be the welfare of their affairs.

15 Now when the Jews heard of Nicanor's coming and that the nations were assembled against them, they cast earth upon their heads and made supplication to him who chose his people to keep them for ever and who protected

signis evidentibus protegit. 16 Imperante autem duce, statim inde moverunt et convenerunt ad castellum Dessau.

17 Simon vero, frater Iudae, commiserat cum Nicanore, sed conterritus est repentino adventu adversariorum. 18 Nicanor tamen, audiens virtutem comitum Iudae et animi magnitudinem quam pro patriae certaminibus habebant, sanguine iudicium facere metuebat. 19 Quam ob rem praemisit Possidonium et Theodotium et Matthiam ut darent dextras atque acciperent. 20 Et cum diu de his consilium ageretur et ipse dux ad multitudinem rettulisset, omnium una fuit sententia amicitiis annuere. 21 Itaque diem constituerunt qua secreto inter se agerent, et singulis sellae prolatae sunt et positae. 22 Praecepit autem Iudas armatos esse locis oportunis, ne forte ab hostibus repente mali aliquid oriretur; et congruum conloquium fecerunt.

23 Morabatur autem Nicanor Hierosolymis et nihil inique agebat gregesque turbarum quae congregatae fuerant dimisit. 24 Habebat autem semper Iudam carum ex animo, et erat viro inclinatus. 25 Rogavitque eum ducere uxorem filiosque procreare. Nuptias fecit; quiete egit, communiterque vivebant.

26 Alchimus autem, videns caritatem illorum ad invicem et conventiones, venit ad Demetrium et dicebat Nicanorem rebus alienis adsentire, Iudamque, regni insidiatorem, successorem sibi destinasse. 27 Itaque rex, exasperatus et pessimis huius criminationibus inritatus, scripsit Nicanori, di-

his portion by evident signs. 16 Then at the commandment of their captain they forthwith removed from the place where they were and went to the town of Dessau to meet them.

17 Now Simon, the brother of Judas, had joined battle with Nicanor, but was frightened with the sudden coming of the adversaries. 18 Nevertheless Nicanor, hearing of the valour of Judas' companions and the greatness of courage with which they fought for their country, was afraid to try the matter by *the sword*. 19 Wherefore he sent Posidonius and Theodotius and Matthias before to present and receive the right hands. 20 And when there had been a consultation thereupon and the captain had acquainted the multitude with it, they were all of one mind to consent to covenants. 21 So they appointed a day upon which they might commune together by themselves, and seats were brought out and set for each one. 22 But Judas ordered men to be ready in convenient places, lest some mischief might be suddenly practiced by the enemies; so they made an agreeable conference.

23 And Nicanor abode in Jerusalem and did no wrong *but* sent away the flocks of the multitudes that had been gathered together. 24 And Judas was always dear to him from the heart, and he was well affected to the man. 25 And he desired him to marry a wife and to have children. So he married; he lived quietly, and they lived in common.

26 But Alcimus, seeing the love they had one to another and the covenants, came to Demetrius and told him that Nicanor assented to the foreign interest, for that he meant to make Judas, who was a traitor to the kingdom, his successor. 27 Then the king, being in a rage and provoked with this man's wicked accusations, wrote to Nicanor, signifying that

cens graviter quidem se ferre de amicitiae conventione, iubere tamen Macchabeum citius vinctum mittere Antiochiam.

28 Quibus cognitis, Nicanor consternabatur et graviter ferebat si ea quae convenerant irrita faceret, nihil laesus a viro. 29 Sed quia regi resistere non poterat, oportunitatem observabat qua praeceptum perficeret. 30 At Macchabeus videns austerius secum agere Nicanorem et consuetum occursum ferocius exhibentem, intellegens non ex bono esse austeritatem istam, paucis suorum congregatis occultavit se a Nicanore. 31 Quod cum ille cognovit fortiter se a viro praeventum, venit ad maximum et sanctissimum templum et sacerdotibus solitas hostias offerentibus iussit sibi tradi virum. 32 Quibus cum iuramento dicentibus nescire se ubi esset qui quaerebatur, extendens manum ad templum 33 iuravit, dicens, "Nisi mihi vinctum Iudam tradideritis, istud Dei fanum in planitiem deducam et altare effodiam, et templum hoc Libero Patri consecrabo." 34 Et his dictis abiit.

Sacerdotes autem, protendentes manus in caelum, invocabant eum qui semper propugnator esset gentis ipsorum, haec dicentes: 35 "Tu, Domine universorum, qui nullius indiges, voluisti templum habitationis tuae fieri in nobis. 36 Et nunc, sancte sanctorum omnium, Domine, conserva in aeternum inpollutam domum istam, quae nuper mundata est."

he was greatly displeased with the covenant of friendship and that he commanded him nevertheless to send Maccabeus prisoner in all haste to Antioch.

28 When this was known, Nicanor was in a consternation and took it grievously that he should make void the articles that were agreed upon, having received no injury from the man. 29 But because he could not oppose the king, he watched an opportunity to comply with the orders. 30 But when Maccabeus perceived that Nicanor was more stern to him and that when they met together as usual he behaved himself in a *rough* manner and was sensible that this rough behaviour came not of good, he gathered together a few of his men and hid himself from Nicanor. 31 But he, finding himself notably prevented by the man, came to the *great* and *holy* temple and commanded the priests that were offering the accustomed sacrifices to deliver him the man. 32 And when they swore unto him that they knew not where the man was whom he sought, he stretched out his hand to the temple 33 and swore, saying, "Unless you deliver Judas prisoner to me, I will lay this temple of God even with the ground and will beat down the altar, and I will dedicate this temple to Bacchus." 34 And when he had spoken thus he departed.

But the priests, stretching forth their hands to heaven, called upon him that was ever the defender of their nation, saying in this manner: 35 "Thou, O Lord of all things, who wantest nothing, wast pleased that the temple of thy habitation should be amongst us. 36 *Therefore* now, O Lord, the holy of all holies, keep this house for ever undefiled, which was lately cleansed."

37 Razias autem, quidam de senioribus ab Hierosolymis, delatus est Nicanori, vir amator civitatis et bene audiens, qui pro adfectu pater Iudaeorum appellabatur. 38 Hic multis temporibus continentiae propositum tenuit in Iudaismo corpusque et animam tradere contentus pro perseverantia. 39 Volens autem Nicanor manifestare odium quod habebat in Iudaeos, misit milites quingentos ut eum conprehenderent. 40 Putabat enim, si illum decepisset, se cladem maximam Iudaeis inlaturum.

41 Turbis autem inruere in domum eius et ianuam disrumpere atque ignem admovere cupientibus, cum iam conprehenderetur gladio se petiit, 42 eligens nobiliter mori potius quam subditus fieri peccatoribus et contra natales suos indignis iniuriis agi. 43 Sed cum per festinationem non certo ictu plagam dedisset et turbae intra ostia inrumperent, recurrens audenter ad murum praecipitavit semet ipsum viriliter in turbas, 44 quibus velociter locum dantibus casui eius, venit per mediam cervicem. 45 Et cum adhuc spiraret, accensus animo surrexit, et cum sanguis eius magno fluxu deflueret et gravissimis vulneribus esset saucius, cursu turbam pertransiit, 46 et stans super petram quandam praeruptam et iam exsanguis effectus, conplexus intestina sua utrisque manibus, proiecit super turbas, invocans Dominatorem vitae ac spiritus ut haec illi iterum redderet. Atque ita vita defunctus est.

37 Now Razis, one of the ancients of Jerusalem, was accused to Nicanor, a man that was a lover of the city and of good report, who for his affection was called the father of the Jews. 38 This man for a long time had held fast his purpose of keeping himself pure in the Jews' religion and was ready to expose his body and life that he might persevere therein. 39 So Nicanor, being willing to declare the hatred that he bore the Jews, sent five hundred soldiers to take him. 40 For he thought *by ensnaring* him *to* hurt the Jews very much.

41 Now as the multitude sought to rush into his house and to break open the door and to set fire to it, when he was ready to be taken he struck himself with his sword, 42 choosing to die nobly rather than to fall into the hands of the wicked and to suffer abuses unbecoming his noble birth. 43 But whereas through haste he missed of giving himself a sure wound and the crowd was breaking into the doors, he ran boldly to the wall and manfully threw himself down to the crowd, 44 *but* they quickly making room for his fall, he came upon the midst of the neck. 45 And as he had yet breath in him, being inflamed in mind he arose, and while his blood ran down with a great stream and he was grievously wounded, he ran through the crowd, 46 and standing upon a steep rock, when he was now almost without blood, grasping his bowels with both hands, he cast them upon the throng, calling upon the Lord of life and spirit to restore these to him again. And so he departed this life.

Caput 15

Nicanor autem ut conperit Iudam esse in locis Samariae cogitavit die sabbati cum omni impetu committere bellum. 2 Iudaeis vero qui illum per necessitatem sequebantur dicentibus, "Ne ita ferociter et barbare feceris, sed honorem tribue diei sanctificationis, et honora eum qui universa conspicit," 3 ille infelix interrogavit si est potens in caelo qui imperavit agi diem sabbatorum.

4 Et respondentibus illis, "Est Dominus vivus ipse in caelo, Potens qui iussit agi septimam diem," 5 at ille ait, "Et ego potens sum super terram, qui impero sumi arma et negotia regis impleri." Tamen non obtinuit ut consilium perficeret.

6 Et Nicanor quidem, cum summa superbia erectus, cogitaverat commune tropeum statuere de Iuda. 7 Macchabeus autem confidebat semper cum omni spe auxilium sibi a Deo adfuturum. 8 Et hortabatur suos ne formidarent ad adventum nationum sed in mente haberent adiutoria sibi facta de caelo et nunc sperarent ab Omnipotente adfuturam sibi victoriam. 9 Et adlocutus illos de lege et prophetis, admonens

Chapter 15

Judas, encouraged by a vision, gains a glorious victory over Nicanor. The conclusion.

But when Nicanor understood that Judas was in the places of Samaria he purposed to *set upon him* with all violence on the sabbath day. 2 And when the Jews that were constrained to follow him said, "Do not act so fiercely and barbarously, but give honour to the day that is sanctified, and reverence him that beholdeth all things," 3 that unhappy man asked if there were a mighty one in heaven that had commanded the sabbath day to be kept.

4 And when they answered, "There is the living Lord himself in heaven, the Mighty One that commanded the seventh day to be kept," 5 then he said, "And I am mighty upon the earth, and I command to take arms and to do the king's business." Nevertheless he prevailed not to accomplish his design.

6 So Nicanor, being puffed up with exceeding great pride, thought to set up a public monument of his victory over Judas. 7 But Maccabeus ever trusted with all hope that God would help them. 8 And he exhorted his people not to fear the coming of the nations but to remember the help they had before received from heaven and now to hope for victory from the Almighty. 9 And speaking to them out of the law and the prophets, and *withal* putting them in mind

etiam certaminum quae fecerant prius, promptiores eos constituit. 10 Et ita animis eorum erectis, simul ostendebat Gentium fallaciam et iuramentorum praevaricationem. 11 Singulos autem illorum armavit non clypei et hastae munitione sed sermonibus optimis et exhortationibus, exposito digno fide somnio, per quod universos laetificavit.

12 Erat autem huiusmodi visus: Onian, qui fuerat summus sacerdos, virum bonum et benignum, verecundum visu, modestum moribus et eloquio decorum, et qui a puero in virtutibus exercitatus sit, manus protendentem, orare pro omni populo Iudaeorum; 13 post hoc apparuisse et alium virum aetate et gloria mirabilem et magni decoris habitudine circa illum. 14 Respondentem vero Onian dixisse, "Hic est fratrum amator et populi Israhel; hic est qui multum orat pro populo et universa sancta civitate, Hieremias, propheta Dei." 15 Extendisse autem Hieremiam dexteram et dedisse Iudae gladium aureum, dicentem, 16 "Accipe sanctum gladium, munus a Deo, quo deicies adversarios populi mei Israhel."

17 Exhortati itaque Iudae sermonibus bonis valde de quibus extolli posset impetus et animi iuvenum confortari, statuerunt dimicare et confligere fortiter, ut virtus de negotiis iudicaret, eo quod civitas sancta et templum periclitarentur. 18 Erat enim pro uxoribus et filiis itemque pro fratribus et cognatis minor sollicitudo, maximus vero et primus pro sanctitate timor erat templi. 19 Sed et eos qui in civitate erant non minima sollicitudo habebat pro his qui congressuri erant.

550

of the battles they had fought before, he made them more *cheerful.* 10 *Then* after he had encouraged them, he shewed withal the falsehood of the Gentiles and their breach of oaths. 11 So he armed every one of them not with defence of shield and spear but with very good speeches and exhortations and told them a dream worthy to be believed, whereby he rejoiced them all.

12 Now the vision was in this manner: Onias, who had been high priest, a good and virtuous man, modest in his looks, gentle in his manners and graceful in his speech, and who from a child was exercised in virtues, holding up his hands, prayed for all the people of the Jews; 13 after this there appeared also another man admirable for age and glory and environed with great beauty and majesty. 14 Then Onias, answering, said, "This is a lover of his brethren and of the people of Israel; this is he that prayeth much for the people and for all the holy city, Jeremiah, the prophet of God." 15 *Whereupon* Jeremiah stretched forth his right hand and gave to Judas a sword of gold, saying, 16 "Take this holy sword, a gift from God, wherewith thou shalt overthrow the adversaries of my people Israel."

17 Thus being exhorted with the words of Judas, which were very good and proper to stir up the courage and strengthen the hearts of the young men, they resolved to fight and to set upon them manfully, that valour might decide the matter, because the holy city and the temple were in danger. 18 For their concern was less for their wives and children and for their brethren and kinsfolks, but their greatest and principal fear was for the holiness of the temple. 19 And they also that were in the city had no little concern for them that were to be engaged in battle.

20 Et cum iam omnes sperarent iudicium futurum hostesque adessent atque exercitus esset ordinatus, bestiae equitesque oportuno in loco conpositi, 21 considerans Macchabeus adventum multitudinis et adparatum varium armorum ac ferocitatem bestiarum, extendens manus in caelum, prodigia facientem Dominum invocavit, qui non secundum armorum potentiam sed prout ipsi placet dat dignis victoriam. 22 Dixit autem invocans hoc modo: "Tu, Domine, qui misisti angelum tuum sub Ezechia, rege Iudae, et interfecisti de castris Sennacherib centum octoginta quinque milia, 23 et nunc, Dominator caelorum, mitte angelum tuum bonum ante nos in timore et tremore magnitudinis brachii tui, 24 ut metuant qui cum blasphemia veniunt adversus sanctum populum tuum." Et hic quidem ita peroravit.

25 Nicanor autem et qui cum ipso erant cum tubis et canticis admovebant. 26 Iudas vero et qui cum eo erant, invocato Deo per orationes, congressi sunt; 27 manu quidem pugnantes sed cordibus Dominum orantes, prostraverunt non minus triginta quinque milia, praesentia Dei magnifice delectati.

28 Cumque cessassent et cum gaudio redirent, cognoverunt Nicanorem ruisse cum armis suis. 29 Facto itaque clamore et perturbatione suscitata, patria voce omnipotentem Dominum benedicebant. 30 Praecepit autem Iudas, qui per omnia corpore et animo emori pro civibus paratus erat, ca-

20 And now when all expected what judgment would be given and the enemies were at hand and the army was set in array, the beasts and the horsemen ranged in convenient places, 21 Maccabeus, considering the coming of the multitude and the divers preparations of armour and the fierceness of the beasts, stretching out his hands to heaven, called upon the Lord, that worketh wonders, who giveth victory to them that are worthy not according to the power of their arms but according as it seemeth good to him. 22 And in his prayer he said after this manner: "Thou, O Lord, who didst send thy angel in the time of Hezekiah, king of Judah, and didst kill a hundred and eighty-five thousand of the army of Sennacherib, 23 send now also, O Lord of heaven, thy good angel before us for the fear and dread of the greatness of thy arm, 24 that they may be afraid who come with blasphemy against thy holy people." And thus he concluded his prayer.

25 But Nicanor and they that were with him came forward with trumpets and songs. 26 But Judas and they that were with him encountered them, calling upon God by prayers; 27 so fighting with their hands but praying to the Lord with their hearts, they slew no less than five and thirty thousand, being greatly cheered with the presence of God.

28 And when the battle was over and they were returning with joy, they understood that Nicanor was slain in his armour. 29 Then making a shout and a great noise, they blessed the almighty Lord in their own language. 30 And Judas, who was altogether ready in body and mind to die for his countrymen, commanded that Nicanor's head and his hand with the shoulder should be cut off and carried to Jerusalem.

put Nicanoris et manum cum umero abscisam Hierosolymam perferri.

31 Quo cum pervenisset, convocatis contribulibus et sacerdotibus ad altare, arcersiit et eos qui in arce erant, 32 et
ostenso capite Nicanoris et manu nefaria, quam extendens
contra domum sanctam omnipotentis Dei magnifice gloria-
tus est, 33 linguam etiam impii Nicanoris praecisam iussit
particulatim avibus dari, manum autem dementis contra
templum suspendi. 34 Omnes igitur caeli Dominum benedixerunt, dicentes, "Benedictus qui locum suum incontami-
natum conservavit." 35 Suspendit autem Nicanoris caput in
summa arce, ut evidens esset et manifestum signum auxilii
Dei.

36 Itaque omnes communi consilio decreverunt nullo
modo diem istum absque celebritate praeterire, 37 habere
autem celebritatem tertiadecima die mensis Adar, quod dicitur voce Syriaca pridie Mardochei diei.

38 Igitur his erga Nicanorem gestis et ex illis temporibus
ab Hebraeis civitate possessa, ego quoque in his finem faciam sermonis. 39 Et siquidem bene et ut historiae conpetit,
hoc et ipse velim, sin autem minus digne, concedendum est
mihi. 40 Sicut enim vinum semper bibere aut semper aquam
contrarium est, alternis autem uti delectabile, ita legentibus
si semper exactus sit, sermo non erit gratus. Hic ergo erit
consummatus.

31 And when he was come thither, having called together his countrymen and the priests to the altar, he sent also for them that were in the castle, 32 and shewing them the head of Nicanor and the wicked hand, which he had stretched out with proud boasts against the holy house of the almighty God, 33 he commanded also that the tongue of the wicked Nicanor should be cut out and given by pieces to birds, and the hand of the furious man to be hanged up over against the temple. 34 Then all blessed the Lord of heaven, saying, "Blessed be he that hath kept his own place undefiled." 35 And he hung up Nicanor's head in the top of the castle, that it might be an evident and manifest sign of the help of God.

36 And they all ordained by a common decree by no means to let this day pass without solemnity, 37 but to celebrate the thirteenth day of the month of Adar, called in the Syrian language the day before Mordecai's day.

38 So these things being done with relation to Nicanor and from that time the city being possessed by the Hebrews, I also will here make an end of my narration. 39 *Which* if I have done well and as it becometh the history, it is what I *desired,* but if not so perfectly, it must be pardoned me. 40 For as it is hurtful to drink always wine or always water, but pleasant to use sometimes the one and sometimes the other, so if the speech be always nicely framed, it will not be grateful to the readers. *But* here it shall be ended.

Note on the Text

This edition is meant to present a Latin text close to what the Douay-Rheims translators saw. Therefore the readings in this edition are not necessarily preferred in the sense that they are thought to be "original"; instead, they represent the Latin Bible as it was read by many from the eighth through the sixteenth century. Furthermore, in the service of economy, sources for the text are cited according to a hierarchy and consequently the lists of sources following the lemmas and alternate readings are not necessarily comprehensive. If a reading appears in Weber's text or apparatus, no other sources are cited; if it is not in Weber but is in Quentin, only the sources cited by Quentin are reproduced. The complete list of sources for the Latin text, in their hierarchical order, is Weber, the Sixto-Clementine edition, Weber's apparatus, Quentin, his apparatus, the Vetus Latina edition of Pierre Sabatier (1682–1742), the *Glossa Ordinaria* attributed (wrongly) to Walafrid Strabo in the Patrologia Latina, and the database of the Beuroner Vetus Latina-Institut.

When no source can be found for what seems to be the correct Latin, a reconstruction is proposed in the Notes to the Text but the Weber text is generally printed in the edition. Trivial differences between the Weber and Sixto-Clementine editions in word order and orthography,

alternative spellings and inflections of proper names, and syncopation of verbs have not been noted, nor have many differences that do not affect translation, such as the omission or inclusion of forms of *esse,* variant forms of personal pronouns, conjunctions treated by the Douay-Rheims translators as synonymous, and the omission or inclusion of certain pronouns or possessive adjectives.

Whenever it has been necessary to stray from Weber's text (about one thousand times in the first volume), the departures are recorded in the Notes to the Text. These notes by no means constitute a true *apparatus criticus,* but they enable interested readers to see both the deviations from Weber (whose text is preferable for people wanting to get as close as possible to the earliest versions of the many Latin texts which, combined, form the Vulgate Bible) and significant differences among the Weber, Sixto-Clementine, and Douay-Rheims texts.

When the translation reflects a reading closer to Weber's than to the Sixto-Clementine edition, the Sixto-Clementine variation is printed in the Notes to the Text. Less frequently, there are two readings that would translate the same way but that differ sufficiently to warrant noting, as at Gen 19:6, where Weber reads "umbraculum tegminis" while the Sixto-Clementine version has "umbra culminis."

Often the punctuation of the Douay-Rheims edition reflects an understanding of the Latin different from that of the Weber, Sixto-Clementine, or both editions. The Weber edition has no punctuation marks in most books; rather, the editors inserted line breaks to mark new clauses or sentences, a punctuation style known as *per cola et commata,*

which is meant to assist readers without inserting anachronistic markings. These line breaks have been represented in the notes by slashes (/). In general, differences in punctuation among this edition, the Sixto-Clementine Bible, and Weber's edition have been cited only when they demonstrate considerably different understandings of the Latin. Often Weber's presentation is too equivocal to shed light on his understanding; in these cases, his edition is not cited.

While the Douay-Rheims translation belongs to a tradition of exceptionally literal renderings of the Latin Bible, Challoner's revision contains some divergences from the Latin. Any English that does not square with the text *en face* is italicized, and where possible, Challoner's source has been indicated in the Notes to the Text. When Challoner's source is given, it is not necessarily quoted word for word in the lemma; indeed, the Septuagint is cited as a source, yet almost no Greek is quoted in the notes. Whenever there can be doubt of a source based on a slight difference between its reading and Challoner's, the difference has been recorded following the lemma, either in parentheses or in brackets when containing explanatory material that is not a quotation from the source. Sources for the English text are cited in a hierarchical fashion similar to that of the Latin, in the following order: Douay-Rheims, Sixto-Clementine, King James, Septuagint, Hebrew text; this means that if an English reading is found in the King James Version that may also be in the Septuagint, only the King James Version is cited. Also, if Challoner's translation seems to approximate a source that is cited, the distance between source and translation is indicated by a question mark following the siglum.

Words cited from biblical sources are in italics in the notes, and the sigla and any comments are in roman type. Lemmas precede colons; other readings follow them. Occasionally Challoner indicated that he was adding words to his revision that did not appear in the Latin text; he did this by italicizing the relevant words, much as the authors of the King James Version printed occasional words in roman as opposed to black-letter type to indicate an addition. Bracketed explanations or underlinings draw attention to these typographical variations in the Notes to the Text where necessary.

Notes to the Text

Sigla

*D-R = Latin text that seems to give rise to the D-R translation but that is not represented in S-C, Weber, or in any of the manuscripts cited in those editions.

D-R = *The Holie Bible: Faithfully Translated into English out of the Authentical Latin* (The English Colleges of Douay and Rheims, OT 1609–10, NT 1582)

D-Rn = marginalia in D-R

D-R/C = *The Holy Bible: Translated from the Latin Vulgat* (Challoner's 1750 revision, Dublin?)

Heb = Hebrew sources for the text

KJV = *The Holy Bible, Conteyning the Old Testament, and the New: Newly Translated out of the Originall tongues: & with the former Translations diligently compared and reuised: by his Maiesties speciall Comandement Appointed to be read in Churches* (London: Robert Barker, Printer to the Kings most Excellent Maiestie, 1611, rpr. Thomas Nelson Publishers, 1990)

KJVn = marginalia in KJV

PG = J.-P. Migne, ed., *Patrologiae Graecae* (Paris, 1857–1866)

PL = J.-P. Migne, ed., *Patrologia Latina* (Paris, 1844–1864)

Quentin = *Biblia sacra iuxta Vulgatam versionem* (Typis Polyglottis Vaticanis, 1926–[1995])

S = A. Rahlfs, ed., R. Hanhart, rev., *Septuaginta,* 2nd ed. (Deutsche Bibelgesellschaft, 2006)

S-C = *Biblia Sacra: Vulgatae Editionis Sixti V Pont. Max. iussu recognita et Clementis VIII auctoritate edita* (Vatican City: Marietti, 1959)

Sabatier: P. Sabatier, *Bibliorum Sacrorum Latinae versiones antiquae, seu Vetus Italica.* 3 vols. (Rheims: Apud Reginaldum Florentian, Regis Typographicum & Bibliopolam, sub signo Bibliorum aureorum, 1743–1749)

Smyth = H. W. Smyth, ed., G. M. Messing, rev., *Greek Grammar* (Cambridge, MA: Harvard University Press, 1956)

Weber = R. Weber, ed., *Biblia Sacra Vulgata,* 5th ed. (Deutsche Bibelgesellschaft, 2007); in the Psalms this siglum refers to Weber's Psalmi Iuxta LXX

Weber Iuxta Hebr. = Psalmi Iuxta Hebr. in R. Weber, ed., *Biblia Sacra Vulgata,* 5th ed. (Deutsche Bibelgesellschaft, 2007)

The use of sigla from Weber and Quentin's critical apparatus is indicated in brackets following the sigla; Weber's practice of adding a full stop after certain entries to indicate that a citation is limited to the sources referenced has not been followed.

Other abbreviations follow those found in H. J. Frede, *Kirchenschriftsteller: Verzeichnis und Sigel* (Freiburg: Verlag Herder, 1995), and R. Gryson, *Altlateinische Handschriften.* 2 vols. (Freiburg: Verlag Herder, 1999).

HOSEA

1:1 *Ioathan*: *Ioatham* Weber
<1:1 *and* KJV (in roman type in KJV and italics in D-R/C): omitted in D-R>
1:2 *Domino in*: *Dominum in* Weber; *et fac* AOSΦ [Weber's sigla]: *et* Weber, *et fac tibi* S-C

<1:2   *have of her* D-R/C: *make* D-R; *depart* KJV: *fornicate* D-R>

1:3   *peperit ei: peperit* Weber

<2:3   *lest* KJV: *Lest perhaps* D-R>

2:12   *saltum: saltu* Weber

2:16   *illa: illo* Weber

2:18   *cum eis: eis* Weber

2:19   *misericordia et in: misericordia et* Weber

2:23   *terram: terra* S-C

<2:23   *in* S-C: *into* D-R>

<2:24   *that which was* KJV (*them which were*; *them* in roman type): omitted
         in D-R>

2:24   *Populus meus es: populus meus* Weber; *Deus: Dominus* Weber

3:1   *vade: vade et* S-C; *respiciunt: respectant* Weber

<3:1   *and* S-C: omitted in D-R>

<3:2   *bought* D-Rn: *digged* D-R>

<4:1   *the Lord shall enter into judgment* D-R/C: *there is iudgement to our Lord*
         D-R>

4:10   *reliquerunt: dereliquerunt* S-C

<4:10   *his law* D-R/C (in italics): omitted in D-R>

4:11   *auferunt: aufert* Weber

<4:12   *their stocks* KJV: *in their wood* D-R>

4:14   *conversabantur: versabantur* Weber

<4:18   *they that should have protected* D-R/C: *the protectours* D-R>

4:19   *eum: eam* Weber

<5:1   *them whom you should have watched over* D-R/C: *speculation* D-R>

5:4   *Deum: Dominum* Weber; *fornicationum: fornicationis* Weber

5:7   *Dominum: Domino* Weber

<5:9   *that which shall surely be* KJV: *faith* D-R>

5:11   *patiens est: patiens* Weber; *sordem: sordes* S-C

5:13   *Iuda: Iudas* Weber

6:1   *consurgent: consurgunt* Weber

<7:1   *to steal* D-R/C: *spoyling* D-R>

<7:2   *lest* D-R/C: *lest perhaps* D-R; *remember* KJV: *haue remembred* D-R>

7:8   *panis qui: qui* Weber

7:15   *eos et: et* Weber

<8:4   *but* KJV: *and* D-R>

8:5   *eos: eis* Weber

<8:6   *the invention* D-R/C (in italics): omitted in D-R>

8:7   *eo: eis* Weber

8:13   *offerent: adfer adfer* Weber; *et Dominus: Dominus* Weber

9:3   *Ephraim in: Ephraim* Weber

9:4   *comedent: comedunt* Weber

<9:4   *is life* D-R/C: omitted in D-R>

9:6   *congregabit: congregavit* Weber; *argentum: argenti* Weber

9:7   *et multitudinem: et multitudo* Weber

9:8   *ruinae factus est: ruinae* Weber

<9:10   *that* KJV (in italics in D-R/C): omitted in D-R>

9:10   *confusionem: confusione* Weber

9:12   *et si: si et* Weber

9:13   *educet: educit* Weber

<9:16   *And* D-R/C: *But and* D-R; *fruit* KJV (in roman type in KJV): *things*
        D-R>

<10:5   *that* KJV (in roman type in KJV and italics in D-R/C): omitted in
        D-R>

10:10   *et congregabuntur* Sabatier: *congregabuntur* Weber, S-C

<10:11 *corn, but* KJV (*corn* in roman type in KJV): *and* D-R>

10:12   *et metite: metite* Weber

10:14   *Salmana: Salman* Weber

<10:15 *because of* D-R [properly a Hebraism]: literally, *from the face of*>

11:1   *transiit: transit* Weber

<11:1   *so* D-R/C: omitted in D-R>

<11:2   *As* KJV (in roman type in KJV): omitted in D-R; *they* D-R/C: *so
        they* D-R>

<11:4   *that taketh off* KJV: *lifting vp* D-R; *put his meat* KJV (*laid* for *put his*):
        declined D-R>

<11:5   *but* KJV: *and* D-R>

11:7   *eis: ei* Weber

<11:8   *deal with* S: *geue* D-R; *stirred up* S: *disturbed together* D-R>

<12:6   *Therefore* KJV: *And* D-R>

<12:7   *He is* KJV (in roman type in KJV and italics in D-R/C): omitted in
        D-R; *like* D-R/C (in italics): omitted in D-R>

12:11   *ergo: tamen* Weber

12:12   *uxorem* [both times]: *uxore* Weber

13:6   *sua*: *sua et* Weber; *saturati sunt*: *saturati* Weber; *elevaverunt*: *et levaverunt* S-C

<13:6   *and* S-C: omitted in D-R>

13:7   *Et*: *Et ego* S-C

13:10   *reges* S²l [Quentin's sigla]: *regem* Weber, S-C

14:1   *Deum*: *Dominum* Weber; *pereant*: *pereat* Weber

14:3   *et dicite*: *dicite* Weber; *et accipe*: *accipe* S-C

14:5   *eis*: *eo* Weber

14:6   *quasi*: *sicut* S-C

<14:7   *spread* KJV: *goe* D-R>

<14:9   *shall say* KJV (in roman type in KJV and italics in D-R/C): omitted in D-R>

JOEL

<1:3   *let . . . tell* KJV (*tell* in roman type in KJV): omitted in D-R>

<1:5   *take delight in drinking sweet wine* D-R/C: *drinke wine in sweetnes* D-R>

<1:12   *withdrawn* D-R/C: *confounded* D-R>

<2:1   *sound an alarm* KJV: *howle* D-R>

2:7   *Viri*: *vir* Weber; *gradientur*: *gradietur* Weber

<2:11   *can* KJV: *shal* D-R>

2:13   *deprecabilis* $\Lambda^L M^2 \Phi^P$ cum HI (codd. PA Pal¹, ⅓), Θ^A, Θ^G [Quentin's sigla]: *praestabilis* Weber, S-C

<2:13   *ready to* D-R *repent of the evil* KJV (*repenteth him* for *repent*): *readie to be gracious vpon the malice* D-R>

2:14   *vestro*: *nostro* Weber

<2:15   *solemn* KJV: omitted in D-R>

2:17   *Domine; parce*: *Domine* Weber

<2:17   *should they say* KJV: *say they* D-R>

2:19   *eis*: *eo* Weber

<2:20   *the northern enemy* KJV (*armie* for *enemy*; *armie* in roman type in KJV and *enemy* in italics in D-R/C): *him that is from the North* D-R>

<2:21   *done great things* KJV: *magnified to doe* D-R>

2:23   *sicut in*: *in* Weber

<2:25   *and* S: omitted in D-R; *host* KJV (*armie*): *strength* D-R>

2:29   *servos meos*: *servos* Weber

2:31   *vertetur*: *convertetur* S-C

3:2   *vallem*: *valle* Weber

3:3   *prostibulum*: *prostibulo* S-C

3:4   *reddetis*: *redditis* Weber

3:5   *aurum meum* Θ^{S}QΓ^A cum HI (½), HI(G), 175, 176 et HG [Quentin's sigla]: *aurum* Weber, S-C

<3:9   *Prepare* KJV: *sanctifie* D-R>

<3:10   *I* KJV: *That I* D-R>

<3:13   *fats*: colloquially, *presses*>

3:15   *obtenebrati*: *obtenebricata* Weber

3:17   *Sion*: *Sion in* Weber

3:19   *desolationem*: *desolatione* Weber

3:20   *in generationem*: *in generatione* Weber

Amos

1:1   *pastoribus*: *pastoralibus* Weber

1:6   *transtulerint*: *transtulerit* Weber; *concluderent*: *concluderet* Weber

1:10   *mittam*: *emittam* Weber

<1:11   *cast off all* KJV: *violated his* D-R>

1:14   *Rabbae*: *Rabba* S-C

2:4   *abiecerit*: *abiecerint* Weber; *custodierit*: *custodierint* Weber; *abierunt* X(rescr., hab.)ΔΠ^{L}Θ^{S}SQΨ^{D}Ω cum HI in expos., l. 97, JUL-E et AU spe [Quentin's sigla]: *abierant* Weber, S-C

2:6   *pro argento*: *argento* Weber

<2:6   *a pair of* KJV: omitted in D-R>

<2:7   *same* KJV (in roman type in KJV and italics in D-R/C): omitted in D-R>

<2:9   *like* KJV: omitted in D-R>

2:10   *duxi*: *eduxi* Weber

2:11   *Nazareos*: *Nazarenos* Weber

<2:11   *for* KJV: omitted in D-R>

2:12   *propinabatis*: *propinabitis* S-C; *Nazareis vinum*: *Nazarenis vino* Weber; *mandabatis*: *mandabitis* S-C

<2:12 *will present* S-C: *dranke* D-R; *command* S-C: *commanded* D-R>

2:13 *subter*: *super* Weber

3:1 *omni cognatione*: *omnem cognationem* S-C

3:6 *fecerit*: *fecit* Weber

3:7 *faciet*: *facit* S-C

<3:7 *doth* S-C: *wil not doe* D-R; *without revealing* KJV (*but he reuealeth*): *vnles he haue reueled* D-R>

3:9 *penetralibus*: *penetrabilibus* Weber

3:12 *Damasci*: *Damasco* Weber; *grabato*: *grabatti* Weber

4:1 *monte*: *montibus* *D-R

<4:2 *when* KJV (*that*): *and* D-R>

4:4 *offerte*: *adferte* S-C

<4:5 *with leaven* KJV: *of the leauened* D-R>

<4:6 *yet* KJV: *and* D-R>

<4:8 *yet* KJV: *&* D-R>

<4:9 *yet* KJV: *and* D-R>

<4:10 *stink* KJV: *putrefaction* D-R; *yet* KJV: *and* D-R>

<4:11 *some of* KJV (in italics in D-R/C; *some* in roman type in KJV): omitted in D-R; *yet* KJV: *and* D-R>

4:11 *de*: *ab* S-C

<4:12 *Therefore* KJV: *Wherfore* D-R>

5:1 *et non*: *non* Weber

<5:5 *But* KJV: *And* D-R>

5:5 *Galgalam*: *Galgala* Weber

<5:6 *lest* KJV: *lest perhaps* D-R; *with* D-R/C: *as* D-R>

<5:8 *seek* KJV (in roman type in KJV and italics in D-R/C): omitted in D-R>

5:8 *in noctem*: *nocte* Weber; *nomen est*: *nomen* Weber

<5:19 *or* KJV: *&* D-R>

5:22 *obtuleritis*: *adtuleritis* Weber

<5:24 *But* KJV: *And* D-R>

<5:26 *But* KJV: *And* D-R>

<5:27 *go into captivity* KJV: *remoue* D-R>

5:27 *dicit*: *dixit* Weber

<6:6 *are not concerned* KJV (*grieued* for *concerned*): *suffered nothing* D-R>

6:10 *penetralibus*: *penetrabilibus* Weber; *apud*: *penes* S-C

6:12 *mandavit* $\Sigma^T\Pi^L M^*\Phi^{ERG}O\Theta^{SAMG}RYSUQ\Gamma^{A2}\Psi^D\Omega^S$agrel cum HI

(cod. N, ½; cod. C, ⅔), JUL-E (⅔) et G^III [Quentin's sigla]: *mandabit* Weber, S-C

6:14 *nihilo*: *nihili* Weber

6:15 *conterent*: *conteret* S-C

<7:1 *locust was formed* KJV (*he formed grassehoppers*): *former of the locust* D-R>

7:1 *tonsionem*: *tonsorem* Weber

7:2 *dixi*: *et dixi* Weber

<7:4 *Lord* S: *Lord God* D-R>

7:7 *mihi Dominus*: *mihi* Weber

<7:12 *prophesy* KJV: *thou shalt prophecie* D-R>

<7:13 *But* KJV: *And* D-R>

8:1 *Dominus Deus*: *Dominus* *D-R

<8:1–2 *hook to draw down the fruit* [both times] D-Rn (*fruite . . . is dravven vvith a hooke*): *apple hooke* D-R>

<8:6 *a pair of* KJV: omitted in D-R>

8:7 *superbiam*: *superbia* Weber

8:9 *Dominus Deus*: *Dominus* Weber; *sol*: *sol in* S-C

9:1 *cardines* Frede HI Am 3 1086B and 1086C: *cardinem* Weber, S-C; *fugient*: *fugiet* Weber

9:2 *ad caelum*: *in caelum* S-C

9:3 *profundo*: *fundo* Weber

<9:5 *shall* S: *shal al* D-R>

9:9 *concutitur triticum*: *concutitur* Weber

9:11 *illa*: *illo* Weber; *eum*: *illud* S-C; *sicut in*: *sicut* Weber

<9:11 *close up* KJV: *reedifie* D-R>

<9:13 *when* KJV (*that*): *and* D-R>

9:14 *habitabunt*: *inhabitabunt* S-C

OBADIAH

1:3 *petrarum*: *petrae* Weber; *tuum*: *suum* Weber; *dicis*: *dicit* Weber; *tuo*: *suo* Weber

<1:4 *Though* [both times] KJV: *If* D-R; *be exalted* KJV (*exalt*): *shalt be exalted* D-R; *set* KJV: *shalt set* D-R>

<1:5 *till they had enough* KJV: *thinges sufficent for themselues* D-R>

1:5   *racemum*: *racemos* Weber

1:11   *adversus eum*: *adversus* Weber

<1:12   *But* KJV: *And* D-R>

<1:14   *crossways* KJV: *outgoings* D-R>

1:16   *bibisti*: *bibistis* S-C; *absorbebunt*: *absorbent* Weber

<1:17   *possessed* S?: *had possessed* D-R>

1:19   *austrum sunt*: *austrum* Weber

1:20   *omnia loca*: *omnia* Weber

<h2 style="text-align:center">JONAH</h2>

1:2   *et vade*: *vade* Weber

1:3   *Ionas*: *Iona* Weber; *in Ioppe*: *Ioppen* Weber

1:4   *in mare*: *in mari* Weber

<1:4   *raised* D-R/C: *made* D-R>

<1:5   *wares* KJV: *vessels* D-R>

1:5   *Ionas*: *Iona* Weber

<1:6   *that* KJV: *and* D-R>

<1:7   *that we may know* KJV: *and know* D-R>

<1:8   *Of what country art thou* S: *what is thy countrie* D-R>

1:8   *quo vadis*: *quo* Weber

<1:11   *that* KJV: *and* D-R; *may be* KJV: *shal* D-R>

1:12   *grandis est haec* Θ^G [Quentin's siglum]: *grandis haec* Weber, *haec grandis venit* S-C

<1:13   *hard* KJV: omitted in D-R; *but* KJV: *and* D-R; *tossed* D-R/C: *went* D-R>

1:15   *quievit* Frede AM Ps 43.87.1 p. 324.2, PS-AU s Cai I.36.2 p. 55b (*conquievit*): *stetit* Weber, S-C

2:1   *Ionas*: *Iona* Weber

2:2   *Ionas*: *Iona* Weber; *ventre*: *utero* Weber

2:3   *inferni*: *inferi* S-C

3:2   *et vade in*: *vade ad* Weber

<3:2   *bid* KJV: *speake to* D-R>

3:3   *Ionas*: *Iona* Weber; *magna*: *magna Dei* Weber

3:4   *Ionas*: *Iona* Weber

3:5   *Deum*: *Deo* Weber

<3:7 *caused it to be proclaimed and published* KJV: *cried, and sayd* D-R; *beasts* KJV: *beasts and* D-R>

<3:8 *all their* D-R/C: omitted in D-R>

<3:9 *can tell* KJV: *knoweth* D-R; *his fierce anger* KJV: *the furie of his wrath* D-R>

3:10 *a*: *de* S-C

4:1 *Ionas*: *Iona* Weber

<4:2 *what I said* D-R/C: *my word* D-R>

<4:3 *to die* KJV: *death* D-R; *to live* KJV: *life* D-R>

<4:4 *thou hast reason to be angry* D-R/C: *Art thou angrie wel* D-R>

4:5 *Ionas*: *Iona* Weber; *illud*: *eum* Weber

4:6 *Ionas*: *Iona* Weber

<4:7 *But* KJV: *And* D-R>

4:7 *diluculi*: *diluculo* Weber

4:8 *ab ardore aestuabat* Frede AU ep 102.35 p. 575.5 (*a solis ardore*): *aestuabat* Weber, S-C

<4:9 *thou hast reason to be angry* D-R/C: *Art thou angrie wel* D-R; *with reason* D-R/C: *wel* D-R>

4:9 *hedera*: *hederam* Weber

4:10 *et sub*: *et* Weber

<4:11 *how to distinguish* D-R/C [KJV has *cannot discern*e]: *what is* D-R>

MICAH

1:1 *Ahaz et*: *Ahaz* Weber

1:3 *egredietur*: *egreditur* Weber

<1:4 *melted* KJV (*molten*): *consumed* D-R>

1:4 *ignis et*: *ignis* Weber

<1:11 *pass away* KJV: *passe ye to your selues* D-R; *thou that dwellest in the Beautiful Place* KJVn (*fairely* for *in the Beautiful Place*; this is a gloss of the place name): *faire habitation* D-R>

1:11 *Vicina*: *Vicinae* Weber

<1:13 *hath astonished* D-R/C: *of astonishment to* D-R>

1:15 *usque ad Odollam*: *usque Adollam* Weber

<1:16 *thy delicate children* KJV: *the children of thy delicacies* D-R>

<2:4 *melody* D-R/C: *sweetnes* D-R>

<2:6   *The prophecy* KJV (in italics in D-R/C): *It* D-R>
<2:7   *straitened* KJV: *abridged* D-R; *these* KJV: *such* D-R>
<2:8   *But* D-R/C: *And* D-R>
2:8   *sustulistis, et: sustulistis* Weber
<2:9   *their houses, in which they took delight* KJV (*their pleasant houses*): *the
          house of their delicacies* D-R>
<2:10   *that* D-R/C: *the* D-R; *of the land* D-R/C (*the land* in italics): *therof*
          D-R>
<2:11   *of* [both times] KJV: *into* D-R>
2:13   *ingredientur: egredientur* Weber
3:2   *eis: eos* Weber
<3:5   *prepare* KJV: *sanctifie* D-R>
3:9   *hoc: haec* Weber
4:1   *Et erit: et* Weber
4:4   *vineam: vitem* S-C
4:13   *interficies: interficiam* Weber
<4:13   *immolate* KJV (*consecrate*): *kil* D-R>
5:3   *et reliquiae: reliquiae* Weber
6:3   *Popule: populus* Weber; *aut: et* Weber
6:5   *Popule: populus* Weber; *cognosceres: cognosceret* Weber
<6:6   *Wherewith* KJV: omitted in D-R>
6:6   *Curvabo: curvem* Weber
<6:7   *body* KJV: *womb* D-R>
6:8   *requirat: quaeret* Weber
<6:14   *but* [first time] KJV: *&* D-R; *but* [second time] KJV: *and* D-R>
<6:15   *but* [first two times] KJV: *and* D-R; *but* [third time] KJV: *&* D-R>
<6:16   *For* KJV: *And* D-R>
6:16   *Amri: Omri* Weber
7:6   *et filia: filia* Weber; *contra: adversus* S-C; *et inimici: inimici* Weber
7:9   *videbo: videbo in* Weber
<7:11   *shall come* D-R/C (in italics): omitted in D-R>
7:12   *veniet: veniet de* S-C
<7:12   *they* D-R/C: *Assur* D-R; *from* S-C: omitted in D-R>
7:16   *manum: manus* Weber
7:17   *serpentes: serpens* Weber; *perturbabuntur in: proturbabuntur de* Weber;
          formidabunt: desiderabunt Weber

Nahum

<1:3   *will not cleanse and acquit the guilty* D-R/C [after S?] (*the guilty* in italics): *clensing, he wil not make innocent* D-R>

<1:4   *rivers to be a desert* D-R/C [sense from KJV: *drieth vp all the riuers*]: *riuers to a desert* D-R>

1:5   *desolati: adsolati* Weber

<1:6   *can* KJV: *shal* D-R>

<1:8   *But* KJV: *And* D-R>

<1:10   *while they are* KJV *feasting and drinking* D-Rn (*banketing* for *feasting*): *the feast of them that drinke* D-R>

1:11   *exibit: exivit* Weber

<1:12   *Though* KJV: *If* D-R; *were* D-R/C: *shal be* D-R; *yet* KJV: *also* D-R>

1:12   *adtondebuntur* Q [Quentin's siglum]: *adtondentur* Weber, S-C

<1:13   *with which he struck* D-R/C: *from of* D-R>

<1:14   *it* D-R/C (in italics): omitted in D-R>

2:1   *custodiat: custodit* Weber

<2:3   *like* D-R/C: omitted in D-R>

<2:5   *muster up* D-R/C: *remember* D-R; *stumble* KJV: *fal* D-R>

<2:8   *great pool* D-R/C: *fishpoole of waters* D-R; *They cry* KJV (in roman type in KJV and italics in D-R/C): omitted in D-R; *but* KJV: *&* D-R>

<2:9   *for* KJV: *and* D-R; *furniture* KJV: *vessels* D-R>

2:10   *est et: et* Weber; *eorum sicut: sicut* Weber

<2:10   *the* D-R/C: *and* D-R>

<2:11   *now* D-R/C: omitted in D-R>

2:13   *tuas: eius* Weber

<3:2   *rattling of the wheeles* KJV: *violence of the wheele* D-R>

3:2   *frementis: hinnientis* *D-R; *et equitis: equitis* Weber

<3:3   *dead bodies* KJV (*corpses; dead* in italics in D-R/C): *bodies* D-R>

<3:7   *bemoan* KJV: *shake the head vpon* D-R>

3:8   *es: es ab* Weber; *Aquae in: aqua in* Weber

3:9   *eius et: et* Weber

3:11   *et eris: eris* Weber

<3:14   *make* KJV: *hold the* D-R>

3:16   *sint: sunt* Weber

HABAKKUK

1:3   *praedam et iniustitiam*: *praeda et iniustitia* Weber

<1:3   *but* D-R/C: *&* D-R>

1:5   *admiramini*: *et admiramini* Weber

<1:10   *their prince* D-R/C (in italics): *he* D-R>

1:10   *erunt, et* Σ^TS [Quentin's sigla]: *erunt* Weber, S-C

<1:13   *too pure to* KJV (*purer . . . then to*): *cleane, from* D-R; *thou* S-C: *thou not* D-R>

1:13   *non respicis*: *respicis* S-C; *iniqua*: *inique* Weber

1:15   *suum*: *suo* Weber

2:1   *meum super* Ω^{SJ} [Quentin's sigla]: *super* Weber, S-C

<2:5   *desire* KJV: *soule* D-R; *never* S: *not* D-R; *but* KJV: *and* D-R>

<2:6   *heapeth together* D-R/C: *multiplieth* D-R; *himself* KJV: *against himself* D-R>

2:14   *cognoscant*: *cognoscat* Weber

2:16   *es*: *est* Weber

2:17   *hominum*: *hominis* Weber

3:1   *ignorationibus*: *ignorantiis* S-C

3:3   *Pharan*: *Pharan / semper* Weber

3:8   *Qui*: *quia* Weber

<3:9   *according to* KJV (*according* in roman type in KJV and *according to* in italics in D-R/C): omitted in D-R>

3:9   *es*: *es / semper* Weber

<3:12   *anger* KJV (*indignation*): *freating* D-R>

3:13   *usque*: *eius usque* S-C; *collum*: *collum / semper* Weber

<3:13   *his* S-C: omitted in D-R>

3:16   *a voce*: *ad vocem* Weber

<3:17   *fail* KJV: *deceiue* D-R>

3:17   *abscidetur*: *abscindetur* S-C

3:18   *et exultabo*: *exultabo* Weber

3:19   *victor*: *victori* Weber

ZEPHANIAH

1:1   *filii Godoliae*: *filium Godoliae* Weber; *Iudae*: *Iuda* Weber

1:3   *volatilia*: *volatile* Weber

<1:7   *guests* KJV: *called* D-R>

1:9   *super omnem*: *omnem* Weber

1:14   *est et*: *et* Weber

<1:16   *bulwarks* KJV? (*towres*): *corners* D-R>

1:17   *corpora*: *corpus* Weber

<1:18   *Neither* KJV: *Yea and* D-R; *even a speedy riddance of* KJV: *consumma-
          tion with speede to* D-R>

<2:2   *fierce anger* KJV: *wrath of the furie* D-R>

2:2   *indignationis*: *furoris* Weber

<2:7   *bring back* S: *turne away* D-R>

2:9   *eos, et*: *illos* Weber

2:11   *vir*: *viri* S-C

<2:12   *You Ethiopians also* KJV: *Yea and you Æthiopians* D-R>

<2:13   *city* D-R/C (in italics) [cf. Zeph 2:15; KJV has *Nineueh*]: omitted in
          D-R>

<2:14   *singing bird* D-R/C (in italics) [KJV has *their voice shal sing*, referring
          to birds mentioned previously]: *one singing* D-R>

<2:15   *that dwelt* KJV: *dwelling* D-R; *none* KJV: *none other els* D-R>

3:2   *adpropiavit*: *adpropinquavit* S-C

3:5   *lucem*: *luce* Weber

3:6   *Disperdidi*: *disperdi* Weber

<3:6   *towers* KJV: *corners* D-R>

3:8   *et effundam*: *ut effundam* Weber; *eas*: *eos* S-C

<3:8   *my fierce anger* KJV: *the wrath of my furie* D-R>

3:9   *invocent*: *vocent* Weber

<3:11   *thy proud boasters* D-R/C: *the loftie speakers of thy pride* D-R>

3:14   *iubila*: *iubilate* Weber

3:17   *sua*: *tua* Weber

<3:19   *get them* KJV: *make them into* D-R; *where they had been put to* KJV
          (*haue* for *had*): *of their* D-R>

HAGGAI

<1:5   *to consider* KJV (without *to*): *vpon* D-R>

<1:6   *but* [first two times] KJV: *and* D-R; *but* [third time] KJV: *&* D-R;
          earned KJV (*earneth*): *gathered* D-R>

1:8   *ligna*: *lignum* Weber
<1:10   *fruits* KJV (*fruite*): *spring* D-R>
1:12   *Dei*: *Domini Dei* S-C
<1:12   *the Lord* S-C: omitted in D-R>
1:13   *vobiscum sum*: *vobiscum* Weber
<2:1   *they began* D-Rn (in italics in D-R/C): omitted in D-R>
<2:2   *And* D-Rn (in italics in D-R/C): omitted in D-R; *month* D-R/C: *moneth, the one and twentith of the moneth* D-R>
<2:4   *in comparison to that* KJV (*of it* for *to that*; in italics in D-R/C): *so* D-R>
<2:5   *Yet* KJV: *And* D-R>
2:5   *popule*: *populus* S-C
2:6   *pepigi*: *placui* Weber
2:11   *Darii, regis*: *Darii* Weber
2:15   *obtulerunt*: *obtulerint* Weber
2:17   *et intraretis*: *intraretis* Weber
<2:18   *yet* KJV: *and* D-R>
<2:19   *and* D-R/C (in italics): omitted in D-R>
2:19   *in cordibus vestris* Sabatier: *super cor vestrum* Weber, S-C
<2:20   *Or hath* D-R/C: *and . . . hath not* D-R; *you* KJV (in roman type in KJV and italics in D-R/C): omitted in D-R>
2:24   *illa*: *illo* Weber

1:1   *Darii Regis*: *Darii* Weber; *filii*: *filium* Weber
1:4   *et de*: *et* Weber
<1:4   *But* KJV: *and* D-R>
1:7   *undecimi mensis*: *undecimo mense* Weber; *filii*: *filium* Weber
<1:7   *which is called* KJV (*the moneth* for *called*): omitted in D-R>
1:10   *perambularent*: *perambulent* S-C
1:12   *Iste iam*: *iste* Weber
<1:15   *forward* KJV: *toward* D-R>
1:16   *domus*: *et domus* S-C
2:8   *mei*: *eius* Weber
3:1   *mihi Dominus*: *mihi* Weber

3:4   *abstuli* E cum HI (G, cod. N), CY te, AU nu et G [Quentin's sigla]: *abstuli a te* Weber, S-C

<3:7   *to walk* KJV?: *walkers* D-R; *with thee* D-R/C (in italics): omitted in D-R>

3:10   *vineam*: *vitem* S-C

4:2   *et septem infusoria*: *septem et septem infusoria* Weber

<4:7   *Thou shalt become* KJV (in roman type in KJV): *into* D-R>

<4:10   *plummet* KJV [glossed as *stone* in D-R/C]: *stone* D-R>

4:10   *oculi sunt*: *oculi* Weber; *universam terram*: *universa terra* Weber

4:12   *sunt duo* C [Weber's siglum]: *sunt duae* Weber, S-C; *rami* Sabatier: *spicae* Weber, S-C

4:13   *domine mi*: *domine* Weber

4:14   *sunt duo*: *duo* Weber

5:3   *faciem omnis*: *faciem* *D-R

6:3   *varii et*: *varii* Weber

6:6   *qua*: *quo* Weber; *in terram*: *in terra* Weber

<6:10   *them of* KJV (in roman type in KJV): omitted in D-R>

<7:2   *when* KJV: *And* D-R>

<7:5   *month* KJV (in roman type in KJV): omitted in D-R>

7:6   *et bibistis*: *et cum bibistis* Weber

<7:11   *But* KJV: *And* D-R; *to depart* D-R/C: *departing* D-R; *stopped* KJV: *aggrauated* D-R>

7:11   *averterunt*: *verterunt* Weber

7:12   *posuerunt ut*: *posuerunt* Weber

<7:14   *or* D-R/C: *&* D-R>

<8:1   *to me* KJV (in roman type in KJV and italics in D-R/C): omitted in D-R>

<8:4   *man with his* KJV: *mans* D-R>

<8:5   *boys* KJV: *infantes* D-R>

<8:6   *seem* KJV? (*bee*): *shal seme* D-R>

8:8   *et in*: *et* Weber

8:10   *neque exeunti*: *et exeunti* Weber

<8:19   *month* D-Rn: omitted in D-R>

8:19   *laetitiam*: *in laetitiam* Weber

<9:2   *to be exceeding wise* KJV (*be very wise*): *wisedom excedingly* D-R>

9:9   *asinum*: *asinam* S-C

<9:12   *today* D-R/C: *to day also* D-R>

9:15   *vino*: *a vino* S-C

9:16   *elevabuntur*: *elevantur* Weber

<11:2   *mighty* KJV: *magnifical* D-R>

11:7   *Funiculum*: *Funiculos* Weber

11:8   *siquidem et*: *siquidem* Weber

11:9   *vorent*: *devorent* S-C

11:13   *quo*: *quod* Weber; *domum*: *domo* Weber

11:14   *Israhel*: *inter Israhel* Weber

<11:16   *nor* KJV (*neither*): omitted in D-R>

<11:17   *quite wither away* KJV (*be cleane dryed up*): *be dried with withering*
              D-R; *utterly* KJV: *waxing darke* D-R>

<12:1   *Thus* D-R/C: omitted in D-R>

12:1   *Dicit*: *dixit* Weber

12:4   *caecitate*: *in caecitate* Weber

12:6   *illa*: *illo* Weber; *facem*: *faciem* S-C

<12:7   *and* D-R/C: omitted in D-R; *magnify themselves* KJV (*themselves* in
              roman type in KJV): *magnifically* D-R>

12:8   *illa proteget*: *illo proteget* Weber; *eorum*: *eius* Weber

13:1   *domui*: *domus* Weber

13:2   *pseudoprophetas*: *prophetas* Weber

<13:3   *brought him into the world* D-R/C: *begot him* D-R>

13:7   *dispergentur*: *dispergantur* Weber

13:8   *disperdentur*: *dispergentur* S-C

<13:8   *scattered* S-C: *destroyed* D-R; *but* KJV: *and* D-R>

<13:9   *refine ... refined* KJV: *burne ... burnt* D-R>

14:1   *venient dies*: *dies veniunt* Weber

<14:4   *in the midst* KJV: *by the halfe part* D-R>

14:4   *et ad*: *et* Weber

14:5   *eorum*: *meorum* Weber

14:7   *vesperae*: *vesperi* S-C

<14:10   *to* KJV: *of* D-R>

14:10   *prioris et*: *prioris* Weber

<14:11   *people* KJV (*men*): *they* D-R>

14:13   *illa*: *illo* Weber

14:15   *muli et*: *muli* Weber

14:16   *venerunt*: *venerint* Weber

<14:18   *And* KJV: *Yea and* D-R>

14:20   *illa*: *illo* Weber

14:21   *Iuda* CΣ [Weber's sigla]: *in Iuda* Weber, S-C

MALACHI

1:1   *Malachi*: *Malachiae* S-C

<1:3   *given* D-R/C: omitted in D-R>

1:4   *destructa*: *deserta* Weber

1:11   *quia magnum est*: *quia magnum* Weber

<2:2   *yea* KJV: *&* D-R>

2:12   *Disperdet*: *disperdat* Weber

<2:14   *yet* KJV: *and* D-R>

2:17   *quod dicitis*: *cum diceretis* Weber

3:1   *mitto*: *mittam* Weber

<3:4   *in* [first time] KJV: omitted in D-R; *in* [second time] KJV: *as* D-R>

<3:5   *hireling in his wages* KJV (*his* in roman type in KJV): *hyre of the hyred man* D-R>

<3:8   *afflict* [all three times] D-R/C: *fasten* D-R>

3:8   *configimus*: *confiximus* Weber; *primitiis*: *primitivis* Weber

<3:9   *afflict* D-R/C: *fasten* D-R; *even* KJV (*euen* in roman type in KJV): omitted in D-R>

<3:10   *that* KJV: *and* D-R>

<3:13   *unsufferable* D-R/C: *forcible* D-R>

3:16   *timentes Dominum*: *timentes Deum* Weber

<3:17   *my special possession* D-R/C [KJVn has *speciall treasure* later in this verse]: *to me* D-R; *of my doing* D-R/C: *that I doe to my peculiar* D-R>

4:1   *relinquet*: *derelinquet* S-C

<4:2   *But* KJV: *And* D-R>

<4:6   *lest* KJV: *lest perhaps* D-R>

1 MACCABEES

1:1   *filius Philippi* Σ cf. B (*philippi filius*) [Quentin's sigla]: *Philippi* Weber, S-C

1:4   *virtutem et*: *virtutem* Weber; *exercitum*: *exercituum* Weber

1:6   *moreretur*: *moritur* Weber

<1:9   *made themselves kings* D-R/C: *possessed the kingdom* D-R>

1:11   *et septimo*: *septimo* S-C

<1:14   *after the ordinances* KJV: *the iustice* D-R>

<1:17   *had a mind* KJV (*thought*): *begane* D-R>

<1:19   *but* KJV: *and* D-R; *were wounded unto death* KJV: *fel wounded* D-R>

1:21   *et tertio*: *tertio* S-C

1:22   *Hierosolymam*: *Hierosolymis* Weber

1:25   *est in*: *est* Weber

<1:26   *where they were* KJV: *of theirs* D-R>

1:27   *et virgines* ZΩ^{S}arelv cum B [Quentin's sigla]: *virgines* Weber, S-C

1:28   *et quae*: *quae* Weber

<1:28   *bride* D-R/C [KJV has *she*]: *the wemen* D-R>

<1:30   *full years* KJV (*years fully expired*): *yeares of dayes* D-R; *collector* KJV: omitted in D-R>

1:32   *plaga magna*: *plaga* Weber

1:36   *peccatricem*: *peccatorum* Weber

<1:36   *fortified themselves* KJV (*themselves* in brackets in KJV): *waxed strong* D-R>

<1:38   *a place* KJV: *made* D-R>

<1:41   *were brought to* D-R/C: *into* D-R>

1:43   *relinqueret*: *reliquerunt* Weber

1:45   *servituti eius*: *ei* Weber

1:46   *rex*: *rex Antiochus* Weber; *Iudae*: *Iuda* S-C; *legem*: *leges* S-C

1:49   *Et iussit*: *et* Weber

<1:50   *unclean* KJV: *common* D-R>

1:51   *inmunditiis* C [Weber's siglum]: *inmundis* Weber, S-C

<1:52   *would not do* KJV: *had not done* D-R>

1:52   *fecissent*: *fecisset* Weber; *morerentur*: *moreretur* Weber

1:54   *Iudae*: *Iuda* S-C

1:57   *quadragesimo centesimo*: *quadragesimo* Weber, *quadragesimo et centesimo* S-C; *Iudae*: *Iuda* S-C

1:60   *observabat*: *observabant* Weber

1:61   *inveniebatur*: *inveniebantur* Weber; *mense et mense*: *mense* Weber

<1:61   *month* D-R/C: *in euerie moneth* D-R>

<1:62   *of God* KJV (in italics in D-R/C): omitted in D-R>

<1:64   *about their* KJV: *by the* D-R>

1:64   *circumciderant*: *circumciderunt* Weber

2:1   *Ioarib*: *Ioarim* Weber

2:2   *Iohannem*: *Iohannan* Weber

2:3   *Simeonem*: *Simeon* Weber

2:4   *Iudam*: *Iudas* Weber

2:5   *Eleazarum*: *Eleazarus* Weber; *Ionathan*: *Ionathas* Weber

2:9   *senes*: *iuvenes* Weber; *gladio*: *in gladio* S-C

2:11   *ornatus* Sabatier: *conpositio* Weber, S-C

2:12   *ea*: *eam* Weber

2:15   *civitatem*: *civitate* Weber; *accendere tura*: *accendere* Weber

<2:17   *an* KJV: *most* D-R>

<2:18   *obey* D-R/C: *doe* D-R>

2:19   *servitute legis*: *servitute* Weber; *consentiat*: *consentiunt* Weber

2:24   *accensus est*: *ascendit* Weber

2:25   *immolare*: *immolari* Weber

2:27   *magna in civitate*: *magna* Weber

2:30   *et sederunt*: *ut sederent* Weber; *inundaverunt*: *induraverunt* Weber

2:31   *in civitate* X [Quentin's siglum]: *civitate* Weber, S-C

<2:33   *resist* D-R/C: *resist now also* D-R>

2:33   *Regis Antiochi*: *regis* Weber

<2:34   *obey* D-R/C: *doe* D-R>

<2:35   *to give* KJV (*they gaue*): *against* D-R>

<2:36   *But* KJV (*Howbeit*): *And* D-R>

2:36   *eis, nec lapidem miserunt in eos*: *eis* Weber

<2:38   *persons* KJV (*people*): *soules of men* D-R>

2:40   *nostris, nunc*: *nostris* Weber

<2:41   *Whosoever* KJV: *Euerie man whosoeuer* D-R>

2:42   *Asideorum*: *Iudaeorum* S-C [according to the apparatus of Weber and Quentin, but not according to 1959 S-C]

<2:42   *the stoutest* D-R/C: *strong of force* D-R>

2:46   *Israhel et*: *Israhel* Weber

<2:46   *they did* D-R/C: omitted in D-R>

2:47   *manibus*: *manu* Weber

2:50   *patrum vestrorum*: *patrum* Weber

2:55   *implevit*: *implet* Weber; *dux in*: *dux* Weber

<2:56   *for bearing witness before* KJV: *whiles he testifieth in* D-R>

<2:57 *everlasting kingdom* KJV: *kingdom for euer* D-R>
2:59 *et Azarias et*: *Azarias* Weber
2:62 *ne*: *non* Weber
2:63 *periit*: *periet* Weber
2:65 *Simon*: *Simeon* Weber
2:67 *vos adducetis*: *adducetis* S-C
2:68 *Retribuite*: *et retribuite* Weber
2:70 *et sexto*: *sexto* S-C
<3:3 *got his people great honor* KJV: *dilated glorie to his people* D-R>
3:5 *suum eos*: *suum* Weber
3:6 *eius prae*: *prae* Weber
<3:6 *prospered* KJV: *was directed* D-R>
<3:12 *lifetime* KJV (*life long*): *dayes* D-R>
3:13 *fidelium et ecclesiam*: *et ecclesiam fidelium* Weber
3:16 *usque ad*: *usque* Weber
3:17 *contra*: *ad* Weber; *et tam*: *tam* Weber
<3:17 *ready to faint* KJV: *wearied* D-R>
3:19 *quia*: *quoniam* S-C
<3:19 *cometh* KJV: *is* D-R>
3:20 *superbia*: *superba* Weber
3:23 *loqui*: *loquens* Weber
3:24 *persecutus est*: *persequebatur* Weber
<3:25 *of them* D-R/C (in italics): omitted in D-R>
3:27 *autem Rex*: *autem* Weber
3:29 *thesauris suis*: *thesauris* Weber
3:30 *ut*: *et* Weber; *donativa*: *donaria* S-C
<3:30 *formerly enough* KJV (*he did before*): *once and twice* D-R; *for* KJV: *and* D-R>
3:31 *Et consternatus*: *consternatus* Weber
3:32 *Eufrate*: *Eufraten* Weber
3:35 *et ut*: *ut* Weber; *eorum de*: *de* Weber
<3:35 *that* KJV: *the* D-R>
<3:36 *strangers* KJV: *children strangers* D-R>
<3:37 *chief* KJV (*royall*): omitted in D-R>
3:37 *et septimo*: *septimo* S-C
3:40 *cum*: *ut irent cum* Weber; *Emmaum*: *Ammaum* Weber

3:42   *adplicabant*: *adplicabat* Weber

3:46   *Maspha* [both times]: *Masefat* Weber; *ante in*: *ante* Weber

3:47   *cinerem inposuerunt*: *cinere* Weber; *in capite*: *capiti* S-C; *disciderunt*: *destituerunt* Weber

3:48   *libros*: *librum* Weber

<3:51   *For* KJV: *And* D-R>

3:51   *tui facti sunt in luctum et in humilitatem*: *tui in luctu et humilitate* Weber

3:53   *faciem*: *facies* Weber; *tu, Deus*: *tu* Weber

<3:54   *sounded* KJV: omitted in D-R; *and* KJV: omitted in D-R>

3:55   *haec*: *hoc* Weber

<3:55   *this* KJV: *these thinges* D-R>

<3:56   *or* [all three times] KJV: *and* D-R>

3:57   *Emmaum*: *Ammaum* Weber

3:58   *adversus nos disperdere*: *disperdere* Weber

<3:60   *of God* KJV (in brackets in KJV and italics in D-R/C): omitted in D-R>

<4:1   *the best* KJV: *chosen* D-R; *out of* KJV: omitted in D-R>

4:2   *illis*: *illi* Weber

<4:3   *king's forces* KJV (*armie* for *forces*): *powre of the kings armie* D-R>

4:3   *qui erant in Emmaum*: *quae erat in Ammaum* Weber

4:5   *quaerebat*: *quaerebant* Weber

4:6   *qui*: *quia* Weber

4:7   *ad proelium*: *proelium* Weber

4:9   *exercitu multo*: *exercitu* Weber

4:10   *Dominus et*: *et* Weber; *et memor erit*: *et* Weber

4:12   *levaverunt*: *elevaverunt* S-C

4:13   *erant*: *fuerant* Weber

4:15   *autem omnes*: *autem* Weber; *gladio*: *in gladio* S-C; *Gezeron*: *Gesoron* Weber; *usque ad*: *ad* Weber

4:18   *state nunc*: *state* Weber; *sumetis postea spolia securi*: *post hoc sumetis spolia* Weber

4:19   *haec, ecce*: *haec* Weber

4:20   *vidit Gorgias*: *vidit* Weber; *sunt sui*: *sunt* Weber; *succenderunt*: *succensa sunt* Weber

<4:20   *had* D-R/C: omitted in D-R>

<4:21 *Judas* D-R/C: *both Iudas* D-R>

4:22 *campum: campo* Weber

<4:23 *take the spoils* KJV (*spoile*): *the spoiles* D-R>

<4:24 *home* KJV: omitted in D-R>

4:24 *Deum in: in* Weber; *bonus: bonum* Weber

4:27 *consternatus: consternatus est* Weber

<4:27 *discouraged* KJV: *faynted in mind* D-R; *had not* S: *not* D-R; *according to his mind* D-R/C: *as he would* D-R; *had commanded* D-R/C: *commanded* D-R>

4:28 *Lysias virorum: virorum* Weber

4:30 *manu Ionathae: manus Ionathae* Weber

4:34 *proelium, et: et* Weber

<4:35 *that his men were put to flight* KJV (*his armie* for *that his men*): *the flight of his men* D-R; *how bold the Jews were* D-R/C: *the boldnes of the Iews* D-R>

4:35 *multiplicati rursus venirent: multiplicatus rursus veniret* Weber

<4:38 *growing* KJV: *growen* D-R>

4:38 *vel in: vel* Weber

4:39 *Et sciderunt: sciderunt* Weber; *cinerem super caput suum: cinerem* Weber

<4:41 *had* KJV: omitted in D-R>

4:44 *altare: altari* S-C

4:45 *illis: illi* Weber; *destruerent: destrueret* Weber

<4:45 *into their minds* D-R: literally, *to them*; *lest* KJV: *lest perhaps* D-R; *had* KJV: omitted in D-R>

<4:46 *temple* KJV: *house* D-R>

<4:48 *temple* D-R: literally, *house*>

4:48 *domum erant: domum* Weber

4:51 *fecerant: fecerunt* Weber

<4:51 *begun to make* KJV: *made* D-R>

4:52 *die mensis: mensis* Weber; *hic est: hic* Weber

<4:52 *which* KJV: *this* D-R>

<4:53 *had* KJV: omitted in D-R>

<4:54 *had* KJV: omitted in D-R; *dedicated anew* KJV (without *anew*): *renewed* D-R>

4:54 *et in: et* Weber

4:55   *in faciem et*: *et* Weber; *eum*: *ei* Weber

<4:55   *had* KJV: omitted in D-R>

4:56   *sacrificium salutaris et*: *salutaria* Weber

<4:57   *renewed* KJV: *dedicated* D-R>

4:59   *die mensis*: *mensis* Weber

4:60   *eum*: *eam* Weber

4:61   *eum* [both times]: *eam* Weber

<4:61   *against* KJV: *against the face of* D-R>

5:1   *sanctuarium*: *sancta* Weber; *iratae*: *et iratae* Weber

5:4   *ei in*: *in* Weber

<5:5   *devoted them to utter destruction* D-Rn (*vtterly destroyed*): *anathematized them* D-R>

<5:6   *where he* KJV: *and* D-R>

5:8   *Gazer*: *Iazer* Weber

<5:8   *towns* D-Rn (*villages*): *daughters* D-R>

5:12   *veni, et*: *veni* Weber

5:13   *Tubin*: *Tubi* Weber; *abduxerunt*: *duxerunt* S-C; *ferme*: *fere* S-C

<5:13   *taken* KJV (*borne away*): omitted in D-R>

<5:14   *these* KJV: omitted in D-R; *behold* KJV: *and loe* D-R>

5:15   *Repleta est omnis Galilea alienigenis*: *omni Galilea alienigenas* Weber

5:17   *autem*: *enim* Weber

5:18   *Iudaea*: *Iudaeam* Weber; *custodiendum*: *custodiam* S-C

5:19   *illis*: *illi* Weber; *Praeestote*: *praeesto* Weber

<5:19   *but* D-R/C: *&* D-R>

5:20   *partiti*: *dati* Weber

5:21   *Ptolomaidis*: verse 22 starts here Weber, S-C

5:23   *sumpsit*: *adsumpsit* S-C

<5:23   *with him* KJV (in brackets in KJV): omitted in D-R>

5:24   *frater*: *et fratres* Weber

5:25   *acciderant fratribus eorum*: *acciderunt fratribus* Weber

5:26   *Barasa*: *Basara* Weber; *Mageth*: *Macet* Weber

<5:27   *had* KJV: omitted in D-R>

5:30   *adlevassent*: *elevassent* S-C

<5:30   *people* KJV: *much people* D-R>

5:31   *ad*: *in* Weber

5:32   *dixit exercitui suo*: *exercitui dixit* Weber

5:36   *Mageth*: *Maged* Weber

<5:38   *men* KJV (in brackets in KJV): omitted in D-R>

5:39   *conduxerunt*: *conduxit* Weber; *auxilium sibi*: *auxilium* Weber

5:40   *adpropiaverit*: *adpropinquaverit* S-C

<5:41   *on the other side of* S: *without* D-R>

<5:42   *Suffer no man to stay behind* KJV: *Leaue not a man* D-R>

5:43   *omnes gentes a facie eorum*: *ante faciem eorum omnes gentes* Weber; *erat*: *est* Weber

5:45   *Galaditide*: *Galaditiden* Weber; *Iudae*: *Iuda* S-C

<5:48   *But* KJV (*Howbeit*): *And* D-R>

5:50   *adplicuerunt se*: *adplicuerunt* Weber

<5:51   *the city* KJV: *it* D-R>

<5:52   *to* KJV (*into*): *in* D-R>

5:52   *contra faciem*: *contra* Weber

5:53   *venirent*: *venerunt* Weber

5:55   *Simon*: *Simeon* Weber

<5:59   *give* D-R/C: *meete* D-R>

5:59   *illis*: *illi* Weber

<5:60   *and were persued* KJV (without *were*): omitted in D-R>

5:60   *Iudaeae*: *Iudae* Weber; *illa*: *illo* S-C

<5:65   *towns* KJV (in roman type in KJV) [cf. 1 Mcc 5:8 D-Rn]: *daughters* D-R; *burnt* KJV: *burnt with fyre* D-R>

5:65   *igni in*: *in* Weber

5:66   *terram*: *terra* Weber

5:67   *volunt*: *vult* Weber; *exeunt*: *exiit* Weber

<5:67   *some* KJV (*certaine*): omitted in D-R; *they* D-R/C: *whiles they* D-R>

5:68   *terram alienigenarum*: *terra alienigenarum* Weber; *diruit*: *vidit* Weber; *sculptilia*: *spolia* Weber; *regressus*: *reversus* S-C

6:1   *perambulabat*: *perambulavit* Weber

<6:2   *coverings of gold* D-R/C: *couerings thereof gold* D-R [typographical error for *there of*]; *King* D-R/C: omitted in D-R; *Macedonian* D-R/C: *king of Macedonia* D-R; *had* KJV: omitted in D-R>

6:3   *praedare*: *depraedari* S-C

<6:3   *but* KJV: *and* D-R; *design* D-R/C: *word* D-R>

6:4   *est in*: *est* Weber

<6:5   *whilst he was* D-R/C: omitted in D-R; *how* D-R/C: *that* D-R>

<6:6   *store of* KJV: *manie* D-R>

6:6   *multis quae*: *multis quas* Weber; *ceperunt de castris quae exciderunt*: *ceperunt* Weber

6:8   *factum est ei*: *est factum* Weber

6:9   *dies*: *per dies* S-C

<6:9   *came more and more* KJV *(was euer* for *came)*: *was renewed* D-R>

6:12   *unde et*: *unde* Weber; *auferre*: *auferri* Weber

6:15   *eum ut* Sabatier: *eum et* Weber, S-C

<6:15   *for the kingdom* KJV: *to reigne* D-R>

6:16   *nono*: *et nono* Weber

<6:18   *the Israelites* KJV: *Israel* D-R; *to strengthen* D-R/C: *the strengthning of* D-R>

6:18   *semper et*: *semper ad* Weber

6:20   *convenerunt*: *coirent* Weber

6:21   *impii ex*: *ex impiis* Weber

6:22   *facis*: *facies* Weber

<6:22   *delay to execute* D-R/C: *doest . . . not* D-R>

6:24   *abalienabantur*: *alienabant* S-C

6:26   *arcem in*: *arcem* S-C; *in Bethsuram*: *Bethsuram* S-C

<6:26   *of* [both times] S-C: *in* D-R>

6:27   *nec*: *et non* S-C

6:28   *ut haec*: *ut* Weber

<6:29   *There came also* KJV: *Yea and . . . there came* D-R>

6:29   *de insulis maritimis*: *insulis et maritimis* Weber; *conducticii*: *conducticius* Weber

6:30   *exercitus eius*: *exercitus* Weber

<6:31   *but* KJV: *and* D-R>

6:32   *movit*: *admovit* Weber; *Bethzacaram*: *Bethzacara* Weber

6:33   *surrexit rex*: *surrexit* Weber; *in impetum*: *impetum* Weber; *Bethzacaram*: *Bethzacara* Weber

<6:33   *march on fiercely* KJV *(marched* for *march on)*: *into fiercenes* D-R>

6:36   *ibi erant*: *erant* Weber; *ibant, et*: *ibant* Weber

<6:37   *And* KJV: *Yea &* D-R>

6:37   *ligneae*: *ligneas* Weber; *intus*: *Indus* S-C

<6:37   *an Indian* S-C: *within* D-R; *to rule* KJV *(that ruled)*: *the master* D-R>

6:38   *tubis*: *tubis et* Weber; *constipatos*: *constipati* Weber

6:39   *eis, et*: *eis* Weber

6:40   *alia: alii* Weber, *alia pars* *D-R

6:41   *inhabitantes terram: inhabitantes* Weber; *multitudinis eorum: multitudinis* S-C; *conlisione: conlisionis* Weber

6:45   *audaciter: audacter* S-C

<6:46   *between* D-R/C: *vnder* D-R>

6:46   *se ei: ei* Weber

6:47   *deverterunt: diverterunt* S-C; *se ab: ab* Weber

6:48   *adplicuerunt: adplicuit* Weber; *regis: rex* Weber

6:49   *Bethsura: Bethsuram* Weber

<6:49   *year of rest* KJV: *sabbaths* D-R>

<6:51   *sanctuary* KJV: *place of the sanctification* D-R; *instruments to cast* D-R: literally, *darts of*>

<6:53   *them that came* D-R/C: omitted in D-R>

<6:54   *but a few* KJV: *few men* D-R>

6:55   *adhuc viveret: viveret* *D-R; *constituerat: constituit* Weber; *ut nutriret: et nutriret* Weber; *ut regnaret: et regnaret* S-C

6:56   *reversus: et reversus* Weber; *quaerebat: quaerit* Weber

6:57   *Et festinavit* M*Φ^{T}OΩ^{J2}(*et festi* in ras.)agrelv cum LG et G [Quentin's sigla]: *festinavit* Weber, S-C

<6:57   *Wherefore* KJV: *and* D-R; *the affairs of* KJV: omitted in D-R>

6:62   *citius iuramentum: ius iuramenti* Weber

<6:63   *where he* KJV: *and* D-R>

7:1   *primo: et primo* Weber

7:2   *in domum: domum* S-C; *adduceret: adducerent* S-C

7:3   *rex* Δ^{M}* cum X [Quentin's sigla]: *res* Weber, S-C

<7:3   *when he knew it he said* KJV: *the king was known to him: and he sayd* D-R; *Let me not see* KJV: *Shew me not* D-R>

<7:5   *high* KJV: omitted in D-R>

7:6   *eius omnes: eius* Weber; *disperdit: dispersit* S-C

<7:6   *driven* KJV: *destroyed* D-R>

<7:7   *some* KJV: *a* D-R; *and let him* KJV: *that he may* D-R>

7:7   *ut: et* Weber; *puniat: puniit* Weber

<7:8   *one* KJV? (*a friend*): omitted in D-R>

7:9   *ut videret exterminium quod fecit Iudas, et* Ω^{SJ}*aest [Quentin's sigla, without punctuation]: *ut videret exterminium quod fecit Iudas, sed et* S-C; *et* Weber *sacerdotium: sacerdotio* Weber

<7:9   *made high priest* KJV: *appointed to the priesthood* D-R>

7:10   *fratres*: *ad fratres* S-C

<7:11   *But* KJV: *And* D-R>

<7:16   *threescore* D-R/C: *threescore men* D-R>

7:18   *est*: *est ei* Weber; *iudicium in eis*: *iudicium* Weber

7:19   *Bethzecha*: *Bethzetha* Weber; *refugerant*: *effugerant* S-C

<7:21   *but* KJV: *and* D-R; *did what he could* D-R: literally, *was busy*; *to maintain* KJVn (*to defend*): *for the principalitie* D-R; *chief* KJV (*high*): omitted in D-R>

<7:22   *they* D-R/C: *al that* D-R; *the* KJV: *their* D-R;

7:23   *filiis*: *in filios* Weber

7:24   *Iudaeae*: *Iudae* Weber

7:25   *erant*: *sunt* Weber

<7:26   *principal* KJV (*honourable*): *nobler* D-R; *was a great enemy* D-Rn (*the most terrible* for *a great*): *practised emnities* D-R>

7:28   *ut*: *et* Weber

7:32   *Nicanoris exercitu*: *Nicanoris* Weber

<7:33   *this* KJV: *these wordes* D-R>

<7:34   *But* KJV: *And* D-R>

7:38   *gladio*: *in gladio* S-C

<7:38   *any longer* KJV: omitted in D-R>

<7:40   *But* KJV: *And* D-R>

7:41   *quia*: *qui* Weber

<7:41   *blasphemed* KJV: *because they blasphemed* D-R>

<7:42   *even* KJV: omitted in D-R>

7:42   *contere*: *percute* Weber

7:44   *cecidit*: *cecidisset* S-C

7:45   *Adazer*: *Adasor* Weber; *in Gazara*: *Gazera* Weber

7:46   *Iudaeae*: *Iudae* Weber

7:47   *in*: *et* Weber

7:49   *mensis* $\Delta^{L}Z^*$ cum G [Quentin's sigla]: *die mensis* Weber, S-C

<7:50   *short time* KJV (*litle while*): *few dayes* D-R>

<8:1   *and strong* KJV (*valiant* for *strong*): *of power* D-R>

8:2   *Et audierunt*: *audierunt* Weber; *fecerunt*: *faciunt* Weber

<8:2   *had done* KJV: *did* D-R; *how* KJV: *that* D-R>

<8:3   *had done* KJV: *did* D-R; *had brought under* D-R/C: *brought into* D-R; *had gotten possession of* KJV (*had conquered*): *possessed* D-R>

588

8:3   *potestatem*: *potestate* Weber

8:4   *locaque quae*: *locos qui* Weber

<8:4   *had* [both times] KJV: omitted in D-R>

<8:5   *had* [both times] KJV: omitted in D-R>

8:5   *Ceterorum*: *Citiorum* Weber; *tulerant*: *tulerunt* Weber; *in bello*: *bello* Weber

<8:6   *how* KJV: *that* D-R>

8:6   *elefantos et equitatum et currus*: *elefantos* Weber

<8:7   *how* KJV: *that* D-R>

8:7   *regnarent*: *regaverint* Weber

8:8   *Indorum*: *Medorum* Weber

<8:8   *of* [both times] S: omitted in D-R>

<8:11 *had* D-R/C: omitted in D-R>

<8:12 *had* KJV: omitted in D-R>

8:12   *erant longe*: *longe* Weber

<8:13 *That* D-R/C: *But* D-R; *a kingdom* KJV: *reigne* D-R>

8:13   *regnabant, quos autem vellent regno deturbabant*: *regnabant* Weber

8:15   *et viginti* Θ^{S2} cum LXG et G [Quentin's sigla]: *viginti* Weber, S-C

<8:17 *a league of* KJV: omitted in D-R>

8:20   *conscribere*: *conscribi* Weber

8:22   *rescriptum est*: *rescriptum* Weber; *miserunt in*: *miserunt* Weber

<8:22 *graven* D-R/C: omitted in D-R>

<8:26 *or* [first time] KJV: *nor* D-R; *or* [second and third times] D-R/C: omitted in D-R; *or* [fourth time] KJV: omitted in D-R>

<8:27 *also* KJV: *also and* D-R>

8:27   *ex animo*: *corde pleno* *D-R [cf. 1 Mcc 8:25]

<8:28 *either* KJV (*Neither*): omitted in D-R; *or* [all three times] KJV: omitted in D-R>

8:28   *custodient*: *custodiant* Weber

9:1   *ut*: *ubi* Weber

9:2   *Masaloth*: *Mesaloth* Weber

<9:2   *many people* KJV (*much* for *many*): *of men manie soules* D-R>

9:3   *In*: *et* Weber; *et quinquagesimi*: *quinquagesimi et* Weber

9:4   *Beream*: *Berea* Weber

<9:4   *with* KJV: omitted in D-R>

9:7   *et confractus*: *confractus* Weber

<9:9   *But* KJV: *And* D-R; *for we are but* KJV: *and we are* D-R>

9:9   *revertamur: revertemur* Weber; *et tunc: et* Weber

<9:10   *and* KJV: *to* D-R>

9:16   *et eos: et* Weber

9:17   *et ex: et* Weber

9:19   *suum, et sepelierunt eum in sepulchro patrum suorum in civitate: suum in* Weber

<9:20   *for him* KJV: omitted in D-R>

9:21   *faciebat populum: faciebat* Weber

<9:22   *But* D-R/C: *And* D-R>

9:22   *fecit et magnitudinis eius: fecit* Weber

<9:23   *began to put forth their heads* KJV: *came forth* D-R>

9:29   *inimicos: inimicos nostros* S-C; *gentis: genti* Weber

<9:29   *our* S-C: *the* D-R>

9:30   *esse pro eo: esse* Weber; *nobis: nobis in* S-C

9:35   *Et Ionathas: et* Weber; *et rogavit: ut rogaret* *D-R; *commodarent: commendaret* Weber

9:36   *Madaba: Madabas* Weber

9:37   *Madaba: Nadaba* Weber

9:39   *levaverunt: elevaverunt* S-C

9:40   *ex: cum* Weber; *montes: montem* Weber

9:42   *vindictam sanguinis: vindicta sanguinem* Weber

9:43   *magna: multa* Weber

9:45   *devertendi: divertendi* S-C

9:47   *Ionathas: Ionatha* Weber; *devertit: divertit* S-C

<9:47   *but* KJV: *and* D-R>

9:48   *desiluit: dissiliit* S-C; *Ionathas et qui cum eo erant in Iordanem: Ionathan* Weber

9:49   *sunt in: sunt* Weber

9:50   *in Bethel: Bethel* Weber; *Tamnata: Tamnatan* Weber

<9:51   *war* D-R/C: *emnities* D-R>

9:52   *Gazaram: Gazara* Weber

9:53   *custodiam: custodia* Weber

<9:54   *court of the* KJV (*court* in italics in D-R/C): omitted in D-R>

9:55   *paralysi: paralysin* Weber

<9:55   *so that he could no more* KJV: *neither could he . . . any more* D-R>

<9:58 *held a council* KJV: *thought* D-R; *and* KJV: omitted in D-R>

9:58 *confidenter: confidentes* Weber; *omnes in: omnes* S-C

9:62 *Bethbessen: Bethbessi* Weber; *extruxit: struxit* Weber

<9:63 *when* KJV: omitted in D-R; *he* KJV: *and* D-R>

9:63 *cognovit: agnovit* Weber; *Iudaea: Iuda* Weber

9:64 *desuper: desuper a* Weber; *Bethbessen: Bethbesse* Weber

<9:65 *But* KJV: *And* D-R; *of men* D-R/C: omitted in D-R>

9:66 *tabernaculis: tabernaculo* Weber

9:73 *Machmas: Machemas* Weber

10:5 *omnium malorum: omnium* Weber

10:6 *fabricare: fabrificare* S-C

<10:8 *had given* KJV: *gaue* D-R>

10:8 *rex: rex in* Weber

10:11 *struerent: instruerent* S-C

10:14 *Bethsura: Bethsuram* Weber; *remanserunt: remanserant* Weber

10:15 *promisit: promiserat* *D-R

<10:15 *had done* KJV: *did* D-R; *had endured* KJV: *endured* D-R>

<10:16 *Now therefore* KJV: *and now* D-R>

10:19 *potens sis: potens* Weber

<10:19 *of great* KJV: *mightie of* D-R>

<10:20 *now therefore* KJV (*Wherefore now*): *& now* D-R>

10:20 *et quae: ut quae* Weber; *sentias nobiscum: sentias* Weber

10:21 *stola sancta: stolam sanctam* Weber

10:22 *est nimis: est* Weber

10:24 *illis: illi* Weber; *sint: sit* Weber; *adiutorium: adiutorio* Weber

<10:24 *offer* KJV (*promise*; in brackets in KJV): omitted in D-R>

10:25 *scripsit eis: scripsit* Weber

<10:27 *Wherefore* KJV: *And* D-R>

10:30 *hodierno die: hodierno* Weber

10:32 *ut: et* Weber

10:33 *resolvantur: solvantur* S-C

10:34 *dies post: post* Weber

10:35 *habebit: habeat* Weber; *negotia: negotii* Weber

<10:35 *against them or* KJV (*with* for *against*): *and* D-R; *any* KJV: *against any* D-R>

10:36 *Et: et ut* Weber

10:37 *supra: super* S-C; *ambulent in: ambulent* Weber

10:38 *aliae: alii* S-C

10:39 *Ptolomaida: Ptolomaidam* Weber

<10:39 *I give* KJV: *which I haue geuen* D-R; *free* KJV: omitted in D-R>

10:40 *do singulis annis: singulis annis dabo* Weber

10:41 *fuerit: fuit* Weber

<10:42 *shall* D-R/C: *let these* D-R>

10:43 *fugerint: confugerint* S-C; *est in: est* S-C; *obnoxii: obnoxios* Weber; *dimittantur: dimittatis* Weber

<10:45 *as also* KJV: *and* D-R>

<10:46 *for* KJV: *and* D-R>

<10:47 *peace* KJV: *the wordes of peace* D-R; *always* KJV: *al dayes* D-R>

10:48 *ad: contra* S-C

10:49 *duo reges: reges* Weber; *Demetrii: Alexandri* Weber; *Alexander: Demetrius* Weber

10:52 *regressus: ingressus* Weber

<10:54 *now therefore* KJV: *and now* D-R; *thee and her gifts worthy of thee* S-C: *thee gifts, and to her, dignitie* D-R>

10:54 *ero: ego ero* S-C; *dabo tibi dona et ipsi: ipsi* Weber; *dignitatem: digna te* S-C

10:56 *quae: quod* S-C; *occurre mihi: occurre* Weber; *Ptolomaidae: Ptolomaidam* S-C

10:57 *Ptolomaidam: Ptolomaidae* Weber

<10:59 *and* KJV: *to* D-R>

10:60 *Ptolomaidam: Ptolomaidem* Weber

<10:61 *men of a wicked life* KJV: *wicked men* D-R; *to accuse* KJV: *soliciting against* D-R>

10:62 *expoliari: spoliari* S-C; *vestimentis: vestibus* S-C; *indui: induit* Weber

10:63 *principibus suis: principibus* Weber; *medium: medio* Weber

<10:64 *when* KJV: *it came to passe, as* D-R>

10:66 *Ionathas: Ionathan* Weber

10:69 *Demetrius Rex: Demetrius* Weber; *Apollonium ducem: Apollonium* Weber

10:70 *adversum nos exerces: exerces* Weber

10:72 *quis sum: qui sim* Weber

10:73 *equitatum et: equitatum* Weber

10:74 *occurrit: concurrit* Weber

<10:75 *but* KJV: *and* D-R>

10:76 *intra civitatem: in civitate* S-C

10:80 *eius et iecerunt iacula in populum: eius* Weber

10:81 *praeceperat: praecepit* Weber

<10:81 *so* KJV: omitted in D-R>

10:83 *per: in* Weber; *idolium* Sabatier: *idolum* Weber, S-C; *ut ibi: ut* Weber

<10:84 *But* KJV: *And* D-R>

10:84 *omnes: eos* Weber

10:86 *Ascalona: Ascalonem* S-C

11:1 *oram: ora* Weber

11:2 *ei civitates et occurrebant ei: ei* Weber

11:4 *succensum igni: succensum* Weber; *fecerant: fecerat* Weber

<11:4 *suburbs* KJV: *rest* D-R>

<11:5 *had done* KJV: *did* D-R; *but* KJV: *and* D-R>

11:7 *est in: est* Weber

11:10 *Paenitet: paenituit* Weber

11:12 *abalienavit: alienavit* S-C; *manifestae factae: manifestatae* S-C

11:14 *Alexander: Ptolomeus* Weber; *locis illis: locis illius* Weber

<11:14 *had* KJV: omitted in D-R>

<11:15 *when* KJV: omitted in D-R; *he* KJV: *and* D-R; *give him* D-R/C: *him into* D-R>

11:15 *bellum: bello* Weber

11:17 *Zabdiel: Gaddihel* Weber

<11:18 *after* KJV: omitted in D-R>

11:21 *Regem Demetrium: regem* Weber

11:22 *venit: venit ad* S-C; *obsideret arcem: obsideret* Weber

<11:22 *and* KJV: *to* D-R>

11:23 *obsidere: obsideri* Weber

<11:23 *still* KJV (in brackets in KJV): omitted in D-R>

11:24 *Ptolomaidam: Ptolomaidae* Weber

11:26 *in conspectu omnium amicorum suorum: ante conspectu amicorum omnium* Weber

<11:27 *the honours* KJV: *other thinges . . . precious* D-R>

11:28 *Iudaeam et tres toparcias et Samariam et confines eius: Iudaeam toparcias id est et Samariam* Weber

<11:31 *send you here* KJV: *haue sent to you* D-R>

11:34 *Lydan*: *Lyddam* Weber; *Ramathan*: *Ramathae* Weber; *sequestrari*: *sequestra* Weber

<11:34 *the payments* KJV: *these thinges* D-R>

11:38 *videns*: *vidit* Weber; *omnes*: *omnis* Weber

<11:39 *who, seeing* KJV: *and he saw* D-R; *went* KJV: *& he went* D-R>

11:39 *murmurabat*: *murmurat* Weber; *Arabem*: *Arabum* Weber

<11:40 *had done* KJV: *did* D-R; *how* KJV: omitted in D-R>

<11:41 *desiring* D-R/C: omitted in D-R>

11:41 *eiceret*: *eicerent* Weber

11:43 *in auxilium mihi viros*: *viros in auxilium* Weber

<11:45 *to the number of* KJV: omitted in D-R>

11:50 *obpugnare*: *obpugnantes* Weber

11:51 *arma sua*: *arma* Weber

11:53 *alienavit*: *abalienavit* S-C; *Ionatha*: *Ionathan* Weber

<11:53 *but* KJV: *and* D-R>

11:54 *et regnavit*: *qui regnavit* *D-R; *inposuit sibi*: *inposuit* Weber

11:55 *omnes*: *omnis* Weber

<11:55 *Demetrius, who* KJV: *him: and he* D-R>

<11:57 *high* KJV: omitted in D-R; *ruler* KJV: omitted in D-R; *and* KJV: omitted in D-R>

11:58 *aurea in*: *aurea et* Weber

<11:58 *clothed* KJV: omitted in D-R>

11:60 *Ascalona*: *Ascalonem* S-C

11:61 *erant in circuitu civitatis*: *in circuitu erant civitates* Weber; *ea*: *eas* Weber

<11:61 *all* D-R/C *the suburbs* KJV: *the thinges that were* D-R; *about* KJVn (*thereabout*): *about the citie* D-R>

11:67 *Ionathas*: *Ionatha* Weber; *campo*: *campum* Weber

11:68 *ei in* Ω^S [Quentin's siglum]: *in* Weber, S-C

11:72 *est Ionathas*: *est* Weber; *eos in fugam*: *illos* Weber

11:73 *eo*: *eo omnes* S-C

<11:73 *all* S-C: omitted in D-R; *the enemies* D-R/C (in italics): omitted in D-R>

11:74 *regressus*: *reversus* S-C; *Ionathas*: *Ionatha* Weber

12:1 *iuvat*: *iuvat et* Weber; *misit eos*: *misit* Weber

<12:1 *and* S: omitted in D-R>

12:2 *Spartiatas*: *Spartas* Weber

12:3 *intraverunt in*: *intraverunt* S-C; *renovaremus*: *renovetis* Weber; *pristinam*: *pristinum* S-C

12:5 *hoc*: *hoc est* S-C

12:7 *ab Ario*: *a Dario* Weber

<12:7 *then* KJV: omitted in D-R; *to signify* KJV: omitted in D-R>

<12:10 *lest* KJV: *lest perhaps* D-R; *altogether* KJV: omitted in D-R>

12:11 *et in*: *et* Weber

12:16 *Antiochi filium*: *Antiochi* Weber; *Antipatrem*: *Antipatrum* Weber

12:17 *et reddant*: *ut reddant* Weber

12:19 *hoc*: *hoc est* S-C; *Oniae*: *Onias* Weber

12:20 *Arius, rex Spartiatarum, Oniae, sacerdoti magno, salutem*: *Rex Spartiarum / Onias Ionathae sacerdoti magno salutem* Weber

12:23 *vestra nostra*: *vestrae nostrae* S-C

12:24 *regressi*: *egressi* Weber

12:25 *dederat*: *dedit* *D-R

12:28 *formidaverunt*: *formidaverunt in* S-C

12:29 *autem*: *enim* Weber; *lumina*: *luminaria* S-C

<12:29 *for* KJV: *and* D-R>

12:30 *est eos*: *est* Weber; *Ionathas*: *Ionatha* Weber

<12:30 *but* KJV: *and* D-R>

12:32 *perambulavit*: *perambulabat* S-C

<12:36 *mount* D-R/C: *mount of a great height* D-R; *have no communication* D-R/C: *be alone* D-R>

<12:37 *for* KJV (*forasmuch*): *and* D-R>

<12:40 *lest* D-R/C: *lest perhaps* D-R>

12:40 *Bethsan*: *Bethasan* Weber

12:41 *obviam illi*: *obviam* Weber; *Bethsan*: *Bethasan* Weber

<12:42 *when* KJV: omitted in D-R; *he durst not stretch* KJV: *to extend* D-R; *him* KJV: *him: and he feared* D-R>

12:42 *venit Ionathas*: *venit* Weber; *et timuit*: *timuit* S-C

<12:43 *but* KJV: *and* D-R>

<12:45 *therefore* KJV: *And* D-R>

12:46 *fecit Ionathas* Sabatier (*fecit Ionatha*): *fecit* Weber, S-C; *Iudam*: *Iuda* S-C

12:48 *portas civitatis*: *portas* Weber

12:50 *est Ionathas*: *est* Weber

<12:51 *they* KJV: *the matter* D-R; *for* KJV: *vpon* D-R>

<12:52 *Whereupon* KJV: *But* D-R>

12:53 *perdere*: *conterere* S-C

<13:2 *And* KJV: omitted in D-R>

13:2 *et in*: *et* Weber

13:6 *natos quoque nostros*: *natosque vestros* Weber; *gratia*: *gratis* Weber

13:10 *omnes*: *universos* S-C

13:11 *remansit*: *mansit* Weber

13:14 *in loco*: *loco* S-C; *fratris sui Ionathae et quia commissurus esset cum eo proelium*: *Ionathae fratris sui* Weber

13:15 *regis propter negotia quae habuit*: *regis* Weber

<13:16 *But* D-R/C: *And* D-R>

13:17 *loqueretur*: *loquitur* Weber

13:18 *misit*: *misit ei* S-C

13:19 *Et misit pueros et centum talenta, et*: *et* Weber

13:23 *adpropiasset*: *adpropinquasset* S-C; *eius illic*: *eius* Weber

13:35 *respondit ei*: *respondit* Weber

<13:35 *in answer to this request wrote* D-R/C: *according to these wordes answered him, and wrote* D-R>

13:37 *bahem*: *baen* Weber

<13:38 *shall* [first time] KJV: omitted in D-R; *shall* [second time] KJV: *let them* D-R>

13:39 *in Hierusalem*: *Hierusalem* Weber

13:40 *ex*: *in* Weber

13:42 *Simone, summo*: *Simone* Weber

13:43 *conprehendit eam*: *conprehendit* Weber

13:44 *eruperunt qui*: *qui eruperunt* Weber, *eruperant qui* S-C; *civitatem*: *civitate* Weber

13:47 *emundavit*: *mundavit* S-C; *eam*: *ea* Weber

13:49 *ingredi in*: *ingredi* S-C

13:51 *eam*: *ea* Weber; *vicesima die*: *vicesima* Weber

13:54 *quod fortis proelii*: *quod* Weber; *habitavit in*: *habitavit* Weber

14:1 *secundo*: *secundo et* Weber; *exercitum suum*: *exercitus suos* Weber; *abiit in*: *abiit* Weber; *ut expugnaret*: *et expugnare* Weber

14:2 *conprehenderet*: *conprehenderent* Weber; *adduceret*: *adducerent* Weber

14:4 *siluit omnis*: *siluit* Weber

14:8 *terra Iuda*: *terra* Weber

14:10 *Et civitatibus*: *civitatibus* Weber

14:12 *sua, et non*: *nec* Weber

14:16 *esset*: *est* Weber; *Spartiatas*: *Sparta* Weber

14:17 *obtineret omnem*: *obtineret* Weber

14:18 *in tabulis*: *tabulis* Weber; *renovarent*: *renovaret* Weber; *fecerant*: *fecerunt* Weber; *et cum*: *et* Weber

14:20 *principes et civitates*: *princeps et civitatis* Weber

14:22 *amicitiam pristinam*: *amicitiam* Weber

14:23 *Spartiatarum*: *Spartiarum* Weber

14:24 *pondus*: *pondo* S-C

14:26 *Israhel ab eis*: *Israhel* Weber; *Monte*: *montem* Weber

14:27 *Et hoc est exemplum scripturae*: ¶ "*Octava*: *octava* Weber

14:28 *regionis*: *regis* Weber

<14:33 *lieth* KJV: *was* D-R>

<14:34 *lieth* KJV: *was* D-R>

14:35 *posuerunt eum*: *posuerunt* Weber

14:36 *ipsorum et*: *ipsorum* Weber

14:37 *ad tutamentum*: *tutamentum* Weber

<14:40 *had* [all three times] KJV: omitted in D-R>

<14:41 *had* D-R/C: omitted in D-R>

14:43 *ut scribantur*: *scribantur* S-C

14:47 *placuit ei*: *placuit* Weber

15:3 *et electam*: *electum* Weber

15:4 *regionem*: *regiones* Weber

15:5 *me omnes*: *me* Weber

15:7 *struxisti*: *construxisti* S-C

15:8 verse omitted Weber

15:10 *omnes*: *omnis* Weber

<15:12 *had* KJV: omitted in D-R>

15:14 *ingredi vel egredi*: *egredi* Weber

<15:19 *their cities or* KJV: *and their cities, and their* D-R>

15:22 *Ariarathi*: *Arahae* Weber

15:23 *Lampsaco*: *Samsamae* Weber; *Spartiatis*: *Spartanis* Weber; *in Delum*: *Delo* Weber; *in Myndum*: *Mydo* Weber; *in Sicyonem*: *Sicyone* Weber; *in Cariam*: *Cariae* Weber; *in Samum*: *Samum* Weber; *in Pam-*

philiam: *Pamphiliam* Weber; *in Lyciam*: *Lyciam* Weber; *in Alicar-nassum*: *Alacarnasum* Weber; *et in Choo et in Siden et in Aradon et*: *et* Weber; *Faselida*: *Faselida et Choo et Siden et Arado* Weber

15:24 *sacerdotum, et populo Iudaeorum*: *sacerdotum* Weber

15:25 *Dora*: *Doram* S-C

15:26 *ad eum*: *ei* Weber

15:27 *inrupit*: *rupit* S-C

15:28 *Athenobium*: *Athenovium* Weber

15:29 *in terra*: *super terram* Weber

15:30 *quibus*: *in quibus* S-C

15:32 *Athenobius*: *Athenovius* Weber

15:33 *respondit ei*: *respondit* Weber

<15:35 *yet* KJV (in italics in D-R/C): omitted in D-R; *will* KJV: omitted in D-R>

15:35 *Ioppe*: *Ioppen* Weber; *ei Athenobius*: *illi* Weber

15:39 *Caedronem*: *Gedorem* S-C

15:40 *Caedronem*: *Gedorem* S-C

16:1 *Cendebeus in populo ipsorum*: *Cendebeus* Weber

<16:1 *had done* KJV: *did* D-R>

16:2 *filios suos*: *filios* S-C; *mei et domus patris mei*: *mei* Weber

16:3 *fratres*: *fratris* Weber

16:9 *Caedronem*: *Caedronam* Weber

16:10 *est in*: *est* Weber

16:14 *regione Iudaeae*: *regione* Weber; *descendit in*: *descendit* Weber; *hic est*: *hic* Weber

<16:14 *and Judas, his sons* KJV: *his sonne, and Iudas* D-R>

16:18 *traderet ei*: *traderet* We`ber

16:23 *struxit*: *extruxit* S-C

2 MACCABEES

1:2 *locutus est*: *est* Weber; *servos suos fideles* Gryson 135 E: *servorum suorum fidelium* Weber, S-C

<1:2 *made with* KJV: *spake to* D-R>

1:4 *suis*: *eius* Weber

<1:4 *send you* KJV: *make* D-R>

1:11 *gratias agimus*: *gratias* Weber
1:12 *nos et sanctam civitatem*: *nos* Weber
1:13 *sacerdotum*: *sacerdotis* Weber
1:14 *Etenim*: *ut enim* Weber
<1:14 *marry* KJV: *dwel with* D-R>
1:15 *eas*: *eam* *D-R
1:16 *eos qui*: *qui* Weber
1:18 *vicesima die*: *vicesima* Weber; *ut*: *ut et* S-C
1:19 *altario*: *altari* S-C; *altus et*: *altus* Weber
1:27 *Gentibus, et*: *gentibus* Weber
1:28 *opprimentes nos*: *opprimentes* Weber
1:33 *est res*: *essent haec* Weber; *erant*: *fuerant* S-C
<1:33 *had* KJV: omitted in D-R>
1:34 *templum ut probaret quod factum erat*: *templum* Weber
1:35 *cum probasset, sacerdotibus donavit multa bona et alia atque alia munera, et accipiens manu sua tribuebat eis*: *si quibus donaverat rex multa bona accipiebat ex hoc et tribuebat* Weber
1:36 *hunc locum*: *hoc* Weber
2:1 *transmigrabantur*: *transmigrabant* S-C
<2:4 *being warned by God* KJV (*of* for *by*): *by the diuine answer made to him* D-R>
<2:5 *so* KJV: omitted in D-R>
<2:6 *that* KJV: *withal, that* D-R; *but* KJV: *and* D-R>
<2:7 *saying* KJV: *he sayd: that* D-R>
2:9 *Magnifice etenim sapientiam tractabat, et*: *et* Weber
2:10 *holocaustum, sic et Salomon oravit, et descendit ignis de caelo et consumpsit holocaustum*: *holocaustum* Weber
2:11 *comestum*: *mundatum* Weber; *peccato*: *peccato et* Weber
2:13 *regionibus*: *regibus* Weber
2:14 *deciderant*: *didicerat* Weber
2:15 *desideratis*: *desiderastis* Weber
2:16 *igitur*: *ergo* S-C
2:23 *et leges quae abolitae*: *ut leges quae abolendae* Weber
2:26 *facilius*: *facile* Weber
2:29 *auctoribus*: *auctori* Weber
2:30 *curat*: *conatur* Weber

2:31   *et ordinare*: *ordinare* *D-R

<2:30   *for* D-R/C: *also in* D-R>

2:32   *brevianti*: *brevitati* Weber

2:33   *igitur*: *ergo* S-C

3:2   *ut et*: *ut* Weber

<3:4   *one* KJV: omitted in D-R>

3:5   *Et* Gryson 135 E: *Sed* S-C, Weber [without capitalization]

<3:6   *to bring all* KJV: *al might fal* D-R>

3:8   *iter est*: *iter* Weber

<3:9   *And* KJV: *But* D-R>

3:9   *aperuit*: *apparuit* Weber

3:13   *regi ea esse*: *regiae* Weber

<3:13   *the money* D-R/C: *they* D-R>

<3:16   *whosoever* KJV (*whoso*): *he that* D-R>

3:16   *videret*: *videbat* S-C

<3:17   *the man was so compassed with sadness and horror* KJV (*feare* for *sadness*): *there was a certaine pensiuenes powred about the man, and horrour* D-R; *that* KJV: *wherby* D-R; *was* KJV: *was made* D-R; *what* KJV: *the* D-R>

3:17   *quae*: *quem* S-C

3:18   *gregatim*: *congregati* Weber

<3:19   *some* KJV: omitted in D-R>

<3:21   *would have moved any one to pity* KJV (*would haue pitied a man*): *was miserable* D-R>

<3:22   *safe and sure* KJV: *with al integritie* D-R>

3:24   *omnipotentis Dei*: *Omnipotentis* Weber

<3:25   *ran fiercely and* KJV: *with feircenes* D-R>

3:29   *mutus atque omni spe et salute privatus*: *mutus* Weber

<3:29   *of recovery* KJV (*life* for *recovery*): *and health* D-R>

3:30   *magnificavit*: *magnificabat* S-C

<3:30   *had* KJV: omitted in D-R>

<3:31   *Then* KJV: *And then* D-R; *ready to give up the ghost* KJV: *at the very last gaspe* D-R>

3:31   *ut vitem*: *et vitem* Weber

3:34   *a Deo*: *ab eo* Weber

3:35   *promissis*: *promisit* Weber

<3:37   *asked* KJV: *had asked* D-R>

3:37   *esset: est* Weber

<3:38   *that* KJV: *the* D-R>

4:8   *trecenta sexaginta: sexaginta et trecenta* Weber

4:10   *annuisset: agnovisset* Weber

<4:11   *that* D-R/C: omitted in D-R>

4:11   *legatione legitima: legationem legitimam* Weber

<4:13   *increase* KJV: *certaine increase* D-R>

4:17   *hoc: haec* Weber; *declarabit: declaravit* Weber

<4:18   *the* KJV: *and the* D-R>

<4:19   *to carry* KJV: *carying* D-R; *but* D-R/C: *which* D-R>

4:19   *sacrificium: sacrificiis* Weber; *adportaverant: asportaverant* S-C

4:20   *Itaque* Gryson 135 E: *Sed* S-C, Weber [without capitalization]; *haec oblata: hae oblatae* S-C; *misit* Gryson 135 E: *miserat* Weber, S-C; *triremium: triremis* Weber

<4:20   *the money* KJV (*This* for *the*): *these* D-R>

4:21   *Aegyptum: Aegypto* Weber; *primates Ptolomei: primatus* Weber

<4:21   *to treat with* D-R/C: *because of* D-R; *King Philometor* S: *Ptolomee Philometor the king* D-R; *and* D-R/C: *when* D-R>

<4:22   *where* KJV: *And* D-R>

4:22   *inde in: inde* Weber

<4:23   *Three years afterwards* KJV: *And after the time of three yeares* D-R; *to carry* KJV (*beare* for *carry*): *carying* D-R>

4:24   *Iasoni: Iasonem* Weber

<4:25   *high* KJV: omitted in D-R>

4:26   *circumscripserat* Gryson 135 E: *captivaverat* Weber, S-C

<4:27   *took no care* KJV (*good order* for *care*): *did nothing* D-R>

4:27   *arci: arce* Weber

4:28   *regem sunt: regem* Weber; *evocati: vocati* Weber

4:29   *Et Menelaus: Menelaus* Weber; *amotus est a: motus est* Weber; *Cypriis: Cypris* Weber

<4:30   *When* KJV (*While*): *And when* D-R>

4:32   *e templo: templo* Weber; *Tyri: Tyro* Weber

<4:34   *he went* D-R/C: *when he was come* D-R; *persuaded* KJV: *had perswaded* D-R; *and* S: omitted in D-R>

4:34   *de asylo: asylo* Weber

4:35   *sed*: *sed et* Weber

<4:36   *And* KJV: *But* D-R>

4:37   *animo*: *ad animum* Weber; *Antiochus propter Onian*: *Antiochus* Weber

4:38   *Accensisque*: *accensusque* Weber; *iubet*: *iussit* *D-R; *in eodem*: *eodem* Weber; *in quo*: *quo* Weber; *dignam*: *condignam* S-C; *retribuente poenam*: *poenam tribuente* Weber

<4:38   *being inflamed to anger* KJV (*kindled with* for *inflamed to*): *his hart being incensed* D-R>

<4:40   *Wherefore* KJV (*Whereupon*): *But* D-R>

4:41   *arripere*: *arripuere* S-C; *iacere*: *iecere* S-C

4:42   *versi*: *conversi* S-C

<4:45   *But Menelaus, being* KJV: *And when Menelaus was* D-R>

4:45   *pecunias dare*: *pecunias* Weber

<4:46   *to be of another mind* KJV: *from his purpose* D-R>

4:47   *iudicarentur, hos*: *iudicarentur* Weber

4:49   *Tyrii*: *Tyri* Weber

<4:49   *liberal* KJV? (*honourably*): *very liberal* D-R>

<4:50   *so* KJV: omitted in D-R>

4:50   *malitia*: *malitia et* Weber

<5:3   *one against another* KJV: *and that there were encounterings together neere hand* D-R>

5:3   *destrictis*: *districtis* S-C

<5:5   *Now* KJV: *But* D-R>

<5:6   *not considering* KJV: *nor considered* D-R; *they had been enemies, and not citizens, whom he conquered* KJV (*his countrey men* for *citizens*; *they had been enemies* in roman type in KJV): *he should take the victorious spoiles of the enemies, and not of his citizens* D-R>

<5:7   *Yet* KJV (*Howbeit*): *And* D-R; *for the reward* KJV: omitted in D-R>

5:7   *confusionem accepit*: *confusione cepit* Weber

5:8   *exitium*: *exitum* Weber; *tyranno*: *tyrannum* Weber

5:9   *patria sua*: *patria* Weber

<5:10   *But* D-R/C: *And* D-R>

5:11   *itaque*: *ita* Weber

5:13   *seniorum et*: *seniorum* Weber

<5:13   *old* KJV: *old, and* D-R>

5:14   *vincti, non minus autem venundati*: *vincti* Weber

5:15   *est etiam*: *est* Weber

5:17   *Deus*: *Dominus* Weber

5:19   *Deus*: *Dominus* Weber

<5:20   *communicate in* KJV: *be partaker of* D-R>

5:20   *socius*: *socius et* Weber; *omnipotentis*: *omnipotentis est* S-C

<5:22   *He* D-R/C: *And he* D-R; *but* D-R/C: omitted in D-R>

<5:24   *and* KJV: omitted in D-R; *younger sort* KJV: *young ones* D-R>

6:4   *comesationibus Gentium*: *comesationibus* Weber

6:9   *Gentium*: *gentilium* Weber

<6:11   *of the day* KJV: omitted in D-R>

6:14   *venerit*: *advenerit* S-C

<6:16   *And* KJV: *certes* D-R>

<6:18   *Eleazar* KJV: *Therfore Eleazarus* D-R; *mouth* KJV: *mouth gaping* D-R>

6:18   *Eleazarus, unus*: *Eleazarus* Weber

6:19   *gloriosissimam*: *gloriosam* Weber; *amplectens*: *conplectens* S-C

6:20   *oporteret*: *oportet* Weber

6:21   *ut*: *et* Weber

6:22   *veterem viri*: *veterem* Weber; *faciebant*: *facerent* Weber

6:23   *cogitare coepit*: *cogitationem cepit* Weber; *ingenitae*: *ingenuitatem* Weber; *conversationis actus*: *conversationis* Weber

<6:23   *dignity* D-R/C: *worthie preeminence* D-R; *inbred honour of his grey head* KJV (without *inbred*): *houre heares of natural nobilitie* D-R; *good life and conversation from a child* D-R/C: *doinges from a childe of very good conuersation* D-R>

6:24   *aetati nostrae*: *aetatem nostram* Weber; *arbitrantes*: *arbitrati* Weber

6:26   *manum*: *manus* Weber; *neque vivens neque*: *nec vivus nec* S-C

6:27   *vita*: *vitam* Weber

6:29   *versi*: *conversi* S-C

6:30   *possem*: *possim* Weber

<6:31   *Thus* D-R/C: *And . . . certes* D-R>

<7:1   *It* KJV: *And it* D-R; *for which end they* D-R/C: omitted in D-R>

7:1   *una cum matre sua*: *cum matre* Weber; *edere contra fas*: *contra fas ad* Weber

7:4   *praecidi*: *praescindi* S-C

<7:5   *alive* KJV: *breathing* D-R; *and* KJV: omitted in D-R>

7:5   *sartagine*: *sartaginem* Weber

7:6   *aspiciet*: *aspiciat* Weber; *in protestatione*: *protestationem* Weber

7:7   *detracta*: *abstracta* S-C

7:9   *sic ait*: *ait* Weber

7:10   *inluditur*: *inludebatur* Weber

7:12   *nihilum*: *nihili* Weber

<7:15   *the king* KJV: *him* D-R>

7:17   *Tu autem patienter*: *patienter* Weber; *magnam potestatem*: *magna potestas* Weber

<7:17   *a while* KJV: omitted in D-R>

7:18   *ducebant*: *ducebant et* Weber

<7:18   *being ready* KJV: *beginning* D-R>

<7:21   *and* KJV (*Yea*): omitted in D-R>

<7:23   *But* D-R/C: *But in deede* D-R>

7:24   *iuramento*: *cum iuramento* S-C; *necessarias ei*: *necessarias* Weber

7:25   *suadebat ei*: *suadebat* Weber

7:27   *novem mensibus*: *decem menses* Weber

7:28   *nate, ut*: *nate* Weber; *ad caelum*: *in caelum* Weber

7:29   *fiet*: *fit* Weber; *effectus particeps*: *effectus* Weber

<7:29   *thou* D-R/C: *shal it come to passe, that thou* D-R>

7:33   *Dominus, Deus*: *Dominus* Weber

7:36   *superbiae tuae*: *superbiae* Weber; *solves*: *exsolves* S-C

7:37   *sicut et*: *sicut* Weber

<7:37   *like* KJV (*as*): *as also* D-R>

7:41   *autem post filios*: *autem* Weber; *consumpta*: *consummata* Weber

<7:42   *But* D-R/C: omitted in D-R>

7:42   *dictum est*: *dictum* Weber

8:1   *eos*: *amicos et eos* S-C; *permanserunt*: *permanserant* Weber; *ad se*: *ad* Weber; *virorum*: *viros* Weber

<8:1   *friends and* S-C: omitted in D-R; *assembled* KJV: *brought out to them* D-R>

8:2   *calcabatur et*: *calcabatur* Weber

<8:3   *city that was destroyed* KJV (*city sore defaced*): *destruction of the citie* D-R>

8:9   *ei de*: *ei* Weber; *ei et*: *ei* Weber; *militari et in bellicis rebus experientissimo*: *militari* Weber

8:10   *ut regi tributum quod Romanis*: *regi ut tributum Romanis quod* Weber; *talentum*: *talentorum* S-C

<8:11   *wherefore* KJV: *and* D-R; *to invite* D-R/C: *calling* D-R; *they should have* KJV: *he would sel* D-R>

8:11   *Iudaicorum*: *Iudaeorum* Weber

<8:12   *that the enemy was at hand* KJV (*army* for *enemy*): omitted in D-R>

<8:13   *And* D-R/C: omitted in D-R>

<8:14   *others sold all that they had left* KJV: *and others if they had any thing left, sold it* D-R>

8:14   *eis*: *ei* S-C; *comminus*: *in comminus* Weber

8:15   *et si*: *si* Weber; *testamentum tamen*: *testamentum* Weber

8:17   *loco sancto*: *in locum sanctum* Weber; *ludibrio*: *ludibria* Weber

8:18   *potest et*: *potest* Weber

8:19   *et quod*: *et* Weber; *Sennacerib*: *Sennacherim* Weber; *perierunt*: *ut perierunt* Weber

8:20   *e*: *de* S-C

8:23   *adiutorii*: *adiutorio* Weber

8:26   *reverterunt*: *reversi sunt* S-C

8:29   *itaque*: *ita* Weber

<8:29   *When* KJV: *therfore* D-R>

<8:30   *Moreover* KJV: *And* D-R>

8:33   *epinicia*: *epicinia* Weber; *in Hierosolymis*: *Hierosolymis* S-C; *eum*: *eos* Weber; *incenderat*: *incenderant* Weber; *quoddam domicilium*: *quoddam domicilio* Weber

9:2   *in eam*: *ea* Weber, *in eam civitatem* *D-R; *templum*: *templa* Weber

9:4   *in ira*: *ira* Weber; *currum suum*: *currum* Weber

9:5   *Dominus, Deus*: *Dominus* Weber

9:7   *hoc*: *haec* Weber; *adcelerari*: *adcelerare* Weber; *vexari*: *vexare* Weber

<9:7   *so that* KJV: *and* D-R>

<9:8   *Thus* KJV: *And* D-R>

9:9   *viventes*: *viventis* S-C

<9:9   *he lived . . . his flesh* S-C: *his liue flesh* D-R; *sorrow and* KJV: omitted in D-R>

9:13   *hic*: *haec* Weber

9:15   *habiturum*: *habituros* Weber

<9:17   *Yea* KJV: *Besides these thinges* D-R>

9:17 *se futurum*: *futurum* Weber

<9:18 *of life* KJV (*his health* for *life*; in italics in D-R/C): omitted in D-R>

<9:21 *As for me* KJV: *And I* D-R>

9:21 *regressus*: *reversus* S-C

<9:22 *my life* KJV (*mine health*): *of myself* D-R>

9:22 *habens*: *habeo* Weber

9:23 *pater meus*: *pater* Weber

9:26 *Oro*: *orate* Weber

9:27 *meum et*: *meum* Weber

<9:27 *will* KJV: *and that he wil* D-R>

<10:2 *of the idols* D-R/C: omitted in D-R>

<10:5 *was cleansed again,* KJV *to wit* D-R/C: *happened that . . . was made the purification* D-R; *of* D-R/C: *which was* D-R>

10:5 *purificationem*: *purgationem* Weber; *et quinta*: *quinta* S-C

10:6 *montibus et in speluncis*: *montibus* Weber

<10:7 *now* D-R/C (in italics): omitted in D-R>

<10:9 *this was the end* KJV: *his departure out of life was after this sort* D-R>

10:11 *Hic enim*: *hic* Weber

10:12 *instituit*: *constituit* Weber

10:13 *creditam sibi a Filometore deseruisset et ad Antiochum*: *creditus a Filometore* Weber

10:17 *minus*: *minus a* Weber

10:19 *itemque Zaccheo*: *item Macchabeo* Weber

10:24 *At Timotheus*: *Timotheus* Weber; *equitatu*: *exercitu* Weber

10:25 *adpropiante*: *adpropinquante* S-C; *Dominum*: *Deum* Weber

<10:26 *besought him* KJV: omitted in D-R>

10:26 *adversariis adversaretur*: *adversaretur* Weber

10:34 *intus*: *in turres* Weber; *super*: *supra* S-C

10:36 *adgressi*: *adgressi sunt* S-C

10:38 *fecit in*: *fecit cum* Weber; *illis*: *illi* Weber

<11:1 *A short time* KJV (*Not long*): *But a litle* D-R>

11:3 *quaestum*: *quaestu* Weber

<11:3 *high* KJV: omitted in D-R>

11:5 *quod*: *quae* S-C

11:10 *super eos*: *eos* Weber

11:11 *autem more*: *autem* Weber; *hostibus*: *in hostes* S-C; *equitum*: *equites* Weber

11:13 *omnipotentis Dei*: *Dei* Weber; *nitentes*: *innitentes* S-C

11:17 *sunt*: *fuerant* S-C

11:18 *concessi* S-C [1592 and 1593 editions, according to Weber]: *concessit* Weber

<11:18 *he hath* KJV: *I* D-R>

11:19 *etiam*: *et* S-C; *bonorum*: *honorum* Weber

<11:23 *quietly* KJV: *without truble* D-R; *themselves diligently* D-R/C: *diligence* D-R>

<11:24 *and* KJV (*also*): omitted in D-R>

11:24 *patri meo*: *patri* Weber; *postulare a nobis*: *postulare* Weber

<11:25 *Wherefore* KJV: *therfore* D-R; *and* S: omitted in D-R>

<11:28 *we ourselves* KJV: *yea our selues* D-R>

11:32 *Misimus*: *misi* Weber

11:33 *quintadecima die*: *quintadecima* Weber

<11:34 *The* KJV: *And the* D-R>

<11:35 *Whatsoever* KJV: *Concerning these thinges which* D-R>

11:36 *autem ad regem*: *autem* Weber

11:37 *rescribere*: *scribere* Weber

12:2 *Gennaei*: *Gehennae* Weber

12:4 *commune*: *communem* Weber

<12:4 *Which when they* D-R/C: *Therfore . . . & they* D-R; *suspecting* D-R/C: *& . . . suspecting* D-R>

<12:5 *But* S: omitted in D-R>

12:9 *appareret*: *pareret* Weber

<12:10 *And* D-R/C: omitted in D-R>

12:10 *cum iam*: *cum* Weber

<12:11 *a* S?: *there was a* D-R; *in which* D-R/C: *and* D-R>

12:11 *dextram*: *dextras* Weber; *promittentes se*: *promittentes* Weber

<12:13 *He* KJV: *And he* D-R>

12:16 *innumerabiles*: *inenarrabiles* Weber; *duorum*: *duo* Weber; *infectum*: *interfectorum* S-C

<12:16 *with the blood of the slain* S-C: *died with bloud* D-R>

<12:18 *But* KJV: *and* D-R; *for before he had dispatched any thing* KJV: *and nothing being done* D-R>

12:18 *non conprehenderunt*: *conprehenderunt* Weber

<12:22 *But* KJV: *And* D-R; *often* KJV: *rather* D-R>

12:22 *alius ab alio*: *alius alio* Weber

12:24 *Sosipatris*: *Sosipatri* Weber

12:26 *a Carnio*: *ad Carnion* S-C

<12:26 *to* S-C: *from* D-R; *where he slew* KJV: *hauing slayne* D-R>

<12:27 *And* KJV: omitted in D-R>

12:28 *potestate sua*: *potestate* Weber; *confringit*: *confregit* Weber

12:31 *eis, et*: *eis* Weber

<12:31 *exhorting* KJV (*desiring*): *and exhorting* D-R; *and so* KJV: omitted in D-R; *feast* KJV: *solemne day* D-R>

<12:37 *then* KJV (*And*): omitted in D-R>

<12:40 *of* KJV: *that were in* D-R>

12:41 *fecerat*: *fecerit* Weber

12:42 *oblivioni traderetur*: *obliteraretur* Weber; *sint*: *sunt* S-C; *peccatis*: *peccato* Weber

12:43 *peccato*: *peccatis mortuorum* S-C

12:46 *salubris est*: *salubris* Weber; *peccatis solvantur*: *peccato solverentur* Weber

13:1 *Eupatorem*: *Eupatoris* Weber

<13:2 *who had charge over the affairs of the realm* D-R/C (*of the realm* in italics): *and cheefe ouer the affayres* D-R; *five* D-R/C: *& . . . fiue* D-R; *twenty-two* D-R/C: *& . . . twentie two* D-R; *and* KJV (in italics in D-R/C): omitted in D-R>

13:2 *duos*: *duo* Weber

<13:3 *Menelaus* KJV: *And Menelaus* D-R>

13:4 *apprehensum*: *conprehensum* Weber

13:9 *se patre suo*: *se* Weber

<13:14 *all* KJV (in brackets in KJV): *the power and charge of al* D-R>

13:15 *victoriae*: *victoria* Weber; *erant*: *fuerant* S-C

13:16 *hostium castra*: *hostium* Weber

13:18 *difficultatem*: *difficultates* Weber

<13:18 *to take the strong places* KJV (*holds* for *strong places*): *the difficultie of the places* D-R>

13:19 *quod*: *quae* S-C; *minuebatur*: *minorabatur* S-C

13:21 *est et conclusus*: *conclusus est* Weber

<13:22 *and* D-R/C: omitted in D-R>

<13:23 *and* D-R/C: omitted in D-R>

13:23 *honorificavit*: *honoravit* S-C

13:24 *amplexus: amplexatus* S-C; *usque ad: usque* Weber

<13:25 *men of that city* KJV (*people there*): *Ptolemaians* D-R; *for fear* D-R/C: *lest perhaps* D-R>

13:26 *regis: regi* Weber

<13:43 *sins of the dead* S-C: *sinne* D-R>

14:1 *Tripolis: Tripoli* Weber

14:9 *his singulis, oro: oro his singulis o* S-C

14:11 *hostiliter se: hostiliter* Weber

14:12 *misit in: misit* Weber

14:13 *mandatis ut: mandatis* Weber

14:14 *gregatim: segregatim* Weber

14:15 *ut: eum* Weber

<14:18 *the sword* KJV: *bloud* D-R>

14:19 *praemisit: misit* Weber; *Theodotium: Theodotum* Weber; *Matthiam: Matthathiam* Weber

14:21 *singulis: a singulis* Weber

<14:23 *but* KJV: *and* D-R>

14:24 *animo, et: animo* Weber; *viro: vero* Weber

14:25 *Rogavitque: rogavit* Weber

14:26 *adsentire: adsentare* Weber

<14:30 *in a rough manner* D-R/C: *more sternely* D-R; *great and holy* KJV: *most great & most holie* D-R>

14:31 *cum: ut* Weber

14:33 *iuravit, dicens: iuravit* Weber

14:35 *universorum, qui: qui universitatis* Weber

<14:36 *Therefore* KJV: *And* D-R>

<14:40 *by ensnaring him to* KJV (*taking* for *ensnaring*): *if he had intrapped him, that he should* D-R>

14:41 *in domum: domum* Weber; *petiit: petit* Weber

14:43 *audenter: audacter* S-C

<14:44 *but they* KJV: *who* D-R>

14:45 *accensus animo: accensis animis* Weber; *et cum: cum et* Weber; *et gravissimis vulneribus esset saucius: saucius* Weber

14:46 *super: supra* S-C

15:1 *committere bellum: committere* Weber

<15:1 *set upon him* KJV (*them* for *him*): *joyne batel* D-R>

15:3   *ille*: *at ille* Weber; *caelo*: *saeculo* Weber

15:7   *Deo*: *Domino* Weber

15:9   *certaminum*: *certamina* S-C

<15:9   *withal* KJV: omitted in D-R; *cheerful* KJV: *prompt* D-R>

<15:10   *Then* KJV (*And*): *and so* D-R>

15:10   *ostendebat*: *ostendens* Weber

15:11   *exhortationibus*: *hortationibus* Weber

15:13   *hoc*: *haec* Weber

<15:15   *Whereupon* KJV: *And that* D-R>

15:16   *quo*: *in quo* S-C

15:17   *posset*: *possit* Weber; *civitas*: *civitas et* Weber; *periclitarentur*: *periclitaretur* Weber

15:19   *congressuri*: *congressi* Weber

15:20   *hostesque adessent*: *hostisque adesset* Weber

15:21   *manus*: *manum* Weber

15:22   *qui misisti*: *misisti* Weber; *Iudae*: *Iuda* S-C; *Sennacherib*: *Sennacherim* Weber

15:27   *triginta quinque*: *triginta* Weber

15:29   *suscitata*: *excitata* S-C

15:30   *emori*: *mori* S-C; *abscisam*: *abscissam* S-C

15:31   *pervenisset*: *convenisset* Weber

15:34   *conservavit*: *servavit* S-C

15:35   *signum*: *sit* Weber

15:37   *diei*: *die* Weber

<15:39   *Which* D-R/C *if I have done* KJV: *And if wel* D-R; *desired* KJV: *also would* D-R>

15:39   *conpetit, hoc*: *conpetit* Weber; *sin*: *si* Weber

<15:40   *But* S: *therefore* D-R>

Alternate Spellings

In general, the translators of the Douay-Rheims edition of the Bible preserved the transliterations of Hebrew names (and words based on those names) found throughout the textual tradition of the Sixto-Clementine edition of the Vulgate Bible. While these transliterations do reflect the Latin sources for the English presented in this edition, they do not represent what is currently thought to be the likely pronunciation of the Hebrew words or, in some books, words from other ancient languages: for example, the name we see in the New Revised Standard Version (NRSV) as "Ahuzzath" (Gen 26:26) was transliterated by the authors and revisers of the Latin text as "Ochozath." This sort of transliteration renders a few well-known characters harder to recognize, such as Noah, or "Noe" in the Latin tradition. Furthermore, there are frequent inconsistencies in the Douay-Rheims translation as to the spellings of names.

Another quirk of the Douay-Rheims and Vulgate Bibles is that they often identify locations by the names they were understood to have had at the time of the Vulgate's composition rather than the names found in Hebrew scripture. For example, "Mesopotamia of Syria" (Gen 28:2) represents a place referred to in the NRSV as "Paddan-aram."

In presenting the Latin text and the Douay-Rheims translation, the transliterations in the English have been updated for

the sake of accuracy and ease of reference. The Latin has been preserved to reflect its own textual tradition in accordance with the principles stated in the Introduction. However, when names given are not simply a matter of representing vowel and consonant sounds, the Douay-Rheims translation has been left intact so that it remains a genuine translation of the facing text.

There are moments in the Bible where the anachronistic place-names are of significance: at the end of Balaam's last prophetic blessing of Israel, he declares, "They shall come in galleys from Italy; they shall overcome the Assyrians and shall waste the Hebrews, and at the last they themselves also shall perish" (Nm 24:24). The Hebrew word rendered as "Italy" is transliterated in the NRSV as "Kittim," and though the meaning is obscure, it is almost certainly not Italy, for reasons outlined by Milgrom (1990), ad loc. Nevertheless, it is fascinating and important to realize that in the Western European tradition from the fourth century CE until the twentieth century, many read, wrote, and learned that Italians would "waste the Hebrews." Because of this and other instances in which the place-names, however unrepresentative of the Hebrew tradition they may be, are important in terms of what readers of these versions of the Bible may have believed, the Vulgate words have been retained.

Below is a list of the names in the English translation of the Major Prophetical Books (Volume IV) and the Minor Prophetical Books and Maccabees (Volume V). The names are followed by an alternate spelling (or, in some cases, an alternate word) if there is one. An entry presented in italic text signifies a word retained from the Douay-Rheims translation; all other words are the spellings given by the NRSV. An entry in roman

text with no alternative spelling means that the spellings are identical in the two editions; one in italic text with no alternative spelling means that the name is in the Douay-Rheims translation but no parallel was found in the NRSV. In a few cases, words have been based on the spellings of the NRSV and the form in the Douay-Rheims text. For example, the Douay-Rheims text reads "the Sichemites" (Gen 33:18), where the NRSV has "Shechem." To illustrate the translation of the Douay-Rheims while providing an up-to-date transliteration of the Hebrew word, "the Shechemites" has been printed; similarly, in cases where Jerome translated parts of a Hebrew place-name into Latin where the NRSV left the whole name in Hebrew (such as the "temple of Phogor," as opposed to "Beth-peor" at Dt 3:29), the transliterated part of the name has been updated in this edition, but the Latin and English translations have not been changed, yielding "temple of Peor."

Aaron	Adida [Addus]
Abdeel	Adida [Adiada]
Abednego [Abdenago]	Admah [Adama]
Abraham	*Adonis [Tammuz]*
Absalom	Adora [Ador]
Absalom [Abesalom]	Adrammelech [Adramelech]
Abubus [Abobus]	Adullam [Odollam]
Achbor [Achobor]	*Africa [Put]*
Achor	*Agarenes*
Adam	Ahab [Achab]
Adam, children of [mortals]	Ahasuerus [Assuerus]
Adar	Ahaz [Achaz]
Adasa [Adarsa]	Ahikam [Ahicam]
Adasa [Adazer]	Ai

Aiath

Akrabattene [Acrabathane]

Alcimus

Alema [Alima]

Alexander

Alexandria

Alexandria [Thebes]

Almighty [Sovereign]

Amariah [Amarias]

Amaziah [Amasias]

Amittai [Amathi]

Ammon

*Ammon, children of [Ammon-
ites]*

Ammonites

*Ammonites, country of the [Am-
mon]*

Amon

Amon [Ammon]

Amorite [Amorrhite]

Amos

Amoz [Amos]

Anathoth

Anathothite [of Anathoth]

Ancient of days [Ancient One]

Andronicus

Antichrist

Antioch

*Antiochians [citizens of Anti-
och]*

Antiochis

Antiochus

Antipater

*Apadno, tabernacle [palatial
tents]*

Aphairema [Apherema]

Apollonius

Apollophanes

Apphus

Ar

Arabia

Arabian [Arab]

Arabian [Arabs]

Arabians [Arabs]

Arabians [nomads]

Aradus

Ararat

Arbatta [Arbatis]

Arbela [Arbella]

Arcturus [Pleiades]

Aretas

Ariarathes

Ariel

Ariel [altar hearth]

Arioch

Aristobulus [Aristobolus]

Arius

Arnon

Aroer

Arpad

Arpad [Arphad]

Arsaces

*Arvadians [inhabitants of Ar-
     vad]*
Asa
Asaph
Asaramel
Ashdod [Azotus]
Asher [Aser]
Ashkelon [Ascalon]
Ashkenaz [Ascenez]
Ashpenaz [Asphenez]
Asia
Askalon [Ascalon]
Asphar
Asshur [Assur]
Asshur [Assyria]
Assyria
Assyrian
Assyrians
Assyrians, sons of the [Assyrians]
Astyages
*Athenians [citizens of
     Athens]*
Athenobius
Attalus
Ausitis [Uz]
Avaran [Abaron]
Azariah [Azarias]
Azekah [Azecha]
Azotus
Azriel [Ezriel]
Azzur [Azur]

Baal
*Baal, house of him that judged
     [Beth-arbel]*
Baali [my Baal]
Baalim [Baal]
Baalim [Baals]
Baalis
Baal-meon [Beelmeon]
Baal-peor [Beelphegor]
Baasha [Baasa]
Babylon
Babylonia
Babylonia [Babylon]
Babylonians
Bacchides
Bacchus [Dionysus]
Bacenor
Baean [Bean]
Balaam
Baladan
Balak [Balach]
Balas [Bales]
Baruch
Bashan [Basan]
Baskama [Bascama]
Beautiful Place [Shaphir]
Beeri
Beer-sheba [Bersabee]
Bel
Belial
Belshazzar [Baltasar]

Belshazzar [Baltassar]

Belteshazzar [Baltassar]

Benaiah [Banaias]

Ben-hadad [Benadad]

Ben-hadad [Benadad]

Benjamin

Beor

Berea

Berechiah [Barachias]

Berothah [Berotha]

Beth-aven [Bethaven]

Bethbasi [Bethbessen]

Beth-dagon [Bethdagon]

Bethel

Beth-gamul [Bethgamul]

Beth-haccherem [Bethaca-
    rem]

Beth-horon [Bethoron]

Beth-horon [Beth-zur]

Beth-jeshimoth [Bethiesi-
    moth]

Bethlehem

Beth-meon [Bethmaon]

Beth-shan [Bethsan]

Beth-zaith [Bethzecha]

Beth-zechariah
    [Bethzecharam]

Beth-zur [Bethsura]

Bosor

Bosor [Bozrah]

Bosphorus [Sepharad]

Bozrah [Barasa]

Bozrah [Bosra]

Bubastis [Pi-beseth]

Buz

Buzi

Caleb

Callisthenes

Calneh [Chalane]

Calno [Calano]

Canaan [a trader]

Canaan [Chanaan]

Canaanites [Chanaanites]

Canneh [Chene]

Caphar-salama
    [Capharsalama]

Cappadocia [Caphtor]

Carchemish [Charcamis]

Caria

Carmel

Carnaim

Carnaim [Carnion]

Carthaginians [Tarshish]

Caspin [Casphin]

Cendebeus

Chaereas

Chaldea

Chaldeans

Chalphi [Calphi]

Chaphenatha [Caphetetha]

Charax [Characa]

Chaspho [Casphor]

Chebar [Chobar]

Chemosh [Chamos]
Chilmad [Chelmad]
Chimham [Chamaam]
Chislev [Casleu]
Christ
Cilicia
Cnidus [Gnidus]
Coelesyria [Celesyria]
Coelesyria [Celesyria]
Cos
Cub [Chub]
Cushi [Chusi]
Cyprians [Cyprian troops]
Cyprus
Cyrene
Cyrene [Kir]
Cyrus

Dagon
Damascus
Damascus [men of Damascus]
Dan
Dan [Vedan]
Daniel
Daphne
Darius
Dathema [Datheman]
David
Dedan
Dedan, men of [Dedanites]
Dedanim [Dedanites]
Delaiah [Dalaias]

Delos [Delus]
Demetrius
Demophon
Dessau
Diblah [Riblah]
Diblaim [Debelaim]
Diblathaim, house of [Beth-diblathaim]
Dibon
Dioscorus [Dioscorinthius]
Dok [Doch]
Dor [Dora]
Dorymenes [Dorymenus]
Dositheus
Dumah [Duma]
Dura
Dust, House of [Beth-leaphrah]

Ebed-melech [Abdemelech]
Ecbatana
Eden
Edom
Edomites
Eglaim [Gallim]
Egypt
Egyptians
Ekron [Accaron]
Elam
Elamites
Elasa [Laisa]
Elealeh [Eleale]
Eleazar

Eleutherus

Eliakim [Eliacim]

Elijah [Elias]

Elim, well of [Beer-elim]

Elishah [Elisa]

Elishama [Elisama]

Elkoshite [of Elkosh]

Elnathan

Elul

Elymais

Emmaus

Emmaus [Ammaus]

En-eglaim [Engallim]

En-gedi [Engaddi]

Enon, the court of [Hazar-enon]

Ephah [Epha]

Ephai [Ophi]

Ephraim

Ephrathah [Ephrata]

Ephron

Esar-haddon [Asarhaddon]

Esau

Esdris [Esdrin]

Ethiopia

Ethiopia [Cushan]

Ethiopia [Ethiopians]

Ethiopian

Ethiopians [Ethiopia]

Eumenes

Eupator

Euphrates

Eupolemus

Evil-merodach

Ezekiel

Ezra [Esdras]

Gabriel

Gad

Gaddi [Gaddis]

Galatia [the Gauls]

Galatians

Galilee

Gallim

Gareb

Gath [Geth]

Gaza

Gazara

Gazara [Gezeron]

Geba [Gaba]

Gebal

Gebim [Gabim]

Gedaliah [Gedelias]

Gedaliah [Godolias]

Gemariah [Gamarias]

Gennaeus [Genneus]

Gennesaret [Genesar]

Gentiles

Gerizim [Garizim]

Gerrenians [Gerar]

Gibeah [Gabaa]

Gibeah [Gabaath]

Gibeon [Gabaon]

Gilead [Galaad]

Gilgal [Galgal]

Goatha

Gog

Gomer

Gomer

Gomorrah [Gomorrha]

Gorgias

Gortyna

Gozan [Gozam]

Grecian

Grecians [Greeks]

Greece

Greece [Javan]

Greece [the Greeks]

Habakkuk [Habacuc]

Habazziniah [Habsanias]

Hadad-rimmon [Adadrem-
    mon]

Hadrach

Hagar [Agar]

Haggai [Aggeus]

Halicarnassus [Alicarnassus]

Hamath [Amath]

Hamath [Emath]

Hamath [Emath]

*Hamath, as they go to [Lebo-
    hamath]*

*Hamath, till thou come to [Lebo-
    hamath]*

Hammelech [the king]

Hamonah [Amona]

Hamutal [Amital]

Hanan

Hananel [Hanameel]

Hananel [Hananeel]

Hananiah [Ananias]

Hananiah [Hananias]

Hanes

Haran

Haran [Haram]

Harmon [Armon]

Hasideans [Assideans]

Hauran [Auran]

Hazael [Azael]

Hazor [Asor]

Hebrew

Hebrews

Hebron [Chebron]

Heldai [Holdai]

Helem

Heliodorus

Heliopolis [On]

Hen [Hem]

Hena [Ana]

Hercules

Heshbon [Hesebon]

Hethlon [Hethalon]

Hezekiah [Ezechias]

Hieronymus

High Place [Bamah]

Hilkiah [Helcias]

Hinnom [Ennom]

Hittite [Cethite]

Holon [Helon]

Hophra [Ephree]

Horonaim [Oronaim]

Hosea [Osee]

Hoshaiah [Osaias]

House Adjoining [Beth-ezel]

Iddo [Addo]

Idumea

Idumea [Edom]

Idumeans

Igdaliah [Jegedelias]

Illustrious [Epiphanes]

Imalkue [Emalchuel]

Immanuel [Emmanuel]

Immer [Emmer]

Indian

Indians [India]

Irijah [Jerias]

Isaac

Isaiah [Isaias]

Ishmael [Ismahel]

Israel

Israel, children of [Israelites]

Issachar

Italy [Tubal]

Ivvah [Ava]

Jaazaniah [Jezonias]

Jacob

Jacob [Accos]

Jahaz [*Jasa*]

Jahzah [Jasa]

Jambri

Jamnia

Jamnites

Jashub . . . that is left [Shear-
   jashub]

Jason

Jazer

Jazer [Gazer]

Jeberechiah [Barachias]

Jebusite

Jeconiah [Coniah]

Jeconiah [Conias]

Jeconiah [Jechonias]

Jedaiah [Idaias]

Jehoahaz [Joachaz]

Jehoiachin [Joachin]

Jehoiada [Joiada]

Jehoiakim [Joakim]

Jehoiakim [Joakim]

Jehoshaphat [Josaphat]

Jehozadak [Josedec]

Jehu

Jehudi [Judi]

Jerahmeel [Jeremiel]

Jeremiah [Jeremias]

Jericho

Jeroboam

Jerusalem

Jesse

Jew

Jews
Jews [Judeans]
Jezaniah [Jezonias]
Jezreel [Jezrahel]
Joah [Joahe]
Joakim
Joarib
Joarib [Jarib]
Joash [Joas]
Job
Joel
Johanan
John
Jonadab
Jonah [Jonas]
Jonathan
Joppa [Joppe]
Joppites [community of Joppa]
Jordan
Joseph
Josephus
Joshua [Jesus]
Joshua [Josue]
Josiah [Josias]
Jotham [Joathan]
Jucal [Juchal]
Judah [Juda]
Judah [Judea]
Judas
Judea
Judea [Judah]

Jupiter Hospitalis [Zeus-the-
Friend-of-Strangers]
Jupiter Olympius [Olympian
Zeus]

Kadesh [Cades]
Kadesh, Waters of Contradiction
of [Meribath-kadesh]
Kareah [Caree]
Kedar [Cedar]
Kedron [Cedron]
Kedron [Gedor]
Kerioth [Carioth]
Kerioth [Carioth]
Kethim [Cyprus]
Kidron, the torrent [the Wadi
Kidron]
Kiriathaim [Cariathaim]
Kiriath-jearim [Cariathiarim]
Kitteans [Ceteans]
Kittim [Cethim]
Kolaiah [Colias]

Lacedaemon [Lacedaemonians]
Lacedaemonians [Lacedemoni-
ans]
Lachish [Lachis]
Laishah [Laisa]
Lampsacus [Sampsames]
Lasthenes
Lebanon [Libanus]

Levi

Leviathan

Levites

Levites [levitical priests]

Libnah [Lobna]

Libya [Libyans]

Libya [Put]

Libyans

Libyans [Put]

Lord [Sovereign]

Lucius

Luhith [Luith]

Lycia

Lydda

Lydia [Lud]

Lydians [Lud]

Lydians [Ludim]

Lydians [Lydia]

Lysias

Lysimachus

Maachati [the Maacathite]

Maaseiah [Maasias]

Maccabees [Machabees]

Maccabeus

Macedonian

Macer [Macron]

Madmenah [Medemena]

Magog

Mahseiah [Maasias]

Maked [Mageth]

Malachi [Malachias]

Mallus [Mallos]

Manasseh [Manasses]

Manilius [Manius]

Mareshah [Maresa]

Marisa [Maresa]

Mattan [Mathan]

Mattathias [Mathathias]

Matthias [Mattathias]

Mauzzim [fortresses]

Mauzzim [of fortresses]

Mede

Mede [Media]

Medeba [Madaba]

Medeba [Medaba]

Medeba [Nadabath]

Medes

Medes [Media]

Megiddo [Mageddon]

Melchias [Malchiah]

Melzar

Memmius

Memphis

Menelaus

Mephaath

Merodach

Merodach-baladan [Mero-
    dach Baladan]

Merrha [Merran]

Mesaloth [Masaloth]

Meshach [Misach]

Meshech [Mosoch]

Micah [Micheas]

Micaiah [Micheas]

Michael

Michmash [Machmas]

Midian [Madian]

Migdol [Magdal]

Migron [Magron]

Milcom [Melchom]

Milcom [their king]

Minni [Menni]

Miriam [Mary]

Mishael [Misael]

Mizpah [Maapha]

Mizpah [Maspha]

Mizpah [Masphath]

Mnestheus [Menestheus]

Moab

Moabites

Modein [Modin]

Molech [Moloch]

Molech [Sakkuth]

Mordecai [Mardochias]

Moresheth [Morasthi]

Moreshethite [of Moresheth]

Morter [Mortar]

Mosel [from Uzal]

Moses

Myndos [Myndus]

Nabateans [Nabutheans]

Nanea

Naphtali [Naphthali]

Naphtali [Nephtali]

Nathan

Nazirite [Nazarite]

Nazirites [Nazarites]

Nebaioth [Nabaioth]

Nebo [Nabo]

Nebuchadnezzar [Nebuchadrez-
zar]

Nebuchadnezzar [Nebu-
chodonosor]

Nebushazban [Nabusez-
ban]

Nebuzaradan [Nabuzardan]

Neco [Nechao]

Nehelamite [of Nehelam]

Nephi [naphtha]

Nephthar

Nergal [Neregel]

Neriah [Neri]

Neriah [Nerias]

Nethaniah [Nathanias]

Netophathi, that were of [the
Netophathite]

Nicanor

Nile

Nimrim [Nemrim]

Nimrod [Nemrod]

Nineveh [Ninive]

Nisroch [Nesroch]

Noah [Noe]

Nob [Nobe]

Not My People [Lo-ammi]

Numenius

Obadiah [Abdias]
Odares [Odomera]
Oholah [Oolla]
Oholibah [Oolibah]
Omri [Amri]
Onias
Oreb
Orion
Orthosias [Orthosia]

Palestine [the Philistines]
Palestine, people of [Philistines]
Pamphylia
Paran
Pashhur [Phassur]
Pathros [Phatros]
Pathros [Phatures]
Patroclus
Pekah [Phacee]
Pelatiah [Pheltias]
Pelusium
Pentecost
Persepolis
Perses
Persia
Persian
Persians
Persians [Persia]
Pethuel [Phatuel]
Petra [Sela]
Pharaoh [Pharao]

Pharathon [Phara]
Phaselis
Phasiron [Phaseron]
Philarches
Philip
Philistia
Philistines
Philistines [Philistia]
Philometor
Phinehas [Phinees]
Phoenicia [Phenicia]
Phrygian
Posidonius
Ptolemais
Ptolemeans [Ptolemais]
Ptolemy [Ptolemee]
Pygmeans [men of Gamad]

Quintus

Raamah [Reema]
Rabbah [Rabba]
Rabbah [Rabbath]
Rabmag [Rebmag]
Rabsaris [Rabsares]
Rabshakeh [Rabsaces]
Rachel
Ramah [Rama]
Ramatha [Ramathin]
Raphon
Razis [Razias]

Rechab

Rechabites

Regem-melech [Rogom-
melech]

Remaliah [Romelia]

Rephaim [Raphaim]

Reuben [Ruben]

Rezeph [Reseph]

Rezin [Rasin]

Rhodes

Rhodocus

Riblah [Reblatha]

Rimmon [Remmon]

Romans

Romans [of Kittim]

Rome

Sabaim [Sabeans]

Sabaoth, Lord of [Lord of hosts]

Sabeans

Salu [Salomi]

Samaria

Samgarnebo [Semegarnabu]

Samos [Samus]

Samuel

Sarah [Sara]

Sarsechim [Sarsachim]

Satan

Saul

Saura [Avaran]

Scenopegia

Scythians

*Scythopolitans [people of Scy-
thopolis]*

Seba [Saba]

Second [Second Quarter]

Seir

Seleucia

Seleucus

Senir [Sanir]

Sennacherib

Sepharvaim

Seraiah [Saraias]

Seron

Sesac [Sheshach]

Shadrach [Sidrach]

Shallum [Salom]

Shallum [Sellum]

Shaphan [Saphan]

Sharezer [Sarasar]

Sharezer [Sereser]

Sharon [Saron]

Shealtiel [Salathiel]

Sheba [Saba]

Shebat [Sabath]

Shebat [Sabath]

Shebna [Sobna]

Shechem [Sichem]

Shelemiah [Selemias]

Shemaiah [Semei]

Shemaiah [Semeias]

Shephatiah [Saphatias]

Shephelah [Sephela]
Sheshach [Sesach]
Shiloah [Siloe]
Shiloh [Silo]
Shimei [Shimeites]
Shinar [Sennaar]
Shittim [Setim]
Sibmah [Sabama]
Sibraim [Sabarim]
Sicyon
Side
Sidon
Sihon [Seon]
Simeon
Simon
Sivan
Sodom
Solomon
Sosipater
Sostratus
Spain
Spartans
Sud [Sodi]
Susa
Susanna
Syene
Syria
Syria [Aram or *Edom]*
Syria [Aram]
Syria [Coelesyria]
Syriac [Aramaic]
Syrian tongue [Aramaic]

Syrians
Syrians [Arameans]

Tabeel
Tabor [Thabor]
Tahpanhes [Taphnes]
Tahpanhes [Taphnis]
Tahpanhes [Zoan]
Tamar [Thamar]
Tanhumeth [Thanehumeth]
Tanis
Taphsar
Tarshish [Tharsis]
Tarsus [Tharsus]
Tartan [Thathan]
Tekoa [Thecua]
Telassar [Thalassar]
Tema [Thema]
Teman [Theman]
Tephon [Thopo]
Tharseas [Tarsus]
Thassi [Thasi]
Theodotius [Theodotus]
Thou hast obtained mercy [Ru-hamah]
Thracians
Ticon, the house of [as far as Hazer-hatticon]
Tigris
Timnath [Thamnata]
Timothy [Timotheus]
Tirhakah [Tharaca]

Titus
Tob [Tubin]
Tobias
Tobijah [Tobias]
Togarmah, house of [Beth-togarmah]
Topheth
Topheth [Topeth]
Toubianites [Toubiani]
Tripolis
Trypho [Tryphon]
Tubal [Thubal]
Tyrannus [Auranus]
Tyre
Tyrians

Ulai
Uphaz [Ophaz]
Uriah [Urias]
Uz [Hus]
Uzziah [Ozias]

Without Mercy [Lo-ruhamah]

Xanthicus

You are my people [Ammi]

Zabadeans
Zabdiel
Zabulun [Zabulon]
Zacheus

Zadok [Sadoc]
Zarephath [Sarepta]
Zeboiim [Seboim]
Zechariah [Zacharias]
Zedad [Sedada]
Zedekiah [Sedecias]
Zephaniah [Sophonias]
Zerubbabel [Zorobabel]
Zimri [Zambri]
Zimri [Zamri]
Zion [Sion]
Zoar
Zoar [Segor]

Bibliography

Carleton, J. G. *The Part of Rheims in the Making of the English Bible.* Oxford: Clarendon, 1902.

Cartmell, J. "English Spiritual Writers: x. Richard Challoner." *Clergy Review* n.s. 44, no. 10 (October 1959): 577–587.

A Catholic. "A new Version of the Four Gospels, with Notes, Critical and Explanatory." *Dublin Review* 2, no. 2 (April 1837): 475–492.

Biblia Sacra: Vulgatae Editionis Sixti V Pont. Max. iussu recognita et Clementis VIII auctoritate edita. Vatican City: Marietti, 1959.

Challoner, R. "The Touchstone of the New Religion: or, Sixty Assertions of Protestants, try'd by their own Rule of Scripture alone, and condemned by clear and express Texts of their own Bible." London, n.p.: 1735.

———. ed. *The Holy Bible translated from the Latin Vulgat: Diligently compared With the Hebrew, Greek, and other Editions in divers Languages. And first published by The English College at Doway, Anno 1609. Newly revised, and corrected, according to the Clementine Edition of the Scriptures with Annotations for clearing up the principal Difficulties of Holy Writ.* 4 vols. Dublin(?): 1752.

———., ed. *The Holy Bible, translated from the Latin Vulgate, Diligently compared with the Hebrew, Greek, and other editions in divers languages. The Old Testament, First published by the English College at Douay, A.D. 1609 and The New Testament, First published by the English College at Rheims, A.D. 1582. With annotations, references, and an historical and chronological index. The whole revised and diligently compared with the Latin Vulgate Published with the approbation of His Eminence James Cardinal Gibbons Archbishop of Baltimore.* Baltimore: John Murphy, 1899.

———., ed. *The New Testament of Our LORD and SAVIOUR JESUS*

CHRIST. Translated out of the Latin Vulgat; diligently compared with the original Greek: and first published by the English *College at* Rhemes, *Anno 1582. Newly revised and corrected according to the* Clementin *Edition of the Scriptures. With Annotations, for Clearing up modern Controversies in Religion; and other Difficulties of Holy Writ.* 2 vols. Dublin(?): 1752.

Cotton, H. *Rhemes and Doway: An Attempt to shew what has been done by Roman Catholics for the Diffusion of the Holy Scriptures in English.* Oxford: University Press, 1855.

de Hamel, C. *The Book: A History of the Bible.* London: Phaidon, 2001.

Dodd, C. [H. Tootell]. *The Church History of England, From The Year 1500, to The Year 1688. Chiefly with regard to Catholicks.* 8 vols. Brussels [London], 1737–1742.

Duffy, E., ed. *Challoner and His Church: A Catholic Bishop in Georgian England.* London: Darton, Longman & Todd, 1981.

English College of Doway. *The Holie Bible Faithfully Translated into English, out of the Authentical Latin. Diligently conferred with the Hebrew, Greeke, and other Editions in diuers languages. With Arguments of the Bookes, and Chapters: Annotations. Tables: and other helpes, for better understanding of the text: for discoueirie of corruptions in some late translations: and for clearing Controversies in Religion.* 2 vols. Doway: Lavrence Kellam, at the signe of the holie Lambe, 1609–1610.

English College of Rhemes. *The Nevv Testament of Iesvs Christ, Translated Faithfully into English, out of the authentical Latin, according to the best corrected copies of the same, diligently conferred vvithe the Greeke and other editions in diuers languages: Vvith Argvments of bookes and chapters, Annotations, and other necessarie helpes, for the better vnderstanding of the text, and specially for the discouerie of the Corrvptions of diuers late translations, and for cleering the Controversies in religion, of these daies.* Rhemes: Iohn Fogny, 1582.

Frede, H. J. *Kirchenschriftsteller: Verzeichnis und Sigel.* Freiburg: Herder, 1995.

Gilley, S. "Challoner as Controvertionalist." In E. Duffy, ed., *Challoner and His Church: A Catholic Bishop in Georgian England.* London: Darton, Longman & Todd, 1981, pp. 90–111.

Greenslade, S. L., ed. *The Cambridge History of the Bible: The West, from the Reformation to the Present Day.* Rev. ed. Cambridge: Cambridge University Press, 1975.

Gryson, R. *Altlateinische Handschriften: Manuscrits Vieux Latins.* Freiburg: Herder, 1999.

The Holy Bible, Conteyning the Old Testament, and the New: Newly Translated out of the Originall tongues: & with the former Translations diligently compared and reuised: by his Maiesties speciall Comandement Appointed to be read in Churches. London: Robert Barker, Printer to the Kings most Excellent Maiestie, 1611; rpr. Thomas Nelson, 1990.

Kaske, R. E. *Medieval Chirstian Literary Imagery: A Guide to Interpretation.* Toronto: University of Toronto Press, ca. 1988.

Knox, T. F. Introduction. In *The First and Second Diaries of the English College, Douay, and an Appendix of Unpublished Documents, Edited by Fathers of the Congregation of the London Oratory, with an Historical Introduction.* Records of the English Catholics under the Penal Laws. Chiefly from the Archives of the See of Westinster 1. London: David Nutt, 1878.

Metzger, B. M., and R. E. Murphy. *The New Oxford Annotated Bible: New Revised Standard Version.* New York: Oxford University Press, 1991.

Milgrom, J., comm. *The JPS Torah Commentary: Numbers.* Philadelphia: The Jewish Publication Society.

Pope, H., and S. Bullough. *English Versions of the Bible.* St. Louis: Herder, 1952.

Quentin, H. *Biblia sacra: iuxta Latinam Vulgatam versionem.* Typis Polyglottis Vaticanis, 1926–[1995].

———. *Mémoire sur l'établissement du texte de la Vulgate.* Collectanea Biblica Latina 6, 1922.

Rahlfs, A., ed., and R. Hanhart, rev. *Septuaginta: Id est Vetus Testamentum graece iuxta LXX interpretes, Editio altera.* Stuttgart: Deutsche Bibelgesellschaft, 2006.

Sabatier, P. *Bibliorum Sacrorum Latinae versiones antiquae, seu Vetus Italica, et Ceterae quaecunque in Codicibus Mss. & antiquorum libris reperiri poterunt: Quae cum Vulgata Latina, & cum Textu Graeco comparantur. Accedunt Praefationes, Observationes, ac Notae, Indexque novus ad Vulgatam è regione editam, idemque locupletissimus.* 3 vols. Rheims: Apud Reginaldum Florentain, Regis Typographicum & Bibliopolam, sub signo Bibliorum aureorum, 1743–1749.

Weber, R., ed. *Biblia Sacra Vulgata.* 5th ed. Stuttgart: Deutsche Bibelgesellschaft, 2007.